THE
FATAL ART OF
ENTERTAINMENT

INTERVIEWS
WITH
MYSTERY WRITERS

———

THE
FATAL ART OF
ENTERTAINMENT

INTERVIEWS
WITH
MYSTERY WRITERS

Rosemary
Herbert

FOREWORD BY
Antonia
Fraser

G.K. Hall & Co.
An Imprint of Macmillan Publishing Company
New York
Maxwell Macmillan Canada
Toronto
Maxwell Macmillan International
New York Oxford Singapore Sydney

G. K. Hall & Co.
Imprint of Macmillan Publishing Company
866 Third Avenue
New York, NY 10022

Maxwell Macmillan Canada, Inc.
1200 Eglinton Avenue East
Suite 200
Don Mills, Ontario M3C 3N1

Macmillan Publishing company is part of the Maxwell Communication Group of Companies.

Library of Congress Catalog Card Number: 93-22862

Printed in the United States of America

printing number

1 2 3 4 5 6 7 8 9 10

Library of Congress Cataloging-in-Publication Data

Herbert, Rosemary.
    The fatal art of entertainment : interviews with mystery writers/Rosemary Herbert.
        p.   cm.
    ISBN 0-8161-7279-X (alk. paper)
    1. Detective and mystery stories, English—History and criticism—Theory, etc. 2. Detective and mystery stories, American—History and criticism—Theory, etc. 3. Novelists, American—20th century—Interviews. 4. Novelists, English—20th century—Interviews. 5. Detective and mystery stories—Authorship. I. Title.
PR888.D4H47   1994   93-22862
823'.087209—dc20   CIP

The paper used in this publication meets the minimum requirements of American National Standard for Information Sciences—Permanence of Paper for Printed Library Materials. ANSI Z39.48–1984. ⊚™

For my parents,
Barbara Herbert
and
Robert D. Herbert,
with love and gratitude

And with special thanks to
Brian W. Aldiss
and
Lady Antonia Fraser

▶ CONTENTS

▶ FOREWORD

I once attended a dialogue at English PEN between P. D. James and Ruth Rendell. Looking at these two sympathetic, charming, middle-aged women on the platform, it was easy to imagine that they were members of the caring professions: doctors, nurses, social workers. . . . But we were in fact there to listen to them discuss the Gentle Art of Murder! The contrast between their personalities, as evinced in their dialogue, and the subjects they were actually discussing could not have been more forceful. On my way home, I ruminated all over again on the strange paradoxical nature of the crime writer.

Rosemary Herbert's brilliantly enjoyable work has reminded me of that particular evening, and has brought the paradox into focus yet again in the most stimulating way. She has chosen to act as Boswell to thirteen Dr. Johnsons, ranging from eighty-year-old British author Julian Symons, rightly regarded as the dean of crime writers, to the African-American Barbara Neely. I compare Rosemary to James Boswell, incidently, not necessarily in all respects (her scholarly character is certainly not that of the roisterer), but in the vital one which makes us love Boswell for loving Johnson: her enthusiasm. In one particular exchange the great doctor observed to Boswell, "Well, we had a good talk," Boswell replied, and I imagine him saying the words with shining eyes,—"Yes, sir, you tossed and gored several persons." Although Rosemary's selected authors are not literally tossing and goring persons in their conversations, they are certainly contemplating methods of doing so. And I can imagine Rosemary's eyes, like Boswell's, shining.

Certain important themes emerge from this book. This is the result of Rosemary's method of steering each author—without forcing it—in the direction of certain specific topics. Foremost amongst these is the actual status of crime writing as a genre. Is it any more than "the fatal art of entertainment," the phrase of Brian Aldiss which Rosemary takes for her title? *Should* it be more? Is it secondary art compared with mainstream fiction? Or is it perhaps to be regarded as equal yet different? Alternatively, is crime fiction simply to be regarded as part of the broad spectrum of fiction writing, in no way separated from it? Readers will find that the answers vary enormously.

John Mortimer, for example, creator of Rumpole, believes that the detective story "comes, really, into everything." He cites *Hamlet* and *Agamemnon* as crime stories. Julian Symons, on the other hand, while defending the best crime novelists as being "very much underrated in comparison with what people call the best novelists," still thinks that you cannot compare them to Dickens and Dostoevsky. Jane Langton states firmly that it is "a noble ambition" simply to entertain people—and yet at the end of the day mysteries do not rise above "A-minus."

Another interesting theme is that of order—the detective or mystery story as a way of bringing order into a world which is by its nature frighteningly diffused and violent. Patricia D. Cornwell, for example (who keeps a Smith and Wesson .38 in her workroom— for real), talks of "a bogeyman at every turn of the road"; writing mysteries she describes as "my way of dealing with it." Patricia Cornwell also reveals herself as a born mystery writer, in that she did try to write straight novels, but "there was always a body at every turn." Robert Barnard puts this desire for order another way: he tells Rosemary Herbert that such activities "minister to your power lust," or as Jeremiah Healy observes, "you get to play God."

Sue Grafton talks of "facing my own demons": the creation of her sleuth, Kinsey Millhone, was an alternative to feeling impotent rage at the circumstances of her private life. Sue Grafton's admission that crime writing helped her deal with an imperfect life points to the fact that quite a number of these writers have had to deal with challenges and tragedies which are certainly abnormal. When Rosemary asks them in turn whether they have a particular sense of the fragility of life, you are not surprised to find that the question elicits some painful responses. At the same time, as P. D. James points out, crime writing is a form of literary work in which writers do feel that "their essential privacy is protected." P. D. James is indeed yet another who points to her books as hopefully "small celebrations of order" in a world where too much is out of control.

Despite the obvious differences among these writers, differences of culture as well as nationality, I myself found the feeling of sister-and-brotherhood which emerges from this book quite strong. Of course there are differences. For example, Tony Hillerman refers to the Navajo concept of "hosrah," or harmony, and regards his works as "a painless way to learn Native American customs." Hillerman is, however, one of those who is quite clear on the quality of entertainment in even the greatest literature and as he says, there are no footnotes allowed in his books. The instruction on the subject of Native American culture is not an end in itself. Barbara Neely, on the other hand, is aware that she is raising consciousness about the lot of the African-American domestic worker through the adventures of her sleuth, Blanche White, and is happy to be dealing with serious issues in a nonserious way. Beneath this superficial difference, however, I sensed that both Hillerman and Neely stand for deep seriousness in their work, which really makes the question of whether crime fiction is a secondary genre or not superfluous.

This seriousness, combined with Rosemary's infectious enthusiasm, is indeed my abiding impression of this book. It will, I believe, appeal widely to readers of mysteries, as well as practitioners of the art. I myself, for example, have never read the works of one writer, and only dipped into the oeuvre of another. I am left with a strong desire to read anew and reread as well. This art of entertainment may be fatal, but it is certainly compelling.

–Antonia Fraser

▶ ACKNOWLEDGMENTS

In addition to the writers here interviewed who shared not only their thoughts but their generous hospitality with me, I wish to thank my daughters, Eliza Samphire Partington, Daisy Trevigue Partington, and Juliet Gazelle Partington, for their love and patience.

I am indebted to my editor, Catherine E. Carter, and to the following individuals for everything ranging from literary insights and encouragement to photographic advice, hospitality, and practical help: Fawzi and Callie Abdulrazak, Dominick Abel, Nadya Aisenberg, Margaret and Brian W. Aldiss, Jane Andrassi, Marian Babson, Jane S. Bakerman, Louise Barnard, Linda Barnes, the Cadaver Club of Boston, Elinor Dare, Lady Antonia Fraser, Sara Ann Freed, Pamela Grant, Mary Harmon, Barbara and Robert D. Herbert, Pat Hill, Elizabeth Holthaus, Margaret Ittelson, Susan Kelly, Susanne Kirk, Liz Kubek, Kate Mattes, John McAleer, Susan and Stephen Moody, Penny Mortimer, Elaine M. Ober, Susan Oleksiw, Diana O'Neill, David H. Partington, Otto Penzler, B. J. Rahn, Lorraine Reardon, Eileen and John Robinson, Harry Roe, Medora Sale, Sybil Steinberg, Kate Stine, Harriet Swire, Kathleen Symons, William G. Tapply, and Ira Weisman.

My dedicated transcription helpers are Matthias Ferber, Robert D. Herbert, Dierdre Livingston, Anna Macmillan, Jane Merrill, and Brad Skillman. Special thanks are due the Reference Librarians—including Marion E. Schoon and Henri J. Bourneuf—and security staff of the Harry Elkins Widener Memorial Library, the heart of Harvard University.

Acknowledgments _____

Segments of the P. D. James interview first appeared in *The Armchair Detective* 20, no. 4 (Fall 1986):341–348.

Segments of the John Mortimer interview first appeared in *The Paris Review* 30, no. 109 (Winter 1988):96–128, in *The Armchair Detective* 20, no. 4 (Fall 1987):340–349, and in *Lawyers Monthly* (August 1988):3–4, 6.

The Patricia D. Cornwell interview was excerpted in *The Armchair Detective* 25, no. 4 (Fall 1992):388–397.

Segments of the Robert Barnard interview first appeared in *The Armchair Detective* 17, no. 3 (Summer 1984):290–294.

Segments of the Jeremiah Healy interview first appeared in *Lawyers Monthly* (April 1988):5–7.

The Barbara Neely interview was excerpted in *Harvard Review*, no. 5 (Autumn 1993).

Photos of mystery writers Copyright © 1993 by Rosemary Herbert.

▶ INTRODUCTION

"The thing that absorbs me most in our age is the violence behind respectable faces." So confides Julian Symons in the first interview in this volume. The baker's dozen of writers who share their thoughts in the pages that follow share Symons's preoccupation, resulting in thirteen fascinating bodies of work that wrestle not only with puzzling crimes and their solutions but with the even more intriguing question of human character gone criminal.

Just what sort of person entertains a lifelong fascination with the darker side of human nature? What kind of character spends his or her days calculating methods of murder? What type of life experience leads a person to write volume after volume centered around violent death? In short, what manner of mentality comprises a mind to murder?

This volume will answer these questions and others by acquainting readers with thirteen masters of fictional crime. The portraits of these artists are threefold. For each author there is a photographic portrait taken in the author's working environment; an essay that places the author within the literary traditions of the crime and mystery genre, describes the circumstances of the interview, and sheds light on the character of the novelist; and finally there is the interview itself, in which the content is selected to reflect both the subject's views and personality. A reading of the whole may cause the reader to agree with me: "The thing that absorbs me most about these authors is the contrast between their exploration of violence and the respectable and comforting pleasure of their company."

The fact is that these perpetrators of violence on the printed page are without exception charming, hospitable, and downright fun to be with. Ask a probing question— for instance query that fascination with death—and the reply is apt to be humorous. Take Catherine Aird's remark "Death comes to us all at the end, but perhaps for the crime writer it comes earlier, and more frequently." Or John Mortimer's quip: "Murder goes on in the family circle like Christmas."

And speaking of families, what has led these individuals to their criminal pursuits? Is the child father (or mother) to the mystery writer? Two of this company—Symons and Jeremiah Healy—mastered the art of strategy by means of war games with toy soldiers. Mortimer admits that as an only child he acted out *Hamlet* and *Macbeth*, duelling with himself for hours on end. Sue Grafton, too, physically acted out her fantasies, rescuing herself when tied to a neighborhood tree. Barbara Neely picked up the art of storytelling while braiding her grandmother's tresses, and Reginald Hill gleaned inspiration from movie theatre melodramas. And P. D. James confides that when as a child she was told the story of Humpty-dumpty, her response was to wonder, "Did he jump or was he pushed?"

As this volume will show, these authors are also forthcoming with more serious and revealing confidences, some of them involving painful memories and brushes with death or tragedy. Remarkably, all those who have faced extraordinary difficulties have risen above their tragedies to make genuine peace with their pasts. Some, like Cornwell, Grafton, and Robert Barnard, use their experience to drive their narratives and inform their understanding of victims and victimization or family dynamics. All have used their painful experiences to good effect in the crafting of their crimes. Grafton reveals that even the anguish of growing up in a household with alcoholic parents is useful to the writer: "It teaches you early on to be a very careful observer of human nature. . . . you observe: you scan your environment; you try to figure out what's going on and where you're safe. . . . there's a whole sense of the darkness and jeopardy in life." And James asserts that "Something in me believes that . . . if you want to be a writer you should have as much trauma in your early years as you can bear without breaking." Cornwell has a similar attitude. "If somebody deals me a blow, then I will take it and make something out of it that ends up being to my advantage. . . . It all ends up in some form or fashion in what I write."

Occupational experience is also used to advantage by these writers. Cornwell employs knowledge gained at the Richmond City Morgue in providing forensic detail for her novels while Gash uses his experience on the barrows of London's Petticoat Lane district to provide readers with detailed knowledge of the antiques trade. Barnard uses universities he has known in the Australian outback and northernmost Norway to provide two of his settings. And Healy draws upon his work in a New Jersey sheriff's department and as a lawyer to inform his police procedure and structure his plots.

These writers share much more with us than quips about death, glimpses into their childhoods and adult work lives, and more serious ruminations about personal difficulties. In talking about the craft of crime they reveal a few well-kept secrets about how the crime writer manipulates the reader. They may even confess, as Cornwell does, that they are quite capable of scaring themselves. They discuss their sources of inspiration and, in some cases, admit how surprisingly out of control the process of writing the highly structured mystery novel can be. Jonathan Gash, for instance, confides, "I don't go through any kind of conscious thinking at all. . . . I don't plot; I don't plan; I don't know when I pick up a piece of paper if it's going to be part of a poem, part of a play, a doodle, or the next Lovejoy, or the *finish* of the next Lovejoy."

These authors also take us along on research expeditions. Jane Langton describes a trip to a quaking bog, a reservoir, and the bowels of a garbage compactor—all of which serve in her fiction as fine and private places to dump the inconvenient corpse. Gash recounts his encounters with witches and ramraiders. And Hillerman discusses the writer as "bag lady," picking up information ranging from details of escape holes in ancient grain storage structures to Native American puns.

Also addressed here is the question suggested in the title of the book, which is inspired by a remark made by Brian W. Aldiss. When asked about the entertaining quality of his work he replied, "When I think about this I grieve about it because I have discovered in me the fatal art of entertainment. But I have always wanted to write the *undeniable* book which, in the words of Pushkin, would 'lay waste the hearts of men.' And the two are at war, this talent to entertain and the desire to write the undeniable book." While Aldiss is known as a writer of science fiction, mainstream novels, and literary criticism—all of which critics agree is of undeniable literary quality—his concern is one that must be shared by all authors who chose to work in any genre that has been considered over the years to be merely an escapist and entertaining form.

Inspired by Aldiss, this book asks the question, "Does the entertaining nature of the mystery genre in any manner limit the potential for this work to reach the highest levels of literary achievement?" Further, in a genre where surprising the reader often depends on keeping secrets about character development, the interviews query the capacity of crime and mystery writers to succeed as novelists of character. The answers reflect the ongoing debate in academic and critical circles, ranging from James's belief that the author can satisfyingly portray moral ambiguity and psychological subtlety within the constraints of the detective novel to Symons's assertion that "I don't think the crime writer can be a novelist of the highest stature" to Neely's cry, "Who *are* these people" who determine what is literary!

While some have doubts about the genre's capacity to do more than entertain, the tally is seven to six in favor of crime and mystery writers potentially producing the highest order of literature. And even if the literature merely amuses, Langton reminds us that it is "a noble ambition to entertain the reader." Barnard adds that the immediate goal of popular fiction is "to entertain and to arouse interest and excitement. . . . I think popular literature has kept storytelling alive during a rather dark age in the novel, and I think we should be proud of that."

James points out another purpose for the crime writer. "I hope that my books serve as small celebrations of order and reason in our increasingly disordered world." Similarly, Mortimer testifies that the sleuth ought to be "the man who can understand everything in a wicked world and who also imposes order upon chaos." Cornwell declares, "I like the sort of fearful symmetry of having very civilized and humane people . . . warring against" violence in society. And Aird agrees that the appeal of the mystery novel is to those "in search of an orderliness"; she notes that "although personally you may inhabit a world that is not reliable—within the hard covers of a book you know perfectly well that justice will be done."

But a desire for orderliness is not the whole story here. These authors also share sheer enthusiasm for their work. As Grafton puts it, "Each book is always a brand new adventure. The exciting thing is how you keep learning about yourself. That's what mystery writing is about . . . it teaches us about ourselves."

May this volume acquaint its readers with thirteen crafters of crime, with their personal histories and their personalities, with the preoccupations and the occupations or research that inform their work, and with the common concerns and individual impulses that have led them to pursue the fatal art of entertainment.

THE
FATAL ART OF
ENTERTAINMENT

INTERVIEWS
WITH
MYSTERY WRITERS

▶ JULIAN SYMONS

As an octagenarian with twenty-seven crime novels to his credit, and the third edition of his groundbreaking literary history of the genre, *Bloody Murder: From the Detective Story to the Crime Novel: A History*, newly published, Julian Symons cannot escape being regarded as the elder statesman of crime and mystery writing. After all, not only did he stretch the boundaries of crime writing—a branch of literature that he defined as separate from the traditional mystery or detective story in its intent and in many of the conventions employed by its authors—but he has been the most persistent and persuasive proponent of the notion that the best of crime and mystery writing deserves to be taken seriously by the critical and academic community. It is safe to say that no one has done more to legitimize this genre than this man whose own works demonstrate the successful literary risk-taking that is at the heart of all novels of character.

In novel after novel, Symons demonstrates his fascination for "the violence behind respectable faces" by focusing upon the interplay of serendipitous circumstance and personality flaws that cause his characters to step over that boundary between civilized and uncivilized behavior. Always a keen observer of the quirks of human conduct, Symons's detached insight into human motivation was formed during his childhood in a close-knit and strangely isolated family of which he was the youngest child. A severe Victorian father, whose financial well-being seesawed like the fortunes of Mr. Micawber, never demonstrated approval or affection for Symons, who suffered from a stammer so crippling that at one point he attended a school for backward children. Otherwise Symons was loved by his mother and talented older siblings and encouraged intellectually and socially by a varied

1

circle of friends who shared his tastes for everything from endless games of snooker and cricket to deep discussions of politics and poetry.

As a young man, Symons conquered his stammer and plunged into self-education with passion. He recalls living "from the age of about sixteen, for years in a state of permanent intellectual intoxication." He numbered among his friends George Orwell, Wyndham Lewis, Dylan Thomas, and Roy Fuller. Symons published some of their works in *Twentieth Century Verse*, a "*little* little magazine" that he supported entirely by his secretarial work at a small, slightly seedy company called Victoria Lighting and Dynamo. This outfit was headed by another Dickensian character who was forever supporting money-making schemes that came to nought with capital from misled investors and with profits from the sale of very used electric dynamos.

During his "tedious" eleven-year stint with Victoria Lighting and Dynamo, Symons led a highly active intellectual life but found that his early idealism was profoundly tempered by the revelations of the Holocaust. The dark side of human nature is a theme he was to deal with in many of his crime novels. But Symons's interests were not limited to fiction: after teaching himself research techniques while imbibing a rich mix of literature free from the canonization he would have encountered in a university environment, Symons succeeded as a "minor poet" (his own verdict), military historian, biographer, literary critic, and, of course, novelist.

It is chiefly as a crime novelist and literary historian of the genre that Symons spoke with us in this interview. Seated by a coal fire in his double house near Dover, England, or in his kitchen with his charming wife of over fifty years, Kathleen, Symons shared his thoughts with a characteristic earnest thoughtfulness, and with great personal warmth and generosity. Ever unflinching from the truth as he sees it, Symons offered a surprising assessment of the potentialities and limitations he regards as inherent in the literary genre that he has worked so long and hard to promote.

Herbert   I have read with fascination your comment, "The thing that absorbs me most in our age is the violence behind respectable faces." P. D. James has said that an author's body of work reveals something about the writer's inner landscape. Is it fair to say that yours reveals a fascination with the secrets that individuals may harbor?

Symons   Yes.

Herbert   And that we are *all* capable of harboring dark secrets, no matter how respectable we may appear to be on the surface?

Symons   Well, that would be my feeling, yes. I think that everyone is potentially a murderer if the circumstances are right—or wrong

(Smiles.)—and if the pressures are sufficiently great, then we're all potential criminals. And the point at which the pressures operate so that the facade of respectability is fatally cracked: ah, that's something that absorbs me; that's something that I really, myself, find very fascinating as, I suppose, somebody who has led a respectable life.

Herbert   And if you had not led a respectable life would you be equally fascinated?

Symons   Perhaps not. I don't know. But I feel [crime] is an option for everybody. We've all felt the inclination to do things at times that might have taken us to prison. Perhaps we *have* [done them] and have been lucky not to go to prison. That's something that I find absorbing: simply the barrier between what you can do, and remain a respectable member of society, accepted as such, and what happens when you go over the barrier—and you step perhaps almost accidentally over the barrier, and you're on the other side.

Herbert   Yes, in a number of your books you show crime as coming about through an odd combination of circumstances and character. It is almost as if the crime might not have happened at all—no matter how profound the preexisting motivation had been—if a final, exacerbating circumstance hadn't occurred.

Symons   That is so.

Herbert   This notion of the violence behind respectable faces makes me think of a whole range of detective stories and crime novels, from those of Agatha Christie—who in real life imagined that her own relatives harbored murderous thoughts behind the smiles over the dinner table—to your own recent novel *Something Like a Love Affair* in which the outwardly respectable architect has both a sleazy personal history and financial secrets. I would love to have you expand on this thought.

Symons   Yes, of course, to a certain extent it's a cliché of the crime story—or if not a cliché, it's a pillar of the crime story—that it isn't always true that the murderer is the least suspected or most unlikely person. But certainly most crime stories, at least of the kind that I write, and [the detective stories] that Agatha Christie wrote, do depend upon some element of surprise. I mean there are quite a lot of crime stories—modern, recent ones, especially American ones— that don't depend on that sort of element of surprise at all and are not concerned with the violence hiding behind respectable faces, but only with violence on a sort of obvious level. The short stories of Chandler and Hammett are really not concerned with any *hidden* violence; they're only concerned with violence itself. That doesn't seem to me so interesting or, perhaps I ought to say, it's not of interest to me.

Herbert   This brings to mind the difference between the detective story and the crime novel, as you have defined the terms in your literary history of the genre, *Bloody Murder*. As you point out there, the traditional detective story is concerned with material motive while the crime novel looks at psychological motivation. And while the detective story tends to be conservative and to proclaim that the standing order of justice is a pretty good thing, the crime novel may question that. I think in the kind of story you're talking about where someone may accidentally step over the edge—or where we understand why someone was forced by certain pressures to go over the edge—the question, "How *just* is justice?" becomes a much more difficult one to answer.

Symons   Yes. This is one of the things that makes what I call the crime novel something much more like a novel: that it is not simply a question of "Who did it?"

Herbert   In the detective story, the answer to the question "Why?" would be the same as the answer given to the question "Who stood to gain?"

Symons   Yes, generally. It would have to do with some complication of the will.

Herbert   And by "will" you don't mean an individual's mental determination?

Symons   (Laughs.) No. I mean as in Last Will and Testament.

Herbert   Whereas in the crime novel, a complication in a character's mental determination could indeed lie at the heart of the crime?

Symons   Oh yes. But in the crime novel, it wouldn't be right to say such things [as complicated legal documents] don't operate at all, because there are lots of gradations between the crime novel and the detective story. But in the crime novel, what one would be chiefly concerned with is probably the psychology of the main figure; certainly you would be concerned much more with *why* things were done than with discovering the secret of who did them.

Herbert   Exactly.

Symons   Although, I don't mean to say that in no crime novel will you ever be worrying about the secrets of who the villain is—I always like to provide some sort of surprise, which may not be the orthodox kind of surprise. I wrote a book called *The Man Who Killed Himself* which I thought very successful indeed. That is to say, it did the kind of thing I was trying to do. This is about the little timid man who, as you know if you've read the story, adopts a separate personality in which he really becomes, he feels, somebody different. And in order to get clear of the problems involved in his two personalities, he has to kill, so there is no puzzle. You know who the murderer is; the murderer is the little man, Arthur Brownjohn. What you don't know is what's going to happen to him. And it's in devising what's going to happen to him, or the element of surprise, which belongs to the old-fashioned detective story, if you'd like to call it old fashioned—it's in *that* that the element of surprise comes. It's quite a different sort of surprise from the surprise of—well, is it Colonel Mustard? Or is it Mrs. White? Or is it Miss Scarlet? It's a different sort of surprise from that but it is still a surprise.

Herbert   This reminds me of the classic crime novel *Strangers on a Train* in which Patricia Highsmith thoroughly informs the reader of the progress of the crime.

Symons   *Strangers on a Train* . . . has got no problems to be solved in the old-fashioned detective story sense, but it keeps you reading because you can't think how is the pattern going to work out, how can it possibly turn itself into a pattern of the kind that one recognizes as the crime story pattern; and it does very successfully.

Herbert   Another example of this is John Fowles's *The Collector*, where you see what forces made this man kidnap the young woman and you see his point of view throughout as he keeps her in captivity.

Symons   Yes. I wonder whether you'd consider *The Collector* a crime story. I'm not sure. My inclination would be to feel that it wasn't a crime story, although obviously it is a crime to kidnap somebody. There's no question in that sense it's a crime story. But again the line that divides books which have got material about crime in them from what almost any afficionado would think of as crime stories is a very odd one and it's drawn by different people in different places.

Herbert   That's true. That's true. What do you think about *Crime and Punishment*, then?

Symons   Well, I used to say that *Crime and Punishment* was an example of a crime story of a very superior kind. I don't think it is now. I've changed my mind about that. And about *The Brothers Karamazov* and about *Bleak House*. Those are three examples of books which are generally—not generally, *always*—regarded as classic novels. You hear people saying, "Well, Dickens was the first real crime writer" or Dostoevsky, of course. Well, it doesn't seem to me really so. Because the part of *Bleak House* that is concerned with crime is too little a part of the novel. It's not the main stream of the novel by any means.

Dickens's basic concerns weren't with the crime story as [were] the concerns of Dashiell Hammett, whom I only mention because I regard him so highly. Hammett's concerns *are* with the crime story, although I think he was a very good novelist. But Dickens's concerns and Dostoevsky's are much too wide to be pinned inside the crime novel; so I've changed my mind over this. I wouldn't any longer think that *Bleak House, The Brothers Karamazov, Crime and Punishment* are more than books which have some details of the crime story in them. In *The Brothers Karamazov*, there's interrogation and some actual detective work, which is really rather like a crime story. But they're not crime stories, their concerns are altogether different from those of Hammett and Chandler and me, to make up descending ranks.

Herbert   In other words, a very important aspect of your judgment of what makes a good crime novel or a detective story is the intent of the author?

Symons   It's the intent of the author, yes. And it does seem to me that that places a limit on the merits of the crime story. I think crime novelists, the best crime novelists, are very much underrated in comparison with what people call the best novelists. I don't see why one shouldn't consider Phyllis James's crime stories in the same breath and on the same level as novels by Margaret Drabble and Angus Wilson and so on. But then if one is considering on the very highest level—if you're trying to make comparisons with Dickens and Dostoevsky or Chekhov or Flaubert, they really do not work. Because the crime novelist's intentions are never as serious as they ought to be. The problems of the puzzle—as Chandler said—you've got to have a puzzle of some sort. That's almost demanded. You've got to solve it. Well, that's bound to take away from the merit of the story if you're thinking of it on the very highest level. So I think we crime writers ought to be clamoring away for more notice and I think we ought to be saying, if we feel we are, "I'm as good as Wilkie Collins," who was a crime writer—and a very, very good crime writer, and also was a very good novelist but not a novelist of the very highest class. I don't think a crime writer can be a novelist of the very greatest stature.

Herbert   Does this have to do with the fact—perhaps not quite so much in a crime novel but certainly in a detective novel—that you have to trick the reader about character and therefore you must undermine the honest exploration of character?

Symons   It's a built-in flaw. Yes, yes it is. Well, much the same thing applies in a crime novel. You're almost certain in some way or other to be providing bits of surprises. These are the essence of the book. They may not be the sort of surprises that you're providing in a detective story; they won't be the surprise of saying "Ah ha! Surely you see that these footprints have not been made by feet; they have been made by somebody walking on his hands," or something of that sort. They are not that sort of surprise. But they are surprises and they are essential to the novel and they are very good. There is nothing against using these devices that I can see, but they are not the devices that are used in general by the greatest of novelists.

Herbert   Since I view you as the chief advocate for gaining academic and critical attention for the genre, I am a little bit surprised to hear you express this.

Symons   I [used to] feel very resentful that the crime story should have been regarded for so long as Cinderella and I hope *Bloody Murder* in its three editions has helped to correct that and has elevated the crime story. But when Philip Larkin says, "My two favorite novelists are Thomas Hardy and Dick Francis," he is in part joking, but he's not entirely joking; he's meaning to puncture pretentiousness and pomposity. Well, that's fine, but at the same time, I'm not sure that he's doing great service either to the novel in general, or even to Dick Francis. Or similarly, when Kingsley Amis says that Ian Fleming is a much more interesting novelist than Saul Bellow, I don't feel that's— in part they're intending just to provoke, but in part they are meaning what they say, and I don't really approve of saying things like that, in a moralistic manner.

Herbert   You feel there is a distinct difference in the literary aspirations of the great novel and the detective or crime novel?

Symons   In practice it doesn't seem to me that the crime story does ever fulfill the requirements of a great novel. It is in fact sensational writing. It's sensational material, but however you deal with it, even if you deal with it as skillfully as Wilkie Collins, it doesn't aspire—Collins didn't aspire to being the very highest kind of novelist.

Herbert   What *is* the business of the highest kind of novelist?

Symons   I would have thought the distinction is the sort of seriousness that doesn't mark the crime story. If one takes Collins—who I think was marvelous at his best—it's still all tricks. He's not deeply involved, not truly, deeply involved with his characters; as splendid as Count Fosco is, splendid though the villains are, excellent as Sergeant Cuff is. It's not on the same level as Joseph Conrad and *The Secret Agent* for example. I mean you could call *The Secret Agent* a thriller or *Under Western Eyes* a thriller, but they're much more than that.

7

Herbert But there are crime writers, surely, who write with a very high degree of seriousness. Certainly Phyllis James is very serious about what she does.

Symons Well, it's serious on its own level. I think I would have, in the end, to say that crime writers, myself included, have got something lacking in them, if one is speaking on the very highest level. I would think—I don't especially want to name names, but I would think that P. D. James or Ruth Rendell, they are excellent novelists. They are as good novelists as almost any of the novelists who are around now, but they are not in the same league as great novelists, of whom there aren't all that many.

Herbert For the purposes of argument, let's determine by example what we mean by the term "great novelist." Shall we say that Dostoevsky is one?

Symons And Tolstoy, too, of course.

Herbert What about George Orwell, who has had a profound impact on so many readers?

Symons Oh, no, certainly not. He's not a great novelist. A great man perhaps but not a great novelist. Don't think he would aspire to that, even.

Herbert So what you're saying essentially is that the crime novel has the potential of reaching much higher levels than anyone ever considered but in terms of its reaching the very highest levels of literary achievement there are some limitations that are, if not absolutely insurmountable, likely to cause problems. I think you first demonstrated this in the earliest edition of *Bloody Murder*, a volume that caused the academic world to open its eyes to the genre.

Symons These limitations certainly could be surmounted in theory. It's just in practice—I mean certainly nobody could say that P. D. James and Ruth Rendell aren't absolutely serious about what they're doing or, indeed, in my better books that I'm not very serious about what I'm doing. I suppose what I'd have to say is that on the highest level there is a failure of imagination, a failure of moral intensity or some rather pompous term like that. You would absolutely find that moral intensity, in Henry James or Saul Bellow. I mean in a way, Bellow is much inferior as a technical writer of novels to P. D. James or Ruth Rendell. He doesn't have all that much interest in plot. What he's interested in is a kind of moral lesson rather of the kind that P. D. James is trying to teach us in *The Children of Men*.

Herbert And perhaps significantly, that is not a crime novel. I know what you mean. The spirit of delivering a moral lesson is similar.

8

Symons   There is of course also with crime writers—not James or Rendell or, I hope, myself or indeed a number of others—but with a generality of crime writers [it is true that] they write sloppily.

Herbert   The use of the series character may encourage laxity on the part of the author. It's so easy to rely on what the reader has already built up in his or her imagination about the series character. As a result the writer does not need to be so careful and the readers remain happy and the publisher is indeed very happy to have that manuscript just that much sooner.

Symons   One stumbling block for crime writers is that what publishers want, quite naturally, is something that will sell, and really this is all they expect from crime writers.

Herbert   Certainly in this day and age of publishing, my goodness.

Symons   Especially this is so now. It seems to me that one has seen, in the States particularly, books being pushed and publicized—writers being pushed and publicized like Elmore Leonard, who has really only a very average talent, or a slightly better than average talent, but whom we were seeing it was possible to boost into somebody who was the equal, as he certainly is not, of Chandler or Hammett or Ross Macdonald. So crime writers aren't encouraged to be good writers or serious writers. They are *dis*couraged. I mean Chandler said something of this when he said something like "to be taking a mediocre form and doing something good in it; that's a real achievement. It may not be the highest achievement but it's a real achievement." That's all that most crime writers can hope to do.

Herbert   I was talking to Sue Grafton about this and she noted that a very predominant concern of the mystery writer is the order of delivery of information. In a mainstream novel you may elucidate an aspect of character whenever you like but in a crime or mystery novel you may do so only if you can continue to keep that secret as to what the character has been up to in the woodshed.

Symons   Well you can reveal that now to a certain extent, can't you?

Herbert   More so than in the past but, as you pointed out, there still has to be some element of surprise regarding character.

Symons   Mm hm.

Herbert   Taking the question of authorial intent into the personal realm, when you sit down to write a crime novel, how conscious are you of your own literary intentions? Do you see a book like *Death's Darkest Face*, which many have said "succeeds as a novel with elements of crime" in it, as a "crime novel" right from the start?

Symons   It started, just on the face of it, [as] a novel. (Pauses.) Yes, but it also started out—I had clearly in my mind that it was going to be about the disappearance of a poet. That would be the core of the book. The material in this case somehow was the relationship between a son and his father. That . . . took it away from the class of the crime story, but it is still a crime story; it had its inception as a crime story.

Herbert   But it also succeeded as a study of character. And the ambiguous ending emphasized the fact that this was no ordinary whodunit. I loved that ending.

Symons   Well, in *The Progress of a Crime* I was intending to make some comments on the way that justice is administered. That sounds very pompous on my part, but if one starts out with an aim like that it need not be pompous as you do it.

Herbert   And it certainly isn't a pompous book.

Symons   But that was the intention, and it spawned simply from my reading the account of a court case, an actual court case in which half a dozen boys had killed another boy on a bus in Clapham—which is where I was brought up and so that drew my attention. And the police simply didn't know which boy had done it; so they grilled all of the boys, as they do, and they picked on the one that seemed to them most likely. And there was another thing extraordinary about it. There was a marvelous eyewitness who was on the top of another bus and who had actually seen it all happen and she really was a splendid witness. She was totally unflurried in the box and she became more positive the more time went on. The boy she accused was found guilty, sent to prison for life. By the time he came out, it had been made clear that he wasn't guilty at all, but like so many very good eyewitnesses of something you see only for a moment or two, she'd been mistaken or she'd exaggerated and probably another boy did it. All that background I was able to turn into a book about the way, in my view, justice gets done or *doesn't* get done. But it was also a crime story and a crime puzzle. You know, one wants to put that in too.

Herbert   Your mention of Clapham leads me to ask you about your childhood and any incidents within it or traits of character that may have led to your becoming a writer. Did you know from an early age that you wanted to be a writer?

Symons   Before I was in my twenties I wrote poems, but when you say "become a writer," a writer in a commercial sense and make one's living as a writer, I never dreamed of that until, I suppose, my first crime story was published. It never occurred to me that people could do such things—except rather low-grade figures like Somerset

10

Maugham. So I mean, when I was in my teens I wrote poems and then I started my own verse magazine.

Herbert   And it was during this general period of time that you wrote your first mystery novel, rather as a lark, wasn't it?

Symons   Yes. I was working in an engineering firm when I started my verse magazine. I had no financial backing. It was something one couldn't even conceive of doing now but then one was able to have a thousand copies [of the magazine] printed for I think something like £15. Which of course wouldn't mean £15 now. But even then it wasn't very much. It was possible, one hoped, to be able to get the £15 back from sales. I printed the poems of all of the young poets of the time who were outside what was to us the kind of magic circle of the ordained group of people who'd been to Oxford or to Cambridge who were the fashionable writers of the period. Well, I printed a lot of people who weren't fashionable then, like Dylan Thomas, Roy Fuller, Gavin Ewart—although Gavin Ewart was printed in other places, too—and I also found a place in which I could put my own poems.

Herbert   And then, of course, these writers became literary luminaries. How wonderful that you helped to give them a start!

Symons   So that went on for two or three years, almost three years until the war came. When the war came I thought, and in a way rightly from my point of view, that the sort of poetry I admired and wanted to print wouldn't appeal during the war. There would be a flood of patriotic poems, war poems, the kind of thing I wouldn't want to print, so I closed up the magazine. Well then—at some point before that I'd written a joke crime story with the help of a friend of mine called Ruthven Todd, which was based on the surrealist exhibition.

Herbert   It was quite an amusing book, as I recall.

Symons   The idea was to put all our friends into our crime story, set it in the context of an art movement that we invented, kill off the friend we liked least, make another friend the murderer and so on. And well, my friend never actually wrote any of it. He provided all the ingenious ideas; I wrote it, but it was a joke. I didn't even think of sending it to a publisher. Then the war came, and how it actually survived the war I don't know. But at some point my wife, Kathleen, found this yellowed manuscript and read it and said, "It is quite funny in parts; I wonder what a publisher would do with it? We could *do* with some money." And at that time money was fairly short and I was maintaining my art with a job at the BBC—or more or less maintaining my art. (Smiles.) It really is a very, very bad crime story—per-

11

haps it is funny in parts—but so bad I haven't allowed it now for many years to appear in print again. It was called *The Immaterial Murder Case*, based on a movement I've called "immaterialism," which meant that you painted what was *not* there. And it was fairly successful. Although any book in 1945, when it appeared, would have been fairly successful—almost any one, because paper was so short it was easy enough to sell a reasonable-sized edition of almost anything.

Herbert   You're too modest. What inspired you to continue?

Symons   It didn't really occur to me for quite a little while that one could do anything else with a crime story, I don't know why not. And so I wrote two more books which featured the same detective, a figure called Inspector Bland. And then it wasn't a conscious decision that I wouldn't use Bland and that I probably wouldn't use a detective at all that went through a number of books.

Herbert   In other words, you made no conscious decision to eschew the series sleuth?

Symons   Right. And I then wrote a book, *The Thirty-First of February*, which was based on the three and a half years that I had spent in an advertising agency, which I very much disliked. That is to say, I didn't dislike the people; I was actually very impressed with them and they've actually stayed friends of mine, but I disliked the whole world of advertising. So this was really, I suppose, about advertising, although it is also a sort of horror story as well. I'd been reading Dostoevsky at the time and there are echos of the Grand Inquisitor in the interrogations that my hero, or villain, or victim suffers during the course of the book. So there you are: I've wavered since then between writing occasionally books which I've written because people have said, "Why are you always so gloomy and miserable, Julian, in your books? Why don't you write something that's fairly lighthearted?" And then I've written a lighthearted book and they've said, "My God, you'd better go back to what you write best!"

Herbert   I am still trying to discover the earliest hints that you would become a writer. When you were a small boy did you have the sense of narrating your experiences to yourself?

Symons   Never! I only had a sense of how miserable it was to be a small boy. I mean when I was nine or ten, like many others I read the Sherlock Holmes stories and loved them. And if anybody had said to me, then or a little later, "You know, one day you'll be paid money actually to read crime stories and review them"—which I [later] did for ten years for the Sunday *Times*—I'd have thought that was a fate too lovely to happen! But it did happen and it was very enjoyable. But even now I really very much enjoy doing book reviews. They're what I would call my drug, I suppose. I admit I feel a bit uneasy if I haven't got a book I should be reviewing fairly soon.

Herbert   But the other writers whom I have interviewed for this book have shared with me an image of themselves as a child and as a young person. And you do that beautifully in your wonderful, slim autobiographical volume, *Notes From Another Country*, but I would love it if you would share a few memories for the benefit of this interview. Do you have an image of youself as a small boy?

Symons   Well, I don't have much of an image. I really remember awfully little about my life up to the age of about six. I mean I very much envy those who are able to say precisely what was said to them in their cradle or in their pram.

Herbert   (Laughs.)

Symons   And what reactions they had to their uncle or aunt. I really have nothing of that sort.

Herbert   You have written about your war games with tin soldiers.

Symons   Yes, but that was much later; that was about ten or eleven. Yes, when my father would discover me playing with my soldiers he would tell me to clear them up. When he found me reading an article on Marshal Lannes [one of Napoleon's generals] in *The Encyclopaedia Britannica* he took the volume from me, turned the pages to the article on Linnaeus and, frantic with irritation, he said, "Read that, sir; read something useful!"

Herbert   He sounds very severe.

Symons   I am sure he meant no harm to me, but I think he wrought it. By the time I was seventeen or so, I largely escaped my isolated family life to the common, Clapham Common, in the summer; in the winter, to the local Temperance Billiards Hall, where I played snooker. But as I say, of my early boyhood I have very little recollection. I was marked out as a backward child after the age of about two and a half.

Herbert   A backward child!

Symons   At the age of two and a half I was very, very *forward* in the sense that I was able—I don't know quite how—to recite great chunks of poetry, which I suppose must have been taught to me. I was stood up on a chair and set to recite. Well, whether it was because of that or because of some other cause, by the age of about five or six I had a very bad stammer, the very bad stammer continued to exist and does still exist, as you will have gathered, I daresay.

Herbert   No!

Symons   The very bad stammer persisted until the age of about sixteen when I started to go out with girls! And now it's all but vanished.

Herbert   Most boys would *begin* stammering at that time!

Symons   (Laughs.) I went to one school after another. We lived for a time in Brighton and there I was sent to a school for backward boys and girls.

Herbert   At what age was that?

Symons   From eight to nine. When we returned to Clapham my father's life, during the latter part of his life, was a series of unsuccessful ventures. When the Brighton venture failed, we went back to Clapham and I was sent to a fee-paying school which I disliked very much; there also my stammar was a limitation, and there I played truant quite often, and I was discovered by my parents. They were horrified. And in the end they sent me to the local state school, where I flourished.

Herbert   Was it a particularly good school?

Symons   Well either it was a splendid school, or you might say I got down to my level.

Both (Laugh.)

Symons   No, it really was absolutely an excellent school.

Herbert   Did the stammer cause you to feel set apart from the average person in a social situation, in a way that later has become an advantage to you as a writer?

Symons   It's no use. I can't speculate on that. I really don't know. I only know that that was absolutely the first time I was happy at school. And I was very happy there. [But] I grew up very lopsided: very, very good at English; very, very good at history; very, very good with maths. I was pretty bad at almost everything else, or not very good at geography and so on, and really *hopeless* in science. So I could never have taken any examination, because the examinations I would have had to take to move out of the state school to get a scholarship involved passing in five or six different subjects. I was so hopeless at science that I left school at fourteen—

Herbert   At fourteen!

Symons   —which was the standard age if you didn't go on to a grammar school. At that time you left school at age fourteen.

Herbert   At what age did you get your job at Victoria Lighting and Dynamo?

Symons   I went there when I was sixteen.

Herbert   Do you regret having had no further formal education?

Symons   The answer to that has to be "Yes." Because with a university education I would have learned the techniques of research that I had to work out for myself. But there are rewards in ignorance. I was able to encounter the glories of English literature head-on, without being told which books to admire and the proper reasons for admiring them. I could form my own judgments.

Herbert   Did you mainly study literature or did you take on other subjects, like philosophy?

Symons   I read far more verse than prose; I ignored the great nineteenth-century English novelists; but I read instead Tolstoy, Turgenev, and Dostoevsky. Of course, years later I remedied some of these gaps in my reading! I found much of philosophy uncongenial: I could not understand Kant, but I settled down with Schopenhauer and Nietzsche. I was much absorbed with the problems of free will and determinism.

Herbert   A theme of some of your crime novels.

Symons   My reading choices betray a preference for realism over romance. But in between that time [of leaving school at age fourteen and taking a first job] I really worked for my brother A. J., my oldest brother, making lists of things in catalogs and so on for which he paid me a pound a week. I think really he was just being kind to me and to my mother. We weren't terribly poor, but we weren't terribly well off, and she was very eager for me to have some pocket money.

Herbert   And then you took the job at Victoria Lighting and Dynamo where, I understand, you were employed for eleven years.

Symons   Eleven years. Far too many years! I can't imagine now how I could have stayed so long except, of course, that one was pleased to have a job and not to be sacked; the other is that it was a very small firm, and actually a dotty, silly little firm, in which I was very free to do almost anything I liked. I mean, I had no bosses, except for the man who was the director; and the third thing was that in the latter part of it, I was very much occupied with my magazine, which I used to do on office time.

Herbert   I continue to wonder about the child who developed into a multifaceted writer. In addition to your crime novels, you have written biographies and volumes of literary criticism, even military history.

15

Symons   I'm slightly disproportionately pleased when old books turn up and are brought out again or when I meet someone who refers to the books I've written on Victorian military history or whatever.

Herbert   I am still eager to see how your imagination worked when you were a small boy.

Symons   Well, I used to play war games.

Herbert   By yourself? Or with your brother?

Symons   No, entirely by myself.

Herbert   What would be involved in that? Strategy? Or just "bang, bang"?

Symons   Well, I was fascinated when I was young, nine or ten, or eleven, by historical fiction—Stanley Jay Weyman, *Under the Red Robe*, for instance. This English name is probably unfamiliar to you. Equivalent American ones would be—well, I don't know; fill in with American historical novelists—only of course English ones went back much further because of our having a bit more history.

Herbert   (Laughs.) All I can say is, "Your history is our history, too."

Symons   So I would have two groups of soldiers fighting each other, mostly during the English Civil War: the Royalists and the Roundheads during the English Civil War. The Royalists were defeated and Charles the First had his head cut off. Well, so those were mostly my two sides; sometimes they would have been Napoleon and Wellington.

Herbert   How did you represent these? Did you lay them out and reenact the battle scenes?

Symons   Well, I based myself on a very, very good book by H. G. Wells called *Little Wars,* which I used to play with toy soldiers, in which he and his friends mapped out a terrain with rivers and they had all kinds of rules. They had houses that they had made so that it would be the "battle of the farmyards" or. . . . Well, in a way my ambitions were rather greater because I didn't want farmyards; I wanted Napoleon and Wellington. On the other hand, I found it very difficult to have things like rivers. Then, when our son was small, I played war games with him and we then did play on the H. G. Wells's *Little Wars* basis, on which you could move your cavalry two feet at a move, and you could move all your infantry only one foot at a move, and so on.

Herbert   And you would be limited to what actually happened, historically?

Symons   No, no, *certainly not*!

Herbert   So you might start out with the same river or geography as existed in history, but then you'd say, "Ah, if I were the general here, how would I handle that?" And respond to the unpredictable moves of the other person. But you were doing this solo.

Symons   As a child, I was doing this solo, yes. The one way to make sure of winning.

Herbert   Isn't that the way mystery novelists work?

Both   (Laugh.)

Herbert   We were talking earlier about an author's body of work revealing something about the landscape of his or her mind. Well, your military history certainly stems from this imaginative play. I would suspect that the crime writer's strategizing might owe something to the *Little Wars* experience, too. I would like to pursue this idea further.

Symons   My inner landscape? I suppose you could deduce also from my own books that I'm not much interested in the details of violence, in all the blood and guts, nor indeed very much interested in the forensic details, although I am a bit more about that. But that I'm interested in the motivation of it. I would have thought that you've got all this— well this isn't obvious—one shouldn't expect any writers [to] be producing a pen portrait of themselves when what they're supposed to be producing is fiction, but I would have thought again with almost any writer—with Maugham, say, one can trace through Maugham's best books for the sort of person that Maugham was.

Herbert   A number of crime and mystery writers including Jessica Mann, Catherine Aird, and P. D. James have come right out and told me how they chose the mystery form because they do not enjoy self-reve-lation. They wished to write but they did not want anything autobio-graphical to come out in their work. Now, of course they've revealed a lot of things without intending it, but they certainly haven't revealed a great deal about the circumstances of their personal lives. With Phyllis James you know that she has a love of architecture, the place, the love of language, love of liturgy, all of that, but do you know very much about what essentially has happened to her? No. In Saul Bellow you might. Have you yourself felt that this is one of the appeals of crime writing for you? I would think perhaps less so than the other writers that were just mentioned.

Symons   I'm not quite—(Pauses.)

Herbert   Have you felt that crime writing is appealing because you can say all kinds of things about human character, as Phyllis James points out, but you don't necessarily have to say very much about what personally happens in your life?

Symons   No, but then that would apply to any novelist. That they don't have to do that.

17

Herbert Hmm, but I think the crime writer actually sometimes uses the mystery as a shield.

Symons It applies to crime writers more, yes. I would have thought really—actually any good crime writer, like any other good writer, inevitably puts quite a bit of himself or herself into the books.

Herbert We don't have a sense of Julian Symons's life and the circumstance of your life from your crime novels as thoroughly as we do from *Notes from Another Country*.

Symons Well, of course that's true. But I would have thought that if you read half a dozen books by P. D. James or Ruth Rendell or John Le Carré or me, you would get a pretty fair idea of the sort of preconceptions or conceptions that we've got about life and morality and so on —about the kind of people we are. [But with many] crime writers that doesn't apply. I mean they do deliberately keep themselves out of it. I would have thought that, certainly out of the half dozen books of mine that are among my best books—I would have thought you've got a reasonable portrait of me in the margins of them, just as you would have got a portrait of P. D. James, especially in her later books, as being somebody who was a Christian as you say, or a deist as she says, and—with a small "c"—also a conservative. Some-body who wishes to conserve things and so on. But she's not a radical. I mean she may have been a radical in the past; you would know that. You would know from Ruth's books that she has a tendency towards being a radical, although certainly not a militant one and a tendency towards being a feminist and so on.

Herbert And just which ones do you consider to be your best six crime novels?

Symons I change the six titles according to the day of the week. I mean one would certainly be *The Thirty-First of February*, another one would be *The Blackheath Poisonings*, another one would be *The Man Who Killed Himself*. I think *A Criminal Comedy of the Contented Couple* will have to wait a moment. Another one would be *The Progress of a Crime*, another one I think would be *The Color of Murder*. Very depressing that I'm naming ones which were published so long ago and I might even include *Something Like a Love Affair* because it does seem to me very successful.

Herbert And what do we learn about you from those six books you mention?

Symons About me? Well I suppose a frustrated radical or a frustrated—a socialist who doesn't believe that the socialist world he wants will ever actually happen. I mean my books are full of defeated figures. My biographies—I'm always attracted by people who fail. Poe in a sense was a failure. My brother, whom I've written about, also by the size of his aspirations failed sort of. One could say that Carlyle failed [if] you know what he wished to achieve when he was young [and] what he actually achieved and became and so on.

Herbert   And in your crime writing, you frequently focus upon characters who are, if not failures, leading lives of quiet desperation. This makes me think of Tolstoy's famous line about happy families being alike, while unhappy families have a story. It seems to me that unhappy families make fertile ground for the crime story. Their failures provide that sort of gap between their aspirations and reality that fascinates you.

Symons   Well, my new book at the moment is called *Playing Happy Families*, and the basis of that is that what appears to be at first glimpse a happy family turns out to be divided in all kinds of ways. And the primary cause of the division is the disappearance of a prime member of the family. Again, it's based on an actual case in which a girl disappeared after showing somebody around a house. She was an estate agent or a realtor and she had an appointment to show somebody around a house. She was never seen after that. Her appointments book said "Mr. Kipper," which is a very odd name. Whether she ever did show the house, or whether Mr. Kipper was the murderer—she's never been found. Her parents now accept that she's dead. I mean, nobody knows exactly what happened.

Herbert   Oh, it *must* be a phony name!

Symons   They did actually find somebody who, strangely enough, was Kipper who had been looking for a house, but it turned out he was not involved in it at all. So what the explanation was, whether it was a joke that she put in her diary, whether "Kipper" meant something altogether different nobody knows.

Herbert   Yes. It is interesting how you often use an actual news item to inspire your fiction.

Symons   Yes. Yes. At the moment, [this novel] seems to be all right, except that it seems to be moving out in so many different branches, especially with my having made the detective much the most interesting and important character. Again, the basic problem of the book will be the administration of justice. What is justice? Does one cause unhappiness by adhering to what you think are good principles or not? At least, all that is what I *hope* to be able to bring out in the books. Of course, often what one is hoping to bring out is not what the reader finds.

Herbert   When you write a mystery do you find yourself preoccupied with strategy in constructing it?

Symons   Oh, yes. I've never been able to do what I think mystery writers ought to do in theory, and that is map out the whole course of the book right from the beginning to the end. So that you will know precisely what is going to happen. The nearest I ever get to it is mapping out two or three pages, which gives me an approximate course of the story, but I almost never stick to it completely.

Herbert   Well, you know, this interests me, because one of the things that has surprised me in my conversations with crime writers is the astonishing role of serendipity in what one expects to be a very controlled kind of writing. Jonathan Gash even says that his pen virtually writes for him, you know; he just sits down he doesn't know if he's going to write a cartoon, another chapter of a Lovejoy mystery, a poem, or what it's going to be.

Symons   It might be unfortunate for him if he sat down to write a crime story time and again every day and found himself writing a poem! If that went on for months that would be rather disconcerting. Does he practice medicine now?

Herbert   A little; he acts as a consultant in his tropical disease specialty. In fact, one time I was going to have lunch with him and he said, "I absolutely indemnify you; I will be clean and germ-free when we meet for lunch."

Symons   (Laughs.)

Herbert   I must say he came in smelling like a germicide. Fortnum and Mason's, you know? He'd obviously made the effort.

Symons   I'd certainly go along with the pleasure that one gets out of characters who emerge much more strongly in a given book then you intend them to; when you intend them [to be] minor characters and they really *won't stay down*. Of course the same applies the other way around. In *The Blackheath Poisonings*, in the first version of it, there were two small children. It seemed to me that it would be a good idea to have small children. I simply could not fit them in the story and in the end I had to cut them out. More interesting than that is when characters emerge demanding more attention from you so that you become absorbed in them.

Herbert   Did this happen in *Something Like a Love Affair*?

Symons   Not particularly. The challenge that I set myself in that book was to tell the story from the point of view of the female character.

Herbert   Have you set yourself a challenge in most of your books?

Symons   Well not every one, but that's true of a number of them.

Herbert   You're too modest. As you said before, if you're not employing a series character all the time, you have to look for the right story, plot, and everything else, as well as the right people to populate it.

Symons   Yes, if you use a series character, you start off with a great many advantages and in a way you're making life easier for yourself and indeed [for] your readers, who are very keen to meet Commander Dalgleish again or Chief Inspector Wexford again, and so on. On the other hand it seems to me you do limit yourself, as well. [In] the first three books I used a series character and I thought, "It's not what I want to do at all."

Herbert   What made you impatient with it?

Symons   I suppose I wanted to do something different.

Herbert   Do your books tend to stem from an idea for a crime?

Symons   Well, mostly I take inspiration, if that's the word, from things I've read in the paper. Something or other was clipped. What one almost never gets anything from is friends who say, "I've a splendid idea for a story, if only I could write it, I'd do very, very well. I suspect you can." (Smiles.)

Herbert   I see.

Symons   I think also, the older one grows, one gets to realize one's limitations or, if you like, one's capacities. I know that I'm not very good at describing violent action and so I try to avoid it as much as I can. I'm not tremendously interested in the intricate details of police work, so I avoid that as much as I can. I *am* interested in criminal psychology, so that inspires me to continue.

Herbert   I wonder what inspires you to write on a daily basis? Would you tell me about your typical writing habits?

Symons   Normally I'm at my desk at half-past nine.

Herbert   What kind of things do you feel you need to have in your surroundings when you are writing? Do you have to have at hand any kind of thesaurus or things of that nature?

Symons   I have *The Shorter Oxford* [*English Dictionary*]. I do have a thesaurus but I almost never use it. And I have the *Supplement to the Oxford English Dictionary*, which is pretty well indispensable. But I don't overuse the thesaurus.

Herbert   And you use a manual typewriter? How long have you had this Imperial typewriter?

Symons   Well, I must have had it nearly forty years and when I bought it the chap who sold it to me said, "This will see you out." At that time electric typewriters were very rare. You see, I'm a good typist. But as to my daily habits, I would go on until half-past four. I almost never work on weekends. In a way it's really rather like office hours.

Herbert   Using your forty-year perspective on the crime novel, I'd like to return to the point you made about the author's intent as essential to determining the literary possibilities of a book. In *Bloody Murder* you said that "the intent of the author places a limit on the merits of the crime story," and I wondered if you could comment further on that.

Symons   Yes, what I meant by the intent of the author was that—let's take it on a low, fairly commonplace level—that most authors of crime stories are simply intending to produce a good commercial article. They want it to be a good commercial article, but they don't have any intention beyond that. Now, if one takes Raymond Chandler—Chandler was always pushing at the limits of the crime story; he wanted to do something more than produce a good commercial article. If you want to produce interesting characters, as Chandler did, then really the plot went out of the window. Well, this is one of the problems that confront, more or less, any writer of crime stories, I think. In Hammett's case, I'd say he had a down-to-earth approach in the sense that he really didn't care, and the result of not caring in his case was, I think in the best books, really splendid. But for most writers, obviously, it isn't a good idea not to care. So, my own approach would be, again in my better books—because I'm conscious that some of my books are very inferior—but taking my better books, the intent was first of all—and this *has to be* first of all for a crime writer—first of all to produce an interesting puzzle of some sort. It need not be the orthodox puzzle in which, to take it at its extreme point, all the suspects are gathered together in the drawing room, but some sort of puzzle, some sort of riddle, is one of the great attractions of the crime story, not only to me but I think to all readers. The passion for solving riddles is a human passion that long preceded any orthodox crime story. So that's one of the things you've got to have. So that's part of my intent. But my intent also in various books has been, as I was saying to you earlier, to show in one case the administration of justice; in another case the actual cost to chart the progress of a crime; and in another case still to examine the way in which two people who've each got a little kind of kink of abnormal psychology, which doesn't lead to anything harmful when they're alone, explodes when they meet so that they are led together into violent crime, which neither of them would commit on their own. So that's the sort of thing that I mean by the intent of the crime writer. You can have no more intent than to produce a very interesting puzzle. I think that's probably what is at the root of most crime writing. I would not like to denigrate the crime novel. What I think is not advisable to do is to have too grand an intention in the way of showing some sort of moral and to forget the puzzle. You mustn't do that. So that's a long answer to a short question.

Herbert   No. It's a wonderful answer. I've often wondered if people who read crime novels and write them may be somewhat more sensitive to the fragility of life, more aware of it and preoccupied with it than the average person.

Symons   I don't think I can honestly say that I'm much moved, or that I've been especially moved as a crime writer, to a consciousness of the extreme fragility of life; no. I think I'm pretty conscious of it anyway. And writing crime stories is something separate from that consciousness.

Herbert   You're not a person who feels, "At least I'm in control here, pulling strings here for life and death, whereas in real life I'm not"?

Symons   No, I don't think I feel any of that. I've always thought I had what I suppose is an Eastern feeling, that we place far too much emphasis on the sacredness of life so that in India or China—I don't mean Communist China—I think the consciousness that we may all die at any time is much stronger than it is in the West where, especially in this century, we go through all kinds of machinery to try to preserve our lives for another year or two, or five or ten. And we are deeply resentful, in fact, of the fact that we have to die. I don't consciously have any of that feeling. I accept that we have to die; accept that I shall have to die. I'm not conscious of the sacredness of life. I don't believe that life is sacred. And that will be a fairly unusual answer, I imagine.

Herbert   Yes, it is. Thank you. It seems to me that recently there's a lot of moral ambiguity creeping into the crime novel as compared to the past. In the crime novel today we see the impact of the crime upon people as though it were lasting. It's not just wrapped up in the library, you know, and all the loose ends are tidied up and everyone goes on their merry way. Have you any comments to make about that?

Symons   I agree with everything you're saying. And I'm delighted that that's so. Because it makes the crime story more of a novel, less simply a puzzle. That may sound like a contradiction of what I was saying just now. I think, for me anyway, there has got to be a puzzle, but there absolutely should not *only* be a puzzle: for the crime story really to flower, there has got to be something much more than just a puzzle.

So I welcome very much that, for example, in lots of modern crime stories the emphasis is on the criminal or on the psychology of the criminal, rather than it is on the detective and the academic or automatic working-out of the puzzle. I think that's a great gain, but still I must say I would not want to throw away the puzzle. It's only that I want to have that leading to something more. There's more enriching the whole crime story. And I think that is happening now. I think the crime story, as far as I can make a generalization of this sort, is much better now. It's much better written. It's much more varied. At its best, it's much more subtle than it was, say, half a century ago.

Herbert   Are we in a new "golden age" of the crime story?

Symons   Well, I'm sort of distrustful of the golden age. I think what is still called the "golden age" [of the 1920s and 1930s] was really not a golden age at all. It was a golden age, perhaps, of the crime story as pure puzzle, but—one can't make a generalization of this sort that is wholly true—but in general I think it's true that the crime story now is much, much better than it was in the past.

Herbert   Speaking of the past, from another point of view, what has been the appeal, for you, of setting some of your novels in the Victorian period? What advantages does this distance in time, or the Victorian period itself, offer to the writer?

Symons   Well, I've written three of them. I really only wrote the first of them because I wanted to see if I could write a period crime story, and I was really quite pleased with myself. I thought, "Well, this is really quite successful," and the book, which was called *The Blackheath Poisonings*, turned out to have been commercially and indeed in a critical sense, one of the most successful of my books. I mean, I don't think it ought to have been, but . . . . I then wrote two more, *Sweet Adelaide* and a book called *The Detling Murders*. *The Detling Murders* seemed to me terribly bad. I made quite a muck about it. It caused me more trouble! I rewrote it and rewrote it, which I rarely do, much more than any of my other books. Lo and behold! What happened but that it got very good press and also sold quite well, but it was so gruelling to me, I felt so dissatisfied by that that I thought, "That's it, I shan't write any more period crime stories." And as far as I can see, I shan't. (Smiles.) One should never be too categorical about these things. They were all set in around the fall of Victoria, between 1880 and 1900. To go back much further than that, to go back, I'd have thought, beyond the nineteenth century, well, it's something that doesn't interest me much.

Herbert   I'm actually thinking about your books and Peter Lovesey's.

Symons   Ah, yes, well, Victorian life seems to me near enough to our own, the motivations of people are near enough to our own, and Victorian life was so much the Great Age of Poisoning, that I feel it is a fruitful ground. I think Peter's books have exploited it very skillfully. Mine, not so skillfully.

Herbert   I was most impressed with *Sweet Adelaide*. I really enjoyed it.

Symons   Yes, well, I certainly enjoyed doing it. It's a mixture of fact and fiction.

Herbert   It's a fascinating study of a woman who suffered possibly unjustly from the strength of public opinion going against her.

Symons   I became very much absorbed in trying to trace the origins of Adelaide Bartlett, and all that kind of thing, but in fact the book wasn't greeted very warmly. In part I wrote that because somebody said to me, "Well, you've never really created a convincing woman character in the center of a story!"

Herbert   Oh! That's an insult.

Symons   I thought to myself, "Well, I suppose that's true." I slightly, one might say, cheated a little bit in the sense that after all she was a real woman, and I didn't have to invent her.

Herbert   But you had to be inventive in order to speculate about her character.

Symons   Of course I was free to do a little bit of inventing.

Herbert   Which is fascinating.

Symons   Which I enjoy doing.

Herbert   At one point in *Bloody Murder* you said that the crime novelist is most often a fictionally split personality. Half of him wants to write a novel about people affected by crime, but the other half yearns to produce a baffling mystery. In your own approach to writing a novel do you feel those forces pulling you two different ways?

Symons   They sometimes pull one two different ways, sometimes they don't. My books vary between good novels and good crime stories, and some perhaps are good novels and not so good crimes stories, and some perhaps are neither. It's really when one has the idea for a novel—a novel with a criminal element, but a novel—and then knows that one is expected to—or perhaps one wants to—shape it into the crime story form. It's then the conflict becomes most apparent, at least to me. I think I've dealt with this as well as I can in saying that a crime writer who takes it at all seriously is distinctly pulled two ways. He wants to write scenes which have got the tension and reality of those of any other novelist. At the same time, he knows that he has got to use those scenes—those scenes have also got to contribute towards the progress of the plot, which is the plot of a crime story. Now, there's no reason why this is at all impossible. It's not impossible. It's done, but probably one thing does take away from the other.

Herbert　In a sense you've got two preoccupations.

Symons　You've got two preoccupations, yes. Eliot taught us that very well in different contexts in relation to writing plays when he said it's perfectly possible to write a play on two different levels. What he had in mind—I think it was in answer to a question related to *Murder in the Cathedral*—on one level it's an exciting story, a crime story, you might say—a crime story of death, of villainy, of love—but on the other level, if you want to look at it more deeply, it's a story about faith and the adherence to faith in the face of persecution or something. I'm not comparing it with *Murder in the Cathedral*, but I've written *The Progress of a Crime*, as I mentioned before, in which you can take it as simply being—I hope—an exciting story about some boys who are accused of murder and whether or not they're guilty, or which one is guilty. But if you want to consider it further, it's a book about the administration of justice in Britain and of the behavior of the police in Britain under certain circumstances. But there is no compulsion to read it like that.

Herbert　I see. I wondered about importance of place in the crime novel. Some of your settings are very, very interesting and memorable.

Symons　I don't think I'm much concerned with that in a general way, but there are certain places which make a tremendous impact on us. One of them obviously is Blackheath, where I lived for ten years and enjoyed it very much. That's a rather obvious example. And in *Something Like a Love Affair*, there is a housing estate with a hotel; I wouldn't want to live in one of those. "Housing estate" is a rather downmarket term here. In fact I'd hate to live in one, but they do fascinate me in the sense of "What's inside?" But also in some short stories, for example, that sort of atmosphere, the atmosphere of the respectable bourgeois life confronted by something different, something nasty: a murder taking place. That interests me a great deal.

Herbert　The violence behind respectable *places*.

Symons　(Laughs.) Yes!

Herbert　I know that your crime writing has supported some of your other projects, including biography and other nonfiction writing. If you could have made a fortune on nonfiction, would you have turned away from crime writing?

Symons   There was once an interviewer from the BBC who said, "You know what you've been doing all your life? You've been writing [mysteries] in order to pay for the books that you wish to write and that you couldn't make a living from." And to a certain extent, this is true. And the nonfiction books I've written, with one or two exceptions, they've almost all been well received. I couldn't possibly have lived off them; the exception is the book about Poe [*The Tell-tale Heart: The Life and Works of Edgar Allan Poe*], which did make a very fair amount of money. But I could not even have lived off them at a very low level.

Herbert   To return to a suggestion of your first crime title, was there any validity to that BBC man's verdict? Did it strike you as material or *immaterial*?

Symons   (Smiles.) I would not have wished to be confined to crime writing; I also would not have wished not to have written crime stories. If I had struck lucky with a nonfiction book and made a great deal of money out of it, I'm sure I would still have written crime stories as well. They absorb me. For forty-seven years I have found them to be thoroughly absorbing.

▶ SUE GRAFTON

When in 1982 Sue Grafton created the sassy female private eye Kinsey Millhone, the world of hard-boiled fiction was largely the territory of men. But Grafton's sleuth, modeled on the traditional wisecracking, rugged individualist investigator, had lots more going for her than merely her initially surprising difference in sex. She had a network of memorable friends as supporting characters, an individual voice, a tremendous sense of humor, and an instinct to devote all of her heart and her courage to the interests of the powerless. This winning combination has taken Grafton and her private eye through ten books, beginning with *A Is for Alibi*, each memorably entitled after letters of the alphabet.

Although Grafton says that Kinsey is very much based upon the author's own personal characteristics, the reader who is intimately acquainted with the sleuth may expect a tougher gal in Grafton than her feminine appearance suggests. At book signings, publicity parties, and readings, the author tends to wear flowing outfits graced with long scarves and fluid skirts, hardly the wardrobe for avoiding car crashes and scaling fences! But the author may also be found in old sweats, running several miles each morning to keep in shape for a highly disciplined writing day that Grafton finds physically demanding.

If one imagines Kinsey with a twinkle in her eye as she tosses off witticisms and an intensity of gaze when she is concerned about victims of crime, these are features of Grafton in conversation. She works hard at responding to an interviewer and will go beyond the call of duty in offering hospitality. When this interviewer was unable to visit Grafton's Santa Barbara home, the author herself videotaped her writing environment in a

Monterey-style colonial home, accompanying it with a narration that pointed out everything from the chair in which the interviewer might imagine sitting, to a powder blue VW bug, bearing a "KINSEY" license plate, parked in the rose garden.

Panning around an office that Hemingway would admire for its qualities as a "clean, well-lighted room," Grafton remarked, "Yes, I always keep it this tidy! I like to work in serene surroundings. My feeling is that the creative process is itself so chaotic that it is much better if one's desk and all available surfaces are as clutter-free as you can make them." Mauve drawers and filing cabinets are topped with bookcases filled with autographed works by her many mystery-writing friends as well as an array of reference books ranging from a thesaurus to works on criminal law. Numerous awards are also tidily arranged; perhaps the most interesting are the carved bird Grafton was awarded by the Japanese Maltese Falcon Society and the stuffed, witchlike figure, perched on the computer terminal, embodying the Mysterious Stranger Award presented to the author by the Cloak and Clue Society.

Grafton has come a long way from her childhood in Louisville, Kentucky, to her present success. The daughter of intellectual parents who were afflicted with alcoholism, Grafton experienced a rather unsupervised childhood in a "classically dysfunctional family" before she married at age eighteen and earned a degree in English at Western Kentucky State Teachers College. The mother of three, Grafton believes that she suffered from the limited expectations often held by women growing up in her day as well as by a desire to build the perfect family life that had eluded her during her own upbringing. It took her three marriages to discover real happiness, and in her work life, she tried homemaking, work as a consciousness-raising group leader, and the writing of two mainstream novels and numerous screenplays and teleplays before, inspired by the desire to murder an ex-husband, she at last found her true calling as a private eye writer.

Herbert   I understand that you turned your hand to mystery writing at a time in your life when your law-abiding nature prevented you from carrying out a specific murder. Please tell us about your inclination to do away with your first husband.

Grafton   Well, that, in fact, came about because I was going through a very bitter custody battle in connection with a divorce. I have said on numerous occasions that in those days I'm not sure women were taught how to fight, so that I approached that situation with no skills, and no tools, and no ability to conduct myself with any fierceness whatsoever. What I found was that I was feeling helpless and frustrated and ineffectual, and all I could think to do at night in my bed was to conjure up these fantasies of *doing this man in*, because it seemed to me my life would be so much simpler and so much better if he simply *did not exist*. I would cook up various schemes for doing him in, and in the course of it I came up with a method, a murder method. This was the use of oleander, which, in California, is a very common shrubbery, and it's part of the California mythology. For instance, I had heard years before that when Indian women wanted to, you know, cause the death of a spouse, they would rip down an oleander branch and cook his meat on it. If he ate it, it did him in *quite* effectively. Also, I had heard from a neighbor that an ounce of oleander in a ton of hay will kill five hundred head of cattle. She had also told me the story of two children who were playing and they were using oleander leaves to stir their cereal. It was a make-believe game, and soon after, [they] consumed the cereal and were dead within hours. So this was the sort of information that I had been tucking away, just the way writers tend to do, so that in my fantasy this was the method I used. But I thought to myself, "Well, there's no way I can actually act this out, because I'm a law-abiding little bun. I'm gonna get caught at it; I'm gonna end up in a shapeless prison dress, disgracing the very children I'm fighting to keep!" And so in the end I thought, "Well, maybe the best revenge is to put this murder in a book and get paid for it. It's the best of all possible worlds: I get the satisfaction of eliminating this person who has caused me so much grief and pain, and I also get the satisfaction of fashioning a mystery novel out of it."

Herbert   It sounds like the ideal solution!

Grafton   However, I understood that it would be a mistake to tell the story from the point of view of the killer, because it would be limited to a one-book "series." It would be "*A Is for Alibi*, finito."

Herbert   That's right.

Grafton   So it seemed to me that what I needed was a character to interface between me and the reader, so that the reader would have someone to identify with, and therefore I came up with the character of Kinsey Millhone, who has marched with me steadily nine letters into the alphabet.

Herbert   She sure has. Congratulations! I don't usually like the word "interface" but here it seems especially appropriate because Kinsey—with that genuine ring to her voice—does serve as an interface between you and the reader. Readers and reviewers always say that Kinsey seems to step off the pages and become a character in the reader's private landscape, as it were.

Grafton   I hope so. Thank you.

31

Herbert   And especially when we are discussing a character who also serves as the first-person narrator, it is natural to ask the author, just how much do you identify with your character?

Grafton   Well, she and I are virtually the same person, with some obvious exceptions. Her lifeline and mine are not the same. I'm older than she, and will continue to be older than she at a much more rapid rate as the years go on: she will age one year for every two-and-a-half books, so that when I get to *Z Is for Zero* she will turn forty. I will then be sixty-eight years old.

Herbert   Aha! I deduce that you have a very definite writing schedule planned for the future.

Grafton   Yes. And also, Kinsey and I do not have the same set of parents. We were not raised in the same part of the country. But she and I are both Tauruses—my birthday is April 24 and hers is May 5—and so I think we have the same sensibility; we have the same nature. I tend to say, "We have the same opinions on many, many issues, unless you don't like hers [smiles], in which case I totally disavow any connection whatsoever!"

Herbert   (Laughs.)

Grafton   But I remember, when I first started writing *A Is for Alibi*, I would sit and come up with all this outrageous material, and I would think to myself, "People are gonna be furious! I can't say this!" Sort of like, in my well-bred, Southern manner it seemed to me totally sassy to say some of the things that Kinsey Millhone said as a matter of course. But what I have discovered as the years go on is that instead of being outraged, people are amused by her, and in fact identify with her hidden opinions and her secret observations of the human race. So what happens, in effect, is that people feel connected to Kinsey, and because they feel connected to her, they start feeling connected to me.

Herbert   I think we've already touched upon the two chief elements of Kinsey's success with readers: her genuine—and, I might add, unpretentious—voice, and her spunk. When you started writing, it was a pretty spunky thing for a woman to step into the arena of private eye fiction. What was the appeal, for you, of this hard-boiled genre?

Grafton   Well, I've always liked reading hard-boiled private eye fiction and I think when it finally occurred to me in my life that I wanted to try constructing a mystery novel, the female protagonist just seemed natural. Part of it was that I was already so far out of my element: when I began *A Is for Alibi* I knew nothing about investigative techniques, police procedure, or ballistics or toxicology and it seemed to me very presumptious, when I was already struggling for expertise, to try to write from a male point of view. Being female was the one area where I felt I knew what I was talking about and what I did, in essence, was I made myself my prime character. Since I'm female, Kinsey Millhone is also female.

Herbert Are you also tough? Or is that something you have to work at, not having had the experience of being run down by cars every day?

Grafton I don't have the experience of being run down by cars. I think I am tough in a psychic sense. I'm certainly tough in my persona—and I am also mild, soft-spoken, timid, and genteel. But I enjoy competition; I like to test myself in an arena such as hard-boiled private eye fiction. I am not competitive in sports, but there is a certain joy I take in what I call "playing hardball with the boys." You know, I enjoy being out there with the guys and it's kind of fun, since it's been a male-dominated turf, to get in there and knock elbows with those guys whom I greatly admire.

Herbert I wanted to know what you think is the most fascinating aspect of the life of the private eye for you as you portray it.

Grafton Well, I like to think of what I do as "private eye procedural." I'm personally interested in the methodology of investigating and background checking and that sort of thing. But I also think, if that's all you had you'd have a very dull book because truly, from my understanding, much of what a private investigator actually does is repetitive, routine plodding. It's work on the telephone. It's work in the courthouse looking up old birth and real estate records. But much like a police procedural, this is a kind of foundation for the unraveling of the mystery. The private eye procedure is what gives a reality to the case as it unfolds. The fun of it in some ways is the action. Certainly a fictional private eye sees many more car chases and gun battles than a real private investigator would but, after all, it *is* fiction and our job is to make it exciting and entertaining, so one does take liberties—but you've got to know exactly when you're tampering with reality.

Herbert Yes, well, one of the things I've wondered, too, is what kind of literary possibilities does this offer you, having this loner of a character, even if she has some relationships and a network system?

Grafton I think the private eye has always functioned literally as a private eye, E-Y-E, as an observer and as someone who comments on society and on family relationships and on the state of justice in this country, so to me it is the perfect vehicle through which one can look at the dark side of human nature. And I usually start with my own dark side because certainly I am acquainted with my own rage and with my own deviousness. I simply project that outward into various characters.

Herbert   Starting with *A Is for Alibi* and, as you say, marching onward, Kinsey provides an alternative to the feeling of rage and powerlessness that so many of us experience in life, whether she's acting—as in *A Is for Alibi*— to some degree on behalf of you in a poisoning case, or whether it is Kinsey's ability to rise to the occasion when faced with physical danger, or whether it is her advocacy, really, of the person who's in trouble or in a powerless position. I think that these attributes are very appealing to readers today.

Grafton   Well, I work very hard to stay in my own body when I write, and I work very hard not to become self-conscious about the sound of my own voice, and not to fall in love with that "I" narrator. You know, it is always tempting to imagine that, because you say one witty thing, that everything you say is witty, and I have watched other writers begin to stray from the original clarity of that voice into something that becomes a parody of itself. And I think it's because, with the review process and fan mail and feedback that one gets from a publisher, you start taking yourself way too seriously. I work very hard to keep myself human-shaped and civilized, and to keep Kinsey human-sized. I don't want her to be larger than life; I don't want her to be idealized, or in any way perfect; I don't want her to be consistent; I don't want her to be politically correct. But it means I have to pay very strict attention to the writing process so that I don't lose track of that.

Herbert   I'd love to learn more about the particular aspects of the writing process that most engage your attention.

Grafton   Well, humor is a curious critter, because to *try* to be funny is nearly impossible, and when I watch another writer try to be funny, I find the effect very strained, and that's true of my writing also. If I'm *trying* to be witty, or if I'm trying to be amusing, the effect is flat. [Whereas], if I lose myself in the process and simply focus on the truth as I know it, often the result is a form of humor. But it isn't a conscious attempt to be funny. I think when it's working the humor comes out of simple observations and simple statements about the world we live in.

Herbert   There is a real insight. What about the spontaneity? That must be necessary to continuing Kinsey's voice and to the process of writing humor.

Grafton   Oh, that's taken me a long time to learn because the question always with writers or with artists, I suspect, of any sort is, "How do you stay connected to your work? How do you keep peaceful? How do you keep free? How do you keep your spontaneity?"

Herbert   Spontaneity is vitally important.

Grafton   Well, and plus you add to that the fact that as you're working there is always a voice going, "Oh, man, here come the critics! Oh, man, what is your editor going to think? Oh, will they like it as well as the last one?"

Herbert   A great deal of pressure must accompany your fame.

Grafton   And you have this Greek chorus of voices, like in a haunted house, you know, just driving you insane.

Herbert   Beating their breasts.

Grafton   Yeah, that's right.

Herbert   Right.

Grafton   And so what I am learning is to stay very focused and very concentrated and in fact just make it a question of "Do I want to use the word 'mauve' or 'purple'?" And if I can focus *that* precisely, then all the rest of it takes care of itself.

Herbert   I see. You focus on very specific decisions.

Grafton   That's right. So I regard it strictly as process. It is all process and the question is, "Can you trust the process? Can you trust that on any given day? Even the questions that seem to destroy your work or to overwhelm your work or to dismantle your work, can you trust that those are the very questions that will take you deeper into the work itself?" So, from day to day, the question is, "Do you have the nerve to ask yourself every question that occurs to you? Do you have the nerve to follow all those roads and see where they lead? Do you have the nerve to write what needs to be written even if it doesn't correspond with what you thought this book was?"

Herbert   That's right. Do you have the nerve to break a deadline if you need to do something more?

Grafton   That's exactly right. That's exactly right, because all of that's artificial. You know, some days I think to myself, "What if I got sick, you know, what if I were in a hideous automobile accident?" The world would not come to an end if I failed to turn a book in on the specified date. So in some ways I need to give myself the same freedom I would have if I were in a hideous accident. You know? In which case, guess what? All bets are off.

Herbert   Or, on a more positive note, you could wake up in the morning and find that something wonderful has changed your life and temporarily takes you away from the writing desk!

Grafton   Right. But I'm very careful about the difference between self and ego and I learned this a long time ago from a therapist. I mean, my horror in life is being seduced by ego. My job is to stay as close to self as possible and therefore there are many things I decline. There are many, many moments where I deflect praise and attention because I think, "Oh, man, that's not what it's about and please don't let me ever get led down this garden path."

Herbert   Ah.

Grafton   Because ego will ruin a writer. Ego will ruin a writer. I have seen it too many times.

Herbert   Yes.

Grafton   And so my job for me is to stay as far from ego as possible. So in a curious way, you know, you remember the articles that we've heard over the years about how women can't enjoy their own success and women can't experience success. This was regarded as a fault in women but I think that [is] a mistake. I think women generally are more inclined to live in self than ego. Success is about ego and I think many women don't live in ego the way men do. The men get into their own success and they huff and puff and they strut around and they're just so full of themselves, but women, I think, will often absent themselves from that.

Herbert   And this ability to stay centered in the self is not a weakness, then?

Grafton   Oh, no. It is our great strength, *great* strength because we never take ourselves too seriously and we never get seduced into that business of thinking we're so impossibly wonderful. And therefore I think we stay closer to the truth and closer to sincerity and closer to reality.

Herbert   It sounds like you've faced down your demons and found a way to retain a focus on your work. Are there aspects of the writing process, aspects of the craft itself, that used to be difficult for you that have become easier over the years?

Grafton   Hmm. I'd have to think about that, because for me it is such a continuum. I mean, for me, as you learn things, you forget you didn't know them! And so as I look back, I mean, I always maintain, "My paper is always as blank as the next guy's." Every book is a brand new adventure and I always go back to what Eudora Welty said, which is, every book teaches you the lessons necessary to write that book. The down side is that none of the lessons from one book have anything to do with the lessons I need to learn for the next, so, while in some sense of the word, thirty years of writing has served me well, there is a sense in which every time I go up to bat it's a brand new game and each time out, you know—and I am sure this is true of other writers, too—you give away everything you have. You turn yourself inside out: every line, every gimmick, every device, every insight, every good sentence, every word you *know* you pour into a book so that when you get to the end of it you think, "I have nothing left."

Herbert   But then you have all those letters of the alphabet demanding that you continue your series!

Grafton   (Laughs.)

Herbert   Mystery writing would seem to be a very controlled art form. Would you agree with this, or have there been surprises along the way? I would love to hear about some of the paths that you have traveled along with Kinsey Millhone.

Grafton   The exciting thing is how you keep learning about yourself. That's what mystery writing is about: what it teaches us about ourselves.

Herbert   Please tell me more about that. Have you had some surprises about yourself as you've gone along?

Grafton   In the course of writing a book?

Herbert   Yes.

Grafton   Oh, certainly, because—because I am writing about a person who is an aspect of my personality but not its total summation. I mean, there is, in the course of writing about Kinsey Millhone, an incredible sense of discovery about me because truly when I write about her truth comes through me and it isn't a calculated—I don't even know how to say this—it isn't anything I've thought about. It is in the moment, it is in the process of writing, truth comes through. It's like I know things I didn't know I knew. And it's all because of her. I think that is really special to anyone writing about a single character over the course of many books. I don't know what happens to writers who are writing about a different character every time out. Maybe they make the same discoveries only in a different fashion. But for me Kinsey Millhone's growth is a parallel to my own and my job in life is to make sure I keep progressing and growing and changing and exploring myself so that she can grow, because if I shut down she shuts down.

Herbert   That's right. Can you give an example in your current book, *J Is for Judgement*, of any surprises, personal surprises that you encountered?

Grafton   Oh, the surprises have been amazing. The difficulty in discussing them is their form and content become interwoven so [that], for instance, for most of the book I have felt I was telling a certain story and though I am literally ten pages from the end of this book, this little voice came up and said, "I really think this book is about something else all together."

Herbert   Oh, isn't that amazing?

Grafton   Yeah, of course, however, the question still remains, "Can I pull that off? Can I take the reader to that other place?" And I don't know that I have the skill and, in the end, what I am asking may be too much for the nature of the book itself. If so, it is a course I may have to abandon. I don't know. But what makes my life exciting from day to day is [that] everything depends on my capabilities and my skills as a writer. So for me, it is never just an issue of, "Is it Lady Pemberly in the library with the rope?" It is always about facing my own demons and dealing with my history as a writer and trying to discover whether I have in me enough insight to take this book to some new level. And every book isn't like that. Some books are simpler. Some are more entertaining. (Pauses.) Some are darker, and that's part of the fun too.

Herbert   *D Is for Deadbeat* is a wonderful example of one of your darker works. Could you tell us more about the background for this book, which, among other things, deals with the subject of alcoholism?

Grafton   Yeah, that was a strange book. I always considered that my orphan child, and I felt it was a very dark book *because* it was about alcoholism. And yet I just reread it recently, and the power and the clarity astonished me.

Herbert   I think it is one of your best. What do you think accounts for this?

Grafton   You see, my parents were both alcoholics.

Herbert   I'm sorry to hear this.

Grafton   But there actually was a good side to this. Because they were alcoholics, I had a lot of freedom, and in those days we had no television. There were a lot of kids in my neighborhood. We *played* all day long, and we made up dramas. We acted out these incredible theatrical events. And I could stay out till *all* hours. I could ride the bus line from end to end. There was a 409-acre pond behind my house, and I was allowed to roam [around] it at will because the world was not so dangerous. I mean, nowadays you don't let your child walk to the *corner* by herself, because there is so much evil in the world!

Herbert   The fact that your parents were alcoholics must also have caused you to take on a kind of an early responsibility; at least that's been the experience of my other friends who dealt with that.

Grafton   Well, there was that, and I think it also teaches you early on to be a very careful observer of human nature. You know, you observe; you scan your environment; you try to figure out what's going on, and where you're safe. You know, there's the whole sense of the darkness and the jeopardy in life,

Herbert   And you must be self-reliant.

Grafton   Yes. That's exactly right. So I look back on it, and I see that as such a *gift*.

Herbert   Really!

Grafton   It was the perfect training for a writer. It was the great gift of my life that I was raised not only with intellectuals and with people who valued the language and the written word, but with people who were somehow incapable of parenting me very well, so that I was left to my own devices, and I think in that respect Kinsey and I are very connected at the core.

Herbert   I admire the way you've come to terms with this! A lot of people go their whole adult lives and can't come to that point.

Grafton   No, I know—the minute I understood what was happening—it became my responsibility to take care of me, and to sort out all those issues which, God knows, I have done in the course of many, many years of suffering through my rage and my pain. Now I have come out on the other side of that, and I understand that no one is to blame.

Herbert   And that it's not a reflection on you, or their feelings for you, which must have been very difficult to recognize early on. It does explain a lot about how Kinsey is anchored in a bedrock of self-reliance, if her author has also achieved hard-won self-reliance.

Grafton   Well, I think some of her isolation is related to that, too, in the sense of her not being a very trusting soul. You don't see her in yummy, warm, cozy relationships with very many people. Even her relationship with Henry, who is the father figure in her life, undergoes great shifts. *F Is for Fugitive*—when I got to the end of that book and understood it was a book about fathers, I was astonished, because in the writing of it I hadn't been aware of that.

Herbert   Tell me something about your father, Sue. I understand he was a mystery writer.

Grafton   My parents, for all their failings, were very intellectual and they were into books and part of the escape in our family was into reading. So all of us did a ton of reading and my parents, my father, who was a full time municipal bond attorney, wrote mystery fiction in his spare time. So there was always great value set on the language and on reading and on the imagination. I consider that I had the perfect childhood. And I would not change one minute of it. You know, I did a lot of suffering and learned a lot about human suffering, and I learned a lot about family drama and family dynamics. And all of that is grist! Absolutely all of that, I turn and take into the work with me.

Herbert   All of that really trains you to observe character subtleties.

Grafton   I think the downside is: you don't trust. You believe the world is only okay if you're in charge of it, so—and when it comes to the writing process, of course I believe that I am never in charge—so one of my struggles has been to learn to trust the process.

Herbert   And trust your instincts.

Grafton   And to learn that in fact I am not in charge! It looks like I'm in charge but in fact, my only way to survive is to let go completely; so that's been sort of a paradox for me.

Herbert   Yes, it does sound like a very paradoxical statement.

Grafton   I know one gets older and smarter in this world, thank God! And I wouldn't change my childhood for anything. And the truth is, the minute you understand what your life is about, you're *responsible*. And what I don't have any patience for is people who want to blame, and want to find fault. The minute you understand what's going on, the mantle of responsibility passes to you! From that moment on, your life is your own and you may make of it whatever you choose.

Herbert   Yes, yes, it's true.

Grafton   It's just that those of us who grew up in alcoholic families discovered that at the age of five!

Herbert   Some of us don't learn the lesson in a lifetime.

Grafton   My parents had unusual backgrounds. They were both the children of Presbyterian missionaries in China so my parents were raised in China.

Herbert   Oh, I didn't know that!

Grafton   Yeah. And [they] knew each other in China and came—most of those missionary children came over to the States to be educated. My parents were raised in a very strict, straitlaced environment, and when they got over here to college in the twenties, you know, they lived fast and loose and both of them just had a fatal attraction for alcohol. So while both were alive they sort of fit a very classical textbook mold of alcoholics in that while both were alive, my mother was the alcoholic and my father was the martyr. Once she died, he turned around and married a woman who was the martyr and he became the alcoholic.

Herbert   Oh, for heaven's sake!

Grafton   Throughout their lives they drank themselves insensible. My mother was four-foot-eleven—she never weighed a hundred pounds—so it took very little to inebriate her. She had a college education with a degree in chemistry—which is very unusual for her day—and ended up wasting her life. They were very loyal to each other and they'd been married for twenty-eight years when she died. I don't think they should have been married. Now, I grew up in a dysfunctional—what a popular word these days!—family. And when you grow up in an atmosphere like that you learn first of all to scan. And, point two, you learn to escape and create some other reality that is slightly more palatable than the one in which you're living. So we lived in a neighborhood where there were tons of kids, there were ten or eleven of us at all times. And we would stay out for hours and play these incredible games. We just played and played and played! And they were always dramas of great imagination and theatrics; it was great fun. I always got to be the princess tied to the tree.

Herbert   (Laughs.) Like Kinsey Millhone, always getting out of fixes, right? But did you rescue yourself or was a prince coming along?

Grafton   No. One always rescues oneself in this world!

Herbert   Good! Now your father's most famous title—at least the one that leaps to mind for me—is *Beyond a Reasonable Doubt*. That was a courtroom-oriented drama, wasn't it?

Grafton   Yes, and I never got to talk to him about how he put that plot together. It's very cleverly put together, and I'm not sure how he constructed it, and there is no way now ever to know. It's the story of a young attorney who, in the heat of passion, kills his brother-in-law. When the police begin to fix on his sister as the possible murder suspect, he confesses to the crime and then realizes what kind of corner he's painted himself into. So he renounces his confession, because by then the suspicion has moved away from his sister. He ends up defending himself in court, and gets himself absolved of the murder charge. And since the reader follows from the beginning, you know he *did* it. So he does it in the most amazing way possible, because many of the witnesses are people he knows and people who care about him. So he'll say to them, "Just tell the truth, there's been a terrible mistake. I know we'll sort it out; I don't want you to tell any lies for me," so that it looks on the surface as though he's being totally aboveboard, and you think, "How in the hell is he going to get out of this?"

Herbert   Do you think that as a lawyer your father observed cases where the person whodunit was getting away with it?

Grafton   The kind of law he practiced is called municipal bonds, the most boring form of the law there is, and he used to say to me early on, "Whatever you do, don't become a lawyer. You will hate it." It was very tedious, plodding work, and so I think he did me a service in steering me off it.

Herbert   Were there other ways that he influenced you when you were growing up?

Grafton   Well, part of it was that my parents were both very much in love with the English language and with the process of reading, so that from a very early age we were not only encouraged to read, but certainly what we saw in the *family* was reading. We read all the time, and we were allowed to read *anything*. There was no restraint put on us whatsoever. I've often said when the little girls in my neighborhood were reading Nancy Drew I was reading Mickey Spillane. And certainly, my father talked to me about writing, because he taught college English before he went through law school, and he had a great affection for simplicity and for clarity. I can remember him saying to me that it was not my job to revise the English language, that I must always punctuate correctly, I must spell correctly. He used to say it was miracle enough for a thought to form in his head and for him to make chicken scratches on a piece of paper that another person could look at and have the same thought appear in their head.

Herbert   He really conveyed a sense of wonder, didn't he?

Grafton   Yes. And he said *nothing* should interfere with that process. So his feeling was that anything that tampered with the language itself only impeded the process of communication. So I learned clarity and simplicity from him—*and* I learned to spell correctly.

Herbert   Let's talk about the actual practice of writing for you, about your typical writing day.

Grafton   Okay. I get up at 5:30 every morning in the pitchy black dark, and I put on my sweats and I go get in my truck and drive and pick up my friend Florence and we do a three-mile run. Lately on Tuesdays, Thursdays, and Saturdays we do this with two-pound weights and when I get back I do some weight work for my arms. On Monday, Wednesday, and Friday I do abs and lunges. I then come back and shower and have breakfast and lately I have skipped reading the paper because I realized that is such an incredible waste of time. If I skip the paper I'll come up here at 8:15 or 8:30 and lately, since I'm trying to get a book finished, I'll bring a carton of yogurt or a banana with me and have breakfast at my desk. But I will then work until almost inevitably 11:30, and I break for lunch and I come back to my desk at 12:00 or 12:15 and then work through 'til 3:00 or 3:30 or fourish and about two days a week I do a six-mile bicycle ride. In the old days I used to walk four miles, but I got a heel spur and it's just way too hard on my feet to run and then walk. We almost always eat at 6:00 straight up, which is not at all sophisticated but suits our natures. Then in the evenings I get to read and do anything I want and often I'm asleep by 8:30 or 9:00, because 5:30 is early.

Herbert   Yes, it is. Do you maintain this writing schedule daily?

Grafton   And I will do this—especially if I am on a book toward the end—I'll do that seven days a week. Now, Sundays I try not to exercise, 'cause I just feel you need a day where you don't do anything. And inevitably a day comes along where you think, "You know, the machine just isn't turned on today." I sit down here and this little voice goes, "I'm not gonna do it!"

Herbert   But generally you seem to be highly disciplined.

Grafton   I just feel my job is to keep myself healthy and alert and physically fit for the task of writing, which is very hard physical labor.

Herbert   It is, isn't it? It's surprising. People don't realize that unless they've done it.

Grafton   So I probably exercise two hours a day altogether, otherwise I don't know how to offset the tension and the stress of just the inertia. I'm a big fan of exercise that you do as close to home as possible with no expensive equipment, you know. And I think there's a lot of that out there. I don't believe in joining six-hundred-dollar-a-year gyms and wearing fancy-pants leotards; that just drives me insane. If you can't do it lookin' grubby, forget it!

Herbert   (Laughs.) Do you have any superstitions or fetishes associated with writing?

Grafton   I have a silver bracelet made by the Haida Indians up in Canada. The Haida did wonderful, wonderful things when they were in their heyday. They would tattoo themselves from head to toe, and when they were conquered their conquerers understood how powerful the tattoos were so they forbid them the tattooing. But they would allow them to make the jewelry. And in the jewelry they can only use about three forms. They can use the "U," the ovoid, and the "S" shapes. And so every piece of Haida jewelry is just a variation on these themes—much like the mystery I might add—and so my Haida bracelet is a whale. You can see the teeth and the blowhole and the dorsal fin and I wear that because it makes me feel strong. So I think there are certainly totems like that where you think, "This is a powerful object. I have this close to my person and therefore I take it's power."

Herbert   I see.

Grafton   Then also on my computer I probably showed you my little "Mysterious Stranger" award. She looks like a little witch in a peaky hat and I have to have her up there. I could probably write as well without her but I am very used to her.

Herbert   A moment ago you alluded to the mystery being a variation on a limited number of themes, like the design of your Haida bracelet is based upon a limited number of shapes. Let's talk some more about the structure of the mystery novel and whether or not it limits the author in any way.

Grafton   Why do you suggest that there are limitations?

Herbert   Well, here's what Julian Symons said: he feels that there are some limitations to the crime novel because of the need to entertain and the need to, for reasons of formula or craft, keep secrets from the reader somewhat longer than you might if you were writing the so-called novel of character.

Grafton   Yeah, but see, that's what I disagree with because if you think about it, the art of any fiction is to withhold information from the reader. Otherwise, every novel would be two lines long. "Once upon a time. . . . She died." You know?

Herbert   (Laughs.)

Grafton   Oh, the art of telling stories is about laying out information in a certain order to make it entertaining and to pull from it the fullest depth of its meaning. And to me, that's exactly what makes mystery fiction the more remarkable because mystery writers understand the profound effect of telling stories in the order that maximizes their drama.

Herbert   I like the way you put that.

Grafton   It seems to me that many mainstream writers could learn a lesson from us. I think they know this, which is why they are so busy looking down their noses at us! I think they understand that we, the mystery writers, have a grasp of structure, which I'm not sure a lot of mainstream writers get. They sort of wander stories out like reels of fishing nylon. A mystery writer always understands the order in which information needs to be given.

Herbert   That's true.

Grafton   *All* reading, I think, should be entertaining.

Herbert   I agree with you. But have you ever been in a position where you have wanted to say something about a character and felt that you couldn't because it would tell us too much about whodunit? Have the exigencies of the mystery plot, the need to keep secrets about motivation, ever caused you to feel restricted in developing character?

Grafton   Yeah, but so has any writer writing about a character. Character is about the *development* of a character. Character is about what happens to people over a passage of time and I have to imagine—I mean, having written "mainstream" myself—every writer experiences that. Otherwise, why not give the punch line on line two of any given book? So every writer goes through this. I mean, I don't know why a mainstream writer would pretend that in fact he or she is giving you all the pertinent information at the first rush. That just isn't true. All of us, in the course of telling a story, will withhold information or aspects of a character as we go along. I think it is totally false to imagine that somehow uniquely and specially and with much limitation the mystery does this to its own detriment. Not true at all. And in fact I think mysteries are far more entertaining than the average mainstream novel for precisely that reason.

Herbert   Because the writer admits to herself or himself that there is a need to manipulate information?

Grafton   Yes. We do it consciously.

Herbert   Some would say that the mystery writer needs to be coy with the reader.

Grafton   Yeah, I understand and I think what you see is simply a reflection of their attitudes. I mean, I could make a similar kind of statement about mainstream fiction being "disorganized," or "not dramatic," or "fuzzy," or, you know, your choice of language just reflects your basic stance with regard to a form. I don't think mystery writing is at all "coy." I think it is artful. I think it is cunning and devious in the way all good fiction is. I mean, Tolstoy didn't say on page one, "Anna Karenina fell under a train." You know? The whole point is, you read and you [wonder], "What in the world is going to happen to this incredible woman?"

Herbert   Right.

Grafton   And you agonize with her and you suffer with her and in the end, when she goes under the train, you think, "Oh, my God, how inevitable!"

Herbert   Absolutely.

Grafton   Which is exactly the way a mystery novel works. You know, it's like none of us tell the punch line—although I have seen writers do it and it can be amusing when writers violate the sequence of time or the unity of time and give you the punch line in advance. I'm trying to think [of an example]. I think Faye Weldon has a book where she will say something like, "Who would have guessed when Marie met Charles that within a short time she would be married to him and having an abortion?" There's a sense in which that violation makes it more mysterious and more entertaining.

Herbert   Yes.

Grafton   But I certainly don't think the mystery novel suffers any way, shape, or form. It is certainly true that any mystery writer can do "formula," and write according to form and make a totally flat and boring book, but certainly from my point of view the mystery is the most amazing form. It is the most amazing at its best.

Herbert   Tell me what you think about the "fair-play rule."

Grafton   I think certainly in good mystery fiction you don't go to the end and go, "Oh, and actually I forgot to mention that Charles is a brain surgeon."

Herbert   Right.

Grafton   "And he would know exactly how to penetrate the ear of his victim." You're never allowed to do that. One of the rules of mystery writing is that you need to be as honest with the reader as possible. Obviously there is an artfulness involved but my point is that every novelist uses exactly that *very* technique and yet a mainstream novelist will pat herself on the back for that and look down her nose—actually it's usually a *him*—at mystery novelists for being as crafty as they themselves are.

Herbert   Well, I like that choice of words, instead of doing something just for reasons of craft it's a matter of being "crafty." And I loved your choice of the word "cunning," because that is complimentary.

Grafton   Any time in life that there are rules, one can be a slave to rules and therefore flat and boring. I mean, that is true socially; that's true conversationally. One can always be a strict adherent of the rules and thus flatten one's own personality.

Herbert   I agree with you.

Grafton   I always equate the mystery novel with the game of bridge. Honest to God, I was playing a hand of bridge the other night. Do you play bridge?

Herbert   No, I don't, but I'm really beginning to think I should.

Grafton   Oh, my God, well here it is: I mean, this is just an ordinary evening and a series of hands being played and I've played a three no trump hand. A three no-trump is not the most extraordinary or pressure-filled bid you can make, but there was something about the way the cards laid out that I knew if I were extremely good at what I was doing I could pull it off. My heart was beating so hard, when I did it, the triumph was so sweet, and to me it is exactly like writing a mystery novel. The rules in bridge are as clear as a bell. Because [with] the same number of cards, bidding goes a certain way; cards have to be played; the high card will always take the trick unless it's trump; the rules are *not* negotiable. Within the framework of the rules there is all manner of latitude and that's where the skill of the player comes in.

Herbert   As in the mystery novel.

Grafton   And mystery novels are like that. We all play by more or less the same set of rules, but a skillful player, a skillful mystery writer, can pump the form to the most heartrending level.

Herbert   Oh, I like what you're saying.

Grafton   Oh, I'm telling you! And it is exactly the same thrill for me to pull off a maneuver in writing and to pull off a maneuver at the bridge table. It's like, "*Yes*, yes!"

Herbert   When you're pulling off a maneuver in the novel, especially if you're daring to do it with something that isn't the absolute "high card," does your heart start pounding then, too?

Grafton   Yeah, the difference is, at the bridge table the effect is immediate. You know if you've won the trick or not; you know if the king's sitting in the wrong hand; you know [if] you've miscalculated. And you can't ever control where the cards are, so you play it; you take certain risks and you gamble in a certain way and if you pull it off you just want to kiss everybody at the table. You feel that good about yourself.

Herbert   But with a novel there is a delayed reaction.

Grafton   With a novel, you never know what the effect is. You know what you're aiming for, but given the fact that you might have a million readers, some certain percentage will always outwit you; some certain percentage will always be completely befuddled by your maneuver; and the great middle range will go, "Oh, my God, will you look at this!" You know, in the middle are the people who appreciate the art of it and those are the ones I'm writing for, but you never know. You never know because it is such a heady intellectual maneuver to try for an effect in a mystery novel, you know you never know what the reader is perceiving.

Herbert   But surely at this point in your career you have the experience to know that it's likely when you've done well?

Grafton   No.

Herbert   You don't? I find that surprising.

Grafton   No, every single time I do it the same question arises, which is, "Have I pulled it off?"

Herbert   Mystery reading is a very interactive experience. Now how does this provide challenges to you as an author, if you know that you are pitted against the reader?

Grafton   Oh, it is the best! Well, for one thing, I always imagine that my reader is smarter than I am and the great challenge is to see if I can outwit her. Most mystery readers are fanatics. They'll read seven and ten books a week; they'll remember everything; they tend to be detail people, so you can't slip much by them. They remember all the devices and all the gimmicks, and they are in business to see if they can unseat you. So I always think of mystery writers as the great moralists of fiction, and I also think of us as the magicians, because we are always dealing with sleight of hand. The fun of the game is to see if you can pull a rabbit out of a hat while the reader is watching you perform your magic.

Herbert   And not only watching, but scrutinizing.

Grafton   Now what you need to understand if you engage in this process is, "You cannot fool all the people all the time." And some people, I know for a fact, don't even read my books for the puzzle. They read for the pleasure of Ms. Kinsey Millhone's company, and only peripherally watch the case unfold. Some people I know get very frustrated—the mystery makes them feel inadequate, and they resist that—but I think Ms. Kinsey Millhone sucks 'em right in!

Herbert   I think so, too! Well, if the mystery novel is requiring a sort of a mental game on the part of both the reader and the writer, does this in any way limit it in reaching the highest levels of literature?

Grafton   Well, I don't think so. With the mystery novel, there are rules and regulations that control where you may go and what you may do, but within that framework I have watched mystery writers over the years take the form in a thousand different directions, and the thrill of it is seeing if there is some new truth to be wrung from that very carefully-laid-out set of rules and regulations. I mean, I personally think it is one of the most exhilarating kinds of writing there is. I think it still suffers, the mystery, from the early pulp origins; it was considered the lesser form; it was considered a sort of poor country cousin to mainstream fiction. Now I think there are so many fine writers working in the field that when somebody says to me, "Do you ever intend to write a 'real' novel?," I think to myself, "They don't know beans about the mystery, and what they're describing is just their own ignorance." I think all good writing is about suspense, and all good writing is about conflict and drama.

Herbert   So the predictable aspects of the mystery novel actually enhance our reading pleasure?

Grafton Well, actually, this is a much more profound process, because what you are dealing with is fable and legend and myth and archetypes, so what you are looking at is a very ancient struggle between good and evil. And in fact that's why it always comes down to that final contest, which is generally physical, a physical contest between the good guy and the bad, and you need to know that good will win, but it has to be a contest of equals. If your villain is not with it enough or strong enough or ruthless enough, then the victory isn't as sweet.

Herbert Very often in talking about mystery writing the analogy of some kind of contest or game will come up. Recently Catherine Aird was telling me that there are two kinds of golf: you can play something called a bogey, where you challenge yourself to place the ball in the hole. Pardon my poor idea of golf terminology!

Grafton Sure!

Herbert Or you can play against an opponent, and Catherine Aird feels that what she's doing is engaging in the individual challenge. While you might expect the mystery writer to be actively engaged in a battle of wits with the imagined reader, most say that they are engaged in a much more individual challenge to satisfy themselves.

Grafton I agree. There is a game element to it all. I have read mystery novels where I know fairly early what's going on, but there's a sense in which, ah, it is so delicious, the game itself is so beautifully rendered that the object is not to guess who done what to whom, but just to participate in the writer's world, to be part of it for the duration of the reading.

Herbert Talking about that private world and the setting, would you share with us some of the work that you have undertaken in order to make your scenes as real as Kinsey's voice and personality?

Grafton Well, for instance, with *C Is for Corpse* I went into morgues, because originally at the ending of that book I pictured Kinsey getting into one of the drawers with a corpse, and my real question was, "If she slid herself into a drawer and closed it from the inside, what was the latching mechanism? And could she get herself back out?" When I did the research, what I discovered was that there are very few drawers. The drawers that you see in morgues in films and television shows are largely a fabrication of television writers. And in fact most morgues are not designed that way. So that what I ended up looking at were actual morgues, and those were the settings that I described in the course of *C Is for Corpse*. But certainly in my ordinary life as Sue Grafton, you know, rural writer, you would *never* have had occasion, nor the credentials, to go into the morgue of a city hospital.

Herbert And this, then, does help to explain how these things are so well-written and convincing for the reader.

Grafton Well, it's certainly easier to go and look at reality than to make it up. So one of my strategies is to visit the scenes that I wish to use. For instance in *D Is for Deadbeat*, I needed the top of a building that exists here in Santa Barbara. So I called the building manager and got permission to go with him up into the attic of this building so that I could see what it looked like, and *smell* it. And that way I didn't have to conjure up details that may or may *not* have rung true.

Herbert And you are very good at describing the actuality, so that that works very well for you. Thinking about *C Is for Corpse* makes me wonder about the element of death in the mystery novel. It seems to me that homicide is a central question in your work, obviously, whether it's *H Is for Homicide* or whatever letter of the alphabet it might be. Can you address the question of why death and homicide—rather than other less dramatic kinds of crimes—become central to the mystery novel?

Grafton My personal theory about that is that we live in a permissive age in which nothing matters anymore. There was a time, in Victorian times, when if a man touched a woman's hand with his little finger it could be a great scandal, you know, and his fortunes might rise or fall; her reputation might be lost.

Herbert Reputation certainly doesn't have the same significance today, does it?

Grafton That's right. So that if you consider the notion of building a novel around white-collar crime, so many Americans are involved in it that we think nothing of it. You would have difficulty generating any sense of outrage or jeopardy around stealing paper clips from your company. Everybody does it!

Herbert Even stealing a hundred million dollars!

Grafton And it's, "Who cares?" You know, there's this whole attitude of indifference. But for the most part, homicide *always* matters. I think it strikes at the core of us. The notion of taking another human being's life always has high stakes around it. Now certainly even in this day and age there is something called justifiable homicide; there are occasions when murders are committed and even the law declares that this is not a crime that needs payment in like token, you know. But for the most part, I think we are still appalled by homicide. I am, at any rate. It is that attempt to understand the darkest of our deeds that drives my books.

Herbert And then there are the symbolic possibilities of death.

Grafton I think about it in terms of making sacrifices to the gods. I think if I give the gods bloody victims, perhaps they'll stay away from my family. I have never been touched by homicide or by violent crime—so I think maybe the gods will be fooled. (Laughs.) I can give them Bobby Callahan, and they won't take my child. I do make a big distinction always between real homicide and fictional homicide, and certainly I try to keep that very clear in my own mind. Real homicide is often alcohol-related; it's impulsive; it's ugly; it's dirty; it's stupid. It's poorly motivated: people are murdered for thirty-two cents; they are killed for their basketball jackets; they're killed for their caps. In a murder mystery, the first conceit is that if you are murdered it is because someone devious and cunning with much to be gained has plotted for weeks and come up with terribly clever schemes to do you in, so that if you are murdered, at least it is the end product of somebody's being terribly intelligent and terribly clever. The second conceit of mystery fiction is, if you are murdered, there is a detective who is equally cunning and equally dedicated who will move heaven and earth to see that justice is done. Again, in the real world, we don't see much justice anymore.

Herbert   At least in fiction, then, murder, is personal. However awful it might be, in fiction there is a personal element to it, whereas it might be much more glancing and random in reality.

Grafton   Well, in reality there are many occasions in which the cops know whodunit and they can't prove it, or they bring a case into court and it's dismissed on a technicality, or somebody is convicted and goes into prison for six months and ends up on the street again, so that even in the real world the justice system is not much about justice; it is about technicalities. Whereas in the fictional world of homicide there is retribution and there is a sense of parity again; there is order restored to the universe, as P. D. James has so often said.

Herbert   Yes. Is this something that consciously motivates you to write in this area?

Grafton   I think so, yes. Not that I have a mission, or a cause, or a piece of propaganda to impart, but something in me is satisfied with the notion that in the confines of this book there is a balance restored, there is justice done.

Herbert   Would you also agree that one of the fascinations we have for the mystery story lies in the fact that each of us is capable of murder?

Grafton   Oh, I believe *that*. I believe that without doubt. And I think in some ways the murder mystery allows us to create a false sense of distance, and at the same time allows us to pull that material in a little closer, from the safety of our armchairs. While we explore the dark side of our own natures we can say to ourselves, "Well, it's just a mystery novel. It is just one more trip into the underground, and I know I will come out unscathed."

Herbert That's true, you *do* know you will come out, and you know that the majority of the characters will come out with a better situation than they were in at the beginning of the book. Unless you're reading P. D. James!

Grafton (Smiles.)

Herbert I notice that you never tell the story from the point of view of the criminal. Has this been a conscious decision for you?

Grafton Yes.

Herbert Have you decided that you do not wish to convey the thrill or satisfaction that a killer may enjoy in perpetrating the crime? Have you set out to avoid glamorizing crime?

Grafton Certainly I don't want to glamorize crime. What interests me is the psychology of homicide, the part of our nature that generates that kind of rage and what we do with it and how we work to delude ourselves and conceal the fact of our dishonesty. Certainly the desire not to write from the killer's point of view is in part because I wanted a character that the reader can interface with, but it's also in part because I personally don't like those books written from the killer's point of view. I think they're always extremely cagey and I prefer as straight-ahead a narrative as I can manage.

Herbert How, then, do you get into the mind of your murderer? How do you understand him or her?

Grafton I really see my villains from the outside, as we see other people in real life. I am always interested in the psychology of people who are committing crimes and being dishonest about it. I don't know that I employ any special technique to get into the minds of the killers. (Pauses.) Often I consult my own dark nature and look to the ways in which I delude myself, and look at my own homicidal rages when those come. So, if I find myself having any strong emotion—anger, or fear, or distress, or grief—I analyze that and observe it so that later on I can record it in terms of the writing itself.

Herbert The mystery form was obviously a natural place to turn when you had murder in your heart, because murder was used as a plot device, but are there other reasons why you were attracted to this particular genre?

Grafton In part because my father had done murder mysteries in the forties, I think I always had at the back of my mind that one day I would try the form myself. I look back on it realizing that all of the writing I did before I began *A Is for Alibi* was one long training course for the mystery novel, which, I believe, is where I belong. I did a brief stint of mainstream fiction, I did my tour through Hollywood learning screenplay and teleplay form, and all of it, now, I see as a sort of self-education process preparing me for the mystery novel.

Herbert   Other than your father, who were your greatest literary influences?

Grafton   I've seized Raymond Chandler and Ross Macdonald as true poets. The language is so evocative, the images are so strong, and I think in the course of learning to write this hard-boiled private eye fiction I have had a sense of that as something to work toward—that vivid, brooding prose that both seem to employ in slightly different ways.

Herbert   Are there any female influences on your writing?

Grafton   I would say certainly the Southern writers: Flannery O'Connor, Eudora Welty, Carson McCullers, again, because they tap into the dark side of human nature, and because all three of those women wrote with such poetic and such striking *clarity*—that's the only way I know how to describe it.

Herbert   I can see how those would be influences for you. What keeps you attached to the genre? What continues to keep the mystery form exciting for you?

Grafton   Certainly I credit the mystery novel as being more structured than much of mainstream fiction. I think there is a very strong skeleton buried among the plot—

Herbert   Good choice of words!

Grafton   —and I personally treasure that in the reading process. And often when I read mainstream fiction I feel the writer is wandering in a fog, not quite certain what the story is or how they intend to tell it, whereas in a mystery novel, from page one, if the writer is doing her work well, you know you're in the hands of an expert, and you are off and running!

Herbert   Are there any other dimensions to the writing of mysteries that convince you that you will indeed reach the end of the alphabet, that you will one day complete *Z Is for Zero* ?

Grafton   I look at writing as a spiritual journey, the manifestation of which is a series of novels, but truly the writing process is about my growth as a person, and that's all it's about. If it were not about that I wouldn't be doing it because this is my life. I can't afford to live the next sixteen years without meaning or purpose and somehow these books, because they are such a challenge and because they force me to face my own inadequacies and because they call out of me the most amazing and impossible aspects of my nature, enable me to go forward.

▶ P. D. JAMES

The novels of P. D. James, with their focus on the dark side of human nature and the message that even the process of justice has a contaminating effect on the innocent, does not prepare one for the warmth and gregariousness that the author exudes in person. Whether she is serving tea and cucumber sandwiches in her Regency house in London, or relaxing in her small garden in Oxford, or finding time for the interviewer amid a hectic promotional tour, James's personality is so engaging and her interest in one's own concerns so genuine that it seems as though we've been acquainted over more than ten years since we first met.

James is a marvelous interview subject, who gives serious consideration to all questions put to her. Seated in one of her armchairs covered in William Morris fabric, she will lean forward earnestly and greet each query with firm eye contact often enlivened by a warm smile. Always overscheduled, with her work as a Governor of the BBC, committee work for various literary organizations, membership on the Liturgical Committee of the Church of England, and membership in the House of Lords competing with her writing, she often begins an interview with a request for keeping it brief but then allows her hospitable instinct to prevail as she becomes deeply involved in a conversation that features not only considered talk about death and murder but everyday inquiries about one's children and home life. If the visit is entirely social rather than a formal interview, James reveals herself as capable of infectious laughter over family stories and as rather pleasantly awed at the success she has achieved. At times like these it is nearly impossible to believe that this vivacious personality is capable of envisioning and creating on the page serial murders and mutilations, poisonings, and hangings.

But James recalls that her personality has always been "a curious mix," blending a serious, detached, and intensely private side with a natural social ease. Even during her girlhood in Oxford, and in a town on the Welsh border, and in Cambridge, she recalls herself as the sort of child who, while reading "Humpty-dumpty," would ask herself, "Did he jump or was he pushed?"

James was born in 1920 in Oxford, the daughter of a minor civil servant and a homemaker. She received the most important part of her education at Cambridge Girls' High School—where a favorite English teacher was a Miss Dalgleish—but was discouraged from going on to college by a father who did not believe in higher education for women. In the early days of World War II she met and married a medical student named Connor Bantry White, who was rushed off to serve in the British Army. James gave birth to one of her daughters during the height of the aerial bombardment of London, in 1942.

When Dr. White returned from the war with serious mental health difficulties, James took responsibility for supporting her husband and two daughters by means of jobs in the Civil Service and eventually in the British Home Office. This career experience became invaluable to her when at the age of thirty-nine she determined that she did not want to go through life as a "disappointed writer" and decided to "get on with it" and write her first novel, a mystery introducing the policeman/poet Adam Dalgleish. Writing in the early hours of the morning, she turned out *Cover Her Face* (1962) while also bringing up her daughters and holding down responsible administrative jobs. As years went by she continued to feature Adam Dalgleish in much of her work but also introduced the young private investigator Cordelia Gray and the policewoman Kate Miskin into some of her books. One of her novels, *Innocent Blood* (1980), used none of these characters, but rather follows the quest of a young woman who had been adopted as a child to discover the shocking truth about her biological parents.

James has also served as a magistrate, hearing a wide variety of legal cases, work that she left behind in 1988 when she became a Governor of the BBC. In 1991 she was made a member of the House of Lords and received the lifetime title Baroness James of Holland Park. In addition to her eleven crime novels, James has also written one unpublished play, an account of a historical true crime, and a new novel set in the future.

Herbert　It was thirty years ago that you published your first novel, *Cover Her Face*. Eleven years later you introduced your female sleuth, Cordelia Gray, in *An Unsuitable Job for a Woman*. Cordelia, I recall, had a habit of carefully assembling her scene of the crime kit when she took on the rare case that came her way. And she experienced a feeling of excitement when she labeled her manila folder in readiness for the investigation. Do you experience a similar sense of excitement when you sit down to begin a new work?

James   I think the exciting feeling comes perhaps when the idea begins to generate; when you finally feel enthusiastic about the book; when you finally think, "Yes, I want to write *that* book. I want to develop that *idea*."

Herbert   So the excitement, for you, occurs in the idea stage rather than when you first pick up the pen or face the word processor?

James   Of course, with Cordelia, she doesn't know what's going to happen [whereas] by the time I sit down to write I know *exactly* what is going to happen. I have to know. I don't have that sense which I suppose some writers have when they give themselves over to the characters and they're not quite sure how anything's going to develop. Of course, when you write the classical detective story you can't do that. You've got to control the plot. You've got to know, really, who did it and how and why and what the motives of the suspects were and how you're going to deal with the solution. There isn't quite that sense of not knowing what's ahead or of the unexpected overtaking you.

Herbert   I understand that you have your novels so firmly constructed in your mind before writing them that you need not write the chapters in chronological order.

James   One of the advantages of this method is, certainly, that one can write the type of chapter that appeals at the moment, whether it is passages of dialogue, or whether it's description, or whether it's the finding of the body, or whether it's fast action. I'm not sure quite *why* I do it that way. I think I write a book as if I were shooting a film, in a sense. I see it very much in film sequence, very much dramatically.

Herbert   I do not think it is unusual for authors to view the writing process as analogous to film making but I imagine it *is* quite unusual for first drafts of novels to be written with the chapters out of sequence.

James   Perhaps that's so. Recently I'm moving towards writing more of the first part of the book at the start. But I can never honestly see myself as beginning at the beginning and moving through.

Herbert   This means you have to have all elements of the novel firmly in mind.

James   You have to work firmly, really. You know *exactly* where you're going. This doesn't really mean that the book doesn't develop as it's written, because I think all books *do*.

Herbert In what regards do your books grow and change as you write?

James Sometimes I think up additional contrivances, additional clues, and things change. Certainly much of the dialogue isn't thought up in advance. That really arises as my characters begin speaking to each other. But I *do* have to know precisely where the book is set, what is the time of year, and obviously who the characters are and who's to be killed, and *absolutely* where everybody will be from this stage to that stage.

Herbert Very often your comments reveal the firm control that you exercise over the writing process and over yourself as a writer. Not all writers evidence this, as you know. While a large part of your success, I'm sure, has to do with your ability to control most aspects of the novel, surely there must be occasional surprises in the writing process for you, where the magic of creativity walks hand in hand with the element of control.

James Well, I think the only thing you can say about that, Rosemary, is that however carefully you plot and however carefully you plan, the book you finally produce is always different [from what you've planned], with the changes coming, extraordinarily, during the actual writing, especially because your characters reveal themselves more and more intensely to you. 'Tis very carefully controlled, 'tis very carefully planned, but nevertheless it's subject to that mysterious creative process over which I think writers have, perhaps, only imperfect control in the end.

Herbert If you *do* know a great deal about what your characters are going to do and where they're going to be, in what regards do they further reveal themselves to you?

James Well, Rosemary, the whole of creativity is very mysterious, *and* it's very mysterious to writers. People always expect you to be able to say how did you do that? Why did you do that? And it isn't like that! It's not subject to that sort of kind of interrogation. All that happens is that [pauses] you *feel* the characters. It's as if the characters exist in some limbo of the imagination and then what I'm doing is not so much making them up as getting in touch with them.

Herbert Ah!

James For example, in *A Taste for Death*, you know, one of the victims is this minister of the Crown. On the day he's murdered he goes to put his house on the market and then no one knows where he spends the day and the police have to spend their time trying to find out where he went. And when I was writing the book, for a time *I* didn't know where he went. And then I tried to work on it some more, and then I thought, "Well, *that's* the person he must have gone to see, it's absolutely right, absolutely natural and I knew—it was almost as if he was standing there by the bed and I was saying, "Of course that's what you did! Of course that's where you went! Yes, I see now, where else would you have gone?" And it can be as real as that. But, you know, you can't explain that. If you could explain it, I suppose everybody would do it.

Herbert   Aha! There was a character who had a life of his own. And I believe it is significant that while his author or creator had lost track of his whereabouts, he was turning to the company of the fictional author within your novel! Didn't your character spend the day with the reclusive romance writer across the lake from the crime scene?

James   Yes. It's almost a bit like saying, "Well, I wouldn't have thought that character would have behaved quite like that!" But that's how he *did* behave. And I think that's what some people mean when they say that the characters run away with the book. Well, you *can't* have them running away with the book because you have to control the detective story. I don't think, really, they can run away with *any* book but I think the writer *can* feel that he is getting [the characters'] stories out on paper rather than making them up.

Herbert   There is a limit, then, to the free rein that you will allow to your characters!

James   (Smiles.)

Herbert   What about your sleuths? Are there aspects of their personalities that they share with their creator?

James   I think I identify more with Cordelia Gray than I do with Adam Dalgleish but this may simply be because he's a man. Writing about a man has some problems. I don't mean that I don't understand how he thinks or speaks. It's just the physical fact that one has never been inside a male body, doesn't know what it's like for a man to put on his clothes in the morning, doesn't know what [the process of] shaving off a beard is. It is much easier, really, to identify with a heroine. And I suppose I *approve* of Cordelia very much.

Herbert   Yes, it is in the details of her life that Cordelia comes alive for us. Most readers will never have the experience of climbing out of entrapment in a well, but we can thoroughly believe in the details of her household arrangements and her choice of wardrobe. It is because we believe in these details that we also believe in Cordelia's courage.

James   I hope this is also true of my more recent character Kate. I think this may be one of the strengths of women novelists generally: on the whole we do tell our readers far more about what our characters are putting on, what they're eating, what they're wearing.

Herbert   And domestic detail provides so many clues in your chosen genre.

James   Yes. But with Cordelia, I suppose I try to put myself in the place of a youngish woman: vulnerable, but I think courageous in setting out regardless. And as to Cordelia's domestic arrangements, that is certainly a self-identifying point in that, had I been Cordelia, I would have needed and provided myself with *just* such a refuge. I think psychologically it would have been necessary to have somewhere that was private and expressed me as a person, an *inviolate* place which was a refuge.

Herbert   I expect your books reflect not only some of your personality but some of your life experience.

James   Yes. The experiences in the health service and then the tour in the Home Office, which of course is equivalent to the ministry of justice in other countries, were both very, very valuable in writing the books. I used that experience very widely.

Herbert   Yes. Can you think of any specific examples from these parts of your career that were useful to you when it came to writing your books?

James   Well, I was responsible for awhile for clerking a committee about nurse training and it was all that interest in nurse training that helped me with *Shroud for a Nightingale*. I was responsible later for keeping the list of young chronic sick and finding accommodation for them, and that helped with *The Black Tower*, with all the young chronic sick there. And of course *A Mind to Murder*—at the time that I wrote that I had been administering five psychiatric units and I knew a great deal about psychotherapy and psychiatry so it was all very helpful to me.

Herbert   Did that interest come out of what happened to occur in your career or was the psychiatric interest something that tied in with your husband?

James   Not at all. Not at all. That was the job that happened to be vacant. I would have preferred not to have done it, really, I think.

Herbert   In another part of your work life you have been a magistrate. I wondered if you could comment on how that work provided you with a window on life's tragedies?

James   Well, I don't, I think, use the experience very directly, although one of the characters in *Innocent Blood* is a magistrate in the juvenile court, and of course I knew all about the juvenile courts.

Herbert   Did you ever deal with murder in your capacity as magistrate?

James   Well, you act as the first court in murder. People come up to court to see if there's a case to answer. You have murders come before you but you don't try them. You see if there's a case to answer and if so, you would refer the case to the Crown court.

Herbert   You must have more ideas for writing than you could possibly ever use!

James   Well, quite enough, I think! Yes, it was a fascinating job to do.

Herbert   Returning to your writing, you mentioned earlier that the exciting time for you comes in the idea stage. Do the plotting and planning and the generation of ideas occur mainly at the writing desk or elsewhere?

James   I often do a lot of thinking when I'm walking. I'm awfully fond of walking. Sometimes when I'm in Hyde Park in London a line of dialogue will come into my mind. I'm very fond of dialogue. And obviously the thing is to go back and *get that dialogue down*! It may be a passage of interrogation between the detective and one of the suspects or dialogue between two of the [other] characters.

Herbert   Do you feel you have to rush urgently back to prevent forgetting it, or does it stay with you?

James   I tend to go back fairly urgently. (Smiles.) Or if I have a notebook with me I just sort of settle down under the nearest tree and just scribble.

Herbert   When you are at home, seated at your writing desk, rather than dashing across London from Hyde Park with a line of dialogue in your head, are there conditions that you require for your work?

James   Well, I like to be surrounded by my odd *lares* and *penates*, my Staffordshire figures and solitude.

Herbert   Solitude and silence.

James   Yes. Writing is the loneliest job in the world. Indeed, for me it is impossible unless I am completely alone.

Herbert   Are there additional materials or conditions that you find necessary to a productive writing session?

James   Well, often I write in the mornings. I'm up with the larks. And I find there's a great advantage, certainly, in having everything ready, you know, having the desk ready, having a dictionary and thesaurus, and having enough paper of the right kind and so forth. This is because although life would, I think, be intolerable if I weren't a writer, at the same time when I'm actually sitting down to do it there are other things which suddenly seem more attractive! If you haven't got everything ready, there's always an excuse for fiddling around.

Herbert   Likes Holmes on the violin.

James   Indeed!

Herbert   In your London house you showed me the writing desk at the back of the house, overlooking your garden. Do you continue to write there?

James   Well, you see, Rosemary, I don't have one workplace. I sometimes write there. I sometimes write upstairs in a much bigger writing room. I sometimes like to write in the kitchen on the table where there's a lot of space and I can open the door into the garden and take my coffee out there in the summer. I sometimes write in my Oxford house, increasingly I write in my Oxford house.

Herbert   When we first met in 1982 you told me that most of your books have been first inspired by a sense of place. I wonder if this is still the case?

James   Of course, my latest novel, *The Children of Men*, was a somewhat different case. I had this powerful image and I wanted to write it. It was unusual for me: the idea arose when I read a review of a scientific book which mentioned the extraordinary and unexplained fall, in the last thirty years, in the sperm count in Western man. It caused me to ponder on what the world would be like if suddenly the human race ceased to be able to breed. It was astonishing how quickly it all came together in the new book.

Herbert   But, of course, while *The Children of Men* apparently was inspired more by an idea than by a sense of place, the Oxford setting is one of the most memorable aspects of the novel.

James   Thank you.

Herbert   I think a question that you are going to get quite often is, "Why set the book in such an immediate future?" I have to tell you that this was the first time I ever had to suspend any disbelief in reading any of your work. I found it difficult to accept that a Warden might control England in the near future. I didn't want to give up the fact that you have a democratic form of government!

James   It's over twenty-five, thirty years ahead and I think it made it very easy for me in [that] we shan't have got very much different; it's much the same world. I didn't want it to be a different world. No, I think that things can change very, very quickly and that twenty-five years hence [under the conditions I postulate] people [will] have lost all hope. You see there's not much point in having all the sort of ardours and responsibility of running a country when nobody's going to remember you. I mean, people who become prime ministers must have in mind that future generations will say, you know, "From 1991 to 1995: John Major." But if there's going to be no future, nobody's going to be putting statues up, who wants the responsibility? And I can easily see that all these sort of national institutions break down.

Herbert   Well, use of the near future allows you to anchor us in reality. And when you're going to talk about something that is a scientifically startling question—the lack of fertility in the human race—we need to be anchored.

James   It was necessary to ground it in realistic detail because it's a really frightening book, I think.

Herbert   Yes, I agree. There is a quiet horror in details like the scene at the Cast Museum—the exhibition of plaster casts and marble copies maintained by the Ashmolean Museum—when the reader realizes that there is no future for which to preserve humankind's artistic record. I found that quite chilling. And at the same time the scene illustrated the protagonist's strength of character and resignation to the truth while it was also useful to the development of the plot, since a message was secreted beneath one of the marble figures. I'll never visit that gallery again without thinking of Theodore Faron and that bleak future.

James   That is certainly what I try to achieve. I think the mark of any good novel is whether the characters do continue to exist in the mind of the reader after the book's finish, and also whether they provide part of his or her private landscape, as it were.

Herbert   What actual steps can an author take in order to ensure that a character becomes a part of the reader's imaginative world? What skill must the author command in order to achieve this?

James   Well, I think it's just the power to, as it were, generate the character, the power to create the living character and to put that character into a situation which the reader believes in. So it's a combination of the power to describe character and to describe place, I think.

Herbert   Would you please tell us some more about this sense of place that has inspired so much of your work?

James   People often ask me, "How does a book begin when you're writing a classical mystery? Does it begin with an idea for an original method of death, or with a character, or with a place?" And for me, it's nearly always a place. I think I have a very strong reaction to place. It could be a sinister stretch of coast, an old house, a forensic sciences laboratory; the place comes first, and then nearly always the victims, then the suspects, then other characters. They gradually grow.

Herbert   I would imagine that it is a point of pride for you that you describe your settings accurately. Would you share an anecdote about the sort of research you undertake in order to draw the scene or action accurately?

James   Well, in *The Black Tower* I have two of my characters climb cliffs in Dorset. I did want to get this right and use the right technical words and I wanted them to make a particular climb, a *known* climb, on a known cliff. And, as my son-in-law is a climber, he was kind enough to give me some details and I thought I would get this right. I settled down and I described this climb in great detail with two suspects [making the climb] and I wrote at the end, "Ten minutes later, they flung themselves breathless on the grass on the top of the cliff." When Peter came for the weekend with my daughter I said, "Will you cast your eye over this and see if I've got it right?" And he gave a rich round of laughter and he said, "My God, Mother-in-law, they certainly would have been breathless; they've done an eight-hour climb in ten minutes!"

Herbert   (Laughs.) And in so many detective novels the setting provides not only a milieu into which one can distribute physical clues but an environment that shows something about characterization.

James   Setting, of course, is important in any novel, but I think in a mystery it's particularly important because it can enhance atmosphere, it can influence character, and it can influence events. But it can also provide contrast. There should be contrast between order and normality, decency and goodness and the extraordinary contaminating crime.

Herbert   This makes me think of W. H. Auden's essay "The Guilty Vicarage," where he described the murder as the event that shatters the idyllic situation.

James   Yes, that's a marvelous essay.

Herbert   As the title suggests, Auden also addresses the question of guilt. But in his day, mystery novelists were far more concerned with answering the question "whodunit?" than they were with probing psychologically to discover "whydunit?" How much conscious consideration do you give to the question of guilt?

James   I think I give it quite a lot of thought. I think guilt is a fascinating subject altogether, because to be human is to be guilty, whether the guilt is rational or not. I think perhaps the difference between the cozy detective story and the modern detective story—which may also be called the crime novel—is that the latter does turn its attention to this question of guilt. And of course in the crime novel you may not have much detection, you may know who the guilty person is, and your novel really is about the effect of that deed on the person and on his society. This also bears on the thinking of W. H. Auden, who saw the detective story as a kind of morality play.

Herbert   Yes, the dialectic of guilt.

James   And of course in the cozies we had the satisfaction, I suppose, of feeling that whatever else we may be guilty about, we're not guilty of having slipped the dagger under Sir Gaspar's ribs in the library! I am sure that the attitude of the writer to guilt distinguishes the true crime novel from mere entertainment.

Herbert   I agree.

James   I think one could also say that the crime novel at its best is concerned with the limits of free will, because in this kind of novel you really feel in the end, "Well, how much choice do these people have?" This is the fascinating thing: you are trying to work to an extent within the old-fashioned conventions but at the same time you are trying to write a book which has some claims to be regarded as a novel because it is psychologically true.

Herbert   I see. Obviously writing has been a natural part of your life for many years now. How early in your life did you feel drawn to writing?

James   I think from an early age I was aware that I had what I suppose in common parlance is [known as] "a gift." I knew I had been granted a talent. I don't think I ever doubted that I could write. I mean, obviously one does learn. One learns techniques. One develops—or hopes to develop. But I think I was aware that this was something I could do and the problem was going to be to make myself do it!

Herbert   Do you have an image of yourself that would tell us what you were like as a girl?

James   Well, I think I had a very strong fantasy world from a very early age. I had numerous totally imaginary people who were very real to me to whom I talked and with whom I communicated. This was almost from early childhood. I told stories at a very early age; I used to tell them at night. We had one large nursery when we were young, very young, and I used to tell stories at night to my sister and brother.

Herbert   Were they mystery stories?

James   They were adventure stories. There was also a story about a pig called Percy, Percy Pig. But he had a fairly adventurous life for a pig, I thought!

Herbert (Laughs.)

James I think I lived a strong internal creative life. I was the sort of child who, as my father would say, had "always got her nose in a book." Of course before television that was always regarded as rather a defect in a child, you know. I should have been doing useful things like helping to weed the garden!

We lived in very beautiful places; we were lucky. I was born in Oxford. And then we moved to Ludlow on the Welsh border—it's a very beautiful country town—and then to Cambridge, where I was at Cambridge High School. So I never lived in an ugly town in my youth. And I was wholly influenced by my surroundings and by architecture. I'm very fond of architecture.

Herbert And what were you like in terms of personality?

James I seem to have been a curious mixture because I think I was popular and gregarious at school and yet at the same time essentially very private.

Herbert That is an unusual balance to strike.

James Yes, I think it is. But my mother was a very warm, very emotional sort of person, entirely different from my father, and I can see in myself traits that I've taken from each. My father was very intelligent but I think rather cold emotionally. But he had a sense of humor and tremendous independence and as he got older I valued more and more these qualities in him. I had a very close relationship with him. My mother was sentimental, outgoing, and emotional, fun-loving and generous by nature.

Herbert And you had siblings?

James Yes. I am the eldest of three. My brother and sister and I were spaced by eighteen months.

Herbert So they provided the audience for Percy Pig and your first adventure stories?

James Yes.

Herbert Can you provide any insight into your need for privacy when you were a young girl?

James I just think that's been part of my character all my life, really, and I *needed* to spend some part of every day totally alone. I've never, *never* felt lonely in all of my life. And I don't know why that should be; maybe [it's] part of being a writer. But that's how I am.

Herbert During that private time, did you lead an active life of the imagination or rather, was the need for privacy a self-protective instinct?

James   I suppose if I thought about it for a good many weeks I might come up with something but I can't think of any explanation of it because it's always been there. I suppose it's—I don't know whether it's self-protective or not. I think that I am gregarious and I have a very public life but I still feel that there is a part of me that is intensely private and it always will be.

Herbert   So you don't think it was a matter of your upbringing but rather it was an internal characteristic?

James   Yes. But I had a very religious upbringing. My parents were practicing members of the Church of England so I attended service every Sunday. That has, I suppose, developed in me a religious sense which I think is in my books. It also, of course has a tremendous value because it gave me from childhood—and we were taken to church as *very* young children; we slept through the sermon—a familiarity with the marvelous 1662 version of the King James Bible. How *grateful* I am not to be young now and to be indoctrinated with the modern versions, which I absolutely deplore!

Herbert   So your early experiences in the church seemed to open your mind to the beauty of language.

James   Yes. Most definitely.

Herbert   I wonder if religion also offered you comfort from an unusual sensitivity to death. Do you see yourself as a person who has always been sensitive to the fragility of life?

James   Yes. I think this is so. I think I was born with this sense of the extraordinary fragility of life and that every moment is lived, really, not under the shadow of death but in the knowledge that this is how it is going to end. So that death is in a sense an ever-present thought. It sounds a little morbid, but I don't see it at all as morbid because I think I'm really rather a happy person who was always aware of this. I think for some people detective fiction does help to exorcise this fear. It distances death, really. It almost takes its horror—part of it anyway—and throws it out the window. The reader knows that order will be restored out of disorder.

The world of the murder story is a paradoxically safe world. This was particularly true of the old cozies. They still have their charm. Theirs was an ordered world with everyone moving according to hierarchy, with people knowing where they stand in the scheme of things and no one powerless, no one anonymous, everyone known, recognized, and valued.

Herbert   Do you think that one of the appeals of writing the crime novel is the author's control over matters of life and death?

James　　This is most interesting. Perhaps some people who write detective fiction, and maybe some novelists who write other books, are at heart basically very frightened of violence, are very frightened of a lack of control in themselves and in the world. And this way, as you say, you are taking to yourself the utter control over this situation and these characters. The fact that violence in society and within ourselves might be out of our control is a very unwelcome thought to human beings. And in the detective story there *is* a problem which the reader knows is going to be solved by human ingenuity, human courage, human persistence, human intelligence. Order is restored out of disorder. And therefore in an increasingly disordered world, the classical detective story retains its popularity.

Herbert　　Would you say that your impulse in dealing with crime in society is to show it from the point of view of the person trying to create order out of violence?

James　　Yes. Certainly. I don't know what the need is. I think it certainly is to solve the puzzle and get back *at least* to the fallible justice of man, even if, as I say, you're not getting true justice or God's justice, only men's justice. But you *are* containing the violence in some way. I do think that very often crime writers have a very great fear of violence and I think this is one way in which one can deal with that.

Herbert　　Was there any violent event that affected your life or the lives of your family that stimulated your keen awareness of violence in society?

James　　No.

Herbert　　It's just a general consciousness then?

James　　Yes. I think I was not very secure as a child. I do think I felt insecure.

Herbert　　But you had a loving home life?

James　　(Pauses.) It was all right.

Herbert　　I know you said your parents had very different personalities.

James　　Yes, they did. It was not a—I mean it was a discordant marriage in many ways but nevertheless it was—you know there was no divorce, no separation. And when we got older they got happier and then my mother got ill. At a time when they might have been happier together she took ill, which was very terrible.

Herbert　　Oh, I never knew about that.

James　　Well, that would be in her old age. But she did.

Herbert   I have asked you in the past about your own personal faith and you said that you felt that "no proof had been given" to you of any afterlife—not that you would expect it to be revealed to you more than to anyone else!

James   No, I wouldn't.

Herbert   But it does seem to me from the fact that you are now a member of the Liturgical Committee of the Church of England that perhaps your faith has grown stronger since 1982 when we first met.

James   Well, I am certainly strongly a deist and I pray a great deal. I believe in the Fatherhood of God and it is in relation to God as my Father that I feel most strongly. And that is, if anything, stronger; I think it does get stronger as I get older. And I *want* to believe and I suppose to an extent I *do* believe that the human spirit does in some way endure.

Herbert   But yet still there remains an immense awareness of the fragility of life.

James   Oh, always! Always. Especially of time and of time passing.

Herbert   Yes, it does, doesn't it? It just seems to pass more quickly—

James   —more quickly all the time. It just goes. It just *goes*.

Herbert   When you say that you were not feeling deeply secure as a child, is there any further insight that you can provide about that? Were you sometimes worried about such things as dying?

James   No. I don't think I was worried about dying but I was always aware of death in an odd way. I mean sometimes when I was quite young people used to say, "Well, in another six months we'll go on holiday." Whereas I always used to think, "Well, yes, *if* we're here!" I don't know why I had that feeling.

Herbert   I understand that. I had that feeling, too. I remember that it was very real to me, this fear. I don't know why some people have it.

James   No, I don't know why some people have it. It was more, I think, with me an *awareness* than a *fear* but, my goodness, I am aware of the passing of time! I'm fascinated by time and fascinated in my books with how events in the past overshadow events in the present. I think that's a fascinating part of the crime writer's art, really. So many of the motives have their roots in the past. Old evils. Old hurts. Old wrongs.

Herbert   Just as the crime itself spreads a stain onto the lives of the characters, the past sheds a shadow over the crime.

James　　I like to show how all the lives are touched by the crime. And I dealt with that very much, I think, in *A Taste for Death*.

Herbert　　That's a very strong novel.

James　　It's still, I think, probably my best book.

Herbert　　It's my favorite one. The view of the crime as touching all the innocent people is so powerful. Your religious sense, your love of architecture, and your view of the contaminating nature of crime and its investigation all are revealed in the scene in which the lonely woman realizes that the church, which has been the center of her life, is empty. "He's not here," she says, referring to God.

James　　Yes. She loses the little boy and she loses her faith. Whereas the priest, so depressed, so unsuccessful, at least gets a successful church again and with that, you know, a renewal of life. And the little boy, of course—and that is what I really like—the little boy is saved from his leukemia because *the murderer* saw his illness.

Herbert　　Yes. Isn't that a wonderful twist?

James　　So he was saved. And the Granny died and the girl's life was changed and her attitude to the job was changed—and she has that conversation with Dalgleish about the whole job of policing and being a detective at the end.

Herbert　　And there is the awareness that the crime, even after it is satisfactorily solved, has left indelible scars on all whom it touched.

James　　Yes, exactly.

Herbert　　And the investigation has played an active part in wounding the survivors, too.

James　　I think that one likes to show that the investigation really does as much harm to the innocent as it does to the guilty. It must be a terrifying thing to be a murder suspect.

Herbert　　Oh, it must be. It must be. I think you do convey this. You are also very accomplished at describing violence. I wonder if you ever frighten yourself when writing graphic scenes of violence?

James　　You don't really frighten yourself. I think this is because of the detachment. And I'm sure that you as a writer feel this: that you are involved but at the same time—this is the paradox of it—you are detached. I find that with the awful things that have happened to me in my own life—and some have been very traumatic—that I have been trying to cope with them but part of my mind *has been standing outside watching*. Watching my own reaction!

Herbert　　Does this give you strength, do you think?

James   Oh, yes. Because you don't get lost. And therefore I think when you are writing these horrible parts, when you're with Cordelia Gray looking down on a battered face, part of you is feeling, "I can't be seeing it! I can't be seeing it!" The horrible part for you is feeling the *coldness*. But the writer in you is standing on one side noticing details and observing the emotions. This is what Graham Greene called—

Herbert   —the splinter of ice at the heart.

James   Yes! I don't think that's true necessarily of just detective writers, or writers of mysteries or of crime novels. I think that is true of almost all writers.

Herbert   To take that one step further, if we bring together your thoughts on this with your thoughts about guilt—"to be human is to be guilty"—I wonder whether or not part of you is also thinking, "I can't have done this! I can't have done this!"

James   No, I don't think I ever feel, "I can't have done this."

Herbert   Would you agree that that writerly detachment begins, as it did for me, with a habit of narrating one's actions to oneself as a child.

James   So it does! So it does!

Herbert   I used to narrate my own actions to myself in the third person. Did you find yourself doing this, too?

James   So I did! Do you know, it's not so much now, but when I was a girl, a child, sometimes it was nonstop! It's years and years since I've had anyone mention that to me. I think it was twenty years ago that I read an article by Ethel Mannion—who I don't think now is much known or ever thought of—but she is in *my* memory because she was the only other writer who said that when she was a girl her whole day was one long narration. I think that's very much the sign of a writer. I can't remember when it stopped. It seems to me to be a part of my childhood rather than my girlhood. But there must have come a moment, a turning point.

Herbert   Were you ever observed in the act of narration, or was it more internal?

James   It was internal.

Herbert   I distinctly remember being caught at this while walking over the moors in Wales. Someone was following me without my knowing it. And here I was narrating aloud, "And the sheep. . . . " I think the embarrassment stopped me!

James   (Laughs.) Yes.

Herbert   Speaking of turning points, you have said that you always knew

71

that you wanted to be a writer. Did you always imagine that it would be in the detective arena?

James   No. But by the time I came to settle down to write the first book, there was no particular internal discussion about what sort of book it would be. I knew I was going to attempt a detective story for my first novel.

Herbert   Did this arise out of a love of detective fiction?

James   Well, I certainly read it for pleasure. And Dorothy L. Sayers was certainly a very potent influence upon my youth. I love construction, of course, in novels, and I wanted to write a well-constructed novel. I didn't want to write an autobiographical novel. I didn't want to make use of the experience of my husband's illness or of anything that happened to me directly—but I know that that begs the question of how much any novel must necessarily be autobiographical. And I also thought that a detective novel would have the best chance of being accepted for publication! I also felt that because it's a disciplined and not a self-indulgent form that it would be a marvelous apprenticeship for a serious writer.

Of course, I later discovered that within the detective form I could write a novel that has a moral ambiguity and psychological subtlety like a serious novel. Writing within the constraints isn't, in fact, inhibiting; it's positively liberating! Which is why, I suppose, I'd like to carry on.

Herbert   In terms of crafting your novels, are there any constraints that you have found most challenging?

James   I must say the denouement is always difficult. I mean tying everything up, really. And I've sometimes wondered if the introduction of a second murder—in nearly all of my books there is more than one—whether artistically this is always entirely right, whether that isn't rather seeking after sensation at the expense of truth. But I'm not sure.

Herbert   Coming back to your comment that the constraints of the genre are "liberating," I would like to read you something that Julian Symons wrote in his latest edition of *Bloody Murder*: in a section that he calls "A Postscript for the Nineties," he said, "P. D. James also produced her most assured and accomplished novel in *A Taste for Death* (1986). Here she felt so justifiably confident of the story's power and momentum that she revealed the solution of the mystery two-thirds of the way through. The book showed James moving toward deeper, though never portentous, seriousness in treating the actualities and implications of death but also using as sparingly as possible what she clearly finds at times to be the shackles of the orthodox puzzle plot." I'd love to know your reaction to Julian's assessment.

James   Yes, I think it's the structure, the formal structure, that we need, really, to provide the mystery, to provide the clues, the shape of the novel, which really does attract me very much. I think that certainly the problem, the central problem, is over the characterization of the murderer, as in fact Dorothy L. Sayers said. And I think I have ways of getting over that. What I find fascinating is to *use* the conventions and either stretch them to their limits or to somehow manage to subvert them so that I can do what I want to do while remaining within them. I think, you know, that with Ruth Rendell, Ruth really finds them so inhibiting that, in what I think is her best work, she moves right outside them as Barbara Vine. I don't feel that I want to move outside; I like staying within. But they do certainly present a challenge. I was reading, today, an interview with Graham Greene in which Graham Greene said that he sometimes thought—he loves plots and he wanted action—but he sometimes thought he overplotted. Because what he had set [out to describe] in his book was a man with a major problem or a major failing of character and sometimes he felt the plot got so dense that that character got diminished. I think one has to watch that in plotting, that one doesn't diminish character.

Herbert   So you must be alert to the tendency of the plot to dominate?

James   The plot is so important and I love the plot but the plot must *never*, as it were, twist the character out of true. You must never twist your characters from their true selves just in order to make *them* fit the plot. The plot must fit the characters, not the character the plot. I don't think I'm aware, really, of the shackles as much as Julian seems to think I am.

Herbert   You don't regard them as "shackles"—

James   No! I don't, really.

Herbert   —but rather as a challenge.

James   'Tis a challenge. You're absolutely right. There are certainly aspects of the shape, the form: the need to provide the problem, the need to provide the clues, the need at the end to have the denouement, which can diminish a novel if one isn't careful. But I think the attraction of the form is seeing that they *don't* diminish the novel. And I obviously don't find them too shackling.

Herbert   You say you have ways of getting around them. Will you confide an example?

James   Well, I mean, one thing is that you can't often enter into the mind of the murderer fully because if you [do] we're going to know who's the murderer. But then you can enter *very* fully into his mind before he begins to plan the murder, maybe before he even thinks about it. If you don't have the book open with the murder, if you introduce your little group of characters—among them the murderer—you can then, if you like, see things through his eyes perfectly well *until* the moment when he's planning the murder.

Herbert   And at that point you step back.

James   Yes. And you can have his character seen through other characters, or revealed through other characters.

Herbert   I see.

James   But it is the central problem, I think, of the detective story, to make the characterization true and honest and psychologically real without revealing, you know, that *this* man is the murderer.

Herbert   There's this need to be coy with the reader, then, to keep secrets, would you agree?

James   Well, in a way you have to because, suppose you have five suspects. You're not telling the reader that one of these is innocent, are you? You're not saying, "Well actually he happened to be visiting his grandmother at the time." You conceal from the readers an awful lot about all the suspects. And the readers have to find it out themselves, with the detective.

Herbert   Now, of course, in a mainstream novel there's a certain amount of concealment, as well, because we need to have our understanding of the characters grow in *anything* that can be called a novel.

James   Yes.

Herbert   You start out not knowing all.

James   Yes, you're absolutely right, Rosemary. If everything was revealed even in a mainstream novel we'd be bored. We need at the end of the book to know far more about them than we do at the beginning. So you're absolutely right; this isn't absolutely restricted to detective fiction.

Herbert   But with the detective novel there may be a point where you might have decided to give some information about a character for artistic reasons in developing his or her personality where you would have to say to yourself, "No, I can't do that quite yet. I must hold back somewhat longer on this particular revelation."

James   Yes, that could easily happen, but of course, as I've said, one other way of doing it is to see the character through the eyes of others and really this has got to be intriguing because, after all, that is how we *are* seen: through the eyes of others. So that, for example, if you have a character—perhaps in *Devices and Desires*—Alex, who's head of the nuclear power station, seeing him through his sister's eyes, seeing him through the eyes of the woman he's having an affair with, seeing him through the eyes of his second in command, that is quite intriguing because the reader feels, "Who is this real man? Where is he? They all seem rather different." So I don't see them really as shackles. I think of it more as a technical challenge really.

Herbert   Do you think these technical challenges in any way limit the detective form from becoming the very highest of literary forms?

James   Well, Dorothy L. Sayers said it did.

Herbert   But what do you think? I mean here we are speaking in the light of the fact that you've just published a novel that steps out of the detective or crime genre entirely. Did you feel that it was liberating in some ways not to work within the constraints of the genre?

James   No. I love the detective story. I love the form. I don't know if I agree with Dorothy that it cannot reach the heights of literary excellence. After all, how many novels *do* reach the heights of literary excellence? If we are talking about the heights of literary excellence, we may be thinking about the greatest novels that have ever been written. But if we [ask] "Can it be a really good, lasting novel?" The answer is "Yes, it can." Look at *The Moonstone*. I would think, too, that probably [Margery Allingham's] *Tiger in the Smoke*, possibly Dorothy L. Sayers's *The Nine Tailors* would last, and I think some of Chandler and Dashiell Hammett will last.

Herbert   Well, it seems to me that novels, like yours, that are reaching for the highest of literary levels are ones where somehow the author manages to deliver the final information at a logical point in developing the character artistically as well as at a logical point in the timing essential to the plot of the detective story. And this has to be made simultaneous.

James   Yes, this is it.

Herbert   Because if you're preventing yourself all the time from allowing the character naturally to develop because of the necessities of the plot, then indeed, it is a real limitation.

James   Yes, I think that this is absolutely so and I think that it is difficult to do it successfully. Which is why I think very few detective novels reach the highest levels of literary excellence. I think the general standard of the sort of middle grade is very good, the writing and characterization. I think those who manage, as it were, to *lift* it [provide] cohesion. I think it was Hardy or Henry James said that there should be a central unity. There should be a point at which all the rays converge. There's got to be a unity there and I think there isn't a unity if you are sacrificing character to plot.

Herbert   So that what you have in your mind as you write is not so much a worry about timing as a concern that "I will not let the plot dominate such that I cannot say what I need to about human experience, human emotion, human character."

James   Yes, yes. This is absolutely so. Character must come before plot because character surely determines the plot.

Herbert   Hmm. You just say that easily, lightly. But what a profound statement.

James   Well, I think it has to be that way.

Herbert   You see, there's the pure novelist speaking.

James   You can see it even at a very superficial level. For example, [I might] have a character in a book who on the whole is a gentle old lady who's led a very good life but, you know, a terrible wrong has been done to someone she loves and she's determined to avenge that. [If] she somehow manages actually to psych herself up into a state of committing a murder, it's no good me saying that she goes out and gets a gun and she does this, that, and the other or she concocts something that's tremendously mechanically ingenious. You know, it's against the character! She wouldn't do it that way. She and her emotions have got to be there and *then* you say to yourself, "How is she going to do it?"

Herbert   But you see I think it is the other way around for many mystery writers.

James   I think it is. The approach is, "Who should I create to carry this story forward?"

Herbert   Sadly, yes.

James   It's almost as if, "This is my script and who will I bring in to act it?"

Herbert   The author is populating the plot.

James   Yes!

Herbert   Speaking of populating plots or casting scripts, would you tell us something about your play, *A Private Treason*, and how the writing process for drama differed from your experiences in writng fiction?

James   Well, it was about a man who had betrayed secrets to the Russians, and his mistress's new young husband, but it really was about relationships among the three of them. (Pauses.) I shan't publish it.

Herbert   You told me in the past that it was a novelist's play.

James   Yes, it was. I think it was a novelist's play in many ways because I was exploring some very interesting ideas about the nature of human relations and about the nature of treason, personal treason related to, as it were, national treason. And actually the characters probably spoke rather more than they should have done! (Smiles.)

Herbert   Did you find anything significantly different about the writing process?

James   Well, a play is dialogue and I like writing dialogue very much, but I think it's difficult for a novelist to understand that you don't need many words in a play. The actors do a great deal of it. And I like the *words* to express things, so obviously I felt in myself a bit of a conflict between the novelist and the playwright.

Herbert   And you are more comfortable as a novelist.

James   Absolutely.

Herbert   Focusing again on the novel, can we pursue further your point about the crime novel as distinct from the detective novel?

James   I think there can be little argument that the crime novel, as distinct from the detective story, can be literature. After all, Rosemary, man has always concerned himself with problems of moral choice, with the nature of good and evil, and with that unique crime for which there can be no reparation to the victim, murder. Our earliest myths are concerned with violent death, and with the bringing of order out of disorder.

Herbert   But how do you see the detective story as more limited than the crime novel?

James   The detective story is more limited, I think, in intention and potential than the crime novel. The reader expects a kind of literary formula with the central mysterious death, the closed circle of suspects, and the detective who arrives at a solution by the end of the story. This is not to say that the detective story cannot claim to attain the heights of serious literature. A story of murder and its solution is as valid a plot for literature as any other. But I think the crime novel may be more likely to be taken seriously as literature since its concern is to explore human character, and this concern is placed before the exigencies of the plot.

Herbert   How would you describe the qualities that cause a work of fiction to be regarded as literature?

James   I think it requires originality and imagination on the part of the writer. The author must speak with a clear and individual voice which transcends time and change. Literature is never ephemeral.

Herbert   You said earlier that writing is one of the loneliest professions in the world.

James   Yes.

Herbert   And I wonder if one attraction of writing detective fiction is the fact that, while indeed the process is a lonely one, this is one of the kinds of literature that is very interactive with the reader. The reader of the detective novel is always engaged in trying to outwit the author.

James   What I think I do is always to write to please myself. I just try to do the very best I can with my talent. I think that if I please myself, I will almost certainly please the reader. (Smiles.) At least I hope I shall please the reader. But when I'm writing I don't seem to be conscious very much of the reader. It's always, "This is what is going to make a good book. This is what I think will make it good."

Herbert   Mystery writing can be a form that protects the author from uncomfortable self-revelation. But as you said in your speech at Somerville College, the topography of the writer's mind is revealed in her work. Is it safe to say that a body of mystery writing *does* say a great deal about even the most private author's world view?

James   More in crime writing, I think, than in mystery writing. I do think it is quite remarkable and profoundly true how mystery writers are able, as it were, to hide their essential natures. You can get some character clues—you can get a lot of clues—because after all we *do* reveal ourselves in our books. I've been reading the biography of Margery Allingham and the biography of Ngaio Marsh. Ngaio Marsh was an extremely private person but she is revealed—there's no doubt at all—through those novels. She is revealed. But I do think it is profoundly true that this is a form of literary work in which writers do feel that their essential privacy is protected.

Herbert   It's fascinating, isn't it?

James   It's also a form in which writers are enabled to deal with very violent events without undue trauma because the structure provides tremendous support. In *Devices and Desires* the mass murderer isn't the main murderer, of course; that isn't the main part of the book. But I'm not sure that apart from the mystery I would really be able to write about a mass murderer who killed girls and cut their pubic hairs and stuffed them in their mouths. It's a thing that's very horrific. And I don't think I could write Patricia Highsmith, like that, from the point of view of the murderer, for example.

Herbert   We've skirted around the issue of the trauma in your marriage on a few occasions during this interview. Would you be willing to discuss not only the pain but the positive sides of your life as a wife and mother? I understand that your husband, Connor Bantry White, returned from World War II with a mental disability.

James   That is so.

Herbert   At the time you had two small daughters, one of whom was born during the bombing of London.

James   Yes. That was my younger daughter, Jane. She was born in Queen Charlotte's Hospital in London while the [aerial bombing raids] were at their height. It was very terrifying.

Herbert   It must have been absolutely horrendous.

James   Well, Jane Austen was a great comfort to me, really.

Herbert   You were reading Jane Austen at the time? Did you decide on the spur of the moment to name your baby Jane?

James   Yes. Yes!

Herbert   Has Jane Austen served not only as a comfort to you under duress but also as a literary influence?

James   Absolutely.

Herbert   Which of her many qualities do you admire the most?

James   I think the delicate irony. The humor. The wonderful insight into human nature. And the creation by her of a unique world into which we can enter for our joy and comfort.

Herbert   And what aspect of her work has guided you most as a writer?

James   The way in which she works always within the limits of her own talents so effectively. And, again, that creation of a world into which the reader can enter.

Herbert   I understand that when your husband returned from the war you had to support the family through your work in the Civil Service. This must have been a very difficult time for you. Did you feel especially protective of your children?

James   Well, I wasn't really very able to protect them very much because of their father being mentally ill and they went to school very young. Jane was only three. I'm just grateful that it seems not to have harmed them. They've been the greatest possible joy to me. I do feel strongly protective of them. Yes, I do.

Herbert   You rarely talk about the part of your life when you were a young woman but not yet a writer. What was it like for you at that time? Looking back on those years, do you recall a yearning for self-expression?

James   Well, yes, I think there *was* but, you see, the difficulty was it was such an *unnatural* time. I mean, one was in the middle of war and one was being bombed all the time. In most of the wartime I was actually in physical danger nearly all the time partly because when I was living with my husband in London the bombing was quite intense and then afterwards, when the children were being born, there were the V-1s and the V-2s. When Jane was born in 1942 there were a thousand people killed in the vicinity of the hospital via aerial bombing.

Herbert   Oh, I didn't know it was that extreme.

James   Yes, it was very bad. I mean one in three houses were damaged in the whole of the UK by aerial bombing. And the house where I lived at the beginning of the war with my parents-in-law, in Seven Kings in Essex, was completely destroyed by bombing. Fortunately we weren't there at the time.

Herbert   Oh, Phyllis!

James   So you know, one lived at a very unnatural time and I don't think one had very much time for wondering if you were being frustrated or not because you were just glad to be alive and get on with trying to keep yourself and your children fed. It was a time where, on the whole, I *do* remember being quite hungry.

Herbert   That's quite a surprising answer. I wasn't expecting this; I suppose this betrays the fact that I am neither a member of your generation nor English. I was thinking primarily of you as an embryo author.

James   Well, I was trying to cope with the children and keep them fed. Long amounts of time were spent in queuing for the few things that were not, as it were, on ration. It was a very small ration and one was making do and making over clothes and so on. So I mean, one was in the middle of fighting a very difficult and bloody war, really, and I don't think it was a time for a great deal of introspection. I don't think at that time I felt that I ought to be writing books; I thought I'd see if I survived before I did any of that.

Herbert   Yes, I see. I know that you experienced great challenges with your husband's illness and the need to bring up your daughters, but I wonder if you can provide an impression of the happier moments in your early married life.

James   Oh, well, yes, when we first met, when he was a medical student and he was an undergraduate at St. Catherine's College in Cambridge—and that was in the very, very early part of the war before the real bombing began—that was a *very* happy time. We were young and there were parties and theatres and the river.

Herbert   This makes me think of Cordelia Gray's happy afternoon in Cambridge, in *An Unsuitable Job for a Woman*.

James   Yes. It was a very exciting time and one was in love; even though it was the beginning of the war there was great optimism, I think. But of course you know once [my husband] qualified, he was in the Royal Army Medical Corps and then went overseas, so there was not a lot of that life, really.

Herbert   Was it a matter of months or years?

James   Only months, really.

Herbert   Having had a life that turned out to have been difficult, would you have wished to have had an easy life?

James   Well, it's dishonest to say "No" because I think we all live our lives trying to minimize our pains and maximize our happinesses. But I think as a writer it's better to have experienced a degree of trauma. Someone said if you want to be a writer you should have as much trauma in your early years as you can bear without breaking. I think something in me believes that. Yes.

Herbert   Do you feel that the goodness in people ultimately prevails over the inevitable rougher sides of human nature?

James   I hope it can. I like to think it can. I suppose we all need to believe that love is stronger than death, that the human spirit is indestructible, can surmount almost anything that fate can throw against it. But part of me believes that personal tragedy and, in particular, physical pain can break anybody. There is, I suppose, in my own personality, a dichotomy between the optimism which is part of my nature—probably just a physical thing—and this knowledge of just how dark and dreadful life can be for many people.

Many of my books are—well, they're to do with death—but they're also to do with love, different aspects of human love.

Herbert   This is a wonderful insight into what guides your writing. But what about self-love? In your new book, *The Children of Men*, you say at one point, "There was some dignity and much safety in the self-selected role of spectator. But faced with some abominations a man has no option but to step onto the stage. He would see Xan but was he motivated less by the outrage of the horror of the Quietus than by the memory of his own humiliation, the carefully-judged blow, his body hauled up on the beach and dumped as if it were an unwanted carcass." It seems to me there that the protagonist is not easy on himself; he sees the full range of possible motives in what he's doing; he doesn't grant himself the dignity of having the better motive. Are you that sort of person yourself, about yourself?

James   Well, I hope so because I think that self-knowledge is tremendously important to a happy life. I think it was Tennyson who said, "Self-reverence, self-knowledge, self-control, /These three alone lead life to sovereign power." And I think there's some great truth there. With self-knowledge we know ourselves, reveal ourselves, and control ourselves so I think we need to look at motive and need to have a nurtured and sensitive conscience.

Herbert   A nurtured and sensitive conscience?

James   And I think we do need that. Now I think this character of mine did have quite a lot of self-knowledge. He was very cold; he was very selfish; he was very self-contained: but he does know himself. He *does* know what he is. He doesn't much like what he is.

Herbert   No, he doesn't, does he?

James   But he doesn't fool himself.

Herbert   The reason that I asked about self-knowledge was that I knew, from having been here, that you were describing very much your own home in describing the place where he lived.

James   Yes. Yes.

Herbert   And this led me to wonder "How much does the author identify with him?" I suspect that you are the sort of person who is not easy on herself and who looks at the full range of possibilities of what might be motivating each action that you—or your fictional characters—take.

James   Yes, well I think that that's important to somebody who does write detective fiction because motivation is so important and you have to try and be clear, when you're creating characters, about their motives. Because motives are often very, very mixed.

Herbert   If it is so that the topography of an author's mind is revealed in his or her body of writing, in yours I see some revelations of P. D. James: the need to create order out of chaos and the love of architecture are examples. What else, in your work, do you think shows the most about you personally? What aspect of the novel reveals the most about you?

James   Oh, I don't know that I can answer that. You could probably get others to answer that. (Pauses.)

Herbert   (Waits.)

James I think a dislike of sentimentality, a dislike of dishonest thought, a dislike of humbug come out really quite strongly. And a dislike of self-deceit, a dislike of cruelty.

Herbert An abhorrence of cruelty.

James Yes, an abhorrence of cruelty. A respect for intelligence, respect for a certain decent pride, and a great respect for courage. I think they're all there. And a certain detachment, I think.

Herbert If you could sum up your own achievement in writing, what would you say?

James I hope that my work provides affirmation that we do live in a rational universe. I hope that my books serve as small celebrations of order and reason in our increasingly disordered world.

▶ TONY HILLERMAN

Tony Hillerman's procedurals featuring the Navajo Tribal Police officers Joe Leaphorn and Jim Chee represent all that is best in the American regional mystery novel. Informed with competent research into Native American culture, inspired by the author's conviction that his subjects' way of life offers insights from which we can all benefit, and enriched by the author's deep familiarity with his chosen landscape, Hillerman's work is also strengthened by the author's twenty-year experience as a journalist keenly aware of keeping the reader interested in information conveyed in uncluttered prose.

It is not surprising that the most important of Hillerman's themes, the quest to live in physical and spiritual harmony with one's world, works on three levels in his work. Not only does this concept of harmony—called *hosrah* by the Navajo—provide a cultural insight into Native American culture, but it acts as a guide to the police officers as they seek to restore order after the shattering event of the crime and, finally, it guides Hillerman in his crafting of the novels so that a harmonious and satisfying conclusion is reached. It is not insignificant that the Native Americans also refer to the attainment of *hosrah* as "going in beauty." Hillerman's pattern of taking a disrupted situation and reestablishing harmony with the solution of the crime echoes W. H. Auden's view, expressed in his landmark essay "The Guilty Vicarage," of the detective story as a shattered idyll requiring the sleuth to reinstate order.

Hillerman rebuilds harmony in a distinctly American voice while employing heroes who fall soundly into the tradition of rugged individualism. His heroes can be alone without feeling lonely and they rely on their own skills and resources in a quest for truth. Fortunately for the reader, Hillerman's policemen possess information about and insights into a way of life that is both alien and fascinating to most of us. And the material concerning Native American culture is not merely used as background. It also provides insight into character, which in turn demonstrates that essential ingredient of the detective story: motive or, in the more psychologically sophisticated work of a writer of Hillerman's caliber, psychological motivation. A bonus for the reader and author alike is the ease with which such material as a ceremonial healing takes on a symbolic dimension even as it is the occasion for the occurrence of a crime.

Hillerman's landscapes, too, are steeped in symbolic possibilities, peopled with spirits, and loaded with literal mystery. Take Chaco Canyon, for example, where a crucial scene of *The Thief of Time* is set. Here, as Hillerman puts it, "a thousand years ago at this place the Anasazi were building the Rome and Mecca of their civilization. Why did they, 800 years ago, walk away from this place, literally leaving their dishes on the table?" Here is a location custom-made for the mystery novelist: already imbued with mystery, the ruins in this canyon are the ideal place for Hillerman to play out his struggle between the Anglo world and the culture it seeks to understand and sometimes exploit.

The solutions to Hillerman's crimes always turn on cultural insights that the author thoroughly understands and conveys to us. Hillerman's acquaintance with Native American peoples runs deep and began early in his life when he was brought up in the dust-bowl community of Sacred Heart, Oklahoma. The son of a jack-of-all trades, who supplemented the lean earnings of the family farm with additional jobs, and a registered nurse turned homemaker, Hillerman grew up in a household without a telephone, electricity, or running water and where the family could not afford to keep their one link to the outside world—the radio—supplied with batteries. But it was a household full of love and a place where storytellers were valued.

Hillerman's father, sensitive to events in the greater world and the family's German name, impressed on Hillerman and his brother the need for tolerance, a lesson that came easily to boys who identified with their underprivileged Native American neighbors more easily than with the town boys. Hillerman attended a girls' school run by the Sisters of Mercy, where, he recalls, "The nuns forgave us for not being Indians but they never forgave us for not being girls."

Aspiring to become a chemical engineer, Hillerman attended the University of Oklahoma, where he discovered simultaneously his weakness in mathematics and his talent for English. But his college career was cut short when his brother joined the military and Hillerman returned to run the family farm. Before long he followed his brother into the military and the family farm was sold.

Upon his return from the war, wounded and without a family home to dwell in, Hillerman was encouraged, by a journalist who had used his war correspondence as the basis of a feature article, to take up a career in journalism. At the same time, Hillerman witnessed a Navajo healing ceremony that so deeply impressed him that he drew upon the experience years later when he finally wrote his first novel, *The Blessing Way.*

Hillerman went on to raise five children and become a professor of journalism at the University of New Mexico while establishing a career in fiction writing. He now writes full time from his contemporary adobe home in Albuquerque, New Mexico. His clean, well-lighted office commands a view, across an expanse of wildflowers, of Turquoise Mountain, a peak sacred to The People at the heart of Hillerman's writing. As a person who has never taken financial ease for granted, Hillerman gives the impression of feeling relaxed in his new home and office—he slouches comfortably at his desk— but he also evinces the glee of a child on Christmas morning who has been surprised to receive the gift he dared not hope for.

Hillerman's thoughts, expressed in an appealing western accent and without a trace of pretension, are very much like the man: informed with common sense and profound intelligence, down-to-earth and straightforward, and intensely kind.

Herbert   I'd like to begin by discussing a forte of yours that I admire very much. I expect, when I turn to your books, that I might learn something cultural in the context of a puzzling police procedural. But I often feel that I've been given something more.

Hillerman   Thank you.

Herbert   Here, *The Listening Woman* comes to mind for me, especially that opening scene. There we are with the Listening Woman who will perform the healing ceremony for the stricken man. Along with her is her teenage protégée—

Hillerman   —her niece—

Herbert   —who, once she gets over boys, is going to be quite talented at healing, too. And in this memorable scene the reader is visiting your dark literary landscape, a place out of time, wrapped in the ancient ritual involved in cleansing or healing. And all of that is fascinating enough, but *then* you zoom in on that girl's T-shirt, and it says "Tiger Pep." And immediately the reader realizes, "This is a contemporary scene. This is a teenager who lives in the traditional Navajo world and who is also on a pep team at a high school." This is the kind of thing that is magic for me. It just gives you that extra little jolt that says we're dealing with questions concerning that interface between Indian culture and ordinary contemporary society. I just love that.

Hillerman   Well, thank you.

Herbert   Raymond Chandler may have inspired many mystery writers to use their fiction to elucidate American attitudes but you're enriching this tradition by giving us this other culture within America—

Hillerman   —that we weren't able to eradicate.

Herbert   Thank God!

Hillerman   Thank—yeah, I guess God. Thank droughts, lack of minerals, lack of anything that attracted the Anglo-Americans.

Herbert   Your readers are intrigued by the cultural insights into the Native American way of life.

Hillerman   Yes. This is kind of a shallow statement, and it doesn't reflect everything I mean, but I think this is a little bit of it: it gives them absolution for wasting their time.

Herbert   I *cannot* agree that reading a Tony Hillerman novel is a waste of time on any level!

Hillerman   Don't you think so? They think, "Here I am learning about the Navajos. I really should know more about Native American cultures; I'm learning a little bit; and it's a painless way to learn it." And so [readers] don't feel like they're wasting time.

Herbert   But this is literature, though. You sound like the old-style librarian when you say something like that.

Hillerman   (Chuckles.)

Herbert   You know, in Widener Library at Harvard they used to have a different classification for popular literature. It wasn't *real* literature, so they called it "PZ" while they gave numerical call numbers to everything else. Thomas Hardy and things like that were given bona fide call numbers, while even an undoubtedly literary crime writer like Michael Innes could be found under "PZ."

Hillerman   (Laughs.) How do they catalogue mysteries today?

Herbert   With legitimate call numbers. And this reflects, I think, the rising status of the crime or mystery novel, at least in the eyes of academe. It used to be that popular literature of this type was considered incapable of rising to the level of serious literature.

Hillerman   A lot of people still feel this way. An *awful* lot of people, when I'm signing books [for them], begin with an apology. "I don't normally read mysteries," they say. They don't want me to think they're mystery readers.

Herbert   I'm surprised. In this day and age?

Hillerman   Well, they tend to be older people. You know, they tend to be people my age or so, that have been taught better manners in their youth. (Laughs.)

Herbert   They've had stodgy English professors, I'd say. The readers of this interview will be people who are enthusiastic about mystery writing and who will not be inclined to look down on the genre.

Hillerman   Good.

Herbert   I think many mystery readers don't know very much about the Western novel, and I wonder, since your work is firmly set in the southwest, and it focuses on law and order in a harsh environment, and it usually includes adventurous episodes, does it reflect any literary influences from the Western story?

Hillerman   (Pauses.) It has two influences from the Western. One is western Australia. (Smiles.)

Herbert   Aha! Arthur Upfield's mysteries!

Hillerman   Upfield, yes.

Herbert   Please explain the influence of a western *Australian* writer on your very American work.

Hillerman   Well, in Sacred Heart, Oklahoma, where I grew up, there was no library. The only way to get books was to order them from the mimeographed catalog of the state library. I've often said that this was a guaranteed way to get a broad education. You would order all kinds of adventure stories like *Captain Blood* and the Tom Swift stories, and *Treasure Island*. And then, weeks later, a package would arrive and in it you would find exciting material like *History of the Masonic Order in Oklahoma*! But on rare occasions you would get something about the foreign legion or a novel about a half-breed Australian aborigine policeman who solved crimes in the Outback. That was my introduction to Arthur Upfield.

Herbert   What a serendipitous way to become acquainted with a lifelong influence!

Hillerman   The other Western writer who impressed me tremendously was Raymond Chandler.

Herbert   You're calling him a Western writer because he resided in California, not because he wrote in the cowboys and Indians genre.

Hillerman   Okay. I think Chandler is a heck of a lot more important American writer—and I think he will be recognized as such—than [someone] like Scott Fitzgerald. Chandler had an immense effect on generations of writers by showing you could take this category, detection, and just do wonderful things with it!

Herbert   For instance, what aspect of his work is particularly memorable to you, influencing your writing?

Hillerman   The grand view he gave you of urban culture. I mean, looking back on his books, I don't remember who did the crime, or why, or any of that stuff; I just remember the incredible little scenes of Marlowe going to this old, shabby boardinghouse looking for this missing brother, and what he found there. I was really impressed by Chandler. I still am.

Herbert   Do you think that one of the things you find appealing about him is the way he describes the larger scene of the tenement and then zooms in on details that reveal attitude and character? I ask this because you do wonderful things in this regard.

Hillerman   (Pauses.) Okay. Chandler had Marlowe walking up the walk. He notices what used to be [a] common statue of the black guy who would take your horse, and he kind of lingers on it. I can close my eyes right now and see that lawn with that statue.

Herbert   That sort of statue where the black man stands there with the little lantern?

Hillerman   Yeah! Okay. Chandler uses it to tell you something about attitudes. I mean, he doesn't rub your nose in it, but here's this rich guy and here's this tasteless symbol. Now, later on, he rang the doorbell, nobody comes to the door. I don't remember a damn thing about the plot, who answered the door or anything. But he notices in the grass a sparkle. And he picks it up and it's a diamond. Do you remember the book?

Herbert   Oh, yes.

Hillerman   I can't remember much, and I don't think it has a bloomin' thing to do with the plot. I think probably, had he edited a little bit, he'd have gone back and cut it out, maybe.

Herbert   It's a good thing he didn't because it is such a memorable symbol. How conscious are you of imbuing small details with a symbolic dimension in your work? How consciously are you seeking to teach the reader about the Native American experience?

Hillerman   Well, but see, I've got to fight that all the time. The people who read me have had a hard day at the office; they've got all kinds of problems; they're worrying about God knows what; and they want to be entertained. They don't want some guy out in Albuquerque preaching to them about the sins of their fathers. They don't want me trying to retrain them in American history. They don't want me ser-monizing on religion to them. They want to be entertained. I've gotta keep that in mind all the time, remind myself who I am and what I'm doing. I'm writing what Graham Greene called an entertain-ment.

Herbert   This leads directly into a question that fascinates me. Some years ago, when I interviewed Brian W. Aldiss, we were discussing the fact that his work succeeds not only as thought-provoking literature but also as entertaining fare. When I asked him if he consciously worked at adding entertaining elements to his work, he replied, "When I think about this, I grieve about it, because I have discovered in me the fatal art of entertainment. And I have always wanted to write an undeniable book that would, in the words of Pushkin, 'lay waste the hearts of men.' And I think that the two are at war," this ability to entertain and the urge to write great literature. While Brian Aldiss is a mainstream and science fiction writer rather than a mys-tery writer, I think his comments bear consideration by mystery authors. Because, after all, mystery literature generally is intended as entertainment. I wonder if you find a tension between entertainment and "higher" literary goals, as Aldiss does.

Hillerman   I don't think it's necessarily even a dichotomy. I think the great literature—*Bleak House* is great literature, *Huckleberry Finn*'s great literature—*is* entertaining.

Herbert   But if you're constantly aware of your readers' desire to be entertained, does that ever hold you back from adding other dimen-sions to your writing?

Hillerman   It was holding me back as we sat here. I'm just going to turn on my computer and show you—Joe Leaphorn and Dilly Streib, an FBI man, are driving from Window Rock to Tuba City. The reason they're driving to Tuba City is because there's been a murder there some time ago and not much progress [has been made] on [solving] it. Okay, now. Here's the first paragraph, see, of that chapter. (Extended pause while Hillerman reveals the text of his work in progress at the time of the interview, *Sacred Clowns*.)

Herbert   This is marvelous.

Hillerman   What I want to do here is to develop the character of these two by what they stop to look at. For example, they're going to cross the Hopi reservation. Okay, from this road there you can see literally miles of sagebrush on this great flat [expanse] and the hill rolls away and you can see behind it San Francisco Peaks sixty, seventy miles away. Not a tree, not a bush, not a shrub! It's really pure sagebrush country. And on the fence there, somebody's painted a real neat sign that says, "Woodcutting Prohibited"—

Herbert   (Laughs.)

Hillerman —which is just a huge joke, and it's really there. And they're gonna notice the sign, and they notice it's been repainted. And by showing you their reactions to it, I can illuminate the character of the two men, and also say something about this incredible Navajo sense of humor. This Navajo would go to all that trouble to paint that just to underline the shortage of firewood for a hundred miles!

Herbert   I see.

Hillerman Okay. Then I think, "A lot of my readers want me to get on with it. They know this man's been killed and they're wondering 'Why?'" He's just a shop teacher, see. Somebody hit him on the head. Okay. So I'm beginning to say, "Have I got enough tension built up in this book? Is there enough interest by now?"

Herbert   So you have to think consciously, "Is this a place where I can afford to spend some time in description? Is the reader's interest piqued enough for me to—"

Hillerman —to show 'em a sunset, or—

Herbert   —or a reflection, or a cultural explanation, or—

Hillerman —or spend more time putting them in this immense space, or should I get on with the story? So yeah, I deal with that all the time.

Herbert   And I think you do it effectively with your choice of details. Instead of saying, "Now, we're talking about this interface of two cultures," you zoom in on the telling detail.

Hillerman And remind the reader that it's 1992. Yup. Uh huh. Or should I show 'em a drunk Hopi hitchhiking? And see what they say about the drunk Hopi.

Herbert   So you are consciously concerned to keep the reader turning pages, all the time.

Hillerman Yeah. I mean, hell! I could write, rip this book off, and people'd buy it. I mean, HarperCollins wish they had it a long time ago, and I keep hearing from bookstore people and readers, too. But when you grow up poor, or certainly lower fringe of the middle class at best, and you don't put much value to money, you learn that you don't *need* the money. What you *do* need is to satisfy your urge to be a good writer. This [current novel] is a *son of a gun* to write, though! Are you familiar with the Koshares and the Mudheads and the Pueblo cultures?

Herbert   Only through your work.

Hillerman   Well, they—in Hopi and other Pueblo Indian ceremonialism, traditionally they remind the people that the dance is to celebrate the presence of the Kachinas, the spirits, among the people. Traditionally in most pueblos, either the Koshares or the Mudheads, usually the Koshare, represent the fallible, fallen man, so to speak. They personify everything acquisitive [including] greed [and] all the evils of humanity. And then they'll work with a team of clowns who will meanwhile come in with specifically personifying whatever's wrong with the pueblo, making fun of it.

Herbert   The things in the community that are undesirable?

Hillerman   Yeah, things that need to be *scorned*. Now, for hundreds of years, this system of using mockery and laughter has substituted for having a repressive jail and a police force, and policemen with guns and billy clubs. I thought, "This is really interesting, that they've made this work all these years."

Herbert   *And* it involves a sense of humor.

Hillerman   Yeah. Laughter instead of a billy club. Okay. So, I was going to base a plot on a shop teacher being killed. There's also been a Koshare who's been killed. And of course the two are connected.

Herbert   And what does this particular Koshare represent?

Hillerman   Well, he's a member of the Koshare fraternity in this pueblo. He's an accountant in real life.

Herbert   That's interesting in itself, you know, representing the money and material culture.

Hillerman   That's pertinent to the plot, too.

Herbert   And if you've got a high school shop teacher involved, too, once again you're going to have a variety of age groups represented in your work. A lot of detective fiction focuses on an exclusively adult society.

Hillerman   I noticed that, too. I've got a kind of theory, that while it's hard for people to believe murder and this stuff, if you give them a realistic setting in which all this takes place, where there's a half-empty bowl of oatmeal on the table and children catching school buses, it makes the events seem less Hollywoodish, more down-to-earth and real-life.

Herbert   This makes me think of another scene where the young boy comes back to his hogan with Leaphorn. And the boy doesn't want to enter the hogan because there's been a death. So Leaphorn goes in to retrieve the child's clothes and toys. And when he goes in,

Leaphorn discovers there's hardly anything; the boy has almost no possessions; what he does have is his Snoopy lunch box. And on it it says something like "Happiness is an unbroken kite string." There again, you see that interface between crass contemporary culture—

Hillerman —and the incredible irony of that statement on the lunchbox, when you put it up against real life among poor people.

Herbert And the treasures that the boy had in the lunchbox were all nonmodern, noncontemporary items: he had an arrowhead, various pieces of—

Hillerman I'll tell you, to do that, I was thinking about when I was a little boy, my own little collection of treasures. I had two spools—

Herbert Wooden spools from thread?

Hillerman Yeah, thread spools, and I used to cut a little notch in one end, put a matchstick, put a rubber band on the matchstick, and then wind it up, and it would run.

Herbert Well, I'd love to feel better acquainted with what you were like as a child.

Hillerman I think I had a very happy childhood. I watch TV and I see all these celebrities remembering all of a sudden that they were abused as children. But I got nothing but a lot of love when I was a kid. My mother was a nurse, my father was a—what was my father? He'd been a farmer, he'd been a schoolteacher, he'd been a miner, he'd been a blacksmith, he'd been a horseshoer, he'd been a cowboy, he'd done whatever he could do to make a living. A very interesting man. Both of 'em. My mother was a great storyteller.

Herbert I understand there were times when your household didn't even have batteries for the radio, which was the one kind of outside entertainment available to you, so that it was important to be a good storyteller, to entertain yourself.

Hillerman Well, things *were* quite different. Somebody asked me about telephones one day, and caused me to think about telephones! When I was little, as I said, I lived in Sacred Heart, Oklahoma. Sixty-something population at most. I never could figure sixty!

Herbert You think it was fewer than sixty?

Hillerman Yeah. We used to laugh: "Sixty, counting the dogs." But it had a cotton gin, and then it had a church, and over the hill was a Sisters of Mercy boarding school. There wasn't any telephone for a long time, but when I got to be about ten or eleven there was a crossroads store, which my Dad and uncle had, [and it] was also the post office, and so for some reason they put a telephone in there. I never used it, because I didn't know anybody to *call* on the telephone. I honestly believe the first time I ever used a telephone I was twenty-one years old when I got back from overseas, from the war. They unloaded us off this hospital ship and put us in a hospital on Long Island. And the Red Cross gave you a free telephone call. And I thought, well, "I'll call my mother." My first telephone call.

Herbert   This gives me an insight into your ability to identify with people who belong to a less material culture than most of us live in.

Hillerman   One reason I think I write about the Navajos is because I know I have so much in common with The People in basic ways. Okay. When you get up in the morning what do you do? I look at the sky. Is it gonna rain? You know, city people don't do that so much. Rain is not that important. It was *terribly* important when I was growing up, 'cause it was the dust bowl period in Oklahoma. It's terribly important to the Navajo. I don't care who you are, you know, you're raised in the rural desert where grazing and crops are important, you look at the sky. You *never* think about rain in a negative way. Never. Until we got to be bigger, we pulled our water on a pulley out of a well. And so if you want to take a bath—well, you didn't waste water. I mean, you just did not waste water! You have an attitude about water.

Herbert   Or finding beauty in open spaces that aren't necessarily classically lush. That's something that the Indians share with you.

Hillerman   Yeah, a lot of those things. Yeah, so you relate. Then I check it against the difference between Patowatomie County, Oklahoma, and Apache County, Arizona, to see if it's appropriate. When I'm thinking of a metaphor, I think, "I can't use a metaphor my mother'd use." Or simile. Or the *dicho*, you know, the saying. I gotta come up with one that's appropriate. So I think of one, I take one of my mother's *dichos*, and I change it to fit.

Herbert   Now, would you explain a little further just what a *dicho* is?

Hillerman   The term *dicho* could be Spanglish. It's a saying, an aphorism. The Navajos have 'em just like we do, and you gotta give an appropriate one.

Herbert   This makes me think about your familiarity with Native American language. For instance, in *The Listening Woman* you use linguistic puns: "Leaphorn used the verb 'hodishtal,' which means to take part in a ritual chant. By slightly changing the guttural inflection, the word becomes the verb 'to be kicked,' so the question was,

95

he'd either be cured or be kicked." Now that sounds like intimate, detailed knowledge of the language. How familiar are you with the language?

Hillerman Not very. I don't speak it; I know a few words. I had a great friend who's now dead, Dr. W. W. Hill, who did a book on Navajo humor. He was on the faculty here [at the University of New Mexico]. Long before I was writing about Navajos, I read Hill's book and I talked to Hill. His book is academic and dry—books about humor are always dry—but then I thought, there's so much likeness between Navajo humor and the kind of humor you run into in impoverished, rural places, kind of a self-mocking quality. Another example is this guy called Afraid of His Horse. That's his name. And you'll run into names like that.

Herbert These people are good sports, aren't they?

Hillerman Oh, yeah. Oh, yeah. Oh, *yeah*, they're *great* sports.

Herbert Well, there was another place in your writing where Leaphorn was trying to establish himself—to someone who was a little turned off by the fact that he was a policeman—as a person who respects the Navajo traditions. Here, instead of you writing a whole paragraph on his internal reflections about this, you show Leaphorn indicating a sense of direction by a twitch of his lips in the Indian way. And I thought, "There again, how do you know a detail like that?"

Hillerman Well, you watch 'em!

Herbert Is it partly your reporter's eye?

Hillerman I think so, yeah. I was a reporter for years. You know, you look for details. And you notice that traditional people don't point. Very impolite, to point. And they don't interrupt.

Herbert They listen.

Hillerman They listen. And you'll understand it better when you understand their origin story. Remember when you studied Shakespeare and Bacon and those guys, and you learned about the medieval concept of the body and soul and the balance of forces inside the body and all this; you remember? [The Navajo] have a concept very much like the Elizabethan notion, which attaches great importance to the wind, the breath, that blows through the body. And the human ability to convert that into speech. Speech is very powerful. Was it Sandburg who said that words have big boots? You remember that poem? Boy, the Navajo understands that words wear big boots. They attach great importance, great power, to speech, so they treat it with respect, and they don't interrupt, and they *do* listen, and they *think*: before they say something they get their thoughts organized.

Herbert   And they also do a sort of an introductory span of conversation before they might get down to the main point. I noticed that Leaphorn and Chee, too, have a lot of patience about this, Leaphorn in particular.

Hillerman   I hope my readers do, sometimes! (Chuckles.)

Herbert   You don't always describe the entire conversation. But you *do* show that Leaphorn has waited. And if you do use the lead-in conversation, there's often a clue in it. That pre–conversation *may* indeed have significance later. So we receive a clue while we recognize that there's a dignity afforded each person's thinking process, and style of speaking even, that we don't have in the larger society.

Hillerman   Nobody, I think, in any of my books—I was just thinking about this while you were talking; I never thought about it before—I don't think anybody in any of my books is treated with anything but respect. Including some Gruesome Georges. (Chuckles.)

Herbert   Or, if someone isn't respected to the degree he or she should be, it's highly significant. For instance, not washing the hair of the dead person. In *The Ghostway* it is very significant that this has *not* been done. This deviance from a respectful ritual is highly significant to the policeman acquainted with the custom.

Hillerman   That's right.

Herbert   I've been looking at patterns in your work and noticing how very often the revelation and solution occur through cultural insight. This is fascinating stuff and a very interesting way for a plot to turn.

Hillerman   My attitude is, no footnotes are allowed. If people want to learn about Navajos, there's a lot of books written by people who are very authoritative. So I don't feel that I have a license to teach. But I'm always looking for ways to make an insight germane to the plot. For example, was the guy who was [on the scene of the crime] a Navajo or not? The sleuth is looking at the tracks. He notices that he [the suspect] carefully went to some pains not to step where water has run, which would indicate he was a traditional Navajo. He respected water.

Herbert   And then you also erase some of our cultural assumptions. I remember that at one crime scene, you placed footprints of moccasins as well as footprints of Vibram soles. And then you told us that the Vibram sole was the Indian's. The moccasin represents a non-Indian. By this means, you point out that no Indian is going to wear moccasins except in a ceremony. So this is a wonderful way of erasing an assumption. I wonder how consciously you are wishing to teach us.

Hillerman   I'm always looking for the opportunity. Always. And sometimes you find 'em, and sometimes you don't. When I find one, I like to use it.

Herbert   So it sounds like you're self-editing all the time. Are you doing this in your original draft or are you doing this in the rewrite stage?

Hillerman   I don't do any rewriting in the usual sense. I stay on a page until I get it right. When I used to be pre–computer I stayed on a page till I got it so scratched up and X'd out and written over that I couldn't read it anymore. Now I change the language on the screen until I get it the way I want it. Then, when I call up the chapter again, I go through it again. So the first parts of my chapter are *meticulously* edited, and the last few paragraphs are edited hardly at all. (Laughs.) Then I don't do any rewriting, except maybe I gotta go back to that scene where they show up at Mrs. So-and-so's house and have her know something or have her not know it, or—

Herbert   —or foreshadow something—

Hillerman   —foreshadow something, yes.

Herbert   Do you generally then, control the development of the book in a planned-out manner with few surprises occurring along the way?

Hillerman   I've always been much more interested in *why* the crime is committed than in who committed it. And what you've said for some reason caused my mind to turn to *Talking God*, which I was writing one day, and then I was at Sunday Mass and here comes a guy taking up collection. And he is a man probably in his middle seventies, rigidly straight, Spanish, that dignified face, all that character in his face; hot, it was summer, but he had on a suitcoat, necktie; the suit looked like it had once been a wonderful suit but he'd had it for forty years; and when I got back to writing, he changed the whole nature of that book. He became the body you find by the railroad track. And that body you found by the railroad track became very important. I didn't have much of a plot in mind when I started that book. I just had some ideas, but they began taking shape around this guy taking up collection.

Herbert   You know, one of the things that I've come across in these conversations with a number of mystery writers is the surprising role of serendipity in the construction of essentially tightly plotted books.

Hillerman   Oh, it's incredible! I wasted months in my life trying to outline books.

Herbert   I understand it was serendipity that led, many years ago, to your encountering Indians en route to a healing ceremony. The image that they presented in the landscape inspired you to write your first mystery, *The Blessing Way*. Would you please tell me more about this?

Hillerman   Yeah. There I was. I had a thirty-day convalescent furlough but I changed it. I erased the "thirty" and wrote in "sixty." I met a girl at a USO dance, and her dad was an independent oil man. Small operator. And he had bought some leases out in the Checkerboard part of the Navajo reservation, where there'd been an old shallow oil well developed, but there were no roads in there, see, so they didn't have any way to get the oil out. And they'd haul it out on wagons in tanks. This was way back.

Herbert   Horse-drawn wagons?

Hillerman   Yeah. Understand, this was *way* back. Now, there was a road. And pipelines were going in there and he needed somebody to haul, to drive a truckload of drill stems. How do I describe them? They're steel bars that they connect together to power the bits in. So he was going to drive one truck, and he needed someone to drive the other, and he just couldn't get anybody to do anything, 'cause everybody was in the army or defense industries. So he rather reluctantly, I think, gave me the job of driving the truck. I had a patch over one eye, see, and I couldn't see very good out of the other. But worse, I was in terrible physical condition. I'd been seven months in the hospital.

Herbert   So your stamina must have been low, to say the least.

Hillerman   This bastard would drive twenty hours and then he'd just pull over and sleep. These trucks were shot, and we drove real slow and labored up every hill.

Herbert   And here you were an inexperienced driver, no less, and all those gears and everything to deal with!

Hillerman   One awful day we were struggling up Nine Mile Hill out of Albuquerque, for about the second day in a row. I went to sleep in the middle of the afternoon.

Herbert   Not behind the wheel, I hope!

Hillerman   Behind the wheel. But anyway, he was going slower than I was and I ran into the back of his truck. Not very hard, but it sure destroyed his confidence in me.

Herbert   (Laughs.)

Hillerman   I'm telling you more than you want to know!

Herbert   Not at all!

Hillerman   Anyway, when we got out to the Navajo reservation we drove past these great cliffs that you see in lots of old Western movies, and here came, out of the piñons, this party of people on horseback, and they were ceremonially attired. And I stopped and let 'em go by, and I looked at 'em, and I thought, "Boy, this is interesting." I grew up with Potawatomie Seminole kids, went to an Indian school, so Indians were nothing exotic to me; they were my playmates. But these guys were doing something cultural.

Herbert   It was an impressive sight.

Hillerman   Yeah. So anyway, when I got to where we were going to unload the drill stems, there was a ranch over there, and I asked about it, and found out that there was an Enemy Way ceremonial going on. This Navajo had come back from the Marine Corps, and they were giving this guy the cure.

Herbert   To bring him back into harmony with his people?

Hillerman   That's right. And I was told I could attend the ceremony, as long as I didn't get drunk or rowdy. So I saw a little bit of that. Not much to see, as I recall, because a lot of it goes on inside the hogan, but I saw enough so I was interested. I was interested in the concept.

Herbert   Yes, well, there you were, patch over your eye, not feeling in good shape yourself, and probably—

Hillerman   Walking on a cane, too, as I recall.

Herbert   You probably felt, "I could use a little of this!"

Hillerman   Yeah. I don't think it was conscious, but what I came back to [from the war] was—there wasn't any home! Vietnam veterans had the feeling, I think, that World War II guys were welcomed home with great bands and fanfare. Well, some of them I'm sure were; but a lot of people just came home like I did, sort of slipped in. Not that it bothered me—hell, I was glad to be back! But anyway, the notion of having your family and your clan and your friends all gather and ritually cleanse you of all this you've gone through—I thought, "Boy, that's a good idea." And anyway, that was in 1945. And it stuck in my mind.

Herbert   Now lots of things stick in your mind. You collect things, obviously. Characters walk into your life.

Hillerman   Writers—I'm sure you'll find it's true among all these guys you've interviewed—are kind of like bag ladies. They go through life with a stick and a sack and they get all this baggage: impressions, and characters, and incidents, and plot ideas.

Herbert   It was upon your return from the war that you took up a career in journalism. Had you always nursed the idea of becoming a writer?

Hillerman   Not really. My goal was to make something out of myself, get off the farm. We had a meeting one day, my mother and brother and I, in the kitchen of our house, and decided one of us should go off and go to college. I was about to graduate from high school. We decided that I was more of a scholar than my brother. He was more of a getter-of-things-done and an athlete, and we decided that I would go to college and Barney would stay behind and run the farm. My Dad was dead at this time. So I decided to be a chemical engineer. That sounded romantic to me. (Smiles.)

Herbert   Romantic! I love that!

Hillerman   Anything to get out of Potowatomie County. We had an old Pontiac, drove up to Stillwater, Oklahoma. School had been going on about a week.

Herbert   You went up there without being admitted or anything? Just went?

Hillerman   We didn't know the process! To find out, you went up there and found out.

Herbert   And back then you still didn't have a telephone either.

Hillerman   Right! So they sent me to an advisor, and he was a typical advisor, busy, and [he asked], "What kind of grades you make in math?" and I told him I made As, and so he put me in trigonometry, college algebra. He didn't realize that my high school only offered two math courses. One was beginning algebra, and the other was one semester of plane geometry. So I didn't have nearly as much math now as eighth-grade students do today, and I was not eligible to take either one of those courses. *Far from it.*

Herbert   So that must have been a rude awakening.

Hillerman   Then the next step was to find me a job, a place to live, and we found a condemned old historic building that we could rent. You could rent half a room, half a bed, too, for fifteen dollars.

Herbert   Half a bed? You mean you'd sleep in it part of the day, and somebody else would sleep in it later?

Hillerman   Well, it worked out kinda that way, but we slept together in the same bed, and the room was so small that to move the bed you had to take it apart. But anyway, it was cheap. And, you know, it seemed fine to me. And then we found me a job as a dishwasher at a boarding house for my food. So I had rent paid for a month and my food lined up, I bought all my books but one and I had about ten bucks left. And my mother and brother had to get home because you gotta take care of the livestock. So away they go and there I am. So then I found another job as a housekeeper for a dentist and another job cleaning out ditches and another job with the National Guard. You got thirty-five cents an hour in all these jobs. No money at all in the dishwashing job. Just food.

Herbert   Now how many hours a week would you guess you had to spend in these jobs?

Hillerman Oh, not too many. So, anyway, by the end of the semester I got kicked out of the algebra class. It was just as well; I had no notion what they were talking about! But I kept going to sleep in this class, and the guy behind me was supposed to notice and jog me, because the professor had warned me twice already. And I woke up one awful day; I'll never forget it. I'd fallen out in the aisle. And I was woken up by [the professor] poking me and saying, "Out. Out." Tossing me out. But at least I think I got a W; I think he let me withdraw. And obviously I blew the chemistry and two math courses, but I made an A in English.

Herbert   So there you had a hint that literature might be for you.

Hillerman Yeah. So by then my elder brother [joined] the air force and so I went back and ran the farm.

Herbert   What kind of farm was it? Was it agricultural, animals, or—

Hillerman We had a small farm, and, I mean, nobody would dream of trying to make a living on it. We had a forty-acres and a twenty-acres and an eighty-acres, and we had some cattle. Barney and I were trying to shift it into cattle, and we raised alfalfa and we raised some fruit, raised some corn. And we did real well one year with sweet potatoes, and then the next year for some reason we got the wrong kind of seed and the sweet potatoes were tasteless. So—total wipeout.

Herbert   And then you joined the military?

Hillerman Yes, and then we auctioned everything. We didn't have enough money for a tractor, we had a team of horses. Sold our horses, sold our junky old equipment. Kind of sad thing: it really reminds you of *The Grapes of Wrath*. The auctioneer comes, and all the neighbors come. And they're all friends, but they didn't have any money, and they're torn between wanting to get a bargain and wanting to be fair.

Herbert   I understand it was through letters that you wrote home during the war that you received your entree into journalism.

Hillerman Yes. There was a woman named Beatrice Stahl [who] was a feature writer for *The Daily Oklahoman*. She contacted my mother and my mother dug up all my V-mail letters. Beatrice took them, and she wrote a little feature story about me in *The Daily Oklahoman*. And she told my mother that she'd like to talk to me when I got back. So when I got back I went to see Beatrice Stahl down at the paper, and she said, "You should be a writer." Bless her soul. Well, by then I knew I wasn't going to be a chemist, because my notion that I was good in math had been—

Herbert —rather decimated.

Hillerman And so I thought, "Well, hell, why not be a writer?" I loved to read, and I was a pretty good writer, I thought. In college the only thing I made As in—

Herbert —was English.

Hillerman Yeah, and my English teacher! Bless her heart. Imagine: she'd give me an A with a line under it and an F for spelling. And she said if I would come in on Saturdays, she'd give me a list of spelling words, and she'd be down there grading papers and working, I'd be sitting in her office like a third grader, learning how to spell. But wasn't that sweet?

Herbert What a service she did you there. And then you went back to college to study journalism.

Hillerman Yes. On the GI Bill. What a wonderful thing that was for guys like me.

Herbert So then you were in journalism for quite a few years, and eventually you became a journalism professor. It sounds like your family members, particularly your wife, have supported you, even when you made a risky decision. At the time you decided to further your education you had a number of children to support.

Hillerman Five.

Herbert And your wife was behind you a hundred percent.

Hillerman In fact, she said, "Look, Tony, you've always wanted to be a novelist, and you're almost forty"—or maybe I *was* forty. She said, "You need to think about doing it now." So I thought, "You know, she's right." Then I got an offer from the University of New Mexico. The chairman of the journalism department there knew, apparently, that I was looking [for part-time work], so he came up to see me and said, "Look, I'm gonna retire in a couple years, and we're gonna need somebody like you to take over," because it was a two-man department, a little bitty department. So I got a part-time job and we moved down. But Marie, yeah, Marie was all for it.

Herbert What was the nature of the work that you did for the president's office?

Hillerman They needed a kind of doer-of-undignified-things who would understand campus politics and that sort of thing.

Herbert And prevent the president from getting into fixes.

Hillerman (Laughs.)

Herbert   Talking about fixes, and getting out of them, makes me think about one of the hallmarks of so many of your books: the hero getting out of a fix. Often your policemen get into situations where the odds quite literally are stacked against them. The great excitement for the reader lies in recognizing, "If that had been me, I'd have been a goner there!" Yet the character somehow manages to survive. What kind of research do you have to do to make those scenes so immediate? I'm thinking about the scene in *The Listening Woman* where Leaphorn is being pursued by a vicious dog and villains are trying to burn him out from his sanctuary on a high rock. The hero's pants are steaming; he's put his head through a crack in this crevasse so that he can breathe some air; and the reader begins to think the hero may not survive this crisis.

Hillerman   Oh. Well, in that particular case I didn't have anything planned. I knew I had to get him out of there, see, and my first instinct was, I'll just have him climb, you know, scramble up and get over the top. But then I'd think, "No, they'd shoot him or something." So then I'd think, "Hey, I gotta have him find this cave anyway."

Herbert   So you knew in advance that caves would be important to the plot but you didn't know you would rescue the character from the fire by means of the passages into the caves.

Hillerman   Yeah. I knew the plot was going to turn on these caves, early on. But actually, there's one of the big, notable failures of my research. That is not limestone country, see. And you need limestone to have that kind of cave. Every geologist who ever reads that book who knows anything about this part of the world knows that there's no limestone out there.

Herbert   Well, sandstone does some remarkable things.

Hillerman   Well, yeah, it does, but it doesn't make that kind of cave; that's a seeping cave.

Herbert   Formed by erosion?

Hillerman   Yes.

Herbert   Well, how about the example of the grain storage structure from which the hero escapes via the escape hole built in by the Anasazi Indians hundreds of years ago?

Hillerman   Okay, there, all right, that's not research. That is the bag lady syndrome. I used a remembered fact. I asked myself, "How can I have him *know* something that a[n] anthropologist would know that these city guys wouldn't know?" And I'm thinking about that. What am I gonna do? And I remember that the Hopis who occupied these Anasazi ruins always built these escape holes out of 'em and an anthropologist would know that. You gotta have an escape, and so maybe these caves and this kind of stuff are really—what do you call it? The "God on the Cable," you know, *deus ex machina*?

Herbert   That's right. Still, while you may have the information about the scene available, I continue to wonder about how you establish the immediacy of the suspense. Some of these scenes read as if they are reports on actual experience. Have you, for instance, ever been in one of those grain storage structures in the dark, with no ladder, no means of escape?

Hillerman   Not in a *grain* storage structure, per se, but I've been in old ruins in various places—not surreptitiously, but in ones where they let you in 'em, without violating any rules.

Herbert   When you were in there, did it occur to you to think, "I wouldn't want to be in here in the dark"?

Hillerman   I don't remember consciously [thinking] that, but I do remember seeing a place where the little arch had been built as an escape, and it was full of rubble, and wondering why it was there, and then finding out why it was there.

Herbert   Do you keep notebooks of these facts?

Hillerman   You look at this desk. Do I look like the kind of guy to keep a notebook?

Herbert   No. But you've got a reporter's background. You've got to remember things, you've got to—

Hillerman   Even as a reporter I would jot down numbers, I would make some notes if I wanted the exact flavor of a quote. But then I would put the notes there by my typewriter and I wouldn't ever look at them. (Smiles.)

Herbert   Speaking about your reporting experience, another place in which you make the suspense very gripping is in *The Fly on the Wall*, which is not part of your mystery series but focuses on a journalist hero.

Hillerman   All right. I want a buildup. If this book works, this has got to be tense. I gotta pull the reader right in there. I want to bring the reader in there with me in the dark when he's hiding in that broom closet: so I have you feel things under his fingers; I have you hear what he hears; I try to bring in the maximum number of senses, even what he smells.

Herbert   So you seek to place the reader in the character's mind and body in these suspenseful scenes?

Hillerman   Yeah. So you're right there with his nerve endings; you hear him *breathing*. Listening tensely, he hears somebody breathing right next to him. See?

Herbert   (Shudders.) Thinking about suspense in the mystery story leads me to ask you about the personal side, for you, of another element of the mystery genre. Since mysteries are books that generally center around a question of death, I have wondered whether or not those who write in this genre are individuals who are particularly sensitive to the fragility of life.

Hillerman I'm *interested* in it, I think.

Herbert   Just interested? Not worried about it?

Hillerman No, I think children who grow up on farms, where you see the fried chickens' heads chopped off before they go in the frying pan, and you know that the pig that is such a funny character is going to be butchered and scraped as soon as it gets cold enough so the meat will [keep], [these children] who see death all the time around them, are less shocked by it than children who grow up in cities, who don't witness it.

Herbert   I see.

Hillerman Also, then, growing up where I did, when somebody died, the body stayed home; they stayed in the living room; and relatives would come over and stay up with the body. There was Uncle Arthur, and Uncle Chris, and you knew them, and there they were dead, and you would go help dig the grave. That was also traditional.

Herbert   Really?

Hillerman Relatives would dig the grave so the main family didn't have to. So death was more around you and part of the nature of things.

Herbert   Hmmm, the *hosrah* . . . .

Hillerman Yeah, it was just part of life. Death was part of life, odd as it sounds, and funerals were great family reunions. They always delayed them because people took a long time getting there, they came by bus, and then you sat around and you—you remembered. Okay. Well, John Donne said it beautifully in that "Death where is your sting?"

Herbert   Hmmm . . . .

Hillerman And then when I was wounded—I had an illuminating [experience]. I was blown up by something. I thought it was a hand grenade, but I don't know for sure since I subsequently went back to this tiny little place and talked to a guy who lived there, and the place was so heavily mined, it might have been a mine. Anyway, it blew me up in the air. It was the middle of the night in the winter, and by then I'd seen enough wounded people to know how quickly they die, even if they're not badly hurt, when it's cold and they bleed. And so, I was laying there in shock, I'm sure, and I was thinking, "Well, you know, it was fun while it lasted." I thought I was dying. Your mind is logical, and all logic told me that I was going to die.

Herbert   Were you in pain at that time?

Hillerman   No, not much. My face was badly burned, and my face hurt, but—

Herbert   —the shock may have—

Hillerman   —sure. I think it pretty well turns off the pain. But I have memories of thinking I was dying, and that sense of kind of falling away, and a sense of relief, and comfort, and kind of joy. A sense of welcoming love and, you know, just a *good* feeling. And I remember when I came out of it, when they were putting me on a jeep, I remember being kind of faintly disappointed.

Herbert   Coming back to my question that led us into this discussion of death, then, it seems apparent that it is not a preoccupation with death that has led you to write novel after novel centered around puzzles involving death.

Hillerman   I'd agree with that. It's more a question of greed that preoccupies me.

Herbert   Yes, greed is a terribly destructive emotion, as are jealousy, envy. What has caused you to be particularly sensitive to this aspect of human nature?

Hillerman   I guess, maybe family background. When my Papa died I was fifteen. And my brother was, in his odd way, a very wise young fella. And we were talking one day—or *I* was talking and he was listening is more likely—and he said, "Tony, think about this, now. Think about what you're saying. Your plan here is to get a lot of money." He says, "After you've got shelter and food, and you've got the basic necessities, what can you buy with money that's any particular good to you?" I thought, "Gosh, I don't know!" And I thought about that.

Herbert   Your brother does sound wise. In one of your books you noted that if an Indian has extra money and it becomes noticeable, people feel there's something wrong. This is not something that the rest of the community admires—

Hillerman   —accumulating wealth.

Herbert   Yes.

Hillerman   Well, you know anthropologists who studied witchcraft believed, and found that way back, the people who are likely to be suspected of being witches are people who had accumulated wealth. The very fact that they're visibly well-to-do would indicate—surrounded in an ocean of poverty—that they're doing something that's morally wrong.

Herbert   Here is another way in which you have a natural companionship with the Native Americans: you do not value material gain so highly as does the average American.

Hillerman   I suppose so.

Herbert   I'd love to talk to you a bit about the rich sense of place that is one of the most appealing aspects of your work for many readers.

Hillerman   (Smiles.) I generally have gotten very good reviews, but one reviewer said, "One trouble with Hillerman is that just when things are going along rapidly, Hillerman will stop and describe a thunderstorm or a cloud."

Herbert   Where's that reviewer's eye for symbolism? I mean, sometimes these things you put in are giving us another dimension.

Hillerman   Well, I justify it on two grounds. One, is on the grounds of plot. A storm is germane to the plot in *The Listening Woman*. You remember that I had to get him out of the car, away from his radio. You could do it in one sentence by having him blow a tire or break an axle. On the other hand, if you want to describe a thunderstorm, a rainstorm, one of those incredible little hailstorms we have in the summer, you can use the hailstorm and it washes out the wash so he's separated from his car. So I give you about two thirds of a page of the storm coming, and engulfing the car, all the noise of the hail hitting the roof and it is still germane.

Herbert   Yes, it is.

Hillerman   But the other grounds is, I *like* to do it, and I indulge myself. And it gives you a sense of the chancey-ness of life out there.

Herbert   I think the sense of place in your work also highlights the spiritual quest undertaken by your characters to bring harmony back to the community. You know, one of the things you said in *Hillerman Country* was that in this kind of landscape "you are reminded that out here man has never been a dominant force." I know that readers would be interested to learn what spiritual aspect of this landscape you most respond to.

Hillerman   You know, I have to say that I don't think of the landscape in quite those terms.

Herbert   Okay.

Hillerman   I think of it in two ways. One, a very pragmatic, practical way: frequently in the plot, the isolation, the lack of somebody to hear and see and so forth, and the distances involved are important in understanding what happened, why it could have happened, and why it happened the way it did. In most it's just geography. And I'm very conscious of that. Okay. So I think of that in a very pragmatic way. Then, two, I think about this: for a reader to understand these people, and what's going on here in some nebulous level, deeper level, higher level, he needs to see the kind of place that surrounds them. Distance, mountains, dryness, the landscape—a landscape where if you break an axle, it's a hell of a long ways to water. Where if you get caught by a snowstorm, you can be cold for a long time, where you can freeze to death in the winter. Where people have very legitimate economic interest in wondering whether that rain cloud brewing up over Black Mesa's gonna drift this way, and if it does, you want to remember where it rained because there will be grass there in a couple of months, when they need grass. All that helps in getting a handle on the people. In order to understand this kind of people, I think the reader needs to look at that landscape and see the environment in which they live, just like Elmore Leonard does in his Detroit stories. You need to see the grittiness of Detroit in some of those stories.

Herbert And in your Southwest scenes there's often a wonderful, inherent dimension of mysteriousness, especially in the ruins.

Hillerman Aw, isn't that wonderful? I love that. That's a freebie for a mystery writer, using that as a setting—and it is right in your backyard.

Herbert I'd like to come back to my earlier question about what Brian Aldiss called "the fatal art of entertainment." Have you encountered situations in your writing where you need to keep secrets from the reader for reasons of craft rather than reasons of art?

Hillerman Practically every book, you run into that.

Herbert Does this need to keep back information limit you from revealing all that you would like to say about human character and emotion?

Hillerman I don't think so. It gives you a technical problem, but if you're writing the other kind of novel, the novel of character, you have other technical problems.

Herbert Plot; number one, you need some plot!

Hillerman And yes, you've got to keep up interest! You know what I think, too, about that? I think one reason you're seeing so much good writing done in the mystery field is because of this plague of minimalism that struck like—what's a good metaphor?—like pine chip moth the old forest of mainstream literature and shriveled it up, and it died. And you had all these bright young people trying to write this minimalist stuff. It's easy as hell to write. You don't have to have a story, so people who really are talented writers, but not talented storytellers, thrive. Except the readers are bored stiff with it. So here's a whole bunch of storytellers, who would have been writing mainstream but the mainstream is polluted!

Herbert   I like the way you put that. Turning to technical writing matters, I've noticed that you keep your prose very clean, avoiding unnecessary adverbs and adjectives. Do you consciously edit with this in mind?

Hillerman   Oh, definitely. When I taught writing, I'd say, "Remember always, the adjective is the enemy of the noun; the adverb is the enemy of the verb. If you use an adverb, it almost inevitably means that you didn't find the right verb. Throw out the adverb and find the right verb. If you have to modify a noun with an adjective, maybe you've got the wrong noun. It's less likely you found the wrong noun because if you want to say a 'red barn,' you've got to have an adjective. But be suspicious of both; look on them as failures, adverbs particularly."

Herbert   Does any of that come from your journalism background?

Hillerman   I'm sure it does, but it also comes from a feeling that any time you have any unnecessary word in a sentence, it diminishes the impact of the sentence. It's just like putting corn starch in soup; it just clogs it up and bogs it down. An unnecessary sentence in a paragraph's the same thing. And an unnecessary paragraph in a page. Almost all of my editing is cutting. Do I really need that sentence? Does it move it along? What does it do for me? Do I need that word? Ah, take it out. I have a kind of sense that the reader is a busy person, got a lot of things to do, needs to get letters written and bills paid, and needs to do other things, and I don't want to waste their time. They're gonna be impatient with me.

Herbert   But Tony, can you, within the mystery form, write "the undeniable book"? That's my question. You know, the book that "lays waste the hearts of men" and women?

Hillerman   Well, how about Scott Turow's work?

Herbert   Personally, I think that's a bunch of tricks and double tricks, gripping as they may be.

Hillerman   You weren't impressed by that?

Herbert   Well, I thought it was very impressive manipulation of the reader's focus but it—

Hillerman   —it didn't lay waste—

Herbert   —it didn't lay waste my heart.

Hillerman   How about *Crime and Punishment*?

Herbert   Yup. That certainly does. But you see, I think that in *Crime and Punishment*, we know whodunit; it's not in that formula.

Hillerman   See, in some of mine people say, "Gosh, I knew who did it in the third chapter." And I think, "*I* hadn't decided who was going to do it yet!"

Herbert   Really! You see, my feeling is, that in order for a mystery book to potentially lay waste one's heart, somehow the author has got to work it so that those revelations about character come out simultaneously with the need for the revelation of factual information in the plot. I don't think it happens often. And I think that is the problem with the mystery; I think that's the limitation. Mystery writers are often too engaged with the puzzle to put enough emphasis on natural character development.

Hillerman   I think you've hit the nail on the head there. Look at Leonard's—was it [Elmore] Leonard who wrote the book about the mobster who had left a woman his wonderful house and all his money, but his pride is wrapped up in keeping her chaste and single? And she's a—well, you think—a stage prop character. When you've finished it, you finish it with total surprise and with immense satisfaction. You discover that the woman is really the principal character and she found a way to outsmart them all and escape from her dilemma. And while it doesn't lay waste the heart, it gives you this great satisfaction. It had revealed a lot about human character. I guess I don't think there's any reason that, rare as they are, mystery novels can't end up being these "undeniable books."

Herbert   I see.

Hillerman   And even when you talk about keeping secrets about character from the reader, I'm not sure I worry about keeping too much from them. Take the victim: I want people to care about who got murdered. I'm going to give him more personality than I normally would if he was just a murder victim in a puzzle.

Herbert   Now there's an insight into your writing. In your books you *do* develop a sense of caring on the part of the reader. These are not just puzzles; we care. We get to know the victim as the book develops. At the start of the book, we might only see shoes placed on the wrong feet of a partially buried corpse but by the time that book is finished, we care about an individual whom we've gotten to know. The shell of a corpse takes on real humanity.

Hillerman   If I succeed at what you say, I'm satisfied.

▶ JOHN MORTIMER

John Mortimer's stories about the very British, very eccentric, rumpled and poetry-spouting barrister Horace Rumpole have taken on a life of their own much in the way the Sherlock Holmes stories do. It will be no surprise if historians of crime and mystery writing soon begin to refer to them as the Rumpole canon. Centered around life in barristerial chambers in London's historic Inns of Court and enlivened with wit and marvelous dialogue, Mortimer's stories feature Rumpole both as a sleuth who gets to the real truth that underlies events in the courtroom and as a spokesman for Mortimer's own decent and liberal attitudes about justice and human character.

The only child of a highly literate and eccentric barrister and his wife, John Mortimer was born into a life in literature and the law. After his birth in April of 1923, he was raised in his parents' flat in the Inner Temple in London and later in the Chiltern Hills, in a home and garden designed by his father. Mortimer led a rather solitary childhood, enlivened by play with the daughter of a local chairmaker and long walks in the company of his blind father, who recited Sherlock Holmes stories to him from memory.

Mortimer was educated at the Dragon School in Oxford, then at Harrow where he escaped the sports program to attend the theatre, and at Brasenose College, Oxford. During the war he served in the Crown Film Unit as an assistant director and then scriptwriter making documentary films. He studied law and was called to the bar in 1948, subsequently working as a divorce barrister and later as a Queen's Counsel, in criminal law. His later law career included defending in cases concerned with the question of censorship and freedom of expression.

Mortimer retired from the law about thirteen years ago but not before he had established himself as a playwright for stage, screen, and radio, and as a novelist, journalist, translator, and author of non-fiction volumes— even while pursuing a full-time law practice. He has written more than sixty-five scripts for film and television, some forty scripts for radio, eleven novels, several volumes of Rumpole stories, five volumes of nonfiction, and countless articles for newspapers and magazines. A lifelong opera lover, he has also written a translation of the Strauss opera *Die Fledermaus*.

Mortimer was married to the writer Penelope Mortimer for 23 years, during which the couple produced two children together and were parents to Penelope Mortimer's four children from a previous marriage. They also wrote one travel book and a screenplay together.

In 1972 Mortimer married Penny Gollop with whom he has two daughters. The family resides in London and in the expanded house in the Chilterns, in Oxfordshire, where they maintain the lovely gardens established by Mortimer's parents. The Mortimers also spend considerable time in Italy, where Mortimer has set his novel *Summer's Lease*.

Mortimer spoke with me during a series of interviews in his homes in London and Oxfordshire, and in his favorite local pub, the Bull & Butcher, a stone's throw away from the idyllic churchyard where his parents are buried. He also conversed while taking me on a tour of his garden. There he spoke about his father while pointing out various flora that his parents had cultivated and the very tree where the accident occurred that destroyed the elder Mortimer's vision. Mortimer also treated me to a magical drive through the scenes of his boyhood. While we whooshed through the Chiltern Hills in his red Mercedes with opera gently emanating from the stereo and my laughter punctuating his many humorous remarks, he recalled his boyhood and showed me the settings filmed for productions of *Voyage Round My Father* and *Paradise Postponed* and *Titmuss Regained*. Scenes of dalliance in the television series, sites of his own actual hijinks, the local churches and a windmill, the homes of the local gentry, even the grave of a pet monkey, were all pointed out in due course and with revealing comments disclosing that *this* rural outbuilding actually houses a jacuzzi, and *that* one is owned by a rock star. It seems the chairmakers and field-workers of Mortimer's childhood were driven from their beautiful real estate years ago. But the bulk of our conversation occurred in Mortimer's study in the Oxfordshire house on Turville Heath, where he relaxed on a sofa with his dog beside him, and where he frequently bestirred himself to stoke a blazing wood fire.

Herbert   Because of the popularity of your character Rumpole of the Bailey and because you practiced law for the greater part of your working life, one thinks of you as a barrister *and* writer. In your autobiographical novel, *Clinging to the Wreckage*, you said, "As a barrister who wrote, or, as I wanted to think of it, as a writer who did barristering, I was stretched between two opposite extremes." Did your dual professions make you feel sometimes as if you were leading a double life?

Mortimer Yes, but then that's what I like. I liked it! I mean I love leading double lives because I have a very low threshold of boredom. My happiest thing was to go to court and do a murder case and then come out and go to a rehearsal and see a lot of actors acting something I'd written. And I'd always had a feeling that the real life was in the acting and the pretend life was in the murder trial!

Herbert Which was the more real to you as a person, the role of the writer or of the barrister?

Mortimer Life as a barrister never was terribly real to me and courtrooms were always a place of fantasy to me. They had nothing to do with discovering the truth, really, of course. (Chuckles.)

Herbert Your father was a barrister so presumably the idea of a barristerial career came to you early in life. Did you also, at a young age, dream of becoming a writer?

Mortimer I knew early on that I was going to be a writer. I think it's something rather like a curse that you're born with. I knew I wanted to be a writer and my father was far too intelligent to tell me not to be one. Instead of that, he said, "Of course you'll be a writer. Of course you'll be a very successful writer but just till you make a fortune by writing, just divorce a few people. You know, just a few. There's nothing in it." He thought that writers' wives led such terrible lives because the writer was always at home brewing tea and stumped for words. And he said, "Your marriage will be much happier if you go down to Temple tube station and go to the law courts and divorce people." And he told me there was really nothing to being a lawyer except a certain amount of common sense, and relatively clean fingernails. I managed the common sense but the fingernails have never been absolutely wonderful.

You see, I was practically born into the divorce courts. My father was the *doyen* of the divorce barristers. He was an extremely erudite and very famous divorce barrister. So that when I was a little boy in the nursery, instead of a story like "Snow White and the Seven Dwarfs," I used to get "The Duchess and the Seven Co-respondents."

My father used to return to me flowing with his triumphs in the divorce courts and gave me wonderful lines which I was afterwards able to use in a play I wrote about him. He did really come home to me one night in the nursery and said, "I had a wonderful day in court,

John. Terrific trial," he said. "Managed to prove adultery by evidence of inclination and opportunity," he said. "The only piece of evidence we had was a pair of footprints upside down on the dashboard of an Austin 711 parked in a Hampstead garden suburb."

That was my father. You read *Voyage Round My Father*, my play about him, so you know that my father went blind and my mother had the task of reading aloud to my father all of this terrible evidence in all of his divorce cases. And they used to travel up to London from Henley-on-Thames, where we lived, and they used to sit in the first-class compartment on the Great Western Railway. If you may picture the scene: my mother was reading out all this terrible evidence about stained sheets and male and female clothing scattered around hotel bedrooms—and the train would grind to a halt, somewhere around Slough, and the entire first-class carriage would fall absolutely silent, listening to the ever-diminishing tale, in the hope of catching the name of some close friend or relative who has at last been caught out!

Herbert According to both your play and the novel about your father, his blindness was never mentioned.

Mortimer Yes. That is so.

Herbert Your work about your father is handled with humor and affection, yet it would seem that the circumstances of having such a father would not always have been easy. It appears that there was sometimes a lack of communication and, as in the case of his blindness, an unwillingness even to mention an issue of major importance. How did you achieve your fond comprehension of your parents? I could see similar circumstances, in the hands of many writers today, used as an excuse to make a statement about a *lack* of something, whereas you have a more positive perspective than that.

Mortimer Well, they were very nice to me, my parents. They were extremely nice to me; they were never nasty. And they did treat me as if I was grown up. I try and treat my children from the age of ten months as if they were totally grown up, which I think is the only way to treat children.

But that lack of communication, I'm very fond of that, I think. I hate people saying what they think. If you're an American you must say what you think whereas if you're English you should say everything *except* what you think.

Herbert This leaves much more room for speculation, obviously.

Mortimer And also it's a much more interesting way to write because you have to tell the audience what people think by means of what they're *not* saying, instead of what they are saying.

So, with my parents, I was perfectly able to cope with all of that, really, and the fact that they didn't say things indicated a trust, in a way.

Herbert   And your father's appreciation of literature was also a great influence upon you as a developing writer.

Mortimer   That is so. As he couldn't see, I used to read to him. I read everything to him. I read a lot of poetry and Shakespeare—he knew all of the plays of Shakespeare by heart. We used to go to the theatre every year at Stratford-on-Avon. We always used to arrive about a quarter of an hour after the curtain rose, because my father enjoyed a seven-course dinner. But he was a wonderful help in the audience because he always sat in the front row of the stalls, he knew all of the plays by heart, and he could always recite all of the lines about fifteen seconds before the actors.

And like Rumpole—this was something I used in Rumpole later—my father would always quote Shakespeare extremely inapposite. And when I was about four, every time he saw me, my father would say, "Is execution done on Cawdor?," which, when you're four, is a pretty tough question to answer.

Herbert   You say you knew from an early age that you wanted to be a writer. Aside from your father's love of literature and his influence on you, do you recall any hints coming from within yourself that you might one day write? For instance, did you find yourself narrating your own day-to-day activities to yourself as they occurred?

Mortimer   Oh, absolutely! And also talking to myself in the third person. I remember doing that and I still do it.

Herbert   It's extraordinary that people who write tend to narrate their own lives to themselves in the third person and yet when later they become fiction writers they see the action through the characters' eyes, as in the first person.

Mortimer   That's right.

Herbert   I understand your father was also a great admirer of Sherlock Holmes.

Mortimer   Well, I think everybody enjoys Sherlock Holmes. (Pauses.) Well, I suppose there *are* people who don't enjoy detective stories. But Sherlock Holmes is a great part of my childhood. My father was absolutely besotted with him. We used to take long walks together during which my father would recite the whole of a Holmes story.

Herbert   Your father had an extraordinary memory. Do you think your own memory is similarly excellent?

Mortimer   I don't know. It developed gradually. I think it's a great pity that nowadays nobody ever learns poetry in school because the poetry you learn in school you never forget in your entire life. And of course I learned a lot of Shakespeare because I used to perform the plays for my father. Then, if you're a courtroom lawyer, it's like playing bridge, you do have to remember the evidence; you have to remember what people have said day to day. You have to be able to think on your feet.

Herbert   This well-trained memory must serve you well as a writer.

Mortimer   Absolutely. But of course there are areas where my memory is not so good. I have a very bad memory for people's names, for instance.

Herbert   I noticed that you have made allusions to Sherlock Holmes in the Rumpole stories. Are these ideas that sprang to mind, from your memory of the Holmes canon, as you were writing about Rumpole?

Mortimer   Rumpole is terribly founded on the Sherlock Holmes stories. The structure of the Rumpole stories is very Sherlockian. And there are lots of quotations from Sherlock Holmes in Rumpole.

Herbert   What is, for you, the particular appeal of the Holmes stories?

Mortimer   They're a whole way of looking at life, aren't they? I've always enjoyed crime fiction. I think that the best writing being done today is in crime novels, some of *much* the best writing. The plot and discipline save it from the terrible traps of being sensitive and stream of consciousness and all of that stuff. You do need that discipline, I think, and plot! Life happens in plots all the time; life is absolutely composed of plots!

Herbert   That's the truth of life, I think.

Mortimer   Yes. And coincidences. All of these things happen in life.
   And suspense. I think that Ruth Rendell said the most important thing is suspense. Whatever it is, whatever story you are telling, unless it's got suspense it won't keep people wondering what's going to happen next.

Herbert   Did you learn this lesson early in your writing career? Tell me about your early days in writing, leading to the publication of your first novel.

Mortimer   Well, the war started. And you can't divorce people in the war; it doesn't look good. So I entered a thing called the Crown Film Unit which was making documentary films about the war, and I went into quite a new world, the world of film technicians, of cameramen, of prop men, and actors and actresses and it was all a wonderful world to me. But I was a fourth assistant director in this film unit. The scriptwriter was a wonderful writer called Laurie Lee to whom I owe a great deal.

As a fourth assistant director I found that the only job I was asked to do was to make tea for the director and to say "Quiet please" at the beginning of every shot. And so I used to say "Quiet please" in a very nervous and timid voice—being very nervous and timid as I am to this day. And when I said "Quiet please" everybody on the set went on sawing wood, hammering nails, making love, playing pontoon [a card game], and they took absolutely no notice of me at all. So one day I lost my patience with them all and I yelled, "QUIET PLEASE, you bastards!," and they all went out on strike. So then they decided I'd do a lot less harm being a writer.

Herbert Was Laurie Lee a significant influence upon you? Was he a mentor?

Mortimer He wasn't really a great influence upon me. When I got there he was quite keen on leaving so when I turned out to be a disastrous assistant director he set me a test to see if I could become a scriptwriter. And then he said the work was okay and off he went.

Herbert Can you comment on the differences between writing for documentary films and writing dramatic scenes from your imagination?

Mortimer Well, this was part of the documentary movement which had started before the war. There was a man called John Grierson, who was Canadian, and he was a major force in the documentary idea. One of our precepts was that you didn't use actors; you used the actual people. You *did* write stories and you *did* write scenes but they were played by real farmers or aircraft pilots.

Herbert But since you weren't a farmer or pilot yourself, how did you know what to write?

Mortimer You had them say "Roger!" a lot. But no, you did research. I went down in a mine, for instance. It's a funny trick that you learn, writing documentaries, or being a barrister, for that matter. You *can* prepare yourself to cross-examine a doctor on the vagal nerve. You don't *really* know all about it but you know how to put it so that a jury can understand it.

Herbert Or, in film, an audience; or in prose, the reader.

Mortimer That's right.

Herbert You wrote about your experience in the Crown Film Unit in *Charade*, your first novel, originally published in 1947. The novel was published in its first American edition by Viking in 1987. How was *Charade* received when it was first published?

Mortimer It was quite a success. The first notice I got—and I don't like notices; they make me very frightened—was by a man called Daniel George who wrote in *The Daily Express*, "I have to go back about fifteen years before I can think of the appearance of a young writer with so confident and light a touch." Now if I got that nowadays I would be absolutely delighted. But when I got that when I was twenty-three I was absolutely furious. I thought, "Who is this swine whom he read fifteen years ago who had such wonderful writing?"

Herbert But in any case you were encouraged enough by the critical response to write more novels, even after you returned to the legal profession?

Mortimer Yes.

Herbert How did your service in the Crown Film Unit come to an end?

Mortimer Well, it all *did* come to an end. All the husbands came back from the forces and life took on a grimmer hue. And I didn't really know what I would do. I could have gone on writing films for the Rank Organization. But all of the films of the Rank Organization featured Margaret Lockwood dressed in Regency costumes and flourishing a riding whip. I thought that was rather a distasteful thing to have to write so I went back to divorcing people.

Herbert Would you comment on how your work as a barrister influenced your literary career, even before you created Rumpole?

Mortimer There are a lot of similarities between writing and the law, particularly in the way in which I did the law, which was by being an advocate. If you're a defense person you don't usually open cases. But if you *do* open cases, which you do in civil cases if you're the plaintiff, you have to tell the story to the jury or to the judge, *very*, very simply, and you must tell them a narrative which is going to make them listen. That's very good narrative training, I think. You may have to assemble the facts of some very, very complicated cases and narrate this in a way that will *arrest* them. So that's good training for a writer. And there's the fact that you've got to get up and make a final speech; there's no way you can say you want to go out for a walk or make a cup of tea or you've got writer's block. You've got to stand up and do it.

Herbert Right then and there.

Mortimer Do it then and there! *And* provide a joke if necessary. It makes you able to think quickly.

Herbert Are there ways in which work in the law is not helpful to the writer?

Mortimer (Smiles.) In the law you can bore judges into submission, you know, by going on until they scream for mercy—whereas you can't bore [your readers] into submission!

Herbert In the quotation that I mentioned earlier, you said that as a barrister and writer you felt "stretched between two opposite extremes," but you say you enjoyed the double life. Was this, then, a comfortable balance for you?

Mortimer Well, looking back on it, I probably did the barristering for too long. And I got too good at it for my own good. You know, I was too successful. And I think if I'd stopped it earlier I should have written more. But on the other hand, I don't regret it at all because [without that career] I wouldn't have written the things that I've written; I wouldn't know about the things that I do; I wouldn't have ever met a murderer. And you know, that seems a great privilege, to have met a few murderers in my life.

Herbert You have said before that you handled the question of defending the person "whodunit" by leaving the burden of deciding upon innocence or guilt to the judge and jury. You said, "The thing you, as the defending lawyer, are concentrating on is trying to convince the jury that guilt hasn't been proved beyond a reasonable doubt. Guilt isn't a question you have to decide, really, and you can get quite used to suspending your judgment about that, suspending your disbelief."

Mortimer That's right. Really, you're suspending your disbelief, which is what Catholics do all the time. (Laughs.) So my belief remained hanging in the hall.

Herbert This is what writers do and what readers often *must* do.

Mortimer (Laughs.)

Herbert I picture you hanging up your overcoat along with your disbelief and putting on your barrister's wig. Tell me, please, some anecdotes from courtroom life that were useful to you as a writer. I don't mean simply anecdotes that you have used in plotting Rumpole episodes, but rather memorable moments that opened your eyes to character, language, and other aspects of writing.

Mortimer I learned a lot about literature [by] divorcing people because nothing equips you more for a life in letters than a career in the divorce court. I learned first of all a very important lesson about English dialogue. I learnt the importance of the sporting metaphor in English life, and I remember very well the case in which I learnt that. I was appearing for an admiral. And this admiral had a very unhappy married life because he'd fallen desperately in love with a skating instructress at the Queensway Baths. And this skating instructress was a beautiful little blonde lady who used to pirouette around on the ice in her little white tutu and her little white skating boots. My admiral sat on the corner of the ice rink and he fell so passionately in love with her that he skated across to embrace her. But he was so passionate that he forgot to remove the leather guards from his skates. So the admiral attended the conference in my chambers in a wheelchair.

But in those days in the divorce law you had to ask your client when he'd last made love to his wife. It was very embarassing but you had to ask. And there was I, about a twenty-five-year-old divorce barrister and I said, "Admiral, could you just tell me please—it's very embarassing to have to ask you this—but when did you last make love to your wife?"

It was then that I learnt the importance of the sporting metaphor to the English. Because I'll never forget his reply. He said, "Well, we batted on for the first three years," he said, "but then we drew stumps."

And there was I, a young, innocent, naïve, fresh-faced divorce barrister and I used to leave home in the mornings when I lived at Swiss Cottage [in north London]. I'd had a terrible row with my wife; I had one black eye; I was bleeding at the mouth; my shirt was torn; my tie had been ripped off. I used to stagger down the stairs. All the children were suffering from infectious diseases; the au pair girl was pregnant and had left home. I pulled open the front door and there was a huge mound of bills; the overdraft had been stopped; the mortgage had been foreclosed; the light was about to be cut off. The car had been stolen. I used to thumb a lift to my chambers. I used to sit behind my desk and I was perfectly capable of advising fifty-year-old company directors on exactly how they should conduct their married lives.

Herbert You're referring, now, to the time that you lived with your first wife, the writer Penelope Mortimer, and her four children from a previous marriage and the son and daughter whom you had together? It must have been quite an extreme change to go from life as an only child in a rather insular household to becoming a husband and father in a large family.

Mortimer Yes. That was the appeal, really.

But to tell you more about the law and writing: I also learnt as a divorce lawyer the importance of learning when to end the dialogue, when to cut the scene. And I learnt that when I was doing a rural divorce case. I can just give you a little passage from that case that will show you the importance of knowing when to stop.

If I may just fill in the facts of the case, I had a client who was accused of committing adultery with a young girl in the middle of the Seven Acre Barley Field. And the only witness to this *appalling* act was Farmer Brown, who had been standing at the time at the edge of the Seven Acre Barley Field and had seen it all happen.

And so I got up and I cross-examined Farmer Brown with my usual aplomb. And I said, "Farmer Brown, perhaps on some occasions during your younger years you might have taken a girl into the middle of the Seven Acre Barley Field." And he said, "Ooh ah," or some such rustic reply. And I said, "You might even have sat down in the barley field next to this girl." And he said, "Oh ah." And I said, "Perhaps you sat very close to her." He said, "Oh ah ah." And I said, "Perhaps you kissed her." And he said, "Oh ah." And I said, "Maybe you even laid down beside her, Farmer Brown." He said, "Oh ah." And that was the point, for all students of English literature, for all students of law, at which any decent writer, any sensible barrister, would have cut the dialogue, sat down, ended the scene. But I had to ask the final, fatal question. "So, Farmer Brown, " I said, "any casual witness standing on the edge of the Seven Acre Barley Field at that time might have come to the conclusion that you were committing adultery." "Oh ah," he said, "and he'd be damn right, too."

So it is desperately important to remember when enough is enough, when you've finished the scene.

Herbert   That's wonderful! Thus far you've spoken about your experiences in the divorce court. Have you anecdotes to share from your career in criminal law?

Mortimer   I took to crime rather late in life. But I learnt in all the courts many very, very important lessons about the English language. One of the most important lessons of course is that there isn't one English language; there are about a hundred English languages which are spoken in this island. And the language spoken by judges and the language spoken by clients are totally different. And by and large each is totally unable to understand the other at all. I used to end divorce cases and the judge used to give a most reasoned, brilliant little summary. But at the end of it all, the sort of fifty-year-old lady you represented had absolutely no idea whether she's been condemned to death, or offered huge sums of damages, or been sent for long-term imprisonment. And when one had to explain that she was probably still married to the rather boring person to whom she was married for the last fifty years, a sort of look of puzzled bewilderment used to come right onto her face.

But I never really got to the whole beauty of the difference between judgespeak and clientspeak until I went to the Old Bailey and I met a wonderful judge called Judge Maude. And I would like just for a moment to remember Judge Maude with you. This Old Bailey judge had a gorgeous profile; he had beautiful little grey sideburns; he wore exquisite little golden half-glasses; he always used to adjourn the court at 11:30 every morning for his glass of cold Chablis and a little nibble of cheese. And Judge Maude had the onerous duty of sentencing a totally drunk Irish laborer who had been rightly convicted of urinating down the stairs of Leicester Square tube station, indecent exposure, using indecent language, assaulting the police, everything you can think of! And Judge Maude looked over his beautiful little gold glasses and he said, "I am going to take a most unusual course, a most merciful course, with you my man." And this man said, "Oh, God bless your Royal Highness for your charity." "I'm going to place you upon probation." And the man said, "Ah, Your Holiness, this is the most wonderful thing I've ever heard." The judge said, "But I place you upon probation upon one condition, and one condition only." And the man said, "Oh, I'll do anything for Your Reverence, anything." And the judge paused and said, "Well, the condition is that you must never touch another drop of alcohol for the rest of your natural life." And the man said, "Nothing. Absolutely nothing." And the judge paused and he said, "Look, by nothing, I mean *really* nothing. Not even the teeniest, weeniest little dry sherry before your dinner."

So there is a sort of gap, a sort of language gap, between the judges and the judged.

Herbert   That anecdote makes me think of the opening scene of your first play, *The Dock Brief* (1958), where the barrister talks at cross purposes with the prisoner whom he is chosen to defend. That drama, in which the hopeless barrister seeks to defend an admitted murderer, is the ultimate statement of the notion that barristers are not necessarily in the business of discovering the truth.

Mortimer   Yes. The barrister there, Morgenhall, was a very early Rumpole person, except he was a hopeless barrister, whereas Rumpole is a very good barrister.

Herbert   What inspired you to try your hand at drama at that time?

Mortimer   I'd written about five or six novels and I found writing novels rather a lonely business. You very rarely actually catch anyone reading them. I've heard of a novelist who got onto the tube at Picadilly Circus for the purpose of getting out at Green Park [a distance of one stop]. And as he got onto the tube he found himself sitting next to a girl who was, in fact, reading one of his novels. And he knew that two hundred pages further on there was a joke. So he sat on till Cockfosters [the end of the line] in the faint hope of hearing a laugh which never came.

But somewhere after my fifth or sixth novel I found it such a lonely occupation and Nesta Pain, whom I knew and admired as one of the most distinguished of radio producers, asked me to write a play for the radio. At that time I considered myself a novelist, although it is true that during a lonely childhood I quite often acted out *Hamlet* and *Macbeth*, duelling with myself and pretending I was mad for hours at a time.

Herbert   And of course you had the documentary film experience. In the introduction to the 1958 edition of *The Dock Brief* you note that "documentary films bear as little relation to art as they do to life, existing uninterestingly between the two like the instructions you get with do-it-yourself garden furniture."

Mortimer Yes! Yes, so at first I procrastinated about writing a radio drama. But when I got the idea for *The Dock Brief* I remembered Nesta's request. So I wrote the play. It was about an old barrister and an unsuccessful criminal in the cell and by a wonderful stroke of luck the barrister was played by Michael Hordern, who later played in [the television dramatization of] *Paradise Postponed*.

Herbert   How extraordinary! He played the rector, Simeon Simcox, I believe.

Mortimer That's right. And there he is, on the cover [of the Penguin paperback edition] of *Paradise Postponed*, to this day.

And with *The Dock Brief*, for the first time I actually heard dialogue that I'd written being said by actors and I became intoxicated with the idea of that and the idea of theatre and the idea of dramatic scenes. And the writing of radio plays is a wonderful exercise because they entirely depend upon the imagination of the audience.

Herbert   But surely the playwright exercises some control over the audience. Does the audience response sometimes surprise you?

Mortimer Well, you don't know what the audience response is in radio. The only place you really know about the audience is in the theatre. The response sometimes is surprising. Things that you only put in as an afterthought might draw a big response, as compared to a laugh that you worked harder for.

Herbert   While drama *is* dialogue to a large extent, you also manage, as you remarked earlier, to show us what people mean by means of what they're *not* saying, even in radio drama, where we are not looking at the actors' behavior while they speak. This is remarkable. In much of your drama you delight in presenting the unexpected through marvelous twists of phrasing and unlikely, humorous responses of one character to another. How else do you tell us what people mean by means of what they're *not* saying?

Mortimer Well, you can let the audience have that information and then the dialogue of the character [with another] shows what the character sees or doesn't. Or the other thing that happens in the Rumpoles is that the two characters never answer each other. They have conversations on separate parallel lines.

But *The Dock Brief* was rather successful for me. And if you are successful, if you write a play about two old men in a cell, the moguls of Hollywood immediately think you're absolutely the right man to write *The Decline and Fall of Genghis Khan*! So off I went to Hollywood from time to time and wrote for the movies. And so there I was, barristering, writing, doing all of these things.

Herbert And you were heading a large family. How did you fit your writing in between working as a barrister and leading a busy family life? When did you find the time to write?

Mortimer It was very difficult. I used to get up very early in the morning. And when I became Q.C. [Queen's counsel, or a criminal lawyer] it was much easier because I would do a big case, then have a gap, then do another big case. And by the end I was only doing about five cases a year.

Herbert Was it helpful having another novelist in the family? Did you provide support to one another in literary matters?

Mortimer No. I don't think writers being married to each other is very helpful.

Herbert You can *both* sit home brewing tea, stumped for words.

Mortimer Or else you sit listening to the other person's typewriter rattling and it drives you mad. Also you share common experience so you only have the same thing to write about. We did write a travel book together, *With Love and Lizards*. That was the only book we produced together.

Herbert Did you feel a sense of competition?

Mortimer Yes. I think the problem was, Penelope used to type so I could always hear the typewriter clacking, but I always write by hand.

Herbert You must have together had a number of literary friends. Was that a major part of your life, being involved with other writers?

Mortimer Not really. I think that English writers tend to avoid other writers. I don't think the society of other writers is all that significant to my actual work in writing.

Herbert To get back to a character whom you created both for the screen and the printed page, would you comment on the genesis of Horace Rumpole?

Mortimer Well, somewhere around the mid 1970s I thought I needed a character to keep me alive in my old age and I remembered all of the rather underpaid barristers I'd known, trudging around some very unsympathetic courts, and I thought of my father's uniform, the sort of Winston Churchill set with the black jacket and striped trousers and cigar ash down the watch chain. And I thought of all the barristers I'd known who called the judges "Old Darling." So I thought of Rumpole, and he's been a great comfort to me. You might say he's taken me around the world.

Herbert Are there ways in which Rumpole reflects the barrister John Mortimer?

Mortimer Well, I mean, Rumpole says the things that I think. But if I say them, they sound rather sort of trendy and progressive; if he says them, they sound rather crusty and conservative and nice.

Herbert What about some of the other characters. "She-who-must-be-obeyed," for instance?

Mortimer "She-who-must-be-obeyed" isn't like anyone, really. You can put any scene that happens in marriage into the Rumpole marriage. My wife is not at all like "She-who-must-be-obeyed," but any scene that happens with my wife could be used in the Rumpole.

Herbert Well, from your portrayal of your parents it seems that in their marriage the wife could absolutely take the husband in stride while to others the man must have seemed highly eccentric. This makes me think of Hilda and Rumpole.

Mortimer Oh, yes. They couldn't either one live without the other.

Herbert You seem to have a particular sensitivity to and flair for portraying older, rather eccentric men, and bringing humor to their portraits.

Mortimer Oh, yes. Old men are my specialty, rather! And in my novel *Summer's Lease* I've had rather a good time with another older character; so I'm still at it, portraying old men.

Herbert In 1985 you wrote *Paradise Postponed*. What inspired you to return to the novel after so many years?

Mortimer Well, [several] years ago I went to defend an opposition MP in Singapore. So I flew out of England on Boxing Day to defend this man. I arrived jet-lagged, hung over, with no particular idea of what the case was all about. In short, I was in the usual position of a defending Queen's Counsel in the beginning of an important trial. And I staggered into the Singapore Central Court. There was this robing room, which looked to me exactly like every robing room from Snaresbrook to Bodmin to the Old Bailey to Hong Kong. It was a huge, dirty room with the floor lined with torn-up newspaper. There

127

were barristers lying on benches in their stocking feet, sleeping off their hangovers. There were other barristers ringing up their wives in the vain attempt to explain where they were the night before. And the whole of this familiar environment was presided over by an eighty-four-year-old Chinese woman who was making Nescafe and pouring out Chinese cough mixture for barristers with sore throats. And so I went into there and she looked at me and she said, "Ah, there you are. Lumpore of the Bailey." and I knew that I didn't want to spend the rest of my life being called "Lumpore of the Bailey," so I decided to give it up, for the time at least.

Then what happened was that I was having lunch with Bryan Cowgill, who heads Thames Television, and he said, "When are you going to write a story about England since the war?" At first I thought I didn't want to write a story about England since the war. And then I thought maybe I could. And then I thought, well, I'd adapted *Brideshead* [*Revisited*] for television and it's a long novel. I thought, "Well, I don't want to adapt anybody else's novel so I'll write a novel and *then* adapt it." So I wrote down the idea for it on a piece of paper in handwriting, and I never even typed it out. I sold it to the television company and the publisher. I think they bought it and paid lots of money for it because they never could read the handwriting! So then I set about it and I wrote them both at the same time.

Herbert   The novel reads very much like a Victorian novel, with its episodic nature, its plot centering around a question of money and a debatable will. It calls to mind Wilkie Collins or Charles Dickens. Did you have the Victorian novel in mind when you began *Paradise Postponed*?

Mortimer   I knew that I wanted to write a long novel, as much like a long Victorian novel as possible. I think that Victorian novelists and television writers have got a lot in common because, after all, they have a big audience and their work comes out in parts. I knew it had to have one strong plot which would keep people reading it from beginning to end. Immediately I thought of *Bleak House*. I thought, if you asked anybody what the plot to *Bleak House* was, they would never really be able to tell you, but they would be able to tell you all about the funny things that happened along the way. But if *Bleak House* didn't have a central plot, they wouldn't have gone on reading it and discovered those things along the way.

Herbert   The fact that *Paradise Postponed* revolves around the central mystery of the rector's will ties it in with your first novel, written almost four decades earlier. *Charade*, too, centered around a crucial mystery. And your more recent novel, *Summer's Lease*, involves a mystery, too. In much of your longer fiction you've set out to resolve a central puzzle as well as to discover the truth of character.

Mortimer The detective story comes, really, into everything, I think. And the detective story is hard, much harder to write, than the sensitive novel of adultery in Hampstead-on-Hill. Plots are terribly important. I think they *must* be important because I find them terribly difficult! Plots are the hardest thing for me. But you've got to have that plot in which you find out in the end, as you point out, the truth of the characters. And so the whole detective story reading is the important thing, to my mind. I think it's the hard thing and the important thing; it's the surprise, the suspense.

Herbert Do you have your surprises all planned out? Are you the sort of writer who has to know where everything is going before you start?

Mortimer No, not at all. No, I don't believe in that at all. I only know where everything is going about halfway through. . . . I never have a plan. I know vaguely what's ahead but I never write any plan down because I think that unless the characters come to life and do it for themselves, you're lost. You know, that's the great thing; they've got to do their own living; they've got to be free to do what they feel they *ought* to do.

Herbert That's fascinating. Many authors of fiction will say that they hope for the characters to take on lives of their own, but to add to that the dimension of the characters having an inward compulsion to behave in a certain way is rather different.

Mortimer Absolutely. There's a wonderful remark that Graham Greene said. He said that he writes only about a hundred words a day because his eyes get so tired. So I said, "Is it because you can't read so well?" And he said, "No, it's because you have to watch your characters."

Herbert Do you think the author of the crime novel can allow the characters a free rein, or is the crime writer confined by the necessity of keeping a secret from the reader? After all, if the characters take over, they may let on too much about their motives?

Mortimer (Laughs.) Well, you've got to keep their secrets from the reader but I think they should have some sort of free rein. Obviously in crime novels they're more tightly controlled, but if I write a crime story, which the Rumpoles all are, I don't really know exactly what happens until I'm writing it. I have a vague idea but maybe even the twist at the end is something I don't know until I get to the end!

Herbert So the characters are actually causing the twists to occur at times?

Mortimer Well, it's a combination; we work together.

Herbert   Do you feel that there is any limitation exerted by this necessity to keep secrets, and to keep the characters more tightly under control?

Mortimer   No. Because I think that suspense is the common element to every piece of fiction. You always have to keep the reader wondering what's going to happen.

Herbert   Do you agree with P. D. James that in the crime novel you can say as much about human character as can be said in—for lack of a better term—the mainstream novel; or do you go along with Julian Symons, who says crime novels can be excellent but they are prevented from rising to the highest levels of literary achievement by the fact that the author must keep secrets from the reader for reasons of formula rather than for reasons of art?

Mortimer   I agree with Phyllis [P. D. James] because I think all the great [literary] works of art of the world are crime stories. *Hamlet* is a crime story; the *Agamemnon* of Aeschylus is a crime story. And in a way I think the idea of the contrived secret is not really what it's all about. Ruth Rendell doesn't really necessarily have that in her books. There are surprises and there is suspense but that's not the point of it, really.

Herbert   But some crime novels are completely preoccupied with the contrived puzzle.

Mortimer   Yes, some are. And then they're much worse. Take Agatha Christie, for instance.

Herbert   Does the necessity for a mystery novel to be entertaining in any way compromise its literary quality?

Mortimer   No, because I think all art has to be entertaining.

Herbert   Ah! I thought you'd say that.

Mortimer   That is the primary purpose of the artist: to entertain the audience. There's a very good thing that Matisse said, and I can't quote him exactly, but his meaning was this: people have very busy days; they work hard; and they come home and they need to be given pleasure. And he said that was what his painting was all about. And I mean he was about the best modern painter there is. And you can *also*, by the way, entertain people by moving them or frightening them. However, the first thing you've got to do is not to *bore* them! And the idea that more serious things, or greater literature, has to be more boring I think is absolutely wrong.

Herbert   I was wondering if you had ever considered writing a crime novel of the more usual sort, with an actual sleuth?

Mortimer Well, I think the Rumpole novels are really the nearest I will come to that because in a way he acts as a detective—he finds out the truth. When I thought of Rumpole at first, I thought he was going to be a detective in the tradition of Sherlock Holmes, you know, but he would be a barrister. And there are instances in the Rumpole stories where he *is* just like a detective.

Herbert There are little references to the Holmes canon tucked in—

Mortimer Oh, yes, like his shadow on the blind in "Rumpole's Return."

Herbert And then there's the story in which he, like Holmes, pretends that he is dead.

Mortimer Yes! That is called "The Last Resort."

Herbert And your novel *Summer's Lease* uses Conan Doyle's notion of having the characters unknowingly impersonate others by dining on the terrace in the evenings by candlelight, just the way the character in "The Adventure of the Copper Beeches" is asked to cut her hair and sit in a particular window at certain times of the day.

Mortimer You're very good to catch that one!

Herbert Thank you! Do you think that Conan Doyle exerted an influence on detective fiction that we can still feel today in crime writing?

Mortimer I'm sure he did. I think that all central fictional detectives have been influenced by Sherlock Holmes.

Herbert When you think what Conan Doyle accomplished that we now take for granted: the idea of the rational and inevitable conclusion, playing fair with the reader, and not having information come from—

Mortimer —outer space! Yes. And also the atmosphere, you know. The atmosphere in those stories is so *strong*, the actual physical feeling of them.

Herbert And this is remarkable because he was so very economical in his descriptions. I think your Rumpole stories are like that, too. We get a picture of the courtroom and even the characters based on very economical use of description.

Mortimer Going back to Graham Greene, you have to *see* it in your mind's eye. It's very difficult for me to write about a place I haven't been to. It's very difficult for me to make up a place. And as for the economy of description, you have to find the thing that is unusual about the place.

Herbert What is the greatest appeal, for you, of the Sherlock Holmes stories?

Mortimer I don't know. They're so familiar to me, like Shakespeare and Browning, things that I grew up with. I think there's extraordinary character. I think there's extraordinary atmosphere; you can feel it coming on you like the London fog, it's so strong. And [Holmes and Watson] are such a wonderful matched couple.

Herbert I agree.

Mortimer But I think that Conan Doyle was a very *decent* chap. I mean despite the fact that he had this peculiar belief in faeries at the bottom of his garden, he did devote enormous time and energy to causes and to people in difficulties. He was a decent man who believed in justice and honesty, and I think that quality comes out in the Sherlock Holmes stories. There's a decency in the Sherlock Holmes stories which there is in Dickens, that feeling that somewhere or other there is a goodness in the world. And although there are murderous Moriaritys about, on the whole decency, sanity, and reason can prevail. I think that's very attractive.

Herbert Rumpole, too, seeks to make the right side win, to see that justice is done.

Mortimer Oh, yes. I think that's the common thing that makes up the great detectives. I mean Philip Marlowe is a decent chap. And [Ruth Rendell's] Inspector Wexford is a *terribly* decent chap.

Herbert Is this something you consciously thought about when you created Rumpole? Did you think, "I'm going to have someone who stands up for decency and justice"?

Mortimer Yes. Absolutely.

Herbert Aha! Rumpole may be rumpled and wear a disreputable wig but he *is* an essentially decent fellow. Do you think this may still be one of the chief appeals of the crime novel, that it generally stands for justice and goodness prevailing?

Mortimer Yes. The sleuth needs to be the man who can understand everything in a wicked world and also who imposes order upon chaos, like an artist does.

Herbert Ah!

Mortimer An artist takes the chaos in human life and makes some order out of it. And the detective does the same thing; he imposes order on a mass of mysteries.

Herbert When you think about Rumpole this last remark is telling because the judge may be the one to shout, "Order in the court!" but the one who is *really* making order stand is Rumpole, isn't he?

Mortimer   That's it.

Herbert   Do you have any courtroom anecdotes that illustrate this struggle for justice to prevail?

Mortimer   Yes. Well, I was very good at husband-and-wife murders. You know that murder goes on in the family circle like Christmas. I was very good at husband-and-wife quarrels that ended up with the husband or wife being dead. These quarrels always seemed to take place in bathrooms.

   I had one case that involved the vagal nerve. You can just put your hand on someone's throat and by mistake you can touch their vagal nerve and stop the blood going from their heart and the person dies immediately. Perhaps intendedly. And I had a couple who were quarrelling while in the bath together, and it ended up with the wife drowned. The husband got out and went for a long walk, and finally he turned himself in to the police. And the question was whether he intended to kill the wife whose vagal nerve he had apparently touched in the bath.

   So I started this case by saying that my client, the husband, was sitting at the tap end of the bath. And the judge said, "You mean the woman made her husband sit at the tap end!" So I said, "I'm sorry, my lord, but I'm afraid he always sat at the tap end so that he could wash her hair. "And there was a horrified look on the judge's face. "The tap end? You mean the man had to sit at the tap end?" And, not surprisingly, my client was acquitted.

Herbert   The poor, suffering husband! You have also said that barristers and lawyers are not generally in the business of discovering the truth; rather, there is a contest going on in the court situation.

Mortimer   Yes. That's what really the Rumpole detection is. Rumpole discovers the truth which isn't really emerging in the courtroom. Because a criminal trial under our systems, American and English, isn't an exercise in discovering the truth; it's a contest where the point at issue is whether the prosecution has proved somebody guilty beyond a reasonable doubt. And the fact is when they fail to prove that somebody is guilty beyond a reasonable doubt it doesn't necessarily mean that the person is innocent. And so criminal defense is never an exercise in establishing your client's innocence: it's always an exercise in trying to persuade the jury that the client has not been proven guilty. Therefore the main business of the defending counsel is not to call evidence but to try and stop evidence being called. So therefore it's a perpetual process of narrowing the limits of inquiry.

Herbert   Which is really the opposite of trying to bring out the whole truth.

Mortimer So that really is the drama in the Rumpole stories; it's the actual truth which lies *behind* what the results of the trial are.

Herbert I understand that during your legal career you've always served in the advocate's position.

Mortimer Yes. I only prosecuted in one case, which I lost.

Herbert Was this a philosophical decision?

Mortimer Well, I always felt that cross-examining people into prison, and using all your skills and wiles to do that was rather distasteful. I'd rather use that to keep people out of prison. And also it's much more fun to be a defender!

Herbert In your years as a criminal lawyer you worked with people accused of murder. And in some of your fiction you have created puzzles that center around questions of death. Would you be willing to tell me something about your own attitude toward death? Do you regard yourself as someone who is especially attuned to the fragility of life or do you have a religious outlook that helps you to deal with this question?

Mortimer There are two things I think about. I mean, I find it very difficult to believe in God. But apart from that I would believe in everything else to do with the Christian religion. If you reject the idea of God, still the importance of the individual, and freedom, and all those traditions which are a part of Christianity are very valuable and we cannot throw them out.

Herbert In discussing crime writing and the author's attitude toward death, P. D. James told me that she felt one could have doubts about some essentials of Christianity but still lead a religious life.

Mortimer I think so, too. I [once] did an interview with Graham Greene. And his Catholicism is so near atheism that it's practically the same thing. There's a very good poem which he quoted that says you either have faith interspersed with doubt or doubt interspersed with faith.

Herbert This sounds like a description of English weather! Sunny intervals with cloudy periods or—

Mortimer —cloudy intervals with sunny periods! That's right. Well, I have doubt interspersed with faith.

Herbert And as for your writing career, I hope we may all look forward to your production of more longer novels interspersed with a multitude of Rumpole stories.

Mortimer Oh, yes, you may. One of my latest novels is called *Dunster* and although it is not strictly a mystery story it does include a mysterious element, a crime. The question is, "Should we dig up old war crimes?" I can't seem to avoid a question of crime. And, yes, all this is interspersed with the writing of Rumpole stories.

Herbert   That's very reassuring. Rumpole's in chambers; all's right with the world. Except for the cigar ash down the watch chain and a few mad judges.

Mortimer Ha!

136

▶ PATRICIA D. CORNWELL

Those who have read Particia D. Cornwell's powerful prose exposing violence in contemporary American society will not be surprised to discover that the author in person is an energetic foe of those who would dehumanize others. Whether speaking earnestly before the fire blazing in her fieldstone fireplace, or conversing over an elegant dinner at her health club, or sharing some thoughts with her mentor and colleague Deputy Chief Medical Examiner Marcella Fierro in Fierro's cheerful kitchen, or pointing out the entrance for human remains at midnight at the Richmond City Morgue, Cornwell keeps circling back to her concern for the individual in an increasingly violent society.

Dressed in an FBI Academy sweatshirt and warm-up pants, Cornwell devoted hours to being interviewed in the expansive living room of her Tudor-style home in Richmond, Virginia. The uncluttered environment is decorated with a reproduction of "The Lady and the Unicorn" tapestry and bookcases on which *Black's Law Dictionary* and Whitman's *Leaves of Grass* stand side by side with a well-worn violin missing a string. Two fluffy pink flamingos add a note of whimsey, while a single glass heart is one of the few other decorative objects in the room.

The author also provided a tour of her office where a well-used Lanier printer was shuddering and shaking as it printed out the new manuscript of Cornwell's fourth novel, *Cruel and Unusual*. "I really should get a new one," Cornwell shrugs, "but I'm a little bit superstitious. This one's printed out all of the novels so far." Considering the success of her work she may be wise to stick to the tried and true.

Beside the printer was a .38 revolver. And spread out on the floor and surface areas surrounding Cornwell's desk could be found unusual works of reference including a tome entitled *Sexual Homicide: Patterns and Motives* by Robert K. Ressler et al. and William J. Eckert and Stuart H. James's volume called *Interpretation of Bloodstain Evidence at Crime Scenes* which was spread open to the chapter entitled "Bloodstain Pattern Interpretation." On a nearby shelf stand photographs of Cornwell's father and of Ruth and Billy Graham. Beside these are ceramic mugs emblazoned with the names of some of Cornwell's characters.

Born Patricia Daniels in Florida, Cornwell acquired her nom de plume during her marriage to Charles Cornwell, then a professor, now a minister, seventeen years her senior. Cornwell grew up in Miami until the age of seven when her parents broke up and she moved to North Carolina with her mother and two brothers. When her mother was hospitalized with bouts of severe depression, the family was looked after by missionary neighbors who had recently returned from the Congo. Cornwell was also taken under the wing of Ruth Graham, who became the subject of Cornwell's first published book, *A Time For Remembering: The Ruth Graham Story*, which appeared in 1982.

As a child, Cornwell dreamed of becoming a tennis pro and she went far in tennis competition, but when she discovered that she could not be absolute tops at this, Cornwell followed her inclination to write, and she completed a novel as her thesis for graduation from Davidson College, in North Carolina, in 1979.

Following graduation, Cornwell worked as a prizewinning police reporter with *The Charlotte Observer* before she decided to take her firsthand experience of crime and use it in a work of fiction. She made three false starts before she realized that the forensic procedural was the winning formula for her. Along the way, she interviewed Fierro, who awoke in Cornwell a fascination with forensic science and introduced her to others who would inspire the author. Cornwell found work in the Richmond Medical Examiner's Office as a computer wiz—a talent of which she had previously been unaware—where, while she organized forensic records, she imbibed the atmosphere of the place, and learned a great deal of technical information that would become invaluable to her in crafting her crimes.

During the summer of 1991 Cornwell was shocked to learn that a Florida man, John Benson Waterman, was accused of strangling his neighbor, Jacqueline Galloway, using techniques that had been described in *Postmortem*. It is tragically ironic that the killer, who could undoubtedly have found a method for murder elsewhere, would choose to study the work of an author who made a conscious decision never to portray crime from the criminal's point of view and, in particular, never to show violence as enjoyable in any way, shape, or form.

Cornwell shared her thoughts about the Florida case as well as insights into her writing methods and her life during a day that began with fireside conversation and closed beneath the highways of Richmond, at the doorway to the morgue, where so many of Cornwell's stories begin.

Herbert   On behalf of all the readers who, like me, have stayed up late at night, riveted, scared, and fascinated by the violent society you examine in your novels, I would like to ask you, "Is the random violence that you portray in your books a reality for you as an individual?"

Cornwell   I think for me violence is so real that I cannot seem to escape it; it's like there is a shadow following me over every door and a bogeyman at every turn of the road. Maybe this is because I have been exposed to it in such a real way [in work with the Medical Examiner's Office] that it is something *I cannot dodge* and I feel like I have to deal with it in my books. . . . I cannot know what goes on out there without being frightened of it myself and this is my way of dealing with it, exploring it, and it's a bit of a catalyst for me, or catharsis for me, excuse me!

Herbert   I'd say it's a bit of a catalyst for you, too!

Cornwell   But at the same time, I feel that it's also a comment on the world we live in: you cannot escape that this is what goes on out there! It's not like I'm just fabricating spooks and phantoms. I mean, this is a reality: that people are raped and shot and mugged and murdered and generally there's not necessarily an esoteric motivation behind it. . . . And I like the sort of fearful symmetry of having very civilized and humane people who are warring against this. I think for me, on a subconscious level, this is part of the appeal of Dr. Scarpetta. There is a fearful symmetry of having this humane, civilized, physician, who is sworn by the Hippocratic Oath to do no harm, be the one who is going to these scenes and dealing with the spoils of this hideous irrationality and cruelty.

Herbert   This certainly provides an effective contrast.

Cornwell   It's just such an incredible contrast, more so than a police officer dealing with it because you have no thin blue line that separates the police from the people who do it. There is no "thin blue line" that separates a Dr. Scarpetta from the people who [perpetrate crimes]. You've got a tremendous polarity: she's way over here in one camp representing the paragon of humanity and these people are way over there, the paragons of inhumanity. So I enjoy playing around with all of that. I enjoy exploring it; it intrigues me in a philosophical and even spiritual sense because *there are real people out there doing this*.

Herbert   Your sleuth, the medical examiner Dr. Kay Scarpetta, is sensitized to the potential for violence in her city of Richmond because she comes into contact with slain victims of violent crime in her work. Therefore, it is not surprising that even in the ordinary details of her day she is preoccupied with self-defense, prevention of crime, and the need to keep her home protected with alarms and locked windows. Is this a reality for the average person in your part of America?

Cornwell   I think that unquestionably there are communities that are safer than some of our inner city communities. I live in a city and I would not even *begin* to imagine having a home that is not protected in every form possible. I think that my enhanced awareness of violence makes me much more cautious.

Herbert   So, in this sense, you certainly identify with Scarpetta. Are there other regards in which you identify with your sleuth?

Cornwell   Well, let me tell you, for example, about my police work, because that will provide a little insight on how I can identify with Scarpetta's relationship with Marino.

Herbert   What was the police work like for you?

Cornwell   I rode with the homicide detectives every weekend for three years. And I was actually a first responder on the scenes with them. I also did uniform work, primarily to learn the nuts and bolts of police work. I know what Marino's like. I know what it's like to wear a uniform: how uncomfortable it is. I know what it's like to talk on the radio. I know what it's like to drive an unmarked car and about the constant griping and complaints about how your equipment fails. I've been through all that and I have the utmost respect for the police and I feel every citizen ought to go through a day in their lives to understand what it's like for them. It's tough. That's why I suppose Scarpetta's attitude toward Marino is my own.

Herbert   Can you tell us a bit about the person upon whom your fictional chief medical examiner is modeled?

Cornwell   There is no person that the character's based on. My friend Dr. Marcella Fierro kindly reads my manuscripts and advises me on the accuracy of the medical information. But also the chief medical examiner, Dr. David Wiecking, reviews my work as well. And he's actually my boss, the person I've worked for. So there are elements of both. Marcella is Italian and Catholic; the chief has a law degree and is a forensic pathologist. He went to Johns Hopkins. Dr. Wiecking has been an inspiration because he's very logical; he thinks like a lawyer.

There's some of him in Scarpetta in terms of his influence on me. He's also a good friend of mine.

Herbert   Are there other people who have been invaluable to you in your research?

Cornwell   Yes, Ed Sulzbach, who is an FBI agent, to whom *Body of Evidence* is dedicated, has been a tremendous help and a dear friend.

Herbert   How did you get to know him?

Cornwell   When I was at the Medical Examiner's Office I would audit the forensic science academy. Ed was teaching classes on profiling [criminals] and I sat in on one of his classes. Through him, I got to know what I have to do to profile the killers in my books. I'd go see Ed and he was very patient, you know; he put up with me for three or four years before I got published. I could say to Ed, "If you had this kind of person what would he do?" Or, "If you found this, what kind of person would it be?" So we would go 'round and 'round about that.

Herbert   So you speculated together?

Cornwell   But you get to a point where a lot of that is, in addition to being based on empirical knowledge or information from the past, it is intuitive as well. And I *know* the kind of things that my killer would do. You just have a feel for it.

Herbert   One manner in which you do follow in the traditions of earlier mystery and crime writers is that things are well tied up in the end. And when the killer is revealed, the reader may think, "Oh! Why didn't I think of that?"

Cornwell   Well, thank you.

Herbert   Does part of your success lie in the fact that you have "profiled" the criminal in your mind as you write your book?

Cornwell   Profilers are often remarkably on target. And what they're looking for is that key that links things. As in *Postmortem*, the voice. They always look for the common denominator.

Herbert   Marino seems such a real character in your work. Do you share any personal common denominators with him?

Cornwell   I have a rough-and-tumble side like he does. Marino would be the part of me that's sloppy and lacking in discipline. Scarpetta is a paragon of discipline; he's a paragon of lack of discipline. I'm sure a lot of us can relate to that war within ourselves. I have a Scarpetta in me but I've got a Marino in me and they're always vying to preempt the other.

Herbert The sleuthing team is such an important tradition in crime writing. I noticed this last time when Scarpetta described her first meeting with Marino she actually said, "You're from Richmond City, I presume?" which made me think of Sherlock Holmes saying to Watson, "You have been in Afghanistan, I perceive." I wonder, in terms of crafting your books, how conscious you are of this interplay of the two sides of the sleuthing team.

Cornwell I'm more aware of it as time goes by but in the actual creation of it and the writing of it, it's really more of an intuitive thing: I don't sit there and consciously think [things out.] It just happens. It's like writing music where you just hear the tune and out it comes. It's really intuitive for me. I must say, I do not craft my novels at all. I write them very, very intuitively, and for some miraculous reason it works.

Herbert That's amazing in crime writing because you would expect the writer to be carefully planning in order to lay the clues.

Cornwell But you see I've never read mysteries. I'm rather illiterate when it comes to crime novels. I've never studied them; I've never read them. I read mainstream novels because I like a little poetry in my life. I'd rather read Mark Helprin than something that's very gory or that's about crime. Because I think about that too much as it is. There may be a part of me, too, that I don't like to admit to—I don't want to be influenced. I just don't want to be influenced by what other people are doing so I try to shut it out.

Herbert If you were not a particular fan of the crime or mystery novel, how did you come to be writing in this genre?

Cornwell Before I tried to write the crime novel I decided I would just try to write *the* novel, and every time I would start writing something, somebody would die! There was always a body at every turn.

Herbert But you weren't thinking in terms of the mystery novel?

Cornwell No! There was a body at every turn and one in every room. So I could not seem to escape violence. And it would probably take a psychoanalyst to figure out why some of us seem to be almost obsessed with this, for me maybe more than others [mystery writers] because I don't look at crime as a contrivance or as a form of entertainment. You see death to me is not a game, and violence is not a game, and that's why I do not consider myself a "mystery writer." It's not that I'm disparaging what other people do, but they are creating a *game* in a sense. But I can't do that because my perspective is so different. I'm dealing with the reality of [violence].

Herbert I see.

Cornwell   [My work] starts with a body because that's what Scarpetta starts with. And then you work backwards. It's not a game or a puzzle to be solved. It's a horrific, epidemic, plague, almost, that has been visited upon a city. And it's up to her and the people she works with to try to stop it. It's frightening. "Mystery" implies the game or the entertaining quality that we've mentioned and that formula.

Herbert   Your books succeed in being more than mere studies of violence because they are moving. One of my concerns is to get the authors to talk about how this ability to entertain may be a limitation to the author. Now, in your books you're not intending to entertain us in the ordinary, amusing sense of the word.

Cornwell   Well, *I* entertain by *not* entertaining!

Herbert   But what you do is to entertain us by moving us. John Mortimer spoke about this idea. He said, "You can entertain people . . . by moving them or frightening them." This is a literature that people pick up with the expectation of being entertained, or moved, or engrossed in a "good read," whether you call this cheerful entertainment or not. And, Patsy, your books always succeed as "good reads." And I was wondering if you can say everything you want to say about human character and emotion in a crime novel?

Cornwell   I think, actually, that you can. But I think I find a limitation when I write a scene that I really think is a good one but it really doesn't advance the plot and so it has to be cut. But the truth is, even in a mainstream novel, if it's not advancing the story or the plot, material ought to be cut.

Herbert   I agree.

Cornwell   But I don't believe there is much you *can't* do in crime writing. You have crime and violence, crime and death in so many works of mainstream fiction. You take *Fried Green Tomatoes* and the whole thing centers originally on a death and then later on a homicide. [In a crime novel] you can have some romance; you can have the pathology in families; you can have—I can't think of anything you *can't* have because what is more vital than life and death? What is life without death? What is death without life? The two are the same in a way.

Herbert   Yes. But there is the question in crime writing of needing to keep secrets from the reader for reasons of extending the suspense, and, in effect, for reasons of formula, rather than for reasons of art. You might keep a secret a little bit longer than you would have done in a so-called mainstream novel.

Cornwell   You see, it's much easier for me because [since I'm] writing in the first person point of view, the reader can't know anything that

143

Scarpetta's not going to know. What I couldn't do is have Scarpetta know something for fifty pages that I don't let you know that she knows. Well, I shouldn't say I *couldn't*. It depends. There are times when maybe I could. It might be something personal that she's not admitting to anybody. But in terms of evidence, you can't get away with that with the first person point of view. And so I am not as restricted by the genre because I'm simply working the cases like she is. For instance, the other day the [tennis] pro that I work with three times a week said, "Well, do you know how it's going to end yet?" And here I am on the last chapter of the book! And I said, "No. I'm not sure." He said, "Well, do you know who did it?" And I said, "I *think* I do, I think I do. I think I just saw him in this previous scene." I knew what kind of person he was but I just saw his face. And this is true. This is in the fourth book but I didn't meet him until the last two days I was working on it.

Herbert   How surprising!

Cornwell   And then I knew who it was and it wasn't until the very end that it occurred—you know at three or four o'clock in the morning—that I knew what was going to happen. I was sitting there and I was thinking, "Is she gonna shoot him? Is she gonna run him over in her car? What *is* going to happen?" And then all of a sudden I realized, "Boom!" I knew what was going to happen.

Herbert   It surprises me that the setup of what is going to occur doesn't happen much earlier for you.

Cornwell   It doesn't. Because that's not life. In life Scarpetta wouldn't know 'til she was there.

Herbert   But then, do you have to go back and rewrite and make sure that certain clues are placed earlier to lead to the conclusion?

Cornwell   To a degree, only because—I mean, I know the important things of *why*. You know, *who* in terms of what type of person and what the reason is. But in terms of the name and what he looks like and what the resolution is going to be and how is it gonna end? I don't know. Is he going to get shot? Is he gonna get hit with a frying pan? I don't know that until I'm there, until it's happening right before my eyes. And it's just the same way it would be if it were real life. And in this fourth one, it doesn't end probably anything like you think it's going to, but it works.

Herbert   Amazing.

Cornwell   So I do not feel [generally limited by the genre]. I think a series in some ways might limit somebody because with each book you write you are more and more weighted down by what you've already said and by what background you've given somebody, what history you've given 'em. But, you know, you can look at that as a challenge, too. But I can't think of much you might want to say that you can't say in a crime novel.

Herbert   Can you tell us about some other literary influences that have meant a lot to you?

Cornwell   I do like Pat Conroy a lot. I like Isabelle Allende, the Chilean writer. I love her collection of short stories.

Herbert   What quality of writing do you like?

Cornwell   I think the capturing of the emotions. [This] moves me. In addition to the fact that I admire the poetry of the prose. Mark Helprin's *A Soldier of the Great War* means a lot to me. There are passages of that book that are just so well-written that it's mind-boggling. And I admire that. It's beautiful. He does wonderful things with dialogue. So I'm influenced by people like that. Because I already know about the blood and guts part of it, I like anybody that can help me write better.

Herbert   What are the more challenging aspects of the writing process for you?

Cornwell   Dialogue, interestingly enough, is the easiest thing for me. I hear these people talk in my head and I have no trouble with dialogue. In fact, if you go through one of my manuscripts you will find that almost nothing in my dialogue has been touched. I tend to have a pretty good ear for how people talk and I know what these people sound like. And I hear 'em. The most challenging aspect? Description is difficult because it's tough to maintain a balance where you are not over-writing and oftentimes my descriptions will have to be cut because it slows the plot down. I think the biggest challenge is simply telling the story, where you move from A to Z and you get people there and you have them hanging on by their fingernails. To me that's the ultimate challenge. I think there are a lot of us who have always loved writing but the biggest challenge is to have something to say, to have a story to tell, to be able to do both.

Herbert   And you've solved that problem by opening a window on a field of experience that most readers might never see.

Cornwell   Well, I had to create the story for myself and then report on it, as you put it.

Herbert   Your method relies on the research and on the experiences you're having. As long as you continue to have them, you'll be able to write about them. I mean, you are, after all, trained as a reporter. A reporter cannot indulge in writer's block.

Cornwell   When I get in trouble, then what I need to do is go ride with the police for a night or go hang out with my FBI friend and talk about cases over dinner, or with Marcella and talk about medical things. What I can never do is *just* be a writer: if I ever stop living, then I am failing my characters. And a good case in point is when I travel. My characters are like my children. When I went to Great Britain on the Concorde and I was treated royally . . . my characters wouldn't speak to me for *days*! Because I was doing nothing that was inspiring me towards getting immersed in the world that Marino and Scarpetta live in. And they wouldn't speak to me! [They were thinking,] "You know, you got sent over on the Concorde and you got picked up in this Jaguar limousine and you stayed in this wonderful hotel and got wined and dined, and you come home and you think we will talk to you?!"

Herbert   Especially Marino!

Cornwell   No way! They didn't. It was horrible. Now if I go out and ride with the police like I did a couple of months ago and I ended up climbing up on a rooftop looking at blood up there on the tar paper where some woman had fallen—when I'm getting all down and dirty with these detectives, *then* they talk to me. Especially Marino. It's like, "You're OK." But I've got to ride around in those cars and smell the Armorall and the air freshener and stop off at the 7-Eleven and have coffee or they're not gonna talk to me a whole lot.

Herbert   But in terms of crafting the book then, how far do you go? When you sit down to write the book what do you have in mind? Do your books usually stem from a concept?

Cornwell   The parts that are deliberate when I write a novel are: I have a crime that I want to use. In *Postmortem* I wanted to use serial rape strangulations. And I wanted one of the victims to be a woman physician because I knew the projection that was going to go on with Scarpetta, that that was going to be hard for her. In *Body of Evidence* I knew that I wanted to use the notion of erotomania where you have this woman being threatened by an anonymous person and she fears for her life. Because I find that very terrifying. In *All That Remains* I knew that I wanted to use the concept of the couple killings and to see how Scarpetta would deal with that. And I also have some ideas of the evidence that I want to use. Now that is deliberate, almost shamefully, because I'm not going to use the same thing in each book. I have to say [for example], "In *Postmortem* I want to use the sparkly residue with DNA and some things like that." "In *Body of Evidence* I'm gonna use the paper ashes and the fibers." "In *All That Remains* I wanted to use forensic anthropology." I hadn't done anything with bones. And it was appropriate for that kind of crime. And I also wanted to do something with firearms because I hadn't really done anything with bullets, with guns. So I kind of pull some things out of my magic hat.

Herbert So your writing and crafting of the book is a process of discovery for you.

Cornwell Exactly!

Herbert It's as if you have a body there and you must determine, just as Scarpetta does, what it all means.

Cornwell Right. Exactly. I write my books exactly the way somebody works the crimes. I am working the case *with* Scarpetta and I am following the evidence the same way [she does]. As I say, it's an amazingly intuitive process with me.

Herbert If your writing process is so intuitive, must you rely on being in a particular mood in order to write or do you work systematically?

Cornwell I generally am pretty disciplined about it. I try to go in there every day but I do have long periods where nothing much happens. Like anybody else I get writer's block and I get in the doldrums or I might fool around with the same 150 pages for four months and then I might write 120 pages in ten days. It comes in spurts like that. I do write my books in spurts but I keep at it steadily.

Herbert Is there a certain kind of writing day that you find most productive?

Cornwell My typical habit is I get up and I work for the morning and then I start taking care of all kinds of other concerns in the afternoon. And I used to write at night but I generally do not write at night anymore [because] I have found, strangely enough, that I scare myself easily.

Herbert If, as you say, you are "living the books," I don't find that surprising! When I read of Scarpetta opening the door to her barbecue with some trepidation I thought, "I wonder if Patsy experiences this?"

Cornwell Oh, I do. A number of times I'll be sitting there at nine or ten o'clock at night and I hear an ice cube drop in the ice machine or the floor creak upstairs and I start getting jumpy and decide, "I can't think about this at this hour. I can't do it." But my normal routine is I generally socialize in the evenings. I usually have dinner with people; I play tennis with people; I have a very busy social life as a rule. Evenings are usually when I get with folks. Writing is an isolating job.

Herbert Do you have any superstitions or fetishes involved in your writing habits? Must you have certain conditions for writing?

Cornwell Yeah, I do. I have to have absolute quiet. And, if you'll notice, back there [in her office] I keep the blinds shut. I don't want to look out a window because I think that will be distracting. So my office is aesthetically the least appealing place in the house. It's not there to look good; it's there to simply [hold] the things I need surrounding me, my books. It's just like a little nest I make back there, with my filing cabinets, my research materials, my books, my weapons, whatever it is! It's all right there. And oftentimes at night I'll keep the door shut. I'll shut myself in there. I feel very secure. But blinds closed, curtains closed: I don't let the outside world in at all.

Herbert I noticed there is a gun in there. What kind of gun is that?

Cornwell A Smith and Wesson .38.

Herbert Scarpetta has a .38.

Cornwell She has a Ruger .38 but she got a new one in the fourth book.

Herbert Do you actually sometimes sit around and just handle the gun to get the feeling of how Scarpetta must handle it?

Cornwell Generally I don't handle it because it's loaded. I keep it there because there's no point in having it in a room where I'm not. And the reason I do keep it is if my burglar alarm goes off—and it has once when somebody tried to get in—I want to have that with me while I'm waiting for the police to come.

Herbert In that incident did someone actually enter your house?

Cornwell They tried but they got scared off by the alarm.

Herbert So this *is* quite a reality then?

Cornwell Sure it's a reality. Richmond's got one of the highest homicide rates in the country per capita. It's always in the top ten. A couple of years ago it was number two. And there are burglaries all over. But you're not sure if that's why someone's coming in or do they want something else. I'm not a gun fanatic but that's just something that I choose to have and I choose to know how to use it and I go to the indoor firing range to practice.

Herbert I expect the fact that you are familiar with the use of a weapon and with the forensic lab work adds verisimilitude to the technical events that occur in your writing. Would you provide an example of an event that occurred in the forensic lab that had a direct impact on your writing?

Cornwell Well, in *All That Remains,* I never would have imagined that a medical examiner would roll the skeleton out of the conference room, onto the elevator, take him downstairs, and prop his hands on a table, but I saw it one day on a table down there and I couldn't believe it! And it made perfect sense.

Herbert   And it also works symbolically in your book.

Cornwell   Yes. Death assisting life.

Herbert   Speaking of death assisting life, what was it like for you to work in the morgue? The first time or times that you went to the morgue did you feel surprised at your ability to face it?

Cornwell   Yeah, I did. I did. I guess I was just so intensely interested and caught up in what they were doing and what they were looking for that I just refused to think about it.

Herbert   I guess it takes a certain kind of stamina.

Cornwell   But I couldn't even dissect worms in the ninth grade! I was squeamish as could be. I couldn't even bait my own hook back then! I couldn't stand any of that. To think that I could put gloves on and pick buckshot out of some body today when there was a time that I couldn't even put a worm on a hook! Don't explain that to me!

Herbert   It seems you have a wonderful ability to rise to the occasion.

Cornwell   Well. I think that's probably true. I am fortunate in that regard, I guess.

Herbert   It must take a certain amount of detachment to handle this sort of thing. I love the expression "beside oneself." Do you feel you're standing beside yourself when you're witnessing an autopsy?

Cornwell   I guess I learned at a very early age to detach myself in certain ways to survive what was going on around me. And it's not that I escape into fantasy down in the morgue but I do think that I can play a role, become whatever it is I need to become to accomplish things.

Herbert   Do you feel you are observing yourself in such situations?

Cornwell   No, I don't think I'm observing myself. I just become whatever I need to be. I become the clinical physician when I'm down there at the table.

Herbert   It sounds a bit like acting.

Cornwell   It is. It's like Sir Laurence Olivier, who would turn around 360 degrees before he walked out on stage and someone said, "Why are you doing that?" And he said, "Because I'm walking into my character." And I do that. I walk into my characters. I'm certainly glad that I have the capacity to do it.

Herbert   Your research, whether or not you have done all of it consciously, lends an immediacy to your writing. And the very straightforward, unembroidered style of your writing complements this.

Cornwell   And this is just something that is God-given, because I don't think you can learn it: I'm very fortunate in that I see things in terms of symbols and metaphors. And I use a lot of similes, and originally I wrote a lot of poetry. And my favorite thing to do was to go someplace and simply write down images. And in fact you'll see this in this fourth book because I have a brief setting in Fort Meyers Beach, Florida.

Herbert   Is the sense of place vital to your work? Must you visit your settings before writing about them?

Cornwell   I went down there because I have to go to a place or in some way witness it. And what I'll do is I'll go there and I'll write images. And you have this scene where Scarpetta is walking along the beach and she's watching sea gulls that are tossing back fish; it looks like they're tossing back shots of bourbon, the way they're doing it. And you have to read it. It reads better than I can say it. (Smiles.) That's a very natural proclivity of mind, to look at things in terms of symbols. I mean I don't even have to think about it: it's just subconscious, like the death assisting life, like the skeleton coming down on the elevator. And you could certainly see that when I studied literature in college because I'd pick through Joseph Conrad or Melville and I could see the submerged metaphors. I mean I really get into that sort of thing. But fortunately that is all tempered by this very strong analytical side, which makes it possible for me to tell the story in a straightforward way like Scarpetta would think.

Herbert   And you have a reporter's voice, too.

Cornwell   It's very matter of fact.

Herbert   This is much more interesting writing than just a straight news story, but even straight news stories can be darned interesting!

Cornwell   Well, sure!

Herbert   When you're a news reporter you have to decide upon the priorities of what to get across and that's what you're doing. I don't know how consciously you're doing this but it must be going on in there somewhere.

Cornwell   It is going on in there but if I try to step back and analyze my own work I would seem very narcissistic. But part of me knows why it works. I mean I don't know how I pull it off; it just seems to be me. You know, the things that Scarpetta is observing: she is very analytical about it but yet there is an undercurrent there that's very forboding.

I'm a person of contrasts and my work is something of contrasts. You've got this kind of very straightforward voice but at the same time it's wildly symbolic beneath the surface.

Herbert   It's a nice tension that you have there.

Cornwell   It does create a tension.

Herbert   The forensic science milieu is certainly rich ground for symbolism. After all, you're talking about pulling the whole fabric of a crime together by finding fibers. What could be better? At first, the question is wide open and then you finally narrow it down and discover the truth based on a physically minute, but nonetheless incontrovertible, shred of evidence. I like the way this ties in with your mission in writing, if I may draw conclusions about your mission. If what you are seeking to do is to pit a small but dedicated team of individuals against the massive problem of violence in contemporary society, it seems fitting that their solutions should hinge on tiny pieces of evidence that can convict criminals whose work is huge in its potential for terror.

Cornwell   Thank you. I like that.

Herbert   The symbolic dimension with which you are able to imbue your work causes it to become something more than brutal. You are not just describing harsh facts. If you can reflect on the symbolism, the terrible truths become more bearable.

Cornwell   Without that clinical side, that poetic part, that symbolism, it would be too much. I try to keep the two in balance.

Herbert   Do you think about this consciously as you're writing?

Cornwell   No. It's just the way my mind works.

Herbert   And your novels also succeed in showing human reactions to events. Would you tell us something about your experience of getting to know victims of crime?

Cornwell   My greatest exposure to the relatives of the victims and to victims is when I've been out with the police. I've been with the police on several occasions when they've actually gone into a house to tell somebody that their son has just been murdered. And so I have seen that sort of thing. Generally I remained silent and didn't have a whole lot to say because that was not my purpose in being there and I didn't want to interfere.

Herbert   I see. Have you observed anything that would seem to be wildly inappropriate in such a situation, like humor, or laughing?

Cornwell   Yeah, you see humor. I'll give you an example. It's not funny and you sort of want to laugh and you sort of want to cry but one day I'd gone to the office and there was nobody else there except one of the people from the Anatomical Division. The Anatomical Division is where the bodies are donated to science; it's downstairs. It's also where the crematorium is. And one of the people who works there said, "While you're here, I need another signature on this particular document." It was basically saying that I was a witness to giving this old man who was there the cremains of his wife, which were ashes in a little, teeny urn. And the little package that held her ashes was put inside of her pocketbook, which I guess had come in to the morgue with her. And here was this old fellow, and his hands were all trembly. And he just said, "Oh! You know that was her favorite pocketbook anyway." I mean no morbidity at all; it was just a remark made. And that was sort of appropriate to him. And you almost wanted to laugh but at the same time— (Pauses.)

Herbert   It probably gave him some sort of comfort.

Cornwell   —but you almost wanted to cry. And I thought to myself, "Now I'd have to be there to see this because it would never occur to me to have that in dialogue. You have to see these things, because you never would imagine the things that people do and say!"

But when you're talking about my involvement with victims, I would say that when I've had an opportunity, I've been very involved with victims. When I was a reporter [in a case where] two little girls who were murdered, with one of them I spent a lot of time with her family. I mean I got to be just a fixture in her house and I would very much get involved in what they were going through and talking with them and finding out everything that I could. I was very interested in that side of it. And I guess I felt I wanted to *do* something and writing was the only way I knew how. And sometimes that helps and sometimes in their minds it didn't help. It's like the cricket: it's the only song I know how to sing and some people like it and other people want to squash me.

Herbert   What an interesting way of putting it.

Cornwell   But I'm not afraid of getting involved with the victims or with the relatives of the victims. I'm not somebody who is going to avoid somebody who has undergone a tragedy; I would probably go to their side of the room but I probably wouldn't do anything unless they want to talk about it. But I feel comfortable with that. I am able to do it because I understand what they've seen and the one truth that I know *without* being the victim is that it's so isolating. Because people don't know how to deal with you if you've even been a victim so they tend to avoid you, thereby making your misery even worse.

Herbert   I think you may have a particular sensitivity to the individual who is suffering. You seem to be able to imagine what the people are going through.

Cornwell   Well, I know what it is to—it's the loneliest thing in the world to be suffering and to have no one that cares, *no one*, and to be frightened and not understand what's going on and there's no voice even in the darkness. No warmth, no light. I can remember when I was a kid and my mother had moved us up to North Carolina. She moved us when I was just turning seven. This was when my father and mother had split up so I didn't see him anymore; he stayed down in Florida. But I can remember the couple of times when [my mother] had to be hospitalized. The first time was when I was in the fourth grade and we were sent to live with neighbors that we did not even know and this was for four months. And it was an unbelievable experience. I was just a little kid; I was nine years old, and I would say, "When is Mommy coming home?" and they would say something like, "Don't ever ask that question because she may never be home again."

Herbert   Oh, my God! Did she have a life-threatening illness?

Cornwell   She had emotional problems. You never did know if she was coming back because of the seriousness of her depression. And I know what it's like to feel isolated, where you feel that your whole life is out of control. I've lost my father and now I've lost my mother and you were so—I mean anybody that showed you the slightest kindness or warmth—it meant so much to you! And that happened more than once when I was coming along, and I suppose early experiences made me sensitive because I can really empathize.

Herbert   Did you have no other relatives who looked after you?

Cornwell   No. I don't really have any relatives. I have an aunt and uncle in Chicago and they were tied up with four sons. And there was no way that we could just be transplanted to Chicago in the middle of a winter. And we were in school. And there were these neighbors and they were missionaries and they'd just come from the Congo, if you can imagine! It was like something out of Charles Dickens. Talk about Victorian, I'm telling you!

Herbert   Were they Americans?

Cornwell   They were Americans and they tried to change me into a little lady. If you've watched *Fried Green Tomatoes*, I was like Iggy, the young girl who refused to wear the petticoat to the wedding and goes to the wedding in a boy's suit. That's me! I was Iggy to a T, if you watch the movie, which is why I loved it so much. And there were

153

these Victorian people that taught me to drink with my pinkie out and I had to wear petticoats and learn to embroider and I wasn't allowed to go out and play with the boys.

Herbert And you had siblings?

Cornwell I had two brothers. They seemed to fare better. I think all of that is harder on girls. Boys, it was OK for them to go out and play basketball. And one weekend they all went skiing. That was OK but not [for] me. This wasn't allowed; I was a girl.

Herbert It sounds like a very difficult time in your life but you have made a strength of it.

Cornwell Well, I think my survival was—I just escaped in my head.

Herbert Into an imaginative world. When you thought about other worlds, other imaginative worlds, did you ever also think about narrating your own life?

Cornwell No.

Herbert I know a lot of authors who narrated their own lives to themselves and put it into the third person.

Cornwell I probably did that to a degree [in] the novel that I worked on in college. It was very autobiographical. But beyond that and before that I didn't really think of writing my life story. But I think I felt a great compulsion to deal with the things that had happened in my life because there were gaping wounds and I didn't know what to do with them. There was just a lot of pain and a lot of anger. When you go through something like that you are mad as hell! You're mad as hell. I mean nobody should do this to you. I mean I'd be mad as heck if someone did this to someone else's little kid. When you're the one you just feel sad and despondent and you have a lot of anxiety and a lot of strange little things that happen to you and you don't know why. You don't understand what's going on. You're not able to react with the sort of appropriate rage that you should. You act out in strange ways. And I've probably acted out in ways that I'm not even aware of. But then as you get older you have to find ways to cope with all of this because it's not going to go away. It's there. And I'm sure I cope with a lot of things through my characters.

Herbert You were saying before that you had to live the lives of your characters. What about the lives of your criminals?

Cornwell I don't live their lives. My regard for them is the same way that my good people would regard them. In fact, I've been asked before if I would want to interview any of these people in prison and I've said, "No." I don't want to get close to any of them. I could not do what

Thomas Harris does, you know, walk around in the mind of Hannibal Lechter. For one thing, I honestly think it would do something to me because I immerse myself so wholly in my characters that I do not want to dine with the Devil that closely, or at all.

Herbert   In other words, what do you do about understanding these characters? If you understand Scarpetta because you've worn the bloody shoes—or what do you call that footwear—

Cornwell   Footies. Or the bloody gloves.

Herbert   —and you know what the feel of a cold cadaver is. But how do you reach your understanding of the criminal mind?

Cornwell   I look at the profiling techniques that are used at Quantico and I've talked to people who have actually interviewed these people in prison; I've looked at some of the cases. These people are not an abstraction to me; they are evil to me and I do not want them to connect with me at all. And I think that when you've seen enough of the signatures of what they do, if you've been to the crime scenes, you've seen the bodies, and you have talked with the profilers, *believe you me*, if you've got any intuition at all you can piece together what you're dealing with and that's about as close as I want to get.

Herbert   Well this brings up the question of that case in Florida where someone may have imitated some of the techniques used by a fictional killer in your work. My general feeling is that that person would have found *something* to imitate *somewhere*. If it hadn't been your murderer's technique, it would have been someone else's.

Cornwell   Exactly! I did not cause this person to do something like that.

Herbert   It is quite surprising that he would have had decent literary taste! One of the things that I wanted to ask you about is the care with which you seem to approach this whole question of violence. You never show the criminal's point of view or describe his sick enjoyment of the crime. Do you consciously refrain from doing so?

Cornwell   Yes, I have very strong feelings about that. I take great exception to people who make violence sexy, and unfortunately some of the men writers particularly are guilty of this. They may have a woman who is raped and brutalized, raped and murdered, or whatever. They show it in such a way that they make it almost attractive. It's sexy. I'd love to walk them into the morgue and have them look at the dead body of someone who's been treated this way and say to them, "Now, you tell me that is sexy" because it's not. It's repulsive. Violent death is not pretty. It is not attractive; it is not sexy. And I think that you add to the problem by describing it in such a way as to make it appear that way.

155

Herbert   If there is a message that you could get across through your writing, what would you like readers on the whole to perceive about your views?

Cornwell   I would like them to feel about violence the same way I do, which is *not* to be desensitized to it.

Herbert   One of the things that comes out loud and clear in your work is the sense that we may not be able to control everything that other people do but what we *do* have is our intellect.

Cornwell   The intellect as *well* as our morality—

Herbert   —and our decency.

Cornwell   Yes, our decency. [Scarpetta] fights the good fight and she uses her intellect and she's lucky that her intellect is formidable compared to most people's. (Smiles.) But I've always said it's really difficult writing about characters who are so much smarter than I am.

Herbert   (Laughs.)

Cornwell   I mean it's a great challenge, constantly. But anyway she also has her decency. We should say "We're not going to fight evil with evil."

Herbert   One of the things that John Mortimer said to me about Sherlock Holmes was that there was a basic decency in Conan Doyle's work. Holmes uses his formidable intellect to further the cause of decency.

Cornwell   That may come from the literary tradition that I am somewhat steeped in as a [literature] major in college, but I think a lot of that may come from my own background—even though I have departed in some ways from my religious upbringing, which was very stringent and in some ways Fundamentalist. It was Presbyterian but more of an evangelical Presbyterianism because it was a Billy Graham town.

Herbert   I was brought up Presbyterian, too, so I remember lots about Job.

Cornwell   Right! But even though I have departed from that in so many ways, there are elements of it that I'll never depart from.

Herbert   When speaking to writers who, like you, are creating novels centered around a puzzle concerning death, I am very interested to learn something about the author's attitude toward death. Do you consider yourself someone who has always been particularly attuned to the fragility of life?

Cornwell   I think certainly with what I have experienced, I am very much attuned to the fragility of life and the randomness of the end of it. I think that I do have a strong sense of the *finalitude*, of the fact that I'm not going to be here forever in the manifestation that I know now.

But the irony is that I tend to be very optimistic about things in general because of knowing this. One: I tend to take advantage of the moment in not putting things off. Because you don't know how long you'll be here, you should "seize the day," as the saying goes. And two: I give as much as I can, as long as I can. I go at it with everything I've got, no matter what it is I'm doing, because I live as if this moment is all there is. It might be, although I don't want to think it.

Herbert   You don't strike me as a morbid person.

Cornwell   No, I'm not a morbid person. I also am convinced this is not all there is. I have seen the bodies in the morgue and you see the energy that is gone. It's like a light bulb that has gone out and I *know* there's electricity, so to speak, somewhere. This thing that has been left behind is not all we are. The light is gone from this person and I know it went somewhere. It didn't just disappear. But I don't believe in streets paved in gold, either, so I don't know what—my feeling is that what we are now is a continuum of something else. I don't want to understand where I was before; where I am now is fine; and I don't understand where I'm going to be next. But I think I'm going to be somewhere. And I have a great deal of faith about all that because I believe we are spiritual creatures. I will say the more I know about death, the more I find in life that is mysterious.

Herbert   I would imagine anyone who has experience of the morgue must wonder about the dividing line between life and death and where it is, really? You can quantify, you can measure, you can do all kinds of things scientifically, but where is that dividing line? Have you witnessed someone actually dying, ever?

Cornwell   I've never actually seen somebody die.

Herbert   Do you think you could face it?

Cornwell   Yeah. I would face it. The closest I've come to it is when I saw a prisoner who'd been executed who was autopsied when he'd only been dead about twenty-two minutes. And with that sort of invasive procedure beginning on somebody like that and it goes through your mind, "Where was the dividing line?" And you start thinking, "Gosh! This is so soon." And it's unnerving. And you think, "Who says that this person's dead? I mean, how much do we really know?" It's creepy.

Herbert   Oh, I see what you mean. The establishment of the fact of death is crucial.

Cornwell   But what does it mean? We know what it means clinically but, you know, some of the tribal people of Africa used to believe that the spirits stayed around the body for a certain period of time and you

157

weren't allowed to do anything to [the corpse]. There have been all sorts of beliefs and I'm not saying that I ascribe to that because I tend to be a little bit more scientific, I guess, but there is so much we don't know!

Herbert   Well, one of the things that runs through your work is that while the psychopaths may have dehumanized their victims, there is a dignity, an unfailing dignified treatment of the cadavers on the part of Scarpetta and even on the part of Marino. One of the things I find reassuring about crime novels is, however realistic they might be about dealing with violence and death, people become important. Even where they were at a certain moment becomes important. Each individual is imbued with significance. It is like something out of Thomas Hardy. You might be on Egdon Heath, a huge expanse, but as Thomas Hardy does in his description of Egdon Heath, the thing that gave balance to the entire landscape is the human figure. That's the kind of thing I think you're doing. You're saying, "Look. These terrible things do occur. There can be a dehumanization of the individual. But to me the individual is significant."

Cornwell   Well, this may come from my background and I did grow up with some decent people. And of course Ruth Graham was one of my greatest influences. She was like my adopted mother. And no matter what you might say about Ruth Graham, whether you ascribe to her religion or not, she is a very decent person and a kind person and a moral person. And it's got nothing to do with the sins of the flesh, whether people drink, smoke, or have affairs: in my book, it's whether people are kind. And she is that. And Scarpetta is that.

Herbert   It is Scarpetta's—and your own—commitment to the dignity of the individual that raises your work far beyond a mere description of violence.

Cornwell   Thank you. Yes. So when you're dealing with the Scarpetta character and you think of all the inhumanity she's seen—one of two things are going to happen to somebody like her. Either she's going to become callous to it and kinda throw in her towel with the aggressor and become a combative, cynical, harsh person herself or she, above and beyond all people, will hold herself to a standard that is much greater than most people's. If she ever changes, I hope somebody will kill her off, or tell me to. If she ever becomes intolerant and unkind and judgmental and all those things that are dehumanizing to other people, then she is no better than the people who bring her her business. Then she's finished in the series as far as I am concerned. She's an example to me. I mean, I a lot of times wish I could handle things as well as she does. [She] is fascinating to me and that is what I enjoy about writing the series: there is always something new that will try her talents and make her grow.

Herbert   And test her essential decency.

Cornwell   Yes, that is so.

Herbert   Can you tell us something about your writing of the Ruth Graham biography and how the writing of a biography is similar to crime writing?

Cornwell   Well, Ruth would probably say that what I did to her was a crime! (Laughs.) I think that writing a biography probably helped to some degree because you can use a bit more creative license in a biography than you do in straight news reporting because you are taking very very old information and trying to piece together a story. When I was writing about Ruth's childhood, in particular, I had to piece together days of her childhood, which was spent in China, although the China of her day no longer existed and I had never been to China, period!

Herbert   You had to collect and follow evidence.

Cornwell   It *is* evidence. You are following the clues of somebody's life and you don't quite have the luxury to do that in newspaper stories. You don't have the time. I learned a lot about human nature doing that. You learn a lot about the tricks that memory plays on people and if you translate such details into crime novels it is very useful. And for Scarpetta, it's more than just following scientific evidence; she is following psychological evidence. And you can't do that unless you understand people. And so the biography was very useful to me in this way.

Herbert   It is an effort to get at the truth of someone's life.

Cornwell   That's exactly right. I mean, how can you get to the truth of someone's death if you can't get at the truth of their life? Like we say in the [Medical Examiner's] Office, "People die the way they live." And in the main that's true. It's not always true but in eighty-five to ninety percent of the cases they died the way they lived.

Herbert   Not when they're innocent victims?

Cornwell   No, but in the main. You've got to understand someone's life to understand [his or her] death.

Herbert   I understand you met Ruth Graham when you were about nine years old. Other than the fact that you honed many writing skills in writing her biography, has she exerted any other influence on your work? For instance, I wonder if part of your portrayal of the Lucy character in your work is based on your relationship with Ruth.

Cornwell   Oh, sure. A lot of times the way Scarpetta deals with Lucy is the way Ruth would have dealt with me. And I even think there's a little bit of Ruth in the Sterling Harper character, even though Ruth isn't crazy like that, but there's a certain elegance in Sterling Harper. I think that when you have people that are very significant in your life you keep writing about them over and over again. They turn up all over the place. It's like George MacDonald, you know, the Scottish preacher who wrote the fairy tales, sort of a predecessor of C. S. Lewis. He had this character called the Wise Old Woman, to whom I dedicate Ruth's biography. And the Wise Old Woman was beautiful and ageless and wise and whenever little kids would get lost in the forest they would see smoke coming from somewhere and there would be this house and there would be this woman. Or a little child would open a door, lost in a house, and there would be this woman. And you only found her if you believed in her. But she turned up over and over and over in his work. And it was really kind of this perfect mother figure in his mind. And so I think we have characters that make such incredible impressions upon us when we were coming along that they get translated in fifty different forms in our work. And if anybody did some huge critique of all of my novels they could not do it without knowing about Ruth. I don't know how else she'll turn up, but I'm sure she will again.

Herbert   It seems to me that an essential component of your work and your personality is this drive to survive and succeed, to take disadvantages and make them into strengths.

Cornwell   Well, some of us can survive. Like black cats, we keep landing on our feet. I've been through enough that some people [in my situation] would almost not be able to put one emotional foot in front of the other. And it hasn't made me bitter. I mean I do have anger over a lot of things. And it's probably part of my energy, part of my fuel.

Herbert   But instead of turning it in upon yourself you're making something constructive of it.

Cornwell   I'm a fighter! I don't know why, but from my earliest memories I was always so *tenacious*, I mean just a fighter. Whether it was playing baseball and being the only girl out there with the boys or whether it was in high school being the only girl on the men's tennis team (and I never lost a match in my four years in high school). I don't know where that comes from. It's probably something in my genetic code that I can't really take any credit for but it's there. My saying has always been, "The best revenge is success." If somebody deals me a blow, then I will take it and make something out of it that ends up being to my advantage. For example, if you went through the experiences that I went through when I was younger, you could let them ruin you. But I've said, "Hey! I've had some experiences that other people haven't and I'll do something with them." It all ends up in some form or fashion in what I write. There's probably nothing that's ever happened to me that I would change. I would not undo anything that's ever happened to me because of what it's given me in terms of insight and experience. Well, I wish I'd never broken my arms, which I did when I was jogging ten years ago.

Herbert   How could that happen while jogging?

Cornwell   Somebody left a newspaper binder on the sidewalk. It was a loop of plastic and I didn't see it. It caught both my feet like a noose and I fractured both of my elbows. And that I wish I could undo. Skeletal damage, anything physical like that that causes permanent problems I wish I *could* undo. But in terms of the rest of it: the human spirit is pretty resilient. Don't ask me where that resilience comes from: I don't take credit for it as if I'm something special. It just seems to be something I was born with. Just don't *ever* say "never" to me!

▶ JONATHAN GASH

Within the crime writing genre, Jonathan Gash is a true original. His novels, focusing on scams in the antiques world, reflect the author's humor, spontaneity, ear for dialects and slang, passion for fetching women, and extraordinary wide-ranging knowledge about antiques from cabinets to nipple jewels. Gash's novels are probably the only place in fiction where you are entertained by a character's repartee with everyone from a snake-toting soothsayer to the lady of the manor, where you can simultaneously discover the truth about human character and the integrity of an apparent antique, and where you may be asked to ruminate upon the environment of greed that surrounds objects of beauty—*and* find that all of this is accompanied by specific tips on "antiques" to avoid acquiring.

In the tradition of antiques peddlers in the streets of London, Gash's antiques dealer/sleuth is known by one name only: Lovejoy. And the name, with its suggestion of fun, provides a hint of the author's approach to the character and to the fiction in which he appears: Gash regards the business of writing as a "game" that provides an escape from the author's long-established medical career as a forensic pathologist and later as a specialist in tropical diseases.

From the start of his career as a novelist, Gash did not think of his work as falling into any specific literary category and, even as he has become well known in the field, he continues to pursue—or be pursued by—a spontaneous method of writing that does not involve plotting in advance or conscious rumination about placement of clues, or development of material motive or psychological motivation. Needless to say, this virtually unconscious method of writing without plan and with scenes written out of chronological order is highly unusual in crime writing and may account for the fact that Gash's work does not read like the classic whodunit. While murder and the solution of a crime or crimes frequently figure in Gash's novels, it is often the case that the central focus of the book is a revelation about human greed, rather than a mere preoccupation with the question of "Whodunit?"

Many will be surprised to learn that Gash does not confine himself to writing the Lovejoy books. Using his birth name, John Grant, he has produced a massive corpus of poetry, including epic poems. Much of his verse is written in the Lancashire dialect that he used as a child. He has also penned two volumes of a trilogy of historical novels, also under the name John Grant. In addition he has authored five plays, which take up subjects ranging from euthanasia to the life of Vivaldi. The latter reflects the author's enthusiasm for music and understanding of Vivaldi's religious training, both acquired during Gash's years of study for the priesthood, a vocation he gave up in favor of pursuing a medical career.

Gash grew up in Bolton, Lancashire, during World War II, the son of a mill-working couple. With his parents at war and at work, his was a wild, relatively undisciplined childhood lived out on grey, cobbled streets and anchored by Catholic faith and the proximity of many loving relatives. The environment was economically depressed and visually bleak, and in his teens Gash was happy to escape into the beauty of the seminary where he received the heart of his education. But after taking his first vows toward the Catholic priesthood, Gash left for London, tempted by the lure of the opposite sex and the fact that he had won a scholarship to medical school. At the University of London, Gash trained in medicine while supplementing his scholarship monies with work on the Petticoat Lane antiques market barrows.

Following medical school, Gash served in the British Army Medical Corps and has practiced medicine in London, Essex, Hanover, and Berlin. He was Lecturer and Head of the Division of Clinical Pathology at the University of Hong Kong from 1965 to 1968, and a member of the Faculty of Medicine at the University of London from 1970 to 1988. Since then he has been a private consultant in infectious diseases.

Gash met and, in 1955, married a nurse named Pamela Richard with whom he has three daughters and several beloved grandchildren. He and his wife live in a thirty-five-year-old house in an East Anglian village of some three hundred homes centered around a Saxon church. Literary and artistic associations surround the village of West Bergholt, which was one of the strongholds of the Roman figure Cunebelin, whom Shakespeare called Cymbeline. The landscape and nearby River Stour were favorite haunts of the painter John Constable, who lived two villages away from West Bergholt.

The Gash home is spacious, bright, and uncluttered. Family photographs abound and the furniture is largely contemporary. Gash says he doesn't surround himself with antiques because to begin aquiring them would be "to invite the progress of the incurable disease which is antiques collecting."

Gash is able to write in any environment and over the years has done a great deal of writing during his train commute to London. But in his home he often pursues his work in a good-sized room filled in part with floor-to-ceiling book stacks that house, among many other volumes, his considerable collection of dialect and technical dictionaries. He will not keep a clock in his room but, to appreciate a general sense of time's passing, he uses a large hourglass that was a gift from his children.

Thanks to the author's generosity, this interview was continued in Fortnum & Mason's, Piccadilly, London; the George Inn in Colchester, England; and in a California art gallery, where I spent a day in Gash's company and observed his pleasure as well as some of his negative feelings about the collection. Among other things professional and personal, Gash discusses the joys and woes of the divvie, an individual who can intuitively recognize a genuine antique, in the pages that follow.

Herbert   While of course you are now well known as the creator of the antiques dealer/sleuth called Lovejoy, I understand you have also pursued a career as a forensic pathologist and as a specialist in tropical medicine. Can you tell us something about how you decided to try your hand at crime writing?

Gash   It makes me worried that I still don't know what a crime novel *is*. When I wrote *The Judas Pair*, my first, and sent if off just on spec, [the publisher] Collins wrote and said, "Oh we're delighted to add you to our crime list." And I spoke to them and said, "*Crime* list?" And they said, "Well, there *are* a couple of murders in your book." And I said, "Well, yes, I know but . . ." And they said, "Well, there's a lot of thieving and stealing and grievous bodily harm." And I admitted, "Well, yes." And they said, "There's a spot of fornication and cruelty and sometimes vicious behavior, one to another person." And I said, "Well, *yes*, but . . . . " And I was astonished. You see, at the time I was a forensic pathologist and I have done the associated work, or I've done myself, over 2,000 postmortems, some for heavily forensic reasons. And I wonder if it was that [I] sighed so heavily, so intensely [because] I have such experience of the consequences of one side of crime that this is why I never write a medical or a forensic novel.

Herbert   So when you began writing the Lovejoy novels, you did not consciously set out to follow the crime or mystery writing formula?

Gash   No, not at all, luv.

Herbert   That fact alone provides insight on the refreshing quality of your work.

Gash   You see, there's so much I don't know about writing. So yes, I was astonished at what a crime novel is because of my unlearned approach.

Herbert   Maybe your more original approach!

Gash   Oh, you're very kind, luv; you're very kind to say that. I don't know what it's like in the United States but here we [medical doctors] are not educated [in subjects other than medicine]. Of course we go into university, medical school for six years' intense study and then we come out *blinking at the light*. Three hundred and ninety examinations, all of which you must pass or be out on your elbow! But the trouble is we don't usually see any other students and I imagine we're singular in this respect. We don't see a student of geology or a student of acting. I mention those two because I couldn't afford to go into students' hostel; I had digs in Drury Lane, two doors down from Shakespeare's White Hart pub. And there were a group of students there and we all shared a pad, as it were. Again, this was in the '50s before that became fashionable, so to speak. I didn't write home and say, "There's a girl here doing astrophysics; and there's two students of dramatic art here." But I learned a great deal from them, I would say, because they were very professional. In fact the girl I was with at the time, she was always being Electra in the dawn and asking, "If I said *that* line like *this*, would it be better?" And I asked myself why I wasn't doing a proper job or studying something more worthwhile because I'd learned that they were doing a much more professional job than I. So I learned a great deal from them. It was the only education I had, really.

Herbert   How many people were living together?

Gash   Seven. Two rooms, you know, sharing two tins of beans and seeing how much money we'd got. Sharing half a pint of beer in the tavern, all four of us.

Herbert   And how did you actually support yourself in those days, if I may ask?

Gash   I had to work part time in the antiques trade on Petticoat Lane barrows to get the money to work through university medical school, in a way that's now no longer fashionable, I may add, and thank God for that! And so I did that in the very early dawn of each weekend, which I suppose is where my liking for antiques first budded, as it were.

Herbert   Aha! So is this the place where you acquired your first expertise in antiques?

Gash   Yes, it was. It was at Cutler Street Antiques Market. I think I was about nineteen when I first got my part-time job there, in the rain, in the early dawn.

Herbert   Is there anyone in particular who trained you regarding antiques? Did you have a mentor there?

Gash   I can't say that I worked for any one person because I wasn't that exalted a personality at the time; I was the real dogsbody. There were usually just myself and two or three drunks and two or three displaced persons—"tramps" we used to call them—and we used to put the stuff out in the early dawn and then they would clear off and I was just left there. And I would run about for about sixteen dealers there. So I would learn bits and bats from any of them. But I don't remember any one person that I was especially attached to. I knew them only by their first names or by their nicknames. None of them [was] ever identified by such a posh thing as a nameboard or a shingle or a special awning like some of the clothes traders were in Petticoat Lane market proper, or the welk stalls or the fish-and-chips places. They had real names over the top. But we had none of that. It was more incognito. I'd not thought of that until you've just asked.

Herbert   It sounds like it was a wonderful way to learn about all different kinds of antiques rather than apprenticing yourself to a dealer in a specialist trade.

Gash   Oh, yes. Indeed it was.

Herbert   This was not an indoor shop, but it was out on the street, on the pavement?

Gash   Completely. And really, some [dealers] would arrive with, say, three or four suitcases filled with stuff; others would arrive with maybe just a small shopping bag, or a small briefcase, even. And one chap only ever brought, I remember, a cutlery box, a mahogany cutlery box, and it was entirely empty. He would have a serious stall. He would pay his five shillings to the market man who came round for the rental for the day, and he would just stand there with this cutlery box completely empty, all the time. He'd just stand there with his trilby on and his overcoat.

Herbert   If you put this in a novel nobody would believe it!

Gash   Ah, yes! It was the real thing, luv. And he never, ever brought any antiques at all. And it was the same box, I swear, three and a half years later when I went for the last time.

Herbert   He may still be there!

Gash   Yes! Absolutely.

Herbert   So when it came to writing crime novels you drew upon your Petticoat Lane experience whereas it appears that right from the start you were reluctant to use the medical setting in these books.

Gash   Absolutely. Everybody was pressing me two years ago to write a medical novel with Lovejoy in it simply because they thought I could use my experience. Which would spoil writing for me as a game, of course.

Herbert   I like your choice of word there: "game." After all, you're writing in a genre that lays an emphasis on the puzzle element, and Lovejoy himself is in a business that is often referred to as the antiques "game," and Lovejoy's approach to life is rather like that of a player in a game. You could say the antiques trade is one of the ultimate gambles, isn't it?

Gash   Indeed it is.

Herbert   How did you determine Lovejoy's name? Did you choose it because it's got that fun quality?

Gash   I don't remember making a conscious choice about this and I don't remember ever having known some great pantomime character who was a barrel of laughs who was called Lovejoy. I've never known anybody by that name. Maybe that's the appeal or maybe the combination of "joy" and "love." I just don't know. I've no idea where it came from. It just seemed so apt.

Herbert   Yes, it is, isn't it? But you must tell me more about how you entered into the writing game. After all, you did establish yourself as a doctor before you became a writer. When you were a child, did you aspire to be just one or the other?

Gash   No, I went into a seminary school and I did two years and four months toward the priesthood. It was a Roman Catholic school. Although my father was a Low Church Protestant, my mother was a Roman Catholic, so I was brought up as a Roman Catholic. Yes, [smiles] I was Brother John for awhile.

Herbert   Where was that seminary located?

Gash   That was in Lancashire, where I was born. I'm a Boltonian. I came from a town called Bolton in Lancashire.

Herbert   That's very near Manchester, isn't it? On the Manchester ship canal?

Gash   Yes, it is. It's a very grim place, Rosemary. But the seminary was *too beautiful*. It was too beautiful, Rosemary. It was too pure.

Herbert   Oh, you must tell me what you mean by that! "It was too beautiful." Was it an unreal life, is that what you mean?

Gash   It was *perfect*. I remember when I was four and a bit my father took me along to the library, to the town library, which was magnificent. It was the only thing in the town that *was* magnificent. And he realized that I could read really well by that age and he wrote on the form that I was five so I could go in the children's library. And so I was thrilled by this and I would take two books home and read them in a day and try and take them back in the same day. I was really that terrible! So to me a library became a refuge from the town that we lived in, an awful slum, and of course wartime it was, soon. So there was this carnage outside and this sacrosanct library inside and it was beautiful, where escape was possible, anywhere! So when I went into the seminary as a young man, all of a sudden there was a complete transition from this slum environment and from the rather grudging learning that one did as a schoolboy. All of a sudden [I could] read anything! Any two words stuck together I would read! In the seminary if you read twelve hours a day, great. And I took no notice of what was on the spine, the index, or the heading; I would read and read and read *indefatigably*. And I had this lucky memory and so I was very fortunate in that I was able to assimilate, by osmosis almost, a great deal of learning in a short period of time, just by a fluke!

Herbert   So this was a major part of your education.

Gash   Oh, yes! And there was this lovely garden. And I remember I saw a fuschia—now, living in a mill town slum as we did, all of a sudden I saw fuschias. I'd never seen colors like it *in my life*. And there were rhododendrons. And I thought it was bliss. And you could smell them. Everything was clean; food was plentiful; you were encouraged to learn. It was absolute bliss. And yet, vaguely in my subconscious, I suppose, was this reality of the slums from which I came. And after awhile I knew I wasn't good enough, morally, because I *knew* the attraction of the opposite sex. So I thought, "No, it's too good to be true: it's pure; it's wholesome; it's marvelous; it's great scholastic learning; *but* . . . ."

Herbert   So you left the seminary because it was too good, too pure? What led you from there to medicine?

Gash   Our town had this competition at the end of school when you were seventeen or so. Everybody's marks went into competition and you took an exam for the purpose of scoring the highest mark. And the ones with the highest marks—a group of about thirty—were offered exhibitions or scholarships to various universities. I was one of these. And on mine I had put "medicine"—quite blindly—I don't know why—and so all the while I was in the seminary I had this knowledge that at any time I could walk out and go and do medicine in London.

Herbert   I see.

Gash   And I suppose that was the catalyst. That was the trigger or whatever the metaphor is. And off I went.

Herbert   Oh, what did your family think?

Gash   They thought it was awful. They saw me going from this heaven to this terrible sin city that is London-on-Thames, and I'm sure the brothers made novenas for me and prayed all the time. So that was how I came to London. But of course I was green and raw and knew nothing about life at all. I was just a raw, provincial youth who came out blinking at the light, really.

Herbert   Let's talk about your family and your childhood for a bit please. Your choice of a career in medicine was a schoolboy's momentary inspiration, you seem to be saying, but what kind of a child were you? Was religion a major part of your life, leading to the seminary?

Gash   Well, my father worked in a mill, in a cotton mill. My mother was a seamstress, again in a mill. Everybody worked in a mill.

Herbert   And did you have a large family of brothers and sisters?

Gash   No, just myself and my older brother. And my father went off to the war at the start of the war of course and my mother was conscripted. [My] mother had to leave the mill [to] be a conductress on the trams, taking miners to the mines and cotton workers to the mills. And so my brother and I were five years old and four years old, respectively; I was the younger. And we were just children left in the house. And we ran wild, I mean hoards of children! There were twenty-seven first cousins of mine all in the same street. And very few of them were girls. We had one girl and we regarded her with great suspicion as though she were something *ectopic* or something really rather strange. She couldn't play football very well and she was no cricketer: we knew that at the age of four! You know, we regarded her as very anomalous.

Herbert   At the ages of four and five you were actually left on your own without parental supervision?

Gash   Oh yes, but there were enough relatives in the street sort of casting an eye over us. But I was brought up more or less by my brother.

Herbert   Who was just one year older!

Gash   Who, of course, *knew everything*. My brother knew everything. I could ask him anything and he would *know*. I remember once—it must have been about 1943 and your nation was well into the war—and we woke up in the middle of the night and there was a terrible rumbling. And of course the house was empty but for us two. And I said to him, "Kid, what's that noise?" And he said, "I don't know, Kid. It's not bombers." Because we knew the sound of bombers, and there were no sirens. We used to go down into the cellar if there was a siren. And he said, "I'll tell you in the morning." And I thought, "It's all right because our Kid knows what this noise is" and I went to sleep. And in the morning we went to the top of the street and there were these huge army vehicles with a white star on the side. They were khaki, rumbling past the top of the street. *Our* troops had no vehicles; they marched. And near us, in the town, on the outskirts of the town were stationed a mixed regiment—it was our own regiment, the Lancashire Fusiliers. And then there was another group of free Poles and Czechs. It was a mingled regiment like that and there were French Canadians, Italians. But they had nothing like this. And suddenly here were these vehicles rumbling and they must have been going past all night and I said, "Where did they come from, Kid?" Because we'd never seen *such affluence*. And he said, "Where did they come from? They're from God." So that was all right. And of course we'd seen our first Americans heading south to join the invasion. But the scale of this wealth of so many vehicles, so much petrol, was beyond our comprehension. But that's an example of the sort of question I could ask him and *know* I would get a very truthful answer.

Herbert   Your brother's name is Kid?

Gash   Brian, his name was. Everybody in Lancashire calls their siblings "Kid." For example a sister would call her brother "Kid." And they would say, "How's your kid?" meaning "your brother."

Herbert   It is evident from the Lovejoy books that you are very interested in regional English slang as well as Americanisms. You are very good with our slang in *The California Game*. Very good.

Gash   Well, you're very kind. But I only discovered America three years ago and I was stunned by the inflections and I enjoyed just listening.

Herbert   A mutual friend, Catherine Aird, told me that you have quite a collection of dictionaries. Have you always been fascinated with words?

Gash   I have this theory of word reverence, which I've never read of anywhere. I think there is, when a writer writes, a reverence for fact like, you know, you can't throw a saddlebag [containing] 100,000 doubloons, each weighing an ounce, as though the saddlebag weighs nothing. So there's a reverence for fact and a reverence for detail and I think that's good, and a reverence for plot and motive, all right. But I think ultimately they all culminate to a kind of word reverence. You just have to examine what you've created [during] that terrible toxicity, that exhilaration which is writing, in which you don't know what's going to arise; you just write blind; you write oblivious, ferociously, and out it comes. You've got to read it and say, "Is *that* word right? Is *that* word right? Is *that* word right?" Every word has to justify its presence on the page or *go*. Or be substituted [for]. *Every word* has to justify itself.

Herbert   I wonder when you know you're doing it right and it's coming right, do you experience the feeling that Lovejoy does when a true antique resonates for him?

Gash   Yes! You don't know the process; you don't know the techniques; but you know it's right.

Herbert   It's magic, isn't it? It's a kind of magic.

Gash   That's right. Yes. (Muses.) I think it is a creative thing. But I think of it as a toxicity.

Herbert   That's an interesting choice of words. Is there a medical connection with that word?

Gash   You know toxicity [applies to] a variety of diseases, a variety of medical conditions, and even some of the states of delirium and delusion are very very closely linked. I hope I'm not being blasphemous when I say this, but it does seem that the physical, physiological state seems to be almost akin to the states of religious exaltation. And writing seems so like that: that you're not there in a way, that you're elsewhere, that you're in the land you're writing about. If you're writing about somebody drowning in the sea; *you are drowning in the sea*, you are experiencing it. And it is almost completely total. I mean you're obviously sitting there on the train writing, or wherever it is, but you are elsewhere. It's a trance. And I think that toxicity is about the nearest I can come to it because it is something so compelling, something so alluring. You are just carried away in a fit of self-delighting.

Herbert   I see.

Gash   And I think also [there is] a kind of ferocity in writing and the kinetic as I call it, the kinetic, which is the form that the book takes.

172

But I think there are only these three things, says me, uneducated in the subject. One is the generative toxicity that is the creative process, the writing, the incoherence, the excitement. It's almost as complete a pull as the sexual. [It's] certainly a dream time. And it has *not* to be planned. It isn't just unplanned, it singularly, must never, *ever* be planned or guessed as to what you're going to do. The second bit is the word reverence, the reverence for knowing that *that* word is the right one. I had a terrible argument with an editor, a word editor.

Herbert   A copy editor?

Gash   Yes, a "word clerk," we call them in medicine.

Herbert   I like that.

Gash   Which rather puts them down, I'm afraid. Now "trial" to me is three of a thing. Like "one" is one of a thing; a "pair" is two of a thing; and "trial" is three of a thing. And I know it's rather archaic English except in local dialect. But it persists in gambling, strangely enough. Why? Who knows? But this word clerk canceled this word, deleted this word from my manuscript.

Herbert   And isn't that an example of using words to enrich the text? Using a gambling term in a book about antiques when antiques are the ultimate gamble, really?

Gash   Oh well, it seems there's a niche there that some academic has to explore, Rosemary! (Smiles.) That's an example of word reverence, my using that word, because the person speaking was a person of that ilk, who *would* use that otherwise archaic word. And the word was right. So I think there's that toxicity of the creative stage, and then there's the word reverence in which the writer goes over and justifies to himself every single word. Then after that he has this terrible obligation to read the work as a total stranger, *as a total stranger.* Maybe he'd have to put it, like I do, aside for a week, maybe a month, until he feels, "Right, I'm ready to separate."

Herbert   I've always liked the expression "beside oneself," which seems to apply here. I mean, obviously it *is* your work and you can't forget that, but you are referring to developing a distance that causes you to be beside yourself, critic and writer working together.

Gash   Yes. And then when you've read it, if it flows and feels right and feels warm and it feels *just*—and not just familiar—then it doesn't matter what errors of plot, inconsequentialities of motive, are there. [Or] what inherent flaws in police procedure there are; then it's right. Now that doesn't mean it's commercially viable. The publisher may say, "Oh, good heavens!" (Grins.) It's the Dickens factor. Not that I compare myself with him! But he knew. Dickens, I'm sure, had that feeling. And that's all I know and believe about writing, Rosemary. I'm sorry; that's it. Sorry, Kid.

Herbert   Does this mean I'm part of your family, when you call me Kid?

Gash   Ahh, yes.

Herbert   I'm honored. I'm very interested in this notion of word reverence. It strikes me as a poetic notion. I understand you have published a few poems using the Lancashire dialect. And I felt very privileged, last night, to be able to read a number of your poems.

Gash   I've got this huge corpus of dialect poems of the past quarter of a century, perhaps sixteen, seventeen hundred poems.

Herbert   I had no idea there were so many. I noticed that some use the Lancashire dialect and some poems contain both dialect words and standard English. I also noticed that you use the dialect even when you are describing the very contemporary experiences of the doctor at the deathbed, or the experience of viewing a scene in an exotic locale like Tripoli. It's fascinating to see language that has such a specific local connection for a particular part of the world being used to reflect upon exotic places.

Gash   Do you mean the incongruity of it?

Herbert   Well, it makes perfect sense to me because it is your natural reaction, your natural voice. A poet has to write in the language in his heart, otherwise it isn't poetry.

Gash   Yes, that is interesting. [I wonder about] the relevance today of this dialect poetry. I could ask myself, "What's the point of writing a poem in Lancashire dialect? You're an anachronism."

Herbert   But you could keep the dialect alive in the written record through your poetry. Do you have any plans to publish it?

Gash   In the coming year I'm going to have them produced in typescript. There is a place in the north where they have a repository and they wish to record these. I published one or two in *The Record*, a Lancashire dialect small magazine, and the following three issues were on my phonetics, letters on my phonetics and letters on my expression! So I was so frightened by that I never published any more. Because I thought, "Here's the white-hot glare of analysis!"

Herbert   Rather, they probably thought, "Here is something lively to sink our teeth into." That's what scholars need. Some of this poetry was obviously drawn from your medical experience where you were dealing with life-and-death questions all the time.

Gash   I suppose it's inevitable, yes. I don't bring medicine into the Lovejoy novels at all except as a figure of fun.

Herbert   Then, is it the the topic about which you wish to write that determines that you use the form of the novel or a poem? What kind of thinking do you go through?

Gash   I don't go through any kind of conscious thinking at all. Not that I know of. I don't plan; I don't plot; I don't know when I pick up a piece of paper if it's going to be a part of a poem, part of a play, a doodle, or the next Lovejoy, or the *finish* of the next Lovejoy. I don't know if it's going to be one of the novels under another name, or if it's going to be an historical essay, I just don't know; I don't care!

Herbert   So you actually get up in the morning and you go down and write something and you do not know what it's going to be?

Gash   Literally, I do not know what it's going to be.

Herbert   What about these "novels under another name," your fiction under the name John Grant? Can you describe how they come about?

Gash   I know this must seem very unlearned and raw to you, Rosemary, because I have no illusions. I just do it all by feel. But I'd got so many letters saying, "You're a doctor; you do forensic pathology still. Why don't you write a Lovejoy in a medical setting?" So I thought, "Well, right." So for the very first time I wrote a synopsis—or tried to. It was going to be a Lovejoy with a medical setting and all that. It was the start of a holiday, funnily enough. So I had some time and I was sitting there and I thought, "I *will* write this!" So I wrote a synopsis—it was a good story—and I started writing, *and as always*, the minute the pen touched the virgin page I knew nothing; I was oblivious; I did not know the next word; I did not know what it was going to be; and I found I'd started an historical novel set in 1827 with a medical setting. Now I never had a vision of writing an historical novel in my life.

Herbert   Isn't that astonishing?

Gash   I wrote like a maniac. And it was 859 pages. So I sent it off to my publishers and they were thunderstruck. And they actually said, "Is that Jonathan? Or is it somebody else?" And I said, "No, it's me." I called it *Sealandings*. Sealand here [in East Anglia] is a marsh that's covered at high tide and it's exposed at low tide and there are roads across these marshes that are called stroods . . . and it's really rather remote. You wouldn't really believe it here in Fortnum & Mason's, Picadilly.

Herbert   I was just up in East Anglia. It's Constable country, isn't it?

Gash   Well, it's very dour. I mean on the face of it—I have a great sense of place; I think I must have a great sense of place.

175

Herbert   And how did you find the writing process as compared with crime writing?

Gash   I loved it. I loved it. Very seductive.

Herbert   Well, one of the things that I wanted to ask you is, once you discover the initial idea for a particular book, does it come from a sense of place or especially with a Lovejoy book, does it stem from a particular scam that you might have in mind?

Gash   I simply don't plan. I wish I could, luv. I wish it could be like that. Well, I *do pretend*. If somebody comes who I think is really tiresome I say to my wife, Pam, "I'm very busy." Now, I may not be very busy at all. I may be just reading, looking for some Latin phrase which is suddenly there in my mind. *So* idle, *so* unprofitable, *so* unconstructed that it's just walking about a room with a few books in. Or fiddling with a paperclip, or just looking out, or just being annoyed because the blue tits are upside down tapping on my window saying, "It's time to get the nuts out, man. It's ten o'clock and you're bumming around in that room with your books again." And I'm thinking, "You little sod!" I may just be swearing at a blue tit and I've said to Pam, "Tell him I'm busy." Now, I know I'm not busy. Even the bloody blue tits know this! But I do that just as a defense. But it's terribly important to me to defend that nonwork. I don't know why. (Pauses.) But I feel guilty about it.

Herbert   I know you say you don't know what will be written until you are actually engaged in the act of writing but in the Lovejoy novels you often develop the theme of the greed that surrounds antiques. Is it valid to say your novels are inspired at least in part by this sense of greed that you wish to discuss? I wonder if some of your books begin with just seeing an antique and imagining someone coveting it.

Gash   Yes. (Pauses. Muses.) It's a sense of outrage, I think.

Herbert   Outrage?

Gash   Do you know, it is true what you say. It's very perceptive but it's a bit worrying to me, what you say because I—do you know I was in York about four or five days ago? I'd never visited York before and there was a piece of furniture [in a house open to the public] in the corner by a guy with the strange name of William Vile. And I thought, "Here we go; have a look at this." This piece of furniture in the corner was *beyond belief*. It was just an ordinary—you'd have *not* noticed it. Anybody would *not* notice it. And I looked at this thing and the cabinet shrieked. And I thought, "What is it about that thing?" And I kept going back to the same room and my friends said, "Well, what are you going back to this thing for? It's very odd, that."

And the curator came up and said, "Yes, this is very genuine; it is by William Vile." And I thought, "What the hell is wrong? There's something wrong and incongruous with this." And I suddenly realized that there was a sort of small ballaster, small knob on the top of each, at the end of each corner where you would open the door and there would be hinges on the little cabinet on top. And I suddenly realized that they were floating, they were suspended above—an eighth of an inch at the most—in other words, there was no hinge. They were just stuck by another piece of wood, carved, of course, from another piece of mahogany, for the side. And I thought, "So really it means that the lock in the middle can't turn because you can't open the door because *there's no hinge*. And that lock would be the place where a hinge would be." And I thought, "For somebody to do that in 1720 is fantastic!" And the curator came across and he was chuckling and he said, "How nice of somebody to notice that." And I said, "How the hell does it open?" I said, "It must be an eccentric pin placed from within." And, "Yes," he said. "It doesn't work until you turn one key." And this thing is taller than me, I mean it's quite six foot odd, there's this lovely cabinet only twelve inches deep, you turn one key and the whole cabinet throbs; five layers, some of them frets, some of them fenestrated, some of them solid doors, just opened at a magical turn of the key. And you think, "This is fantastic. It is *really* enthralling."

Herbert   But think about that, how a mystery becomes unraveled, becomes opened, becomes understood. It's just like that; you have to find that *one* key.

Gash   There's some symbolism there, isn't there?

Herbert   Oh, I like that. You must use that in a future novel.

Gash   Vile was a nice guy, in spite of his name. Now that thing shrieks because when you think people worked with no shoes, no heating, no light excepting a guttering piece of tallow, and they made things to a level of perfection that is *breathtaking*. In fact, it is almost sacramental. It is almost sacramental. At the same time we were looking at the roof of York Minster [cathedral] and there's some place there, beyond the beams and the roof trusses, where the top part of the beams are carved—it may not sound very much just to describe it—but the top part of the beam is an inch from the roof underneath and the beam is four foot wide, so no one would ever see it, ever. No one would *ever* in the life of the cathedral *ever* see this carving and it was done with exquisite care. He carved 120 square feet. His short life must have been expended carving that, night after night, all on his own.

Herbert   But he had the satisfaction of doing it.

Gash   Yes, you see it's love; it's self-delighting. He knew he was doing something useful or maybe impelled by the notion of a Godhead that was going to be delighted. We don't know. And this was 1260.

Herbert   "Self-delighting." I must remember that.

Gash   The other day on the BBC radio there were five writers who had this long discussion about writing, about the nature of creativity. One was David Lodge; I don't know the others. Well, they drove me mad. One said, "Oh, the sheer boredom of it, of getting up in the morning and having to go five hours writing."

Herbert   Boredom!

Gash   And then David Lodge said something like, "Yes, the sheer anguish of it and the sheer stress of knowing you've got to do this." And then somebody else said something of a similar kind. And they all agreed "how boring," "how traumatic." And they were all like Rodin's thinker, you know, sort of sitting there with head on fist in anguish, tormented. And I thought, "What hogswallow!" *I really do*. I think it's absolute bombast. [Writing is] self-delighting. Self-delight is the hallmark to me of all art. It's self-delighting.

Herbert   Isn't that nicely put!

Gash   I think so. I really think it's self-delighting. I know I would write exactly as I do if nobody was going to read it or buy it or publish it. I might *mind*, but I would not stop doing it.

Herbert   To get back to the idea of the key that opens the antique and the key that reveals the truth in a mystery, how do you actually construct your mysteries, if the writing of them is done in segments? First of all, do you write the novel in order, from beginning to end?

Gash   No. Completely not. I never know, honest to God, what I'm going to write. I don't know what is going to come on the paper, and this is a terrible flaw. This is a flaw! You know Ruth Rendell, who lives in one of the villages near where I do; she writes from four till six.

Herbert   In the afternoon?

Gash   Evening. Now Ruth Jhabvala writes until one, all day, from nine till one.

Herbert   But you don't have a schedule like that?

Gash   I do it at anytime, anywhere, any order. And I write everything in longhand. I'm a great believer in ink—I never plan at all like P. D. James does—I find that I have written more and more of this

Lovejoy novel and then I'll cobble it together until finally it's done. [First] I'll rewrite it on the same page in very fine, small handwriting in red ink. Then I'll delete the girl in chapter five because I hate her. But I love the one in chapter eleven so I keep her. And then I go over it again in green [ink], and then in blue, so [there are] four rewrites: each page is like a map of the underground, and then when the whole is revised—

Herbert   Oh, I like that because it is the underground of your imagination, too, isn't it?

Gash   I'd not thought of that. No more perceptive remarks, please, Rosemary. (Smiles.) And then I send it on to a friend and she produces it in typescript absolutely infallibly. And then I get back a pristine copy of the fourth draft and I proceed then to alter it and get rid of problems.

Herbert   Do you use a fountain pen, then, with different colored inks?

Gash   No, I have a Biro for the train, different colors of Biro.

Herbert   So you can also write on the train?

Gash   Yes, really, most of the stuff was written on the train, or in a cafe at lunchtime. An hour commute, it takes an hour.

Herbert   So whenever a writing idea occurs to you you are able to pursue it, unless you're at the clinic?

Gash   Yes, that's right. I did thirteen drafts of *Gold from Gemini*. The smallest [number of drafts] is seven for *The Tartan Ringers*. You know the terrible thing is the finish—I find I've really done no changes at all in the last draft except I've put "and" for "also" in a couple of places. And then I think, "Oh, clearly, I'm just procrastinating. I'm just not letting my little child go off to school." And then I take her to the school gates and let her go through and just bite my nails and so forth. Well, you see, I don't know the writing process. You know Dennis Wheatley is supposed to write 670 words a day and when he's written that he stops. And Jack Higgins is supposed to have a great wall of whitewash and he cuts a girl's picture out of a magazine and he says, "That's the sort of girl I imagine except that I'll shade in brown hair instead of this." And he'll put her there because she's wanted in chapter nine. He'll give a biography. This might take him four months to do. And then he just types it off the wall, in two weeks, sends off the manuscript, whitewashes the wall and starts again. So everybody's different.

Herbert   Isn't that amazing?

Gash   Now. John Gardner's a friend of mine. I'm not dropping names.

I don't know Jack Higgins, I *do* know John Gardner, I *do* know Ruth Jhabvala, I *do* know Colin Dexter, and that's all. But John Gardner has a computer and word processor and it goes up to another computer on another floor where his wife gets it all organized and seems to rectify that paragraphs are properly spaced and all of that and then the next morning off he goes again. And I think, "God, how marvelous these people are! They know what they're going to do; they send a synopsis beforehand to the publisher. How do they do that? Can you imagine?" I never am contracted to a publisher. I just write the book, any book I do. It seems to give me a kind of freedom that I wouldn't have if I was to write [according] to a synopsis. I tried to do a synopsis and it was a total failure.

Herbert Then this accounts for the sense of spontaneity in your books.

Gash I mean, we all have a ritual. The computer that has to be upstairs, and the whitewashed wall, 670 methodical words, and the hours from four till six; I think those are rituals.

Herbert I'd rather you confined your ritual to different colored inks and kept the spontaneity. In discussing your writing methods, I've been longing to ask you about your methods of research. When your novels require antiques knowledge that you did not acquire at Petticoat Lane, how do you come up with the details that you need?

Gash The ramraiders who feature in *Lies of Fair Ladies* are very new, started in 1990. A ramraider pinches a car—always a very high performance car—and drives into a shop window, *crunch*. Out come the lads, you see, hooded and masked and with cudgels, and they batter their way around the shop. They go straight to the area of antique that they're told: "There's a painting on that wall of a girl looking out to sea; don't bring the frigging thing next to it, which is bigger."

Herbert Well, how do you find out about these new methods and terms in antiques?

Gash Well, I know one ramraider who's in prison now.

Herbert How did you meet him or her?

Gash I think it was on East Anglia news that so-and-so was up for ramraiding. And I went to him and asked his advice about terminology. It's fascinating to hear these people talk, 'cause they say—and I'll repeat it if you don't mind—"There ya are in the fucking dark, fucking sirens everywhere; there's a bloody dog barking around trying to give its warning; I've dropped the mace can in case it comes; 'arry's being sick because some of the glass is in his neck; and I'm in the wrong [shop]—in a barber shop!" But [a writer] can't put this down because it's too factually true and he's not told this in court.

Herbert   So you're really getting it from the inside then? Now do you take notes on that?

Gash   No. They wouldn't speak to me then. They wouldn't. But they'll often ask to appear as characters or to have friends appear as characters!

Herbert   So a prisoner may help you with details about the experience of thieving. What about the details of faking all sorts of antiques? How do you find out these technical details?

Gash   As you know, I have a great deal of insolence and what I do is,—and I think I've done this as long as I've had time—if I hear of somebody making something or if I hear of somebody who's done a beautiful reproduction and it's not far away from where I am or if it's in London where I work I would contact them and I would say, "Can I come and see you apply this varnish?" "Can I come and see you make this aigrette [a spray of gems worn on the head] or this beautiful lady's Edwardian decoration?" Particularly I remember the first time I saw a nipple jewel ever being made by a very, very august jeweler in Hatton Garden in London between Fleet Street and St. Paul's. This is the center of our jewelery trade, particularly the precious stones. They're tiny little shops but with an astonishing degree of wealth. But this jeweler was marvelous. He showed me [his work] and I was really quite entertained and I realized then—it was about twenty years ago—people want to tell their expertise. I realized that is a general rule. So after that I had no inhibitions at all! None at all! I just go and ask.

Herbert   So this is something that you do often, even after the fact of writing a book? Is that correct?

Gash   Oh, yes.

Herbert   And are there occasions where you hear of somebody doing something and you just go for general interest and maybe it will be used in a book?

Gash   Yes. You've hit the nail on the head, Rosemary. Those are exactly the two ways I do it. But what I have never done consciously is think, "Ah, I'm going to write about a particular man who's going to do a particular thing such as imitate red anchor Chelsea porcelain, so I'd better go to a red anchor Chelsea porcelain faker, find him out, and find how he forges these things, because I'm going to write it in chapter fourteen. I've never, ever done that.

Herbert   Right! Then you could stick it up on your whitewashed wall.

Gash   (Laughs.) Quite! But it's always in the reverse; it's a very strange thing. I write about the thing and then I think, "I don't know how I knew that" or, "I'd better just check this." And then I go and find it.

Herbert That is fascinating. And what about the Far East? Can you tell me about the research, formal or informal, that you undertook there?

Gash Well, you see I was only starting writing in Hong Kong. So I never consciously went about doing any research at all at that time. It was a very odd thing because I was really very comfortable in the Far East, but I also longed for home. What the Far East gave me was the impetus to write, to write about the world I knew at home.

Herbert What about the impetus to write drama? Could you tell us something about your play *Terminus*, for example?

Gash Yes, well, it was rather a gloomy piece. I wrote it for the Chester Festival and it was [set] slightly in the future where euthanasia could be provided by a local council's agreement and it was a discussion of that. And a fatal infectious disease was sufficient grounds for a "terminus" certificate to be provided, which was my name for the euthanasia certificate. And so it centered on the arrival of somebody as a substitute member of such a council having contrary views to the council who were just a little too free awarding certificates of terminus to virtually anybody who applied. And although it was a short play it was very well received.

Herbert You've grappled with the question of euthanasia in your poetry as well.

Gash It's really difficult. I don't know how much my Roman Catholic upbringing—and you know I don't subscribe to faith anymore—actually is a hidden determinant of my attitudes. Because I remember well a woman saying to me when I was working in Exeter thirty years ago, "My husband's really in no fit state for anything. I can't see why you don't finish it." And I said to her, "You want me to kill him? Don't ask me! You can kill him just as well as I can." And I was shocked at myself afterwards, at the cruelty in the answer, but [it's] the same answer that I give now when I sit on [medical] panels that talk about the euthanasia problem.

Herbert And then in your poem "Letter From a Woman Requesting Euthanasia" you reflect on this again.

Gash Yes, this was a person whom I had known some years before [who had] looked me up in the medical register—and here came this letter and I was shocked because here it was presented for the very first time without there being the defense of anonymity. And my feeling is, well, it shouldn't be me. Don't ask me, because I won't do it. I can't see myself ever saying "Sure, I will." The reason being: one: it is a moral imperative. Life is life. Two: we can't be trusted. I can't be trusted and the reason I can't be trusted is in the poem. Because here was I; all things cut and dried; when suddenly somebody whom I knew and had loved, out of the blue wrote, "If you remember me, I am she who—and I am now dying and I'm frightened and I need your help to die. Could you please do it for me?" Up until then I was sure that my football team was going to win; I was sure that my way was better than anybody's; I was sure that my garden was the most pretty in the kingdom; and all of a sudden all of that came unglued and it was as if I'd been living in the emperor's new clothes. All of a sudden I was on sand, everything was quicksand. It was as if I couldn't drive a car anywhere; I'd forgotten the way home. It was for day upon day upon day the most appalling experience. Because it's as if love had reached across that period of time. And so I wrote my received judgment that I'd got from all kinds of religious authorities, medical authorities, political authorities, social imperatives, tra la, tra la, but I felt I'd been stripped of them and I just did not know which way to turn. And I realized that I was not infallible; the judgments I had were simply an enactment of other people's received opinions given to me.

Herbert   But you can see how it could be a loving thing to do.

Gash   Oh, terribly, yes! That was the terrible thing, absolutely.

Herbert   I'd also like to explore your attitude toward death in general. After all, your Lovejoy novels, like so many crime novels, sometimes do revolve around a question of murder or death.

Gash   Well, medicine causes one to be very reflective and not a little shocked—in fact, gravely shocked—by the transient nature of life and the utter finality of the death process. The other thing that has undoubtedly had an impact on my writing is the sheer stupidity of the social occurrences and chance events that lead to accidental death. A quarter of a century ago I was doing a postmortem on a soldier of the NATO forces, in Berlin. He had sunk into sleep, after a bout of drinking, on what he thought was a wooden bench but in fact was a river step. The water rose just a few inches. It didn't cover him; it only covered his breathing as he was lying face down on the step. He drowned quietly and somnolently; his body was drowned but dry. And you think to yourself, "How was it he hadn't gone with his friends instead of being alone there? How frail is our cling to life!" I find this sort of accidental death more upsetting than carcinomas and cancers for which sometimes we can do something and sometimes we can't. I spent the formative years of my life in a seminary. But finally I had to acknowledge that the practice of medicine was really incompatible with the idea of a personal God.

What a fluke life is! This thought is very formative to me and to my notions. When Lovejoy stands over the body of a dead person I know very well his mind. He stands there and he's so, so furious at the whole process. And he says, "I don't know what the gods are playing at sometimes." If there is a God it seems to be the God of lottery, a God of dice, of chance. I share his [Lovejoy's] mind. I do.

Herbert   John, you do write in different forms, such as the crime novel and short story, the historical novel, fiction, poetry, drama, and essays. I'm wondering if you find that in the crime novel you can express everything that you want to say about Lovejoy, about human character, or if there are limitations in the crime novel that lead you to turn to these other forms to express other things?

Gash   The bald answer is "Yes." And it's a very grievous, sad, and intensely awful "Yes." Bearing in mind—you know now, you know the way I write: I just write anything, just watching it come. . . . But then *when finally it takes a pattern*, yes, there, then it's evident, the limitation, the stringencies, the crime novel imposes. There's a limit to how much a jocular—if that's what Lovejoy is—casual—if that's what Lovejoy is—shady, antiques dealer with no money—there's a limit to how much he can say about serious issues. So certainly events have to say it for him, but there comes a time very definitely in a lot of episodes in my books where I can't say all that I wish to say. And that is an—I'll use the word again—appallingly grievous and very distressing thing.

Herbert   What is it particularly about the crime novel that you find limiting? Can you say some of these things in a noncrime novel?

Gash   Yes, you could. And this is why I've turned lately to novels other than just the crime novel, under the thin guise, for example, of romantic historical fiction. Well, about the crime novel, I think what pins you to this is that it's got to be entertainment and it's got to be entertainment à la Agatha Christie. You know my views on her, that there is only one mystery about Agatha Christie and it's not that she wrote only English cozies, where the doctor has no patients, the colonel has no army, the judge has never sentenced anybody, the lawyer doesn't go to work; the only people who ever go to work are the maids and they work with a feather duster. The chauffeur goes to work with an elegant rag and that's it; he's never oily. So it's all caricature, and it's all cipher, and it's great! They're all cardboard cutouts and you can read it with absolute safety and it *never makes your breathing funny*. No, her cleverness at this is not the mystery of

Agatha Christie. The problem about Agatha Christie for me—and it explains a lot about my answer to your question on the crime novel—isn't whether, why, how, what her reasons were that she ran across to Harrogate and vanished for ten days and caused an uproar when in fact her husband was fed up with her and was with another popsie. OK, that's happened before to plenty of people. That isn't a mystery. That isn't the mystery of how deep she was; she wasn't deep, except in one regard and that's [revealed in] the story *Philomel Cottage*. Now in *Philomel Cottage* [there] was this woman alone in a cottage, there's this maniac out in the countryside. You can read this story knowing that nothing will come amiss. Well, she was asked to put that on the stage and instead of defending it and making it still squeaky clean, no trickling of sweat down the back of your neck, instead she refused to do it herself and gave it to a young chap, Frank Vosper, who was interested in the violence that can sometimes come from a confrontation of two people and he made it into a play that still makes your breathing funny in the second act, and you think, "Good God, don't go there! You'll get killed." He wrote it in 1947 from her story, her squeaky clean, boring *Philomel Cottage* story, with all the good attributes that a pantomime has. Of course, because it's Agatha Christie, it's a jolly little romp. But he turned it into *Love from a Stranger*, which *puts the fear of God in you*. And I still can remember in the Lido Cinema when I was a lad seeing *Love from a Stranger* and hearing a gasp and the whole place shook as people grabbed hold of the arms of their seats—so something happened there. Why did she not defend that one thing? She defended everything else. She went and saw things; if something was going to be transcribed she was meticulous at editing things; she deliberately wrote vicious people out of her stories; everything was done by simple deception, explaining motive. Hence my dislike of anything that's called motive.

Herbert   Material motive, generally, rather than psychological motivation?

Gash   Yes, oh yes. Because material things could be weighed, could be assessed, could be judged. It's very much schoolgirl fiction; it's very much *Priscilla of the Lower Third*, I think, Agatha Christie. Not to knock her. She did marvelous things. But how does this relate to your question about limitations of the crime novel? In this regard: that stringency is unreal; it's the unreality of pantomime, it is the disreality of the story as a tale. Now you can be very, very powerful with a fairy tale. And God knows, don't knock the story of *Goody Two Shoes*! It sounds silly to say but it's run into 248 editions so far. So don't let's knock *Goody Two Shoes*. People love it, everybody knows the story; and its familiar and safe. Some things you cannot write about in an entertainment. [For instance] a child murder is something you can't write about. I know that Joseph Wambaugh will write in this way. He will make it a panto, make it an Agatha Christie, and then all of a sudden it will not be because of something that harks back to chapter one or two and then all of a sudden in chapter 38, *bong*! You know that there's something horrendous going on. Mario Puzo does this in what is his greatest novel, called here in England *The Dark Arena*. It is a terrific story. And he can make it look like a safe, English cozy and then all of a sudden in page 71 [snaps his fingers] he will say something and you think, *"That's* what is going on! There is something wrong." And that is brilliant writing and you suddenly realize that from now it's doom and the rest of the book is absolutely grim. It's not a trick; it's *flair*. It's not device or technicality nor is it in fact a knowledge of every single trick of rhetoric in Peacham's 1577 *Garden of Eloquence*, all beautifully listed, telling you how to do it. It isn't any of that. It's actual *flair* in writing and and it's something creative and he's done it entirely by instinct. Why is that book brilliant and *The Godfather* really rather dull? Because he sacrificed flair for technique and allowed the stringencies that will please the editors and please the public and please the sales merchants. That's absolutely it.

So to summarize and answer your question properly, the crime novel has to entertain and it has to entertain in a vein that is now, unfortunately, sadly, traditional. At it's most kindly, banal, affable, pleasant, it is the English cozy, I think you call it in America. In its uttermost it tries to bring in something really rather sinister under the cloak of a crime novel of that pattern, rather like Ruth Rendell does. But it's confining, terribly confining. Which means that there's a temptation here at something rather seductive. Because if you were to recognize this early on and think, "God, this is irritating!" then you know that your duty is to leave it in part at least and devote much of your time henceforth to writing something that will not have that confinement, will not have those chains. So you have to say, "Right, this is going to be creative literature to assuage that need, to assuage that appetite, that thirst for something to deal with a greater issue." And I find more and more and more that when I finish a novel, just like now, I find to my horror it deals with something repellent and appalling in society now. So then the question comes, "How much can I tone [this] down?" I find myself having to think about this and saying, "How can I get by under the cloak of this casual buffoon, this opinionated, hopelessly disorganized bum called Lovejoy and keep those terrible things from pointing up, highlighting this terrible appalling cruelty that's being enacted in our affluent society today?"

Herbert   It seems to me that the answer to this question for you lies in your humorous treatment of Lovejoy. If I'm correct, the humor serves to help you to tone it down, to make it fit into something the publishers are going to accept and that the readers can read with some of their expectations being satisfied regarding a crime novel. The light treatment of Lovejoy's character and foibles makes it possible for him to toss off quite telling remarks in the midst of banter. You've got just the right character for keeping it light. Lovejoy demands lighter treatment of things even though he can say things that cut very close to the bone.

Gash   Yes, that's it. That's it in a nutshell.

Herbert   I wonder, too, if you feel confined by the necessity in a crime novel of having to keep a secret from the reader? I talked to Julian Symons about this and he said that one of the problems for the crime novel that keeps it from being a literary masterpiece is that the writer has to keep a secret from the reader unnaturally long as compared to what might be done in a so-called mainstream novel. The writer is keeping a secret about character from the readers in order to conceal "whodunit."

Gash   I think you're right! I think Julian is right.

Herbert   Do *you* have to think consciously about keeping secrets? And is that a confining thing for you?

Gash   Not consciously, no, because I don't write by plotting. I don't do that. I can't. I wish I could. But I can't do it. So mine are not really so much whodunits, I don't think.

Herbert   I agree.

Gash   But I think Julian's right, that *that* is a terrible confinement if you're going to write like that.

Herbert   In other words, the author is keeping secrets about character for reasons of formula rather than for reasons of art.

Gash   Yes. I think you're absolutely right.

Herbert   The author may know that really here is the place to reveal a new aspect of character from an artistic point of view but the mystery writer cannot do so because such character revelation at that stage will tell too much about motives or motivation. However, I think it *is* possible for a crime novelist to be able to construct a book where the revelations about character are given for reasons of art and reasons of craft *at the same time*, where the timing just works. In that case I think we get the very superior crime novel, the one that breaks the bounds while staying within them.

Gash   Yes. Timing is the essential element there, Rosemary.

187

Herbert   Now with Lovejoy, he discovers his revelations in his own way, whether it's divining the truth about an object of art or about someone's character. Can you provide any insights into his typical manner of going about this?

Gash   He looks at the small detail, luv.

Herbert   It is the small detail that is telling, isn't it? He is aware if a bit of veneer is a new piece added to an older object, therefore the piece does not have complete integrity as an antique. He can determine whether a new layer of varnish on a painting indicates that recent work has been done on it. The same thing with people. His approach to discovering the physical clues to antiques scams and to understanding human character is similar.

Gash   Yes, that's true! He notices the small falseness that resonates— about a cabinet or about a person.

Herbert   When we were in the museum together, you sensed, much in the way Lovejoy does, something false about that room of furniture, didn't you? It upset you.

Gash   (Shudders.)

Herbert   I wanted to ask you, how early in your life did you develop this sensitivity?

Gash   Yes, it's not always nice, luv. Like, well, today in that library it was—I can't even—it was awful, awful. And you know even passing [the room]. (Shudders.) And you know the terrible thing is that the more you become aware of it, it multiplies and resonates and compounds as though something goes loose on a boat; it gets wilder and wilder until finally the bit falls off.

Herbert   You're very wise just to leave when you feel that way.

Gash   And it's hard even to walk past the door. It's very distressing. But it's as long as I can remember, as long as I can remember.

Herbert   For as long as you can remember you've experienced such things? But in the circumstances in which you grew up, were you exposed to much in the way of art and antiques?

Gash   There were so many things that were perhaps religious devotional things.

Herbert   It must have been quite alarming to experience these feelings if you had no context in which to put them.

Gash   But I didn't know, you see, because I was unlearned and I didn't really know that we all weren't like that. I didn't know.

Herbert   Then you didn't feel alone about it? You felt that this was something that other people experienced?

Gash   No, I didn't make that assumption but no, it's a terrible, alone thing, and gradually I learned in my childhood that other people didn't seem to feel it. Other people weren't strangled by the beauty of one candle on each side of the altar at six o'clock in the morning when at the age of seven in my clogs I was serving mass in a church. The beauty of the candle in there in the black dawn was beyond description. And it still is, I think, *it is beyond description* to a child. But at the same time you were shivering with cold and it was terrible if there'd been bombing during the night around the church. So it was a terribly weird world. But it was the only norm you lived. It was the only norm I knew.

Herbert   Now you have a context and then you did not.

Gash   That's right. Oh, yes, I think so; that's well put.

Herbert   Did you never tell your brother about these feelings you experienced?

Gash   No, no. We did not speak of this kind of thing. I didn't want to say, "That is beautiful." I remember I found a budgerigar feather in the back street and I had never, ever seen any kind of color in my life like it. It was this *blue* in the street—they were like loaves, these cobbled streets, great pieces of black stone with dirt in between—and there was this thing on them and I'd never seen anything like it. And I picked it up and I took it home to my mother—I must have been about five—and I said, "What is it?" And she said, "It's a budgerigar feather." And I saved it for years, quite until I left for medical school.

Herbert   When, as a child, you experienced intense feelings about objects in your environment, what did you do when you were too young to articulate this? Now you have language to help you. For instance, you use the wonderful word "resonates." But what did you do then?

Gash   Yes, you're chained as a child. You don't know how to react.

Herbert   This afternoon you didn't have words, either, for that feeling.

Gash   (Shuddering.) No, that was awful. *Malaise.* And it was terrible. But at least you can explain it. But when you are little, you don't have that and all you can be is distressed. You just be distressed.

Herbert   What kind of an emanation are you getting through something like that? Is it a sense of an evil or—

Gash   Oh, something terribly asynchronous, something terribly resonantly out of synchrony, like, for example, colors. I would be made physically sick with juxtaposition of colors that seemed clashing and incongruous and atypical and erroneous.

189

Herbert   The feeling is also on the emotional level?

Gash   Oh, yes. You would feel terribly distressed, you would be absolutely sick.

Herbert   Is it like the feeling you experience when you see certain blues next to red and it makes your eyes sense that the colors flip at each other?

Gash   Yes, they clash. [When I was small] at times it was awful. When I was little I used to serve mass. I'd knock at the vestry door, the rectory door at six in the morning and they'd let me in and I would have to go through the church, clanging all along the way in my clogs, through the back and down a sort of corridor with doors off and alcoves and rather like a late nineteenth-century idea of what a monastery cloisters would be but very, very narrow. And in the alcoves there were left statues they used in processions, little tubs of holy water that had been blessed, and pitchers of this, and pictures of that, and I hated going past the one [alcove] where the crucifix, a huge crucifix, quite man-sized, was lain, just lain at an angle like this. There it was and I was really afraid because I had to go clanging down this corridor all on my own waiting to serve mass.

Herbert   How old were you at this time?

Gash   Six and a half.

Herbert   And did the crucifix engender the same kind of feeling of dissonance for you?

Gash   Yes, that was *exactly the same* and I don't know to this day—I've explored it in my mind—whether it was juxtaposition of all those garish colors, which was so typical in Spain and in Italy, you know, with the heart externalized on the sternum, you know, this kind of gruesome thing—and it's so graphic in the Latinate countries. Is it the juxtaposition of colors or a combination of that and morphology? I don't know, luv.

Herbert   Or even the fact that it was lain on a strange angle?

Gash   [That, or] the fact that I was alone in this whole church that would hold two thousand people at a pinch and I knew that I was going to have to stand there for a half hour changed into my little cassock and little lace collar waiting for the priest and I would have to have the altar ready, the candles lit, and the altar cloth off before anybody came. And you could just hear the pigeons cooing in the church spire and that was it, and the occasional distant hooter of the mill and the constant ch-ch-ch-ch of the mill looms in the distance, of the night workers. And you stand there and you think to yourself, "Is it a whole mixture of the whole thing that called out to be gruesome or was it the simple fact that there was the statue of a dead bloke pinned to a stick?" (Shudders.) It was something more. It feels the same, the same distress, the same malaise.

Herbert   Do you think it had something to do with what was put into the making of it, somehow; is this conceivable? I mean you have said in your writing and in conversation, "That's not by a particular painter, it's a fake, but it's an item that's been made with love which has its own beauty." Is it conceivable that you could have a sense of something negative going into the making of the object?

Gash   Yes, maybe, maybe.

Herbert   In other words, if it's a wonderful thing, it's a wonderful thing, no matter who produced it.

Gash   And you see this is the question that you've asked more gracefully. To me that really doesn't matter so much. All it is is a difference of attribution. We'd like to know that *that* is by Rembrandt or *that* is by Richard Wilson or *that* is by John Constable.

Herbert   So the question for you is not merely "Is something a fake in terms of attribution?" but "Does it have a truth in itself?" And perhaps there is something you're feeling about some of these objects like that crucifix. Perhaps the person made it with some kind of joy in the terror. At six years old, if you were reacting to something about that antique crucifix and not just the *situation* of being alone in a cavernous church with a garish wood carving, it could not have mattered to you whether or not the crucifix was genuinely by a certain woodcarver; it was something else going on there. And the reaction you had in that room today—it seemed to me that it was not just a matter of "There is something false here." It seemed to me that it was something stronger than that.

Gash   Oh, yes. That's right.

Herbert   It was a sensitivity to something in there that was—

Gash   Quite anomalous.

Herbert   And what authors do in crime writing in very different ways— and you especially in an extremely original way—is to deal with different kinds of truth. And I wonder if there's a sense for you of motive in how things are fashioned? And if Lovejoy sees that.

Gash   Yes, yes. Maybe, maybe. Do you know maybe that comes nearer to it? Maybe it does, though, luv. Maybe it does. (Pauses.) Because it offends; it *offends*. Maybe a big element is the recognition of the scorn of the faker.

Herbert   Ah!

Gash   And the sheer insolence of [him]. There is an arrogance, and a scorn.

Herbert   And then there's the question of greed.

Gash   And that is the thing that compounds their scorn 'cause they think, "I've made a living out of your gullibility." And that really is a big element. Fakers often say so. What intrigues me is that when the plug is pulled on their terrible act they very often die very, very quickly.

Herbert   Do they?

Gash   Oh, yes.

Herbert   Or maybe nothing is real—

Gash   —anymore. Anymore. They had to face that they'd no papers on which to hang their reality, their vision. I really think you've hit on something and you've gone further in questioning accurately than I have in providing an answer—

Herbert   Well, I'm really very fascinated by this.

Gash   —maybe because I shun the question. I shun putting questions like this to myself. I just react superficially maybe to shut people away from the truth.

Herbert   Well, you don't want to examine things too much. I don't think any writer should.

Gash   Do you feel that?

Herbert   I think there's a level beyond which you don't want to go because you need your unconscious.

Gash   *I* believe that, too. I believe that.

Herbert   You need the surprises.

Gash   Yes, you need the unconscious element. That's absolutely true.

Herbert   Just think about the word "divining." What a word! Or being a "divvie." It says something right there.

Gash   It's an old one, I don't know how it came to be but strangely in antiques a number of terms have become "marsupialized," so to speak; they've become enshrined in the lacunae of the past and somehow they perpetuate. But you asked me earlier about writing stemming from a sense of place.

Herbert   Yes, I did. And I also wish to know if you share with Lovejoy an uneasiness about the countryside.

Gash   The countryside does worry me a wee bit because I am a town man. Although I fell in love with it right way. In East Anglia the countryside doesn't look much but in the dark hours—not that I'm scared of the dark but—I mean—(Pauses.) It's astonishing how primitive it is and how near everyday normal existence is [to] primitive rural culture. For example, I'd written this book *Moonspender*. And I found I had written about witches. But I'd never met a witch. And I thought, "How extraordinary." So I went up to the tavern in our village and [soon I discovered] the actual interface between suburban living and something really rather primitive. It took three visits to local taverns, not shouting about it or anything, but I let on I was writing one about witches. And I swear it was the third tavern that put me on to a witch.

Herbert   Ah, that's a significant number, three!

Gash   Now don't get into numerology please! And one said, "Oh, you need Elsie down at the music center; she's a witch." And I met her next day. And she said, "If you come up to my house tonight I'll show you the other witches. There are eight of us." And I met my witches' coven! Now, that took about twenty-four hours to find that. And I showed them the bit I'd written. And they fell about, laughing. And they introduced me to some of the rituals in Pillsbury Ramparts. I was thrilled about that.

Herbert   Isn't that wonderful, though! That sort of anecdote causes me to think about the overall appeal of the Lovejoy mysteries. Lovejoy is special because he provides a window on the antiques game, because he takes us into other worlds like Hong Kong and even darkest, bewitched East Anglia, and because he observes and even experiences the fears and foibles and ecstasies that have always been the human condition, no matter how "civilized" we think we have become.

Gash   You're very kind, luv, you're very kind. I think Lovejoy would feel complimented.

194

▶ REGINALD HILL

Edgar Allan Poe himself would have envied Reginald Hill's abode in Ravenglass, Cumbria. To reach the rambling Victorian vicarage one travels over winding roads obstructed by herds of sheep that have broken through the mists and tumbling stone walls of England's dramatic Lake District. Nestled in a hillside, with a view of the Irish Sea in one direction and the literary landscape celebrated by Wordsworth and Coleridge in the other, stands Hill's well-kept former vicarage, which he shares with his wife, Pat, and two Siamese cats. The latter contemplate the passing herons and put the lie to Hill's assertion that his walled garden, as overgrown yet inviting as Frances Hodgson Burnett's "Secret Garden," has been kept in a natural state as a potential sanctuary for the birds.

Actually, the fact that Hill's secret garden remains untended reflects the author's priority to cultivate a writing career that has spanned twenty years and produced thirty-three novels that fall into the categories of thrillers, science fiction, and, of course, crime writing. Under the pseudonym Patrick Ruell, taken from his wife's maiden name, Patricia Ruell, the author has written eight thrillers that combine elements of the mystery with international intrigue. As Dick Morland and Charles Underhill he has explored futuristic problems in four novels. And under his own moniker he has produced his best-known work, nine nonseries mysteries and a dozen novels featuring two mismatched Yorkshire policemen: the brilliant, coarse, egotistical Andrew Dalziel and the sensitive, university-educated Peter Pascoe. In the slim novel *One Small Step*, he proved that he could take the Yorkshire policemen to the moon and blend his factual and futuristic talents, "even if it was with my tongue in my cheek," says Hill. Recently the author has introduced a new series sleuth under his own name: Joe

Sixsmith is an unemployed lathe operator of West Indian extraction from a down-at-the-heels suburb of London, who has invested his unemployment monies in establishing himself as a private eye. The new series will provide Hill with a balance to his often darker works featuring Dalziel and Pascoe and offer him a fresh focus for his energies between the writing of his novels featuring the Yorkshire policemen.

Opening the door to his stone-walled garden, or relaxing in his study with its view of the Isle of Man, the tall, athletic man with sparkling pale blue eyes and an easy laugh seems an unlikely person to spend his days ruminating upon murder and the dark side of human nature. The son of a professional football (soccer) player and a factory worker who valued education, Hill won a scholarship to Oxford and followed his studies there by becoming a schoolmaster and then a lecturer in a teacher's college before he was able to take up writing full time. But while the circumstances of Hill's life have been almost "placid," his imagination is a different story. Inspired by a haunting near-tragic airgun incident and by his keen awareness of social ills and human disappointments, Hill marvels at how chance blesses some and curses others. Although he says he is not a crusader, and his books certainly live up to the "crime writer's contract" to provide entertainment and surprise to the reader, over the years his crime novels have deepened and proved the author to be an astute witness to our times. With laughter and earnest thought, Hill explains how the quiet exterior of his home and persona harbor a lively mentality that is able to identify with and speculate on an extraordinary mix of characters and their experience.

Herbert   The British lawyer and expert on crime writing Martin Edwards has said that your two Yorkshire policemen, Andrew Dalziel and Peter Pascoe, "defy the law of diminishing returns which applies to most series detectives." I heartily agree with him. I'd love it if you would let us in on as many secrets as possible regarding the creation of these characters and your ability to maintain and even increase their appeal to readers.

Hill   Well, they are two very different, even contrasting characters on many levels.

Herbert   Did you set out to pattern them on a Holmes and Watson model, with Dalziel rather more concerned with the intellectual challenges of getting the job satisfactorily puzzled out and Pascoe more centered on helping people in a consciously caring manner?

Hill   I think the way in which Pascoe feels for the underdogs, and Dalziel, too, in a way—in very different ways, they both have very, very strong objections to the abuse of privilege, to the assumption of superiority, to the pretensions of birth, and class, and rank, and wealth and these are things which are very much a part of my own makeup. And yet I'm not a political animal in any practical sense whatsoever. I've never joined a political party. Like Groucho Marx, I don't want to belong to any party that would have me as a member! I'm not even a member of the Groucho Club. If I do anything politically, I do it in my books and they don't make an overt political statement because I think, "That way tedium lies."

Herbert   Very wise.

Hill   And if politics is about people in a social setting I think that the best way to do justice to all is to help the weakest. And I hope that this comes out in the books. And I really do feel that this is basically what policing should be about, or at least a good bit of it. And Pascoe feels this; I mean this is Pascoe's motivation [as] a university graduate joining the police force. But I don't overdo that. I don't want him to come across as a kind of earnest missionary type because he is as uncertain about himself and his own virtues as I think I am.

Herbert   It sounds like you identify particularly with Pascoe; you are motivated to help the underdog but you don't want to make too big a deal of it. In what other regards do you identify with your sleuths? Do they reflect any aspects of your own personality?

Hill   They probably do. Neither of them *is* me but I think there are certainly bits *of* me in both of them. And one would like to say, "Yes, the Dalziel side, that's the artistic, creative side." But perhaps it isn't.

Herbert   Well, all writers play God on some level.

Hill   Yes, well, Dalziel *literally* played the role of God in my novel *Bones and Silence*, as you know.

Herbert   Yes, he was talked into taking the role in a contemporary production of medieval mystery play. A perfect role for a man with his large ego! But please tell me more about how your series sleuths accompany you—in your imagination—through ordinary life.

Hill   You see, I think especially if you use the same characters over and over again, and all the time when you're writing you've got to make their response proper to the situation based upon your past projection of their characters—

Herbert   Yes—

Hill   —I think this is bound to overspill into your life. I mean, it [becomes] not just "What would I do in this situation?" It's "What would Dalziel do in this situation? What would Pascoe do in this situation?"

Herbert   I see. I'm fascinated to hear that there are bits of you in each of them. Could you tell us about the bit of you that's in Dalziel?

Hill   I think that with Dalziel it's sort of sheer delight in being outrageous. He is naturally outrageous in some ways. But at the same time he controls it, you know.

Herbert   Aha.

Hill   He looks at things, people, situations and he will go out of his way just to *explode* the situation. And, I think, frequently I'm either too frightened or, perhaps a better way to put it or, a more flattering way to put it, too *polite* to indulge in this!

Herbert   But you're tempted.

Hill   In my mind, in some situations, I think of what Dalziel would do and I wish I had the *nerve* to do it! Occasionally I've let myself go and done or said a sort of Dalzielesque thing. But I mean it is a delight in outrageousness which I think Dalziel has which I think is part of me. And I think a lot of Pascoe's neuroses are my own. And I've not succumbed yet to the kind of panic attacks which assault poor Peter in the last book, but I understand those very well because this is a response to a situation which is one where you can feel frightened, concerned, agitated, anxious; and I let my mind just run loose with it to the extreme. Rather than let the situation control me, push me over, I run ahead of it! And I sort of stand there, I hope, looking unconcerned, smiling, and then let my mind go mad, you know, start chewing up the carpet or whatever! And then I can come back and step back *from* that.

Herbert   It seems to me that both Dalziel and Pascoe are equally well drawn, although they bring very different personalities and take very different approaches to the same circumstances. It is not surprising that in real life you might look at Reginald Hill's potential reaction to a particular event, along with Andy Dalziel's and Peter Pascoe's possible responses. After all, you have lived with this pair of characters for almost twenty years.

Hill   Oh, yes, and one thing I do remember from a very early age, and which I've still got, is that sense of being outside myself and observing myself in situations and very often—I mean more often than I sometimes feel *comfortable* with—of *selecting* the reaction or the emotional response as if I'm writing myself into a scene, you see.

Herbert   I do. This is very much the mark of a writer.

Hill   I mean, this is very useful for interviews—not this kind of interview—but going for university or job interviews or going into uncomfortable situations because you think, "Right. What shall I do here?"

Herbert   Almost like editing yourself.

Hill   Editing yourself. And it also can enable you to keep control of yourself. I can remember, for instance, I was called up to do my military service at the age of eighteen, nineteen and being harangued by some ghastly drill sergeant who decided, "Ah, this lanky, tall, fair-haired youth is going to be whipped into shape." And I'd done something terribly wrong; I'd dropped my rifle or something, and he had me marching up and down in front of the squad, [while he was] shouting abuse. And I mean my reaction was, you know, to take my rifle and hit him over the head with it, quite frankly. But I can still see myself doing this: knowing that to get through this I had to do what he said and keep my face straight and all this but at the same time I was standing outside of myself telling him what I thought of him and consorting with my bailiff.

Herbert   (Laughs.) It was as if you envisioned a double storyline going on in your view of the events.

Hill   So that kind of thing, as I say, it can be rather worrying because you find yourself, to use Eliot's phrase, preparing a face to meet the faces that you meet.

Herbert   Mm hm.

Hill   I think I use it as a tool, a creative tool, now. And I can sort of switch it off and be myself; I think I can let the real Reg Hill show through rather than be an actor. But I've talked to other people who've felt something of the same thing. Perhaps you've had some sense of this.

Herbert   P. D. James talked about this notion of the icicle at the heart. She agreed with Henry James that the writer does stand apart. She said that someone might grieve at a tremendous personal loss and, while she would comfort them and you can imagine Phyllis being extremely comforting and warm and helpful—she would feel that a part of herself was observing this. I think she, too, finds this distance that comes with being a writer to be somewhat disconcerting, however helpful it may be to the writing process.

Hill   Yes. I can see that. Yes. I can understand what Phyllis said as well, because I mean this is part of it. It is a standing back. I think as Pascoe once used those words, "standing back from myself as well as standing back from the situation." I think a lot of it is to do with an essential shyness, too, for me.

Herbert   Ah, I see.

Hill   I always get very annoyed when I hear people claiming sort of special privileges because they are very shy because I think, quite frankly, ninety-nine percent of human beings are very shy. And I was and I suppose I still am a very shy person. But I mean I don't say this to get any kind of sympathy. I mean the way I've dealt with shyness is to screw up my courage and say to myself, "I've got to go through that door." I mean going into a room full of new people and meeting new people or being introduced on a large platform, and having to stand up there and make a speech: it gives me the colly wobbles. I look for the kind of physical help of having a couple of stiff drinks beforehand if I can. But then also I sort of coach myself into it. I discovered, I suppose, the quintessential defense mechanism: *make people laugh.* And I've found that certainly in my writing and in talking, my tendency always is to try to lighten the situation and to perhaps overdo it by being jokey.

Herbert   I don't think you overdo it.

Hill   But sometimes that can be a nervous response. Sometimes I find myself strutting on the edge of a most inappropriate situation in which to have a laugh.

Herbert   Well, in your Dalziel and Pascoe novels, where the reader may be encountering brutal murder or suicide, one is grateful for a laugh. One is grateful for Dalziel's outrageousness. After all, even Patsy Cornwell, who has firsthand acquaintance with the morgue, can testify to the fact that humor is alive and well—and appropriate to—the grimmest conclusions to life.

Hill   Yes, that's true, isn't it?

Herbert   But while we are on the subject of your bashfulness as a boy and youth, could we explore more about your childhood and the first signposts within it that you were on the road to becoming a writer?

Hill   That's fairly easy. I think that sometime in my preteen years—I can remember it without being specific about the memory—but I can remember realizing or asking and being told that people actually got *paid* for writing stories, for the stories which I loved reading. And I also already loved making up stories. I told them to my younger brother. I had a young brother who is four to five years younger than me and that's a terrible age gap, you know, when you're growing up. You're given the little brat [smiles] to look after so much and the older you get of course, he wants to tag along with his big brother and one way I found of shutting him up was to tell him stories. I was into storytelling. I did find of course that when I was trying to get him to go to sleep—we shared a room some of the time—that in fact the better my stories were, the less they put him to sleep!

Herbert   (Laughs.)

Hill   So anyway, the notion of writing for a living, when I became aware that people did this I thought, "I should like to be that!"

200

Herbert   Were your stories adventure tales? Did they have any elements of the mysterious in them?

Hill   [From] what I can remember of them, they were more verbal versions of the kind of serial films that one saw, like the ABC Minors, you know the junior Saturday morning film club, which would be full of incident and excitement and leave the hero in some impossible position, suspended above a vat of boiling oil with an anaconda 'round his neck and a rope fraying above him. How do you get out of that? Usually with one mighty leap. That kind of thing.

Herbert   I imagine if you wanted your brother to go to sleep, you'd have to resolve the story that night!

Hill   Well, you'd leave the hero dangling. And actually that was the trouble, as I say. It could be counterproductive. (Smiles.)

Herbert   But when you said ABC Minors, that's not something familiar to Americans.

Hill   Well ABC is a film distribution network, Associated British Cinemas or something. I think there two main ones like the Rank Organization. . . . They had cinemas up and down the country and they formed Saturday morning film clubs, where Mom could get rid of her brats on a Saturday morning. We could go along to a big cinema and be entertained. It was utter chaos in there—and there was a theme song, "We are the boys and girls well known as Minors of the ABC."

Herbert   So what does Minors mean? Young people?

Hill   Young people. M-i-n-o-r-s, not miners, not people beneath the ground.

Herbert   Well, I wondered because you were sitting there in the dark! Would you say that these adventure films led you in the direction of the mystery in any specific way?

Hill   I can't answer that specifically. Yes, I liked adventure films and I think my first acquaintance with the mystery was there.

Herbert   And as to your boyhood personality, were there aspects of it that you now recognize as leading toward becoming a writer? For instance, do you remember yourself as being a particularly observant person?

Hill   (Pause.) I can't honestly say that I was. I think that I always had a very active fantasy life. I can remember that. I'm certain it was very commonplace but if I was sitting on a bus or lying in bed at night I'd always be telling myself stories in my head. These were stories that feature oneself as a superhero. So, it was, I think, a very powerful imagination rather than any super powers of observation which I would lay claim to when I was young.

Herbert   What about influential books?

Hill   Our house wasn't a very bookish house; my parents weren't igno-
rant but we were a very working-class family and there'd never been a
lot of money to spend, actually, on books. There were a couple of
shelves for books. There wasn't a library or anything like the number
of books I now own myself. On the other hand, my mother in particular was a great reader and borrowed from the public library and
bought the odd paperback with the raggedy edge. She was a great
reader of thrillers, of detective works, and so that [was a] kind of
influence I suppose. I was introduced to Agatha Christie at a fairly
early age, when I started reading more adult books at ten or twelve or
so. And then it became easier for her because I was a member of the
library, the junior part of the library, and when I was going down
there she'd ask me to go to the senior library and get her a couple of
books. It was first of all, "Ask at the counter whether they have any
good thrillers or romances." But then of course I started wandering in
and being selector myself.

Herbert   And what did you select for yourself?

Hill   I read a lot of the classical, the golden age, crime stuff very early
on. And I read Zane Grey. I can remember sitting around the fire
with my family. These were pre–television days. At least they were
pre–television days for us. And I was reading Zane Grey. I was probably about ten or something like that and I said, "What's rape?" And
I still remember the silence that fell on the family gathering, and my
father reached across and took the book from me and he said, "I
don't think this is a book for you!" And put it away, of course. And
that was it; I didn't rest until I got hold of that book. It was such an
innocent question. I wonder whether at the age of ten they still ask
the same question with the same amount of innocence nowadays?

Herbert   I very much doubt it.

Hill   But I read a lot of the golden age mysteries. And that had to be a
big influence on me. And I can remember sometime—how old must I
have been?—fourteen or fifteen deciding that I was going to write a
book, a novel; it was going to be a thriller. And I got a book out of the
library which was on the art of writing thrillers or how to write a
thriller, by Sidney Horler, whose name you might be familiar with. He
was a British thriller writer of the thirties, forties. I don't know if anyone reads him now. It wasn't much help, I'd say.

Herbert   Did he say *anything* that became memorable?

Hill   Not much. (Laughs.)

Herbert   "Keep the reader's interest"?

Hill   I think I learned a lesson that my subsequent experience has confirmed: you don't need books to teach you how to write, you know. I was still at the stage where you could feel that "there is a secret" that, if only I knew it, would rocket me to fame and fortune. Well, there isn't. But the desire was there. I never wrote the thriller, of course.

Herbert   Not at fourteen anyway.

Hill   It'd have been all right if I could have put an afternoon aside to write it.

Herbert   Yes.

Hill   The realization that it was going to take *rather longer* than that—when there were interesting things to do like sports and, ah, discovering girls and all the other things you do in your early to mid-teens—

Herbert   (Chuckles.)

Hill   So I postponed writing the novel for a long time.

Herbert   While you didn't write a novel at that time, did you undertake any other writing?

Hill   Oh, yes. My earliest memories are of writing a poem at school. I was so proud. The headmaster thought it was marvelous and read it out to the assembled school. And of course this immediately created—not anything like envy. I was accused of plagiarism by all my coevals—entirely falsely. You know, "You couldn't have written that yourself." I did write it myself! I never got as far as finishing anything [else] for a long, long time except the odd short story that no one ever wanted to publish. But I wrote first chapters of novels and first acts of plays. But I always got a feeling that one day I was going to be a writer.

Herbert   Well, you say that you're from a working-class family. What sort of work did your parents do?

Hill   Well, my father, when I was born, was a professional footballer.

Herbert   Oh, I didn't realize that!

Hill   That is, a soccer player. Now, to say that nowadays, you see, with the kind of inflated wages it is possible to earn as a professional soccer player playing in the top divisions, it would suggest that there was a lot of money flying around but, oh, no. This was back in the twenties and thirties. The reason I was born where I was born—West Hartlepool in County Durham—was not because there was any family connection with that part of the country at all. It'd been that my father was playing for Hartlepool United at that time and shortly

203

afterwards he moved to another club and the family moved on. But it was all very much lower-division stuff where the wages were peanuts and also in those days this was before professional sportsmen in Britain got themselves organized, so you really were in a pretty powerless position. So he gave that up by the end of the thirties and became a storeman at an RAF maintenance unit near Carlisle in Cumberland. Again, a rather manual job, keeping stores and moving them around. It had the one good side to it, I suppose, from the family point of view: [it] was a reserved occupation. He didn't get called up during the war because this was essential RAF work anyway. So we had him at home in the war and avoided the awful business of separation or risk from sudden death. Because we lived in Cumberland . . . there was very little activity. The odd bomb got jettisoned somewhere close, you know, but there was nothing there to bomb. The only true risk to the family came with one of my favorite playthings. When I was a little lad my father was a member of the home guard and I used to play with his rifle. (Laughs heartily.)

Herbert   Oh no!

Hill   I don't think they allowed them [the members of the Home Guard] to have bullets.

Herbert   So, it wasn't loaded.

Hill   Oh, no, *no*; I'm sure. I don't think that they even let them have bayonets. What they were supposed to do if the Nazis arrived, I'm not quite certain!

Herbert   Stand there threateningly with a stiff upper lip.

Hill   (Laughs.) So, that's what he did. My mother, when the family got old enough, worked very hard all her life in the metal box factory. She became charge hand on a machine line. Kept them all in order. So that was it, that was our family. We lived on a council estate in Carlisle and so we were never property-owning. Neither was there a little spare money to buy a lot of books. But there was always an interest in education, [my parents were] always very keen that all the kids got a good education. We all managed to get further education.

Herbert   You went on to the university level. Is that right?

Hill   That's right, yes, because, of course, this was the post–war era. It was the year of the "meritocracy," you know, when everyone was supposed to get a fair chance. So I was fortunate to get good enough exam results at school in the public examinations to get awarded what was called a state scholarship.

Herbert　And you majored in English Literature at St. Catherine's College, Oxford.

Hill　It was St. Catherine's Society then, "Societas." Because they were still building the actual St. Catherine's College. The building was finished about the time that I left. It is one of the newest whole college buildings in Oxford. It is a rather fine, modern building. And it's a very great contrast with the older colleges, but worth a look if you ever get down that way.

Herbert　And then you were a schoolmaster following that.

Hill　Yes, I first spent a year working in Edinburgh for the British Council as an Overseas Students' Welfare Officer.

Herbert　What did that entail?

Hill　I was responsible, with others, for looking after the students. I steered them through the adminstrative mine fields such as the registration at the university, et cetera, et cetera. It had its interesting moments but much of it was extremely dull. I was terrified of my secretary, a formidable Scottish lady.

Herbert　(Laughs.)

Hill　She obviously resented this young whippersnapper, an Englishman, turning up to give her orders. I used to invent excuses to get out of the office. (Laughs.) I mean enough is enough. So I went into teaching and then into teaching teachers, which took me to Doncaster in 1967. Which is when I actually managed to finish my first book, almost purely as a result of being on the move. My wife, Pat, was down in Essex trying to sell a house. I was in Doncaster where we'd bought a house and living in there with a bed and a folding table and an electric kettle. And I had time on my hands so I launched myself in a book and lo and behold, I got to the point for the first time ever where I wrote "The End."

Herbert　Was that your first published book?

Hill　No, in fact that was the second published book; *Fell of Dark* was the first finished.

Herbert　I see.

Hill　This is sort of retrospectively following my own advice. It is now the only bit of advice which I give to aspiring authors. I generally don't tell them what to do [but] one thing I *do* tell them to do is, "When you finish the first book send it off. Don't sit around waiting for a publisher to come to your door with a wheelbarrow full of money. It is unlikely to happen." Whatever happens, whether it's rejection or acceptance is going to take a long, long time. And you're sitting there terrified of ringing them up in case you provoke them into throwing the thing back at you, trying to persuade yourself it's taking such a long time because they are all so fascinated—you know, they are all debating "Will he accept fifty thousand pounds? Will he be insulted?" Fortunately, I didn't wait. I was so delighted at having discovered that I could finish a book, that I set off right away and wrote another. And ended up—to cut a long story short—selling them both to Collins. And we decided after discussion, or rather, when it was suggested to me—I was still too terrified to argue in case they took their ball away and wouldn't let me play anymore. They suggested they put the first one out second and the second one out first. I said, "Fine! Any order you like."

Herbert   Just publish me! You've now had a twenty-year career writing crime and other fiction. Can you comment on how your aspirations within the crime novel have grown over the years?

Hill   Consciously I can feel myself trying to do more things with each book, reaching out. I mean, eventually I'll probably overreach myself, but I think unless you really *go for it*, you're never going to know what you *can* do, and I'm conscious more and more of the sheer challenge of the novel. You learn the art. I mean, [as] you get older, I don't think you don't get any wiser, but [laughs] you *do* get more experienced and I'm beginning to realize that it's not a question of *I* can do things with the novel, but *the novel* can do things.

Herbert   The novel offers certain possibilities as a form?

Hill   Yes. I can understand now what I didn't see when I first started out. So that the central growth over the years is not about the way in which I perhaps *tell* stories, but [if] I look back I think that the ideas I'm playing with, the *ideas*—they're coming out of somewhere perhaps deeper in me than [they did] to start with. The core of *Bones and Silence* was the idea of suicide, really, which sounds rather macabre, but I had a very dear friend who killed himself several years ago, and I just found it incomprehensible. Look back, and of course you'll see all kinds of clues—

Herbert   But at the time it came as a real surprise.

Hill   —it came as a real surprise that a man I admired so much and seemed to have so much going for him decides to take his life. So, I mean, I didn't want to write about *him*. It wasn't that kind of an exploration: it wasn't going to be any morbid exploration of my own feelings about David. But it was just that the *idea*, I think, has been simmering around inside me. I felt that I could make it work, because I knew that in real life it *had* worked. And I supply a sufficient number of [additional characters], I think, who had good cause to be melancholy and downcast.

Herbert   But somehow they brave it out and keep going.

Hill   Whereas, the one who [commits suicide], that is perhaps the last one you'd expect. I suppose it's the old Agatha Christie twist. As Robert Barnard said, "We've all borrowed from Agatha." But I think with Agatha it's always [done in] a rather mechanical fashion: it's always the last one you'd expect. Someone once said if you work out who it can't possibly be, that's who it will be. And I thought this was a little truer to life [in *Bones and Silence*].

Herbert   Well, after all, the inspiration for the book *was* true to life; you were surprised by your friend's death.

Hill   But it's got to work for the people who read it as well, and they've got to be surprised, but not [feel], "Oh, no, that's impossible."

Herbert   Well, I think the surprise works and has tremendous impact. I thought it was very effective that you did allow her to jump. It could have been so easy, and so much less real, to have her be readily convinced; "Oh, well, all right, you've saved the day." Because I think when people are at that point, whether or not they actually succeed, they really are in a desperate state and absolutely want to succeed at doing it.

Hill   Well, I mean, that's the thing that I wasn't absolutely certain I was going to do until three quarters of the way through the book. But by the time I was really writing the end of it I knew that she was going to jump to her death. The option—this is the great thing about writing, you have options—well, or at least, you can delay options until the last possible moment—but finally you think this out and say, "I've got to go with it."

Herbert   Well, it's interesting that this book came—the idea of it came— from a personal relationship that made you start to think about suicide. In other words, it was inspired by an event that caused you to ruminate about a certain kind of death. Have you done that before, or was this a new kind of thing? After all, the crime novel so often is centered around a death, or at least some of the *puzzle* is certainly centered around it.

Hill   I think it usually is; I mean, not always something as illuminating as a form of death, but just picking up an idea as in, say, *Under World*. The idea came from just thinking about the *under*-world: miners working, a kind of life which would probably destroy me. It's just a personal thing. I love fell-walking. I've no fear of heights; I love being up high; but I've got a terror of the confined spaces, which I think has got worse! (Laughs.) I mean, my recurring dream is me going up a sort of spiral staircase and down a winding corridor, and it gets narrower, and narrower, and narrower, and I know in the end I'm going to get stuck. "Wake up, wake up! Please wake up before I get stuck!" And I always used to find that, reading *Alice in Wonderland*, the most disturbing bits, especially looking at the pictures, those Tenniel pictures, is when Alice has taken the thing which says "Eat me" and she—she's in the house, like this—[anguished gasps] —now even talking about it I feel a shudder growing inside me. So the idea of working underground—I think, you know, it's something that's deep in my subconscious, and that's what you want to explore, isn't it? (Smiles.)

Herbert   Absolutely. Are there other books of yours that have particularly stemmed from something in your subconscious?

Hill   A lot of them have stemmed from things which have somehow entered into my mind and they've become part of me, in a sense, more than just a simple memory. I sometimes use them in a very, very casual way, or not in a very central way. But in my very first book published, *A Clubbable Woman*, a woman is killed, in fact. She has this rather strange blow to the head and it turns out to have been performed by an air pistol of the kind that was compressed by pressing the barrel down against something hard and a very long barrel went back into itself, in fact. There was a double barrel, the inner one and the outer one. so you were pressing it back against a valve and compressing air so that when you put the pellet in and you pulled the trigger, about four or five inches of solid steel barrel came out.

Herbert   I can visualize this.

Hill   And I can remember when I was about eleven or twelve, I was out playing with some friends and I had to look after my younger brother. And one of the bigger boys had one of these guns and of course we all envied this and finally I managed to get my hands on it. And I knew that there wasn't a pellet in it; it wasn't loaded in the sense of having a projectile in it. And I put it to my young brother's head as one might do with a toy gun. And the lad whom it belonged to said, quite casually, "I shouldn't press that." And he reached across and took it from me and he pressed the trigger and this five inches of solid metal just came shooting out of the end.

Herbert   Oh, my word!

Hill   It would have just gone right through his head. And I've never, *ever* gotten—you know that's something—I say, it's not a memory, it's a shock. I still can wake up in the night with it.

Herbert   Oh, how awful.

Hill   So, I mean I used that. I think I made an attempt at getting it out of my system by making this youth actually kill the woman by accident.

Herbert   And did it help? Did it help to let it out?

Hill   I think it probably did, yes.

Herbert   P. D. James has said that a writer's body of work will, over time, reveal aspects of his or her private emotional landscape. It sounds like this is one of yours.

Hill   I am most certain of this, yes.

Herbert   This particular example elucidates why you chose to write a particular book that dealt with a killing. But I wonder why, overall, you have chosen to write books that, one after another, inevitably deal with questions of life and death?

Hill   Well, the question "Why do you write crime novels?" is one that I've often been asked, and I've usually given the same answer, that is, "I'm not altogether certain." You know, they say that whenever you start asking writers about their books, they start telling you lies, automatically, instinctively, and don't always know it! I started writing because I enjoyed reading, and there was always something in a crime novel which I could creatively catch on to. And after many false shots at writing *novels*—writing the first chapters of "great novels"—and after a while I thought "What am I really doing here? What do I imagine I'm doing?" And, you see, the first book I finished . . . really started off like so many of my books, all these "great novels." It was an exploration of character, of relationships between this chap who was having trouble with his marriage, his best friend, his university friend who is homosexual, who's having all kinds of troubles; their mutual troubles string them together out on a Lake District holiday. And then, not for the first time, I kind of got to this state of, "What the hell am I writing about?" (Laughs.) And that is where murder and detection first reared its head, because it gave a skeleton to the book.

Herbert   I like the choice of words!

Hill   Yes, it did. The book *needs* bones, and this gave it the bones on which I could write—around which I could write. I could flesh them out with the story, and feel there was something in the middle there which was holding it all together. The crime-writing element of my writing provides the bones, and that is the part that doesn't fade away. You know when you cut through, when you slice, when you boil it all up or whatever image you like to use, those bones are still there; if you've got a crime-writer's plot in the middle, the whole thing is going to stand up on that and not just fall around you like a blancmange.

Herbert But do these "bones," does this structure in any way confine you? Do you feel that you can really bring the greatest of your writing skills to this genre and go further each time, a little bit further, and take a little bit more of a risk, the way people do in highblown mainstream novels?

Hill I would like my brain to think, "Why shouldn't it be possible to do this?" I know that Julian Symons says that the trouble is that the crime novel, certainly the novel of detection, by its very essence stops the writer telling everything about his characters, because if you told everything then you'd know who was the criminal from the very start. And I think, "Yes, but really every novel I read doesn't tell you everything about the characters, not all at once! The truth about a character emerges gradually: Dickens, and Trollope, and Forster, and all the great novelists offer some surprise. And they are the kind of surprise, you know, about character, which is exactly the same as the surprise you get in a crime novel." So I don't think that this is a disqualification from writing great literature. I mean, I think there *is* something odd. The other question you're going to ask is, "Well, having said that, where will I point to the great novels that have been written which are crime novels?" and this is worrying.

Herbert Well, with a few notable exceptions, it is only relatively recently that numerous sophisticated writers have turned to this genre. Many authors, including Reginald Hill, are producing very serious literary work. It may be that because crime writing is more "respectable" now, authors with high standards for themselves are finding that if they do push themselves to the limits they can do what they want within the form. I gathered from what you have said that so far you *have been able* to expand the kind of questions you might ask and stretch your writing skills within the genre. You haven't had to say, "Oh, I can't do this, simply because I've got to keep the secret for the next two chapters." Is that so?

Hill No, no, that hasn't happened to me.

Herbert So, this need to keep secrets for reasons of craft has never caused you to feel that you're being a bit coy with the reader?

Hill I've never found it so. I think I'd put it a different way than that: it is a constraint of point of view rather than of characterization.

Herbert Hm!

Hill I mean, for instance, in *Bones and Silence*, quite clearly I never have to take you, the reader, into Chung's mind, and I always have to look at her from the outside looking in. But then I have to say that this doesn't seem to me to be an unusual or indeed an unnatural approach in *any* kind of novel: you choose the characters into whose minds you go, whose eyes you use to look at the situation. I don't find it a problem. I think it makes me exercise an area of my craft of writing which—it keeps me on my toes; it presents a challenge rather than a problem and I can't say that I've ever felt that the shading or the keeping of a secret has interfered with what I think of as the artistic integrity of a book as a novel. I can see how it is possible to make out the argument that it does and therefore this means it [crime writing] is by definition a lesser art. Whereas I should have thought it means that it presents an extra problem to be overcome and that therefore the skill of the best crime writers is in some ways *superior* to the skill of the chap who doesn't have to do this. He has got it comparatively easy!

Herbert   And isn't that the fascination in real life with people? That you don't know everything about them?

Hill   In what we think of as the greatest novel writers, whether it's Jane Austen, Dickens, or the moderns, you don't know everything about everybody; it's a process of discovery. So I can't see any reason why this should be picked upon as a peculiarly disabling feature of the crime novel.

Herbert   I like the way you put that. I have asked a number of crime writers if part of the appeal of writing for them is the ability to be in control of matters of life and death in books which usually center around a murder or unexplained death.

Hill   I've been doing it for a long time now and I do find that after awhile you do get hooked upon it. And I like the killings and resolution of the crimes and I feel that this is a part of the pleasure, that I am the creator, the guy in control of the book. I don't quite feel about my characters as Thackeray felt [about his]—you know, put them back in the toybox, in *Vanity Fair*. There's something of that feeling that we're in an equal partnership, except that I've got more shares—and on the whole they do what I want. You see, once you're writing a crime novel, you do enter into a kind of contract with your readers to surprise them. And I feel, really, that if I keep this contract, [if] I surprise them; as long as I do that, I can do anything else that I'm able to do. And if what I want to do is to write a kind of Greek tragedy, then fine. But I've got to obey that first little bit of the contract.

Herbert   It sounds like the contract hasn't limited you thus far, particularly if you can allow yourself to make decisions about character very close to the end of a novel. This strikes me as very like the freedom enjoyed by a mainstream novelist. That's about as free as you can be with a character.

Hill   Yes, but the contract was that the reader would not guess which one it was, as in the case of *Bones and Silence*. The dilemma was something quite different than the criminous contract that I've made with my readers.

Herbert   A nice way of putting that, as well. You mean that identifying the suicidal character is different than identifying the ordinary murderer in the usual whodunit?

Hill   Yes. And it is an example of doing something different within the crime or mystery form.

Herbert   And then what that "criminous contract" is doing is enforcing the element of surprise that you feel is necessary to any literature.

Hill   I think it well could be. I think another trouble is that the term "crime novel," like all generic terms, is applied to a huge, huge field. And there are things in it at both ends which have got so little connection with each other that you think, "What's the point to lump them all together under this one heading?"

Herbert   Readers do, however, recognize a crime or mystery book when they see it. The universe of crime writing is somehow related enough so that it is an identifiable body of writing to those who enjoy reading it. And this does not simply mean that there is a butler provided to open the door on a body in the library.

Hill   I often wonder, "What is the common element?" I suspect also that readers are rather more stratified than we imagine.

Herbert   There's something for every taste in the crime-writing field. Do you think that basically one of the fascinations for the reader of detective novels is summed up in "There but for the grace of God go I"—that every person is capable of murder if enough pressures are exerted on him or her?

Hill   I suspect that we all think we know ourselves well enough to have some sense of our own limits. We think we know what it would take to push us to an act of violence or we believe that nothing could push us to an act of such violence. But while I might be fairly certain—not a hundred percent—about myself, no offense, but I *can't* be absolutely certain of you.

Herbert   (Laughs.)

Hill   Yes. I think this is one of the appeals of detective stories.

Herbert   That we cannot know what lurks in the heart of our fellows?

Hill   Yes.

Herbert   But to pursue this question of secrets of character as essential to the crime novel, let's look more closely at *Bones and Silence*. The resolution of its central question has to do with understanding character rather than, "Who was where when?" You were concerned with psychological motivation rather than simply material motive and just the plain facts of the crime. And I think when a writer can do that it is a step forward for the crime novel, a step away from the formulaic. When authors can make decisions based not simply on surprising the reader but founded on genuine character development, we are talking of the concerns of the novelist of character. And if fully developed characters can populate a crime novel, I would say it's got a lot going for it in terms of its potential to reach the highest levels of literature.

Hill   Yes. I suppose basically there are two schools: there are those who belong to the "Agatha" school, who, if they've got a good plot, would rather junk the character for the plot. They'd dilute the character, tear it down, squash it, or damage it. Me, I'd rather junk the plot for the character. Anyone can think of a clever idea, but turning that into a character who *lives* is an entirely different matter.

Herbert   In other words, you are more interested in the puzzle of character than in the plot as puzzle?

Hill   Yes.

Herbert   What about the effect of crime on your communities of characters?

Hill   Very early in my kind of book you feel sorrow about the person who is killed. Never any about the person who turns out to be the culprit. Whereas you know murder is a double tragedy. It's a tragedy for the person who is murdered and then there is the double tragedy because of the effect that that has on relatives and family, which in some ways is a greater tragedy. To have your grandmother murdered is dreadful, but to have your grandmother to turn out to be a murderess is something else, isn't it?

Herbert   It certainly is. You can address the question of plot and character from the point of view of Reginald Hill and as Patrick Ruell, the thriller writer, and as Dick Morland, the author of books set in the future. Are there any constraints in the crime series that do not become concerns in your other fiction?

Hill   Well, I find that Dalziel and Pascoe to me are not a constraint; they're a liberating force. Again, I refer you to Julian Symons in matters literary, whom I respect highly. But we never meet quite on this and he always feels that having series characters is almost automatically going to limit the scope of a book. Again, I can see what he means, but I really in my case, I just want to make a special plea. This is one of the dangers, obviously, to a writer: that they [the series characters] can become like old slippers. Sometimes slippers get so old that they can walk by themselves. We've all read books with series characters that are like that. Which is why I have never written two Dalziel and Pascoe books in succession. There has always been at least one other book, and sometimes two between them.

Herbert   This may account for a lot of their freshness.

Hill   I've never yet found myself getting bored with them. Anything that I want to say, anything I want to explore, I can explore in Dalziel and Pascoe books. And I've never found it constricting. I mean I obviously can't write Patrick Ruell–type thrillers using them because I'd have to shove them in situations in which their jobs and characters wouldn't take them, but I suppose in *One Small Step* I have shown that I could put them in a science fiction situation even though it was with my tongue in my cheek. But on the whole I do find it liberating and exhilarating to return to them, rather than restricting. And the fact that Dalziel and Pascoe are in a relationship [in which] I think I've set myself all kinds of problems keeps the character development going. These seem to be the problems of life. Literature should not be a fairy never, never land.

Herbert   That's another question that comes up in some of today's crime writing: moral ambiguity. You think of Phyllis James for instance and her clear demonstration that the investigation of the crime—while it establishes justice—is actually a very destructive process that leaves a trail of devastation in its wake.

Hill   That's right. The people can never be the same again and the communities can be changed. In the book I'm working on at the moment, the next Dalziel and Pascoe, which takes place in a very small Yorkshire rural community, from time to time behind it all there's always the fact that this fairly low-key investigation that's going on is going to explode into a sort of full-scale helicopters and frogmen and the convoys with their lights flashing, and I keep the threat of this as a sort of a foil to this rather peaceful, lovely, and very attractive village. It is the intrusion of real life in the worst possible sense.

Herbert   Yes, you've done that successfully in many locations. And it was W. H. Auden who, in his essay, "The Guilty Vicarage," talked about the detective story as portraying an idyllic world, the "great, good place," that has been disrupted. This is one of the wonderful tensions of crime writing from the golden age to today. You can think of your

Bones and Silence as an example of this, with its glorious cathedral-close setting contrasting with the devastating personal problems in the lives of those who live there. One of the things that you do, it seems to me, is reflect the development of the crime novel by taking some of these settings that we adore—some of them very well used already—and putting very contemporary problems into those settings. The settings may be idyllic visually, but when you learn what lurks within them you soon realize that this is far removed from an idyll.

Hill   Yes. I am very concerned to take what seems to me to be the best of the past and to use it, not to try and discard it. Curiously, I'm very conscious in recent books that I've got—I've almost worn myself out—I've supped my fill of horrors and misdeeds.

Herbert   Really!

Hill   I suppose if I go back—I could go back the whole way. I mean with a book called *Under World*—the metaphor and the actuality of the underworld which meet in Pascoe's own sort of claustrophobia—I mean that is something that I do share; that it's very much a nightmare of my own and ultimately it is tragic as again, in *Bones and Silence*, it's tragic. And I've hoped that *Recalled to Life*, as the title suggests, is a little more uplifting.

Herbert   Are you trying perhaps to deal with things that are more subtle now? You have always been concerned with character development surrounding the killings. But are you saying that you're getting tired of dealing with the gruesome side of things?

Hill   Yet, to say, "I'm getting tired of it" is not quite the same as to say, "I find it tiring." That is, I'm not tired of it in the sense of "bored with it." It does take it out of you. But then, as I say, I always write at least one book between writing Dalziel and Pascoe books, and there is another book which has been written which is coming out.

Herbert   Featuring other characters, and using your pseudonym Patrick Ruell?

Hill   No, it is going to be published as Reginald Hill and it is perhaps the beginning of a new series because it features Joe Sixsmith, the private eye in a couple of my short stories that you might recall, who is a balding, middle-aged, redundant lathe operator of West Indian extraction who lives in Luton and has plowed his redundancy money into becoming a private eye. He has no qualifications whatsoever for the job and, indeed, no natural talent for it, except the very useful ability, which I describe, I think, as serendipity of making choices, of making discoveries by happy accident—and he *has* got this. The first time he appeared was in a short story which, in fact, Pat Craig chose to publish in *The Oxford Book of English Detective Stories*. That was called "Bring Back the Cat." And then in Charlotte Macleod's anthology, *Christmas Stalkings*, which is a pun in American but not in English.

Herbert   There's another example that illustrates George Bernard Shaw's remark, "England and America are two countries divided by a common language."

Hill   And here is another Joe Sixsmith story called, "The Running of the Deer." And I thought I'd like to try him out in a full-length book as well. Anyway, he's a very gentle kind of character, as far away as you can get from Andy Dalziel! But I like Dalziel very much.

Herbert   Well, that's very exciting. What is the title of the book?

Hill   *Blood Sympathy*. My English publisher liked it so much that they insisted on a two-book contract; they wanted to make sure there was going to be another Joe Sixsmith—which I was very happy to promise.

Herbert   Oh, that's marvelous.

Hill   So that was very nice, to turn away from the kind of more traumatic areas of *Recalled to Life* to write this Joe Sixsmith. But then I've started another Dalziel and Pascoe and the further I got, I thought, "I think that the theme of this one is more healing than anything else," and it's almost a book without much crime in it. Though—I won't give anything away but I hope it has a hell of an impact. But I am enjoying writing it, very much, and again it wasn't something conscious. Really, as I was writing this, the scenes, the ideas—they become—they start solidifying and you start understanding why you're writing and I realized that I was writing a bit away from the sort of "killing fields" of *Bones and Silence*.

Herbert   What about Dick Morland and Patrick Ruell? Are they otherwise occupied for the moment?

Hill   Dick Morland, yes, he is in kind of suspended animation which has gradually merged, I think, into death. I think the life support system has been switched off. I mean I'd like to write some more sort of SF futuristic stories, but to find the time is difficult.

Herbert   Well, it sounds like in the past you used to have that as an alternative and now you've got yet another alternative to Dalziel and Pascoe.

Hill   Yes, and Patrick Ruell is still going strong. But the last Patrick Ruell didn't find a mainstream American publisher—a book called

The Only Game—because it has an IRA element in it and I was assured by the American editors that they're always a bit worried about IRA because of the strong IRA sympathy you get among the Irish population [in the States].

But anyway that was a book which got a very good response back home, and the option has been sold to a television company which again have got high hopes of turning it into a series. I mean, so much so that I've done another couple of storylines for them using the character who is an ex-soldier and by the end of the book an ex-policeman called Dog Cicero. The pressures on my writing time are very great [pauses], which is good because I can look into the future and see that all these things that I've got to do and I want to do. . . .

Herbert   But it's exhilarating and difficult at the same time.

Hill   That's right.

Herbert   Tell me about your writing habits. Do you still write most days and reserve Fridays for your fell-walking?

Hill   Yes! Friday is fell-walking day and I do my level best—

Herbert   I love your choice of words, considering how unlevel the fells are!

Hill   (Laughs.)—to keep that up because I still find that's the best therapy of all. You know you walk for ten minutes uphill and turn around and look back and even after such a short time suddenly everything gets put into perspective. You know you're out of reach of the telephone; there's no sheets of paper in front of me; and I'm not worried about the tax man or the VAT man; and it's just you and what's under your feet and above your head: it's just lovely.

Herbert   And actually when you're writing, too. It's just you and the page, which is very nice. How many hours a day now are you putting into writing? Do you have a definite pattern?

Hill   My pattern's the same as it's been for donkey's ears. I write in the mornings, starting as early as I can, but by nine at the latest—why, early as eight or earlier sometimes if I get up—and I work through solidly at writing till one o'clock. Now, afternoons it's a movable feast. Sometimes I feel as if I'm very hot, you know, there's something going: I'll go back upstairs. Or it depends on the weather, you see; if it's a wet day I'll go and do some more work; if it's a lovely day, "I'd better get out and do some work 'round the garden" or do things like go shopping, which always involves me because I drive and Pat doesn't. Where we live, in the Lake District, the market is twelve miles away and little things like shopping do involve an expedition rather than just popping around the corner.

Herbert I'm not certain that Americans will be familiar with the geography of the fells. Would you provide a nutshell description of them for us?

Hill It's mountainous countryside but they're not big mountains. In fact I think by United States standards they are little mountains. In fact I think the highest ones are just over three thousand feet, which doesn't seem very high if you're looking up at the Rockies, I suspect!

Herbert But it's steep climbing, is it not?

Hill It can be. It's serious walking country: let's put it this way, every year quite a lot of people get killed.

Herbert Sounds like a great recreation ground for a crime writer.

Hill (Laughs.) While it's country that can be crossed in a couple of days, or three days, quite easily, it's still possible to get yourself seriously lost and you know if you're up high and you're in mist and you slip and fall down five hundred feet you can seriously injure yourself. And the great thing about it, from the walker's point of view, is that you can get to every top.

Herbert And your early novel *Fell of Dark* was set in this environment?

Hill Yes. It's all of course the English Lake District which means that it's got our lakes in it, Windermere, Grasmere, et cetera, et cetera, which have been made very familiar to huge generations of students of English literature through Wordsworth in particular, and one or two others.

Herbert This leads me to ask how important setting is to you as you create your novels? How essential to you is the sense of place?

Hill (Pauses.) It's pretty important. I mean certainly it is in the Dalziel and Pasco books with their Yorkshire settings, even though it is geographically nonspecific in that I've invented a region of mid-Yorkshire which doesn't exist. There's a North Yorkshire, a South Yorkshire and a West Yorkshire—curiously, there doesn't seem to be an East Yorkshire!

Herbert That's England for you!

Hill In any case, I've invented this mid-Yorkshire which is a central spot, which gives me the option of using all the characteristics—because it's our biggest county; it is the—kind of Texas of England, in more ways than one, I suspect. And by not being specific, it means that instead of having to be geographically and characteristically precise, I've been able to pick up on things from the north, south, and west, and use them at will. But setting is important.

Herbert   When you are preparing to write a book, or while you are in the process of creating it, do you feel that you need to visit the types of scenes of the crimes? I'm particularly curious about *Under World*; did you actually visit any mines as you wrote that book?

Hill   Well, when I was writing *Under World*, I was living then in South Yorkshire, which is the center of the Yorkshire coalfields. It is in fact the spiritual center of coal mining in England. It's where our great leader Arthur Scargill, the one who led the great strike, comes from. And the Coal Board have their headquarters in Doncaster, which is where I lived. So I was very much in the middle of it and really in the middle of the strike. I mean just two miles down the road from our house you came to one of the mines which was at the center of much of the agitation.

Herbert   Did you actually enter some of the mines? I know you don't like enclosed spaces.

Hill   I had been down a mine; it was in Scotland some years ago, and I can't say I cared for it much, but that was certainly an experience, crawling in a very deep mine right up to the coal face. And I was making arrangements through a friend of mine who had connections with the miner's union when I started that book. But I'd just got the first two chapters done, the thing mapped out, and the great miner's strike began, which is referred to in the book and then, of course, because all the mines were being picketed, the opportunity for me to go down went out of the window and I put the book aside because I thought, "This mining world that I'm writing about is not going to be the same! I've got to wait and see what happens." And of course the strike went on for the best part of a year, in which time I wrote another book. And then I came back to *Under World* and suddenly found myself really having to start completely from scratch and writing about the mining community as it now existed after the strike, which was probably the most traumatic and significant we've had in this country since the General Strike of the thirties.

Herbert   I wonder what kind of research is necessary to create your worlds, since you are not yourself a miner; you are not yourself a Yorkshire policeman.

Hill   I do whatever research is possible, usually by reading. There are a vast number of books written about and by miners, both fact and fiction. I also knew a lot of people connected with the mining industry so I was able to talk to them. And of course, during that year of the miners' strike, the newspapers were full of articles about the whole business. So, as it were, I'd got the whole of British journalism, from the tabloids to the serious Sundays, doing my research for me, which

219

was handy. If you happen to be writing something that the newspapers are interested in, really, they do work very hard and much more ruthlessly, than you probably do.

Herbert　How convenient!

Hill　And they've got their big research libraries, as well. So there's a message for budding authors, isn't it?

Herbert　It sure is. "Use the journalists."

Hill　But ultimately, the important things, like being a Yorkshire policeman or being a miner or whatever, I think it just comes down to imagination.

Herbert　You have a wonderful imagination, in that case.

Hill　Well, I've never committed a murder in my life and all the time I'm writing about people who have committed murders and about old people or young people, women, men, gay people, policemen, killers, vicars, prostitutes. And unless you can convince yourself, it's not going to come over convincingly for your readers. So I don't know it you've got to say I'm blessed with or cursed with this power of imagination.

Herbert　I'm also wondering about the dark side of you. It seems as if your books have become darker over the years. And from my brief acquaintance with you, and from what you've told me, it seems as though you've had a well-ordered, generally happy life. Yet in your books you explore themes of disappointment, quiet desperation, rage, personal and political wounds, and the like. I wonder where all this comes from? Have you gone through difficult experiences in your life that help you to identify with and understand your characters?

Hill　I'm aware that my life has been *fairly* even—touch wood—but it's a matter of looking out. I find that if you're a writer of fiction, in the end you are the eye of the storm; you have got to be the stillness at the center of things.

Herbert　That is wonderfully well put.

Hill　And I suppose the danger of this is that you can become too much of an observer, as I hinted before.

Herbert　Yes, that has made you uncomfortable.

Hill　There's that standing back, again, and taking a view, and taking notes. And I think you've got to have this to some extent. Now, certainly in general terms, though the course of my own life and existence has been pretty even and almost placid, it seems to me, looking around, that I've lived through times which are, as the Chinese say, "interesting times."

Herbert   Indeed.

Hill   Well, let's just speak for our own country: England now is in a worse state than it has been for many decades. Things have gone from worse to worse, still! And perhaps the contrast between me being able to make a living out of doing something that I want to do at a time when we've got three million who aren't allowed to make a living out of doing anything at all, I mean that kind of thing strikes me very strongly. So I think there's any amount of material of that kind, the darker side of things.

But as I said earlier, I have been aware of things getting a bit gloomier and in *Pictures of Perfection*, the Dalziel and Pascoe that I've just finished, I've made a conscious effort to break the spiral and to move, if not quite into the sunlit uplands, at least into rather brighter weather.

Herbert   I shall be interested to read it! In response to your thoughts about the writer acting as the eye of the storm, I look around us at your home in one the most celebrated beauty spots of England, and your happy relationship with your wife, and your ordered environment with the occasional heron flying past your window. Here you are in a Victorian vicarage that even features a walled "secret garden," ensconced in tranquility while writing of the trauma of a miners' strike, or a woman's suicide, or bloody murder. Both Auden's title "The Guilty Vicarage"—

Hill   That would be a lovely address, "The Guilty Vicarage"—

Both   (Laugh.)

Herbert   —and Wordsworth's notion of "emotion recollected in tranquility" come to mind. It seems to me that what you are doing is treating "trauma imagined in tranquility." As you say, in the eye of the storm.

Hill   Yes.

Herbert   I wonder why you have chosen to write in a genre that is preoccupied with questions of death and closure? Do you regard yourself as particularly sensitive to the fragility of life?

Hill   (Pauses at length.) Yes, well, that's a conversation killer!

Herbert   (Laughs.)

Hill   I don't think of myself as morbid in any sense. I'm not fascinated by death.

Herbert   Mm hm.

Hill   What does strike me more and more is the sheer fortuity of life. You know, you put your hand in the bran tub and you pull something

221

out and you either end up living happily in the Guilty Vicarage in the Lake District or starving and being shot at and raped in Bosnia.

Herbert   I see your philosophical point quite clearly but I can only imagine what is a "bran tub."

Hill   Ah, yes. It used to be a popular thing at village fêtes and things, for the kids. They have a tub full of bran. And there are gifts in it. You pay money and the kids have a dip in the bran tub, and you'd stir your hand around in this stuff until you'd found something and it was just a matter of chance whether you got the packet of "Dolly Mixtures" [candies] or the model aeroplane. So it's a matter of chance.

Herbert   And luck. This makes me think of a close cousin to chance and luck, serendipity. What role, if any, does serendipity play in your work?

Hill   When I am writing, I know what a book is about but *how* it is going to be about what it is about I don't really know until I come to grips with it.

Herbert   You're beginning to sound like Lewis Carroll!

Hill   (Laughs.) Things suggest themselves as you're writing. For example, I'm working on a book where the detective, Joe Sixsmith, comes across a body in a cardboard box, one of these cardboard boxes which, alas, are becoming all too common in the shop doorways of England, where homeless people sleep. And he finds this body and things develop from there. My notion was it was going to be in a shop doorway in a shopping center. And I wrote this. And then I thought, he sings in a choir, you see, and they are rehearsing Haydn's *Creation*. And then I thought, "Haydn's *Creation*: that's quite an ambitious thing for a small choir to be doing and you'd need an orchestra so perhaps they will join up with another group and so the actual location of this would be a big church." Well, I hadn't got a church, so I invented one. And I thought, "How much better, and how much more symbolic, or whatever you care to think about it, to have the cardboard chock around the back of a big, old, Victorian church full of nooks and crannies and a dark graveyard and have him go there to sleep."

Herbert   That's *much* more atmospheric.

Hill   But that illustrates the way in which I begin the book, knowing a lot of the facts, but the book changes as I'm writing it. And I will have to go back and rewrite.

Herbert   It seems to me to be the business of the novelist to enrich the book. My impression is that the best of today's crime novelists are willing to change with the book in a manner that might not have been so true of the old writers of golden age puzzlers. Earlier, you spoke about the novel's possibilities as a form. Can you embroider on that a bit?

Hill   I am aware more and more of the possible ways of doing a thing. The very simple things you are aware of from the start, such as point of view. I mean the way to start your first novel, I suppose, is with the word "I."

Herbert   (Laughs.) Indeed!

Hill   Whether it is a first person point of view, whether it is a multi-person point of view, whether there is an all-knowing author whose voice comes through and addresses the reader perhaps not quite as directly as "Dear reader," but just about as directly, or whether it is totally impersonal: that's very simple. You know that when you are a beginning writer, but not in the sense of properly having experienced it as a creator. And I think you tend to make up your mind when you first write and you make a commitment to start with. But now, I know you have to start somewhere so I make a commitment but now I can get into a book and say, "*No*, this is wrong."

Herbert   And this judgment is based on sound experience.

Hill   And from the crime writer's point of view, because we do have a peculiar set of rules to adhere to, while the puzzle has become for me less important, I still pride myself on providing the kinds of suspense and revelation proper to a crime novel and I am very much concerned with the ways you can do this by shifting the ways in which you tell the story. After all, the pure goal of the crime writer is to have your reader say, "It's amazing but it's *true*." There must be both surprise and inevitability.

Herbert   Your emphasis on truth is very telling, Reg. I think you've just put your finger on the secret of crime fiction as literature: the reader expects the surprise, which the crime writer enjoys delivering, but the novelist at the heart of the crime writer also demands revelation of truth.

Hill   Yes, truth about human character and experience. That's the ultimate goal, isn't it?

▶ JANE LANGTON

It is not insignificant that Jane Langton entitled her first mystery novel *The Transcendental Murder*. Of course, it was set in Concord, Massachusetts, the home of Ralph Waldo Emerson and Henry David Thoreau, founders of the Transcendentalist Movement. But the term "transcendentalism" also defines the heart of Langton's mysteries for adults: according to *A Handbook to Literature* (Sixth edition, edited by C. Hugh Holman and William Harmon [New York: Macmillan, 1992]) transcendentalism is "a reliance on the intuition and the conscience." These are exactly the qualities that inspire a dedication to discovering the truth and even the detecting methods of Langton's lanky series sleuth, Professor Homer Kelly, as he investigates murder and mayhem in New England and as far afield as Florence, Italy.

A reliance on intuition and conscience as well as a desire to share a transcendentalist sense of wonder at one's experience of nature, human nature, and the world at large informs all of Langton's works, including her numerous children's books. Langton says she came to her transcendental awareness and her career as a writer after several very fascinating but "false turns" in academic and intellectual pursuits.

During a happy and secure childhood spent in Massachusetts and Wilmington, Delaware, where her family flourished despite the Depression, Langton developed a lasting love of books and enjoyed watercolor painting and the collecting and making of paper dolls. For some of her handmade paper dolls—whom she imagined to be "orphans with enormous eyes and beautiful blonde hair"—she penned sad life stories. But her schooling, which emphasized diagramming sentences over English composition, did not prepare her for the rigors of writing college papers, and she was easily discouraged by negative comments from one of her professors at Wellesley College. Although another professor urged her to major in English, Langton remained for a time true to her desire to become a scientist, a dream inspired by her reading of the life of Marie Curie years before. While the mathematics necessary to the study of astronomy was very challenging to her, Langton completed her degree at the University of Michigan—where she also met and married her husband—in 1944.

Together they moved to Massachusetts where Langton pursued a degree in art history at Radcliffe College and entered into childrearing, giving birth to three sons. Settled in Lincoln, near Concord, Langton rediscovered her love of children's books—and her ability to write and later to illustrate them—while she was bringing up small children. Her Newbery-award-winning book, *The Fledgling*, is now required reading in many elementary schools.

Her decision to move from children's books to crime writing occurred after her daily round of passing Walden Pond in the course of doing ordinary errands inspired her to read Thoreau's *Walden*. "There was no overnight transformation," she recalls. "The book sank in slowly, but it saturated everything." Langton says she became "a transcendentalist of the Concord stripe" and created a detective who would share her "affliction."

Although Kelly has strayed from his Concord neighborhood to investigate murders on Nantucket Island, on the campus of Harvard University, in Boston's Isabella Stewart Gardner Museum, in Emily Dickinson's house in Amherst, Massachusetts, and in a villa in Florence, he has come home in Langton's latest novel, *God in Concord*, which takes an Indian student, Ananda Singh, on a pilgrimage to visit Walden Pond. Singh represents the worldwide appreciation that exists for the works of Thoreau and makes a wonderful contrast with the money-hungry land developers who threaten to despoil the landscape surrounding Walden Pond. This novel features Langton's unique blend of humor, and yes, "intuition and conscience."

In a soft-spoken but earnest voice, Langton shared her thoughts about her work over homemade soup and sandwiches in her snowbound Lincoln home. The closest neighbor to the site of Thoreau's cabin for one hundred and forty years, Langton's farmhouse sits on a property with a view Thoreau might have cherished, sloping down to fields cut across with low, hand-built stone walls. Beyond the farmhouse kitchen, along the narrow corridor, is a curious room plastered with posters of Florence, Italy, and artwork by Langton's son. Here, the wide floorboards characteristic of the oldest of our American houses contrast with the word processor on the wooden table, sporting a screen displaying a high-speed passage through the stars.

Herbert   In your latest book, *God In Concord*, you have explored more engagingly and deeply than ever your enthusiasm with transcendentalism and your concerns for the natural and historic environment in which you live. In this novel you use not only your sleuth, Homer Kelly, as your spokesman but you also employ the delightful Indian pilgrim to Walden Pond, Ananda Singh.

Langton   I enjoy Homer Kelly because he is a fanatic about the same things that I am. And he's kind of nutty voice for me, and anything that I think, he can say, and he'll say it out loud and he will say it *loud-ly*. I would hate to give him up because then I would feel I'd lost a voice. And he is much more uninhibited than I am. I'm timid, and of course he's bold and rash. Nothing stops him from saying what he thinks.

Herbert   Oh, he's marvelous. I can even picture the way this very tall man folds himself into a chair. What qualities of his do you identify with the most?

Langton   His ecstasy and rapture. No, that's not the word. There is a word that I am looking for, which I feel very strongly in myself. And it means, a sort of wild abandon and enthusiasm. It's a transcendental response to the world.

Herbert   Would you explain this further for the benefit of our readers?

Langton   (Pauses.) You are constantly aware of how astonishing things are and you see things in relation to the dull normalcy of ordinary life. The world has these *shafts* of astonishment in it. I mean [she gestures at the view] look at the snow coming down!

Herbert   Having been acquainted with you for some years, I've noticed that you don't seem to take even your surroundings for granted. I think this is a quality of writers in general. But it's especially true with you.

Langton   You have to be very suspicious of it, suspicious of one's own enthusiasm. It can be foolish; it can be silly. And there's so much pain and suffering in the very heart of things; there is a cruelty [in] the very heart of nature, all that cruelty, which I can't get over. You just can't get over that. It's just there.

Herbert   That's right. Your mysteries seem to tell us that this is true not only in nature—where there is the unqualified beauty of the woodthrush's song in contrast with the quaking bog that might devour anything that strays into it—but of human nature.

Langton   Yes, yes.

Herbert   This capacity for cruelty is inherent in human personality or character?

Langton   People are *not* good and kind altogether.

Herbert   Well, you see that in *God and Concord*. I think there are a number of places in this book where you point out this rapacious, devouring nature of the people, and then take us into a frightening scene in nature.

Langton   Or into a lovely one. What I really loved doing was to take the odious Mimi Pink—

Herbert   —whose greedy goal in life is to convert the shops in Concord from those that would serve the practical needs of the locals to expensive purveyors of crystal and perfume—

Langton   —and I have her at her perfume store and have this exotic perfume being opened up and then instantly you go to the forest where the elderflowers are just opening up and [their fragrance] is *free of charge*! And then there is the bunny rabbit [for sale], the little furry bunny toy, [whose fur] of course has been taken from a live rabbit, and the woman [in the shop] is thinking how cuddly and sweet it is, and then here in the wilderness they come upon a wounded real rabbit. Contrasting by putting the two side by side: I love to do that.

Herbert   You also succeed at this when you show Ananda Singh's progress through the landscape toward Walden Pond. The garbage dump and trailer park along the way to the idyllic destination of his pilgrimage certainly contrast with the unspoiled world that any reader of Thoreau expects to find there!

Langton   I needed to have someone come in who represents the readership that Thoreau has all over the world and come *as a pilgrim* to this sacred site, this spot where their "god" lived. And so Ananda is that. And having him be from India is appropriate because Thoreau was a great admirer of the sacred books of India, the Hindu books, and [Ananda] is also a kind of a re-creation of a gentle, noble figure in my children's books.

Herbert   Prince Krishna.

Langton   Yes, he appears in *The Swing in the Summer House* and *The Diamond in the Window*.

Herbert   I'd like to know more about your inspiration for the idealistic Ananda Singh.

Langton   I needed to have an objective observer. The people of the town of Concord are so used to Walden Pond and Henry Thoreau and their literary heritage and their Revolutionary heritage and so on that they don't give it much respect. They're kind of sick of having people tell them, "You've got this magnificent heritage! You've got to save this piece of ground and that piece of ground and this other piece of ground and this building and that building. You can't do anything to Concord; you've got to leave it absolutely as it is! You've got to get rid of the trailer park and you've got to get rid of the dump, which do not grace the scene and are an insult to the memory of Henry Thoreau."

Herbert   So the citizenry is weary of all this.

Langton   Yes. So I created Ananda Singh and he comes and walks out the precious pilgrim's way to Walden Pond and comes upon the highway. He comes upon the huge dump and he comes upon the beach and is very much distressed. It's to make people wake up a little bit and see the world view that people have of Thoreau.

Herbert   You mean the worldwide appreciation for his thinking?

Langton   Yes.

Herbert   *God in Concord* may do a great deal for the saving of the landscape. I wondered if it is typical for your books to arise from your concern with an issue, a mission.

Langton   Not usually, no. I don't think that's the case. It comes out of an interest in a place.

Herbert   It seems to me it is often a sense of place combined with another dimension, such as the music that is being rehearsed and performed in *The Memorial Hall Murder*.

Langton   Yes, or the poetry of Dante with the Florence book.

Herbert   Yes, *The Dante Game*.

Langton   I should point out that in most of these cases, there is a whole lot of ignorance behind my superficial enjoyment.

Herbert   You're too modest. You can't deny that you have the background in astronomy to support your use of the eclipse in *Dark Nantucket Noon*!

Langton   I saw the eclipse the first day I saw Nantucket. They were kind of thrilling together. Yes, it *was* a sense of place and the additional dimension, as you say, that inspired me there. And, with *Emily Dickinson Is Dead*, it's been the poetry of Emily Dickinson and her house—it's relation to the poetry—that I responded to. The sense of her presence in that house.

Herbert   With *Emily Dickinson Is Dead*, you also treated the bitter history of the Quabbin Reservoir, which was originally a lovely populated valley that was flooded in order to provide a water source for metropolitan Boston. The bitterness behind the loss of homes and villages there worked in very nicely with the celebration of the Emily Dickinson Centennial during which sophisticated academics flooded the haunts of local people.

Langton   Yes.

Herbert   I would love to hear about some of the research that helped you to construct this and other books.

Langton   I've talked to people who have been removed from the Swift River Valley. They have a little museum, devoted to the history of the area. It's a very provincial little amateur museum, but with lots of things: boxes that remain from the box factory and straw hats they made.

Herbert   How did you learn about the reservoir shaft in which the bodies were disposed?

Langton   I wanted to see Shaft 12, which was this little building, and they wouldn't talk to me at the MDC, the Metropolitan District Commission. They wouldn't talk to me. I assume it's because they didn't want me to throw a gruesome, dead body into their nice clean water, even a fictional dead body.

Herbert   You've had a number of occasions where people have been resistant to your desire to deposit fictional dead bodies on their doorsteps.

Langton   The Gardner Museum didn't like it, and neither did Mrs. Dibble, who was at Emily Dickinson's house. But I always feel that a cat can look at a king and a writer can write about almost anything.

Herbert   Aha!

Langton   But I finally was told where to go to find Shaft 12. You park on a certain place on this highway. You climb over the fence and there is a road there, and you just walk in. It was February and it was cold but I walked and walked and walked. I walked about three miles, I guess. I was cold and I was hungry and I thought maybe I had gone the wrong direction and was in the wrong place. And so finally I turned around. And along came an MDC van and a man called Richard O'Brien, who put his head out and he said, "Lady, you've lost your way to the shopping mall."

Herbert   (Laughs.)

Langton   And I told him what I wanted and he said, "Hop in." And it was just around another corner. And he had a key, he let me into this building. It was wonderful! And I saw the trap doors in the floor and I saw the crane and I saw the big bucket. And I was able to concoct this wild story, which I couldn't have otherwise. It was just wonderful that he came along.

Herbert   What a stroke of serendipity! I often wonder about the role of serendipity in writing mystery novels, because you would assume that a book of this sort would need to be very tightly constructed with the author utterly in control in order to know where every clue is to be laid. But through discussing this with numerous crime and mystery writers, I have discovered that a surprising amount of serendipity is involved.

Langton   It's in the process of finding out things that it occurs. You can't invent the story at home. I couldn't.

Herbert   You have to get out there and meet people and uncover things?

Langton   Yes. It has to grow out of the place. It has to have kind of an organic connection to the environment. You can't just state that your character committed the murder on Fifth Avenue or something and then suddenly: New York, it's all New York. The story has to rise out of Fifth Avenue-ness, somehow, or whatever the crummy street is!

Herbert   (Laughs.) That's right, that's right. So you leave you desk and enter the scene yourself to discover and investigate what might happen, to learn what possibilities might arise out of the scene itself?

Langton   Well, of course one is ready, is eager for impressions and stimulation and for something that one can use. I sometimes feel as though it's a bag—you are putting in all of these things in the bag. And as you begin to write, you've got more and more stuff that's coming out of the bag. At some point you have to draw a string around the top of the bag. You have to put everything together again and close the bag. I do have a tendency to have too many things. (Smiles.) And in the beginning, I think, "This will be like Robert Parker. This will have two characters and maybe three at the most. There will be some tight situation at the beginning, some sort of conflict, some suspense. And then you will just follow these three characters as they interact, and that will be it." [But] pretty soon, I have a *telephone book* of people, and they are sprawling all over the place! And there are subplots, and there are sub-subplots, and so I have a hard time drawing that string—pulling that drawstring.

Herbert And there are details, visual details, and environmental details, that cry out to be used.

Langton In the book that I have just finished, I wanted to write a book about organs, pipe organs. I thought it would be fun to draw pictures of organs; that's where I started. What I really needed was some kind of church, because the organs [of this size] are only in churches. Where was this church going to be? I wanted to use a real setting, as I always do. So I wandered around Beacon Hill and the Back Bay, and I went into all the churches and looked at their organs, and wanted to hear their organs and so on. And I walked into the Baptist Church, which is on Clarendon and Commonwealth—do you know that church?

Herbert No, I'm afraid not.

Langton Well, there are sculptures way up on the tower. Oh, and the church was empty—it was a Saturday or a Monday or something, and the minister was there. He asked me what I wanted, and I said I just wanted to look and see the sanctuary, and I told him some of the details that I was looking for. He said, "Across the street is an empty lot. It has a playground on it." I looked across, and there indeed was this playground. Right across the street, on Commonwealth and Clarendon. I suddenly discovered that I didn't want to use a real church, and here was a place to build a church. So I built a fictional church there, an 1880s church. It was his cleverness. It was really wonderful that this random person I met gave me this suggestion.

Herbert It was serendipity.

Langton Yes. But I had to keep probing. I had to be there. I had to *know* there was something that I needed an answer for.

Herbert It sounds like this book also arose from more than the sense of place; in this case it was your love of architecture and drawing and, again, a musical connection.

Langton It's certain music by J. S. Bach. And it's organ music, and it's the writing of Martin Luther, which I don't know a great deal about.

Herbert What is that book going to be called?

Langton It's called—well, this is sort of a joke—it's called *Divine Inspiration*.

Herbert Great title!

Langton It's a novel of suspense, and it's all about organ pipes and sewer pipes as well. The sewer pipes are just as important as the organ pipes. And it's something that gets one excited. You get a sort of an afflatus of excitement. I think you have to write out of some excitement. For *Divine Inspiration*, I talked to the building manager—the sexton, I guess you would call him—at Old South [Church], and he was wonderful. I have a friend who has been so helpful over and over again. Her name is Libby Blank and she works for the Boston Water and Sewer Commission. And she gave me all kinds of help. She gave me maps of the underground sewers and the underground water supply in the Back Bay, and she told me who I should talk to. The whole Back Bay is built on wooden pilings. And if the pilings dry out the buildings are in danger. And I went into the basement of the Trinity Church, and there is a manhole there. And you can look down the manhole there.

Herbert   It sounds like you researched every historic Boston church until you came upon the right combination of the technically useful and the spooky detail.

Langton   And then I created my own building after all!

Herbert   I notice the twinkle in your eye when you describe this process of investigation. What about the writing itself? Do you agree with Jonathan Gash that the writing process is self-delighting?

Langton   (Pauses.) Well, when it's going well. When it's going badly, you think you are going to bore people to death. And you are not sure you can do it again, and you wonder if you haven't lost it. And then I comfort myself by thinking that I've always thought that each time. It's an awful lot of plodding.

Herbert   Plodding, or plotting?

Langton   Plodding. Grinding away every day, and sometimes you lose faith.

Herbert   Well, what is your daily habit? Do you write daily?

Langton   Every day. *Every* day, because I'm so *slow*. Six drafts of a long book takes a long time. If I didn't keep after it every day, I'd never finish. And so I work on it every single day. Christmas Day I was up fairly early. Of course there are interruptions. You have to keep going out and finding out things.

Herbert   But that is still work.

Langton   So it is not all work at the desk but I do work every day. I sometimes think about the giddy life one might lead and [the] sacrificing of friendship. There isn't very much jollification when you're grinding so hard. And then, after the sixth draft, I have to spend a couple of months doing the pictures, and that's very—it's laborious. I like doing it, but it's hard work.

Herbert But your drawings look so spontaneous, not to mention your dialogue!

Langton I'm a bad enough artist so that I can't draw well the first time. I have to go over it and over it and trace it until it's become like *iron*.

Herbert It may feel that way to you—

Langton It doesn't feel very spontaneous to me. I do make heavy weather of the whole thing. When occasionally you feel you've brought off a good paragraph then of course you are pleased.

Herbert Taking Jonathan Gash's comments a step further, he noted that related to the self-delighting aspect of the writing process is his need to please only himself while writing. He said he has very little awareness of the potential reader as he writes.

Langton I just don't think about people out there. I know that its got to be a certain way, and that's all. I can tell when I'm getting dull; I have to intensify this a bit. But it's myself I'm pleasing.

Herbert Do you work a typical schedule during the day if you're writing at home, and not scurrying around churches or investigating water shafts?

Langton I get at it as early as possible, and go on it until I get sleepy, around one o'clock or two o'clock or something.

Herbert How do you organize your work?

Langton Well, I don't have a system. I charge in anywhere. I don't begin at the beginning with the first draft. I just write anything I can think of. And sometimes, a scene will suggest itself to me as being something that will be amusing and interesting, entertaining. And so, [I] get a few little nuclei like that, notes around which to build the rest. And sometimes they can be fun, set you walking in the right direction. Not that there isn't a great deal of pleasure in it—*of course* there is— but there is a lot of taking the sentence and turning it back to front, or looking at a paragraph and realizing there is no transition here, and having to do that—an awful lot of that.

Herbert Yes. What do you find most enjoyable about the writing process?

Langton Well, taking your finished book and reading over a passage and saying, "Aha! *I* did that." Having chosen the passage very carefully! (Smiles.) I like the thought that a book that you were pleased with is going to be around for awhile, so that the year has not vanished; the year is represented by this object on the wall, on the shelf. I think if I weren't writing books, I would feel, as I get older, that "Oh, gosh, it's all going, it's disappearing—what did it amount to?" I think I'm too much of a Puritan, a hard-working "greasy grind," as we used to say, to ever have had [a] jolly life. I know people who just have a wonderful time all the time. They have many, many friends; they are always going to concerts and the theatre and art galleries and having a thick, dense cultural life—one of great social joy and interrelations with friends. But I think if I weren't writing books, I would be doing something equally grinding. I don't know what. At least there is this object that I have. Painters probably feel the same way; at least they've got a picture on the wall.

Herbert   I don't think creative writing is a process that can be hurried. You must work at your own pace. What about aids to the writing process? I know that from time to time you have used a large board with Post-it notes all over it to help you organize the action. Is that something that you've done commonly for most of your books?

Langton   I've done it three times. It didn't occur to me until about three books ago. And then, it just seemed to be what I needed. It's been a big help.

Herbert   Can you explain the process further?

Langton   Post-it notes are little tiny—they come in all sizes, but I use the tiniest kinds, which is about two inches by one and a half inches. And they are sticky on the back, with such an interesting kind of glue that it can be picked up and put down again and will still stick. So I draw a little episode on each Post-it note, an episode I know I want to have, and I put them down in what I think is the right order, on a big piece of cardboard.

Herbert   When you say "draw" you mean you make a drawing of something from the scene?

Langton   Yes. And when I look at them I think, "No, this should be here" or "This should be there." And they are in the wrong order, and I see it; there is a scene missing. So it helps me visualize it—I'm a very visual person as so many people are.

Herbert   This must be especially useful to a writer who creates scenes *out* of chronological order.

Langton   Oh, yes.

Herbert   You're in good company, Jane. P. D. James is one of the few other few authors I've met who can construct a book without following strict chronological sequence.

Langton   Virginia Woolf talks about that; she talks so eloquently about her own writing. In her diary, she will say, "I'm going to write the scene about the dinner party, and then I'll skip ahead to where James is meeting . . . ."

Herbert   Isn't that amazing?

Langton   It's as if she is carrying a light through darkened rooms. So she wrote not necessarily in absolute sequence.

Herbert   Now, I wonder if the fact that you write out of sequence accounts for your need to write as many following drafts as you do? Particularly in a mystery, every smidgen of information has to be carefully laid out. Do you have to make lots of adjustments so that the clues are delivered in the proper order?

Langton   My first draft is really just a big mess. I haven't got the characters right; they've got the wrong names; I've got too many people or not enough people; and I don't know quite what's happening or how to approach the end. I have to have *some* notion about the end, but I don't quite know how to do it. And so I stop before I get to the end because I just give up on that—at least I know now how to *begin* a book! So I begin it over again, and go through it a second time, and get a little closer to the end. But I've still got things mixed up. By the time I do the third, I've more or less got things in the right order. But they are kind of stenographic, skeletonic, if there is such a word, skeletal. And so I go through it a fourth, a fifth, a sixth time to do three things: to intensify, to [assure that] there is no lapse of logic and transition, and to polish. The polishing of course is laborious: to be sure it is absolutely silken, that there is no clumsiness and no rocks in there. So the reader never stops being in the story, rather than in the construction of the story.

Herbert   So you use multiple drafts not only to refine language but to reconstruct the whole?

Langton   You couldn't read the first, second, or third drafts. You couldn't read them! There would be nothing there to read. And if you read the fourth one, you would think, "My gosh, this is terrible."

Herbert   So you don't really discover the whole of the story until you're on the last couple of drafts?

Langton   [With] the last book, I think I didn't even write the ending until the fifth draft. And then of course I had to rewrite it a number of times to get it right. But everything has to move together toward this end.

Herbert   This is something that P. D. James has pointed out, underlining the thinking of Henry James. He believed that there had to be a unity that he likened to shafts of light finally coming together. In his case, these shafts of light might finally come together to illuminate his golden bowl with its flaw. And when you think about this, it is very applicable to the mystery novel because the insight that one gains from a well-wrought mystery often illuminates a flaw of character.

Langton   Yes. And there is something that is accidental which I enjoy. It is completely accidental; discovering as you write along that anything, say, in the first half of the book, can become an element in a pattern. Anything. A wart on someone's nose can be an element in a pattern. And you can bring it in a second time. You say, "Ah, here's an opportunity for the wart on his nose." And then at the end, the wartiness of his nose is somehow triumphant. And so you bring together all these other little elements. And the real joy is to bring them together in a fist at the end. All those fingers coming together. But of course you're in danger of having too many things and confusing the poor reader and having it not work out into a nice beautiful perfect pattern, but just to be a mishmash. So one is constantly checking.

Herbert   So it is not simply a matter of pulling that drawstring bag shut again, but it's making sure those contents are arranged in some orderly manner?

Langton   Mm hm. I love doing last paragraphs.

Herbert   Do you always write them last?

Langton   Well, sometimes I have the last paragraph in mind before I come to the end. There's a good joke in the last line of the one I'm just finishing. It refers to the title, *Divine Inspiration*. My son David and I were watching television and we had the little wand, the little remote control. And we couldn't make it work somehow. And David said, "What it needs is a button labeled 'divine inspiration.'" So we thought, "Wouldn't it be funny if there were a button labeled 'Div. Insp.'?" So, as the new organ is being constructed in the story, the man who's going to play it wants a stopknob that says "Div. Insp." It isn't connected to anything, but he feels it would help to pull it out. And in the very end it says, "And the Divine Inspiration stopknob continued to be connected to nothing. To nothing on earth at all."

Herbert   Oh, that's marvelous! Having a stopknob for divine inspiration would certainly take the struggle out of organ practice! I wouldn't mind having a key for that on my word processor! And speaking of struggle, I notice that in *God in Concord* you describe a physical struggle at the end.

Langton   The character is actually in the garbage compactor, yes.

Herbert   Sue Grafton told me that she certainly thinks that these physical struggles are an excellent way of showing a real battle between the forces of good and evil, in a very definite manner, and that it appeals to her to write such scenes.

Langton   For me, it's very heavy work, because it doesn't come naturally to me and I've never witnessed violence at all, except in television and movies. My personal experience of violence extends as far as observing little boys having a tussle under the tables at the Sunday school. And I suppose I've spanked my children once or twice when I was in a terrible rage! And so I do a lot of using the thesaurus, looking for synonyms for "fought" and "socked." It is not easy.

Herbert   That's a great use of the thesaurus! I imagine your copy, dog-eared at all the terms of violence!

Langton   (Laughs.) And [the violent scenes] come out, I think, as rather heavy-handed.

Herbert   It must be from all that experience in spanking! Your mention of the thesaurus causes me to ask whether or not there are any superstitions associated with the writing process for you. Some authors have to have a certain object beside them, or they must approach their work in a particular manner.

Langton   You mean, just the mechanics? Or do I have a rabbit's foot? Or do I always read some passage? I used to think I ought to read Joyce Cary's *The Horse's Mouth* every morning before starting because it's so buoyant and this wonderfully rascally character leaps through the pages. I thought it would set my mind in the right direction. I wish I had more spontaneity. I think in youth there is much more of that available, the freedom and spontaneity, the dream-like ability to let go and be a little bit insane. But one loses that, and so if there were an artificial form for bringing it on again, I would be all for it.

Herbert   Well, it sounds like you do have that when you encounter ideas during the research process. You are very receptive, then, to twists and turns that the book might take.

Langton   You snatch at something.

Herbert   Right. I think you should compliment yourself, Jane; I don't know if you do this, because you're so modest. But a lot of writers might go out and, for instance, seek out the sound of the woodthrush for the benefit of their narrative. But then they would hear the woodthrush and leave it at that. Not everyone can see the potential for other things in the scene that could be used imaginatively.

And not every writer would be willing to take the chance—*and* devote the time—to alter an envisioned plot once the book is well under way.

Langton   You have to be on the snatch. You have to be on the snatch.

Herbert   Yes.

Langton   But while we're talking about the writing process, there is something else I try to avoid, and sometimes succeed in doing so and sometimes cannot, and that is having a lot of explanation at the end. I try to avoid it, and hope that the thing will just be so obvious that you can just say, "Aha!" But sometimes it takes pages and pages to explain the crime.

Herbert   That is certainly a hurdle that crime and mystery writers have to deal with.

Langton   It would be wonderful if it just worked out by itself.

Herbert   But of course sometimes that section of resolution is delightful. I think of Michael Innes. There was a real section in almost all of his books where they would really have to sit down in a library and the sleuth would explain what had gone on, with literary allusions dropping out of the sky and everything else. But I can see how you wouldn't want that in every single one of your books.

Langton   Dorothy Sayers, in *The Nine Tailors*, which is such a famous book, has the most dramatic conclusion, the most thrilling discovery. You realize that the last page happened on the first page, and that Peter Wimsey himself was contributing to the death of this man, and it's just overpowering. It's a sensational ending, and it works magnificently well, but she still has pages and pages of explanation. You forgive her for it because of the dramatic discovery.

Herbert   I find it significant that you say, "You *forgive* her for it." It sounds as if you find some of the conventions of the mystery novel to be undesirable. Or perhaps you find the structure to be confining?

Langton   I think I disappoint many readers who do want a puzzle all the way to the end. They want that, whereas I am apt to give it away halfway through and say, "Well, I can't go on any farther keeping this a secret." For one thing, I think it's boring to have a whole lot of red herrings. I think it's a style that's been used so much that it is tiresome. And I would rather show you one person's character development leading up to what he or she is going to do. It's the "whydunit" instead of the "whodunit."

Herbert   Do you think this reflects an inclination to write a novel of character rather than a novel of cardboard characters?

Langton   Don't forget my paper dolls! But yes, it turns out that that's what I hope to have done, but I don't think about that when I start. I think, "I've got to make these characters more interesting. They are such stereotypes; they have got to be more than that." That's another thing that happens as one goes through draft after draft, the characters become more real, I think, and more dense.

Herbert   A moment ago you spoke about your reluctance to write a lengthy resolution section in your mysteries. But while you may feel that you'd like to keep your explanations short and sweet, I wonder how you feel about the fact that most mysteries still do offer a satisfying sense of closure for the reader?

Langton   I don't have that feeling that people often express about a mystery, that they read it because it gives them a sense of closure, or finality or something, and life refuses to do that for them. But having said that, I guess I *do* tidy things up. I enjoy tidying up, getting out my feather duster and sweeping off the crumbs of delinquency. It's perhaps a little excessive but it's always so much fun to do, get everyone straightened out. Put them in the right corners, put the round pegs in the round holes and the square pegs in the square holes. And I *do* get a grisly sort of pleasure out of someone getting their comeuppance. When my character gets his on that garbage dump, oh, I love that! And when the church falls down, I enjoy that. It comes down with a tremendous *crash*. You know, sometimes they blow up a building on purpose, and they show it in slow motion falling down. I don't know why that's so pleasing, but it is. The thought of the labor that it took to build it and all of the care with which it was hammered together, and soldered together, and bolted together, and to see it all just come down, there is a satisfaction in it.

Herbert   Speaking of that ability to give the bad guys their comeuppance, do you see the detective story as an opportunity to write a moral allegory?

Langton   I don't think I'm doing that for that reason. It's a tradition and style in which I am able to work. I think that if I try to write a straight novel—and I often wish that I could do that, and weren't constrained by the necessity to have crime and a solution— I think that it would just be lost. I don't think anybody would pay any attention. I could probably write a creditable, workmanlike novel but I think it would just disappear. It would just evaporate. So I continue to do this, because I feel I can. I don't have any great moral message I am trying to get across. At least that isn't the reason that I do it. I do have good guys and bad guys. I do enjoy my good guys, who are full of flaws. And some of my bad guys are altogether too bad, and I don't think anybody is as bad as all that. I don't know anything about criminal psychosis. It would be good if I did, but I don't.

Herbert   That leads me to ask whether or not you consciously avoid describing the pleasure that the criminal takes in his or her crime?

Langton   I have occasionally been in the mind of the perpetrator. In the book called *Natural Enemy*, I was. I saw him thinking. And who else have I been inside of? Mimi Pink, I think I got into her mind, but it wasn't a very savory experience. You saw her childhood when she was angry at her sister and her mother. But I don't think she is a fully developed person. Winnie Gall—I think I feel happier about Winnie Gall. She's the very fat woman who kills Alison Grove in *Emily Dickinson Is Dead*. I think I've felt a good deal of sympathy with her. *I* could eat twelve dozen donuts. In a moment of depression, it would be a natural thing to do.

Herbert   In other words, the way you get into the mind of your murderers is to to look at their vulnerabilities, to say, "Here is this person's weakness and it is understandable to me."

Langton   I think it's Aristotle who said, "Character is fate." What it means, of course, is what happens to you is what you deserve. And you want to do that with your characters: through their own behavior, they should achieve the result that happens to them; they should be the agents of their own end. And when you can work that out, that's good. That's why I like what happened to Mimi Pink; she went from one kind of trash to another kind of trash. (Smiles.)

Herbert   But another memorable character is rather redeemed by love. I wonder if this is possible in part because she is a young person and not hardened in her ways as the adult characters are? I think one of the refreshing aspects of your work is that you do portray people in different age groups. So often mystery novels just give you the adult circle of suspects. There are not many young people.

Langton   I like writing about babies, and I like writing about old women because I am an old woman. I like writing about different ages, that's true. I have a hard time writing about macho young men. I find myself often having to do it, but I don't think I do it well. Who knows how they really think? I don't!

Herbert   Do you think that your ease in writing about multiple age groups in the mystery has anything to do with your experience writing for the young adult audience?

Langton   They are a very different sort of writing. I don't know that one goes over to the other, but perhaps you put the same sorts of things into it, whatever is in your character as a person goes into both kinds of stories. I think most writers are observers of other people. And I try to grasp what the honest, *honest* thought of someone in any particular situation might be. I think by asking yourself what you would *really* think—

Herbert   —even the most unflattering thoughts, looking to the darker side of the whole range of possible emotions in a given situation—

Langton   —the vain thought, the vanity. Vanity and modesty are such interesting reverses. Two sides of the same thing. Somebody said, "With modesty, I will conquer the world." I go by that. That's my motto.

Herbert   And the vanity in the characters leads them to their crimes and their comeuppance. After all, isn't pride the deadliest of the seven deadly sins?

Langton   Yes, they get their comeuppances but I don't think that I go about murdering people heartlessly and ruthlessly and leaving them there lying in their blood. And, well, I have a sense of, "I've *got* to do it, it's part of what you've got to do." It's kind of like eating your spinach. The mystery writer has to kill people. So, I, in sort of a *dogged* way, I kill them by one means or another. But I don't enjoy that. At one point in *Murder at the Gardner*, there is this awful woman, impossible, Mrs. What's-her-name. She is killed. And Homer Kelly looks at her and realizes—well, let me read you the passage: he realized "the trouble that nature had gone to in the first place in order to create this complex bundle of protoplasm. He couldn't help thinking of his son and the secret beginnings inside his mother. The slow growth in the dark as the microscopic fingers took shape. And the bones formed cavities and prominences, and the miniature organs expanded, and began to function, until at last the perfect infant creature was ready to be born. All that work and preparation, all that miraculous growth and diversity here gone utterly to waste." (Pauses.) That's the way one *should* feel.

Herbert   Yes.

Langton   And often one heartlessly slays people right and left. And they are just bunches of protoplasm on the floor, which *shouldn't be*. I think there should be a sense of pathos in the death of anyone.

Herbert   Well, even in the cases of your most unlikable characters, you always show us that there was a flaw in character that may not have even been the character's fault. There is always something there that gives you that little bit of pity for the individual.

Langton   I want you to feel some pity and not ruthless extinction.

Herbert   Do you consider yourself to be particularly sensitive to the fragility of life, Jane?

Langton   I certainly am aware of the preciousness of life. And how terrible it would be to die young. There have been moments when I thought I was dying.

Herbert   Really? Were you ill, or in danger?

Langton   I had a sort of a heart problem, which seemed like a heart attack at the time but actually was not. It was a long time ago but it was frightening at the time. But I suppose the thing is to feel each day is a gift—sometimes you just plod along and you're not thinking about these things at all, and other times you wonder how many days you have left, and hoard them and think, "This is enough, just to be alive." Emily Dickinson said that, somewhere, the mere sense of being alive is enough. The mere sense of living is enough. You have to keep that before you. This is good: breathing, looking out and seeing things in perspective. To walk around a tree and see the branches move against one another, to look at the fur on a dog's back. All those different colors blending in a wonderful browny, whitey, blacky colors.

Herbert   Since mystery writing is usually centered around a puzzle concerned with death, I have wondered just what causes writers to choose this genre, knowing that death will be a major concern of each of their books.

Langton   Is it some kind of strange and grisly thing about our century, which is so involved with violence and killing people? Are we part of that abnormal fixation on death? Is this a queer thing that people will look back on one day as they looked back on nineteenth-century prudery, and say, "How odd; how strange and sick"? I forget what your question was. (Laughs.)

Herbert   I guess I am trying to determine whether or not the majority of mystery writers is particularly preoccupied with death.

Langton   No. It is something to be avoided.

Herbert   (Laughs.) Do you have a personal faith that would help you in the face of death?

Langton   Well, I certainly don't believe in life after death. I think I've had a happy life and will be ready to die when the time comes, as I would not have been when I was younger. We have a good friend who was a quadriplegic who was often in the hospital with some kind of breathing disorder and we had a really goofy minister who went to see him. And he [the minister] said, "You want to talk about death, don't you?" And our friend said, "It is a subject in which I am not interested."

Both   (Laugh.)

Herbert   Turning to the other end of life, its start, would you be willing to share an image of yourself as a child?

Langton   I was born here in Boston. My father was teaching at MIT, geology. And so we were here for six years, and then we went to Delaware. I grew up in Delaware. But I didn't like Delaware. At six years old I knew it was the wrong place. And one time in school when we were supposed to stand up and sing "Oh, Our Delaware" I remained seated.

Herbert   (Laughs.) Looking back on your childhood, do you see yourself as headed down the road to becoming a writer?

Langton   No. I think I was someone who kept switching and changing as I became a teenager. Before I went to college I read—I made that awful mistake, you shouldn't read books [laughs]—I read a life of Madame Curie, by her daughter. And I said, "Oh, I want to be a scientist like that!" My father was a scientist—I revered my father. But that was the wrong direction.

Herbert   What about drawing and painting, and reading?

Langton   Yes. I can remember being totally intent on watercolor painting and drawing. I always loved to read, as I suppose all writers did love to read. And I never stopped loving children's books. I still love to read them. Especially picture books. There were library books and then there were the ones my father read to us after supper. We would lean against him on the brown plush sofa while he read to us from A. A. Milne's poems and stories. He had a squeaky voice for Piglet and a gruff voice for Pooh and a sad voice for Rabbit. We never tired of the stories. He also read to us from Dumas and Howard Pyle.

     And I recall that one Christmas there was a glorious, stunning, overwhelming present with my name on it. I had never dreamed of asking for it. I didn't know I wanted it. It was a black and shining Remington typewriter, smelling of gear oil and inked ribbon. Instantly I began practicing the exercises in the little booklet. Learning to type without looking at the keys took no time at all.

Herbert   So here were some early signs of the writer.

Langton   But, you see, I didn't stick with it. I veered off, left and right.

Herbert   But you eventually came back to your love of books when your boys were small and you had reason to make children's books a part of your life again.

Langton   Yes, that's so. And then of course after a while I began to write for adults, too.

Herbert   Your mysteries always succeed on a number of levels. They may be thought provoking; they have humor; they tell us something about ourselves. But they are also invariably entertaining. This reminds me of the question that I put to Brian Aldiss a long time ago. And his answer inspired the title of this volume. I asked him if he consciously set out to add entertaining elements to his work or if the entertainment was just a natural result of his personality. He told me, "When I think about this, I grieve about it because I have discovered in me the fatal art of entertainment. But I have always wanted to write the *undeniable* book which, in the words of Pushkin, would 'lay waste the hearts of men.' And the two are at war; this desire to entertain and the desire to write the undeniable book."

Langton   That doesn't worry me because it seems to me a noble ambition to   simply entertain the reader.   You think of someone picking up something that is really just black marks on white paper, and bursting out laughing, when these black marks were put on the paper a hundred and fifty years ago, and the person is *dead* who wrote them, and yet, [those marks] elicit laughter in a contemporary reader. That seems to be a noble, noble thing to have done.   I think entertaining someone's dull, boring life is of immense value, and I don't feel that one has to achieve great literary excellence in order to feel that you have accomplished something.

Herbert   But can a mystery novel achieve the highest levels? Are there any inherent limitations?

Langton   What does it mean to have a high literary level? Does it mean anything more than writing something that stays with you, and that you remember with affection and pleasure for the rest of your life? It seems to me that there are mystery novels that achieve that. A piece of writing doesn't have to be [a] profound, tragic kind of great saga, [or] epic to achieve a level that is enviable among writers. To affect a great many people with a pleasure that comes from reading is the achievement. Memorable scenes, memorable characters: you can have all those things [in a mystery]. If it all hinges upon a puzzle, that doesn't seem to me a bad thing. I don't care what it hinges on if it gives people a memorable kind of pleasure. There are plenty of mysteries you read and you think, "Oh yes, that's who did it." And then you just toss it aside and forget it. But, there *are* others that seem to do more. The fact is, these are books about life and death. This literature is calling into question very heavy problems that every human must face. I don't see why that is not a literary achievement.

Herbert   I agree with you. But to take this a step further, Julian Symons has pointed out that when working within the conventions of the crime and mystery genre, there are occasions when the author must hold back information from the reader. The author makes decisions about description of character for reasons of craft rather than for artistic reasons.

Langton   That is true; that is certainly true. Yes, I do feel that one is constrained by the plot all the time. And there is an artificiality in trying to show a reason, motivation for every action. Often, *actual* life is irrational but here you've got to impose this network of reason upon your story, which may make it a little stereotyped and dull. But there's nothing preventing you from putting in a little jab now and then which is addressed to society and leaves it's little scar.

Herbert   I wish you would elaborate on this!

Langton   To make a tiny digression and express one's own opinion within the novel, to write things that you would never dream of saying aloud.

Herbert   Yes, that certainly is a proper function of serious literature. But I am going to press you further here. Have you felt in any way personally constrained by the exigencies of the plot or structure or conventions of the mystery novel? For instance, Julian Symons has said that in the mystery there is often a need to be coy with the reader so that you will not reveal the motivation of particular characters too early on.

Langton   I don't aspire to write a majestic book. I enjoy keeping little secrets. I enjoy that! Maybe it is coy, but it's a pleasure to think I can keep a little secret and have it pop out at the end. And I don't feel that that's a detraction from a work of literature. I do feel that the leaden hand of necessity can cause you to write an awful lot of dull pages that have to be there. This is why I am not always willing to have a whole lot of red herrings. I'm not willing to go to the trouble— it's a labor—of having all of these characters, all of them having the motivation, the weapon, and the opportunity.

Herbert   Are you saying that unless you relax the structure of the crime or mystery story it will defeat you in saying all that you might wish about human character?

Langton   Mostly one is constricted by the demands of the plot, which, in a mystery, can be onerous and tiresome. (Pauses.) I guess I would be hard put to find a mystery that fits the quality of the greatest works of literature. A-minus, yes! But not soaring beyond grade level.

Herbert   From your own experience in constructing mystery novels, why do you think this is so?

Langton   Because of the rigid necessity to follow the plot and not to be unbuttoned, not to be ungirdled. I think that the plot dominates to the degree that the writer cannot allow some strong theme to carry the story from beginning to end, to obsess the writer throughout, while the characters are entangled with one another in a truly important way. I must say that I do not feel children's books are constricted in this way. Children's books can attain the highest of levels. But mysteries, while they may be immensely clever, while they may be highly memorable, while they may be splendidly written, do not achieve this. Rarely is the mystery writer obsessed with the working out of *life* on the page.

Herbert   More likely the mystery writer is obsessed with working out the solution of a puzzling death. What obsesses you as you write, Jane? What drives your work and preoccupies you?

Langton   What I am trying to do—and the reason it's so difficult, and takes me so long—I'm trying to make a pattern and it has many elements. The character is in it, and the plot is in it, and the setting is in it. And often some kind of theme—in this case [*Divine Inspiration*] the question of divine inspiration and where does genius come from? They all have to be woven together, and events have to happen in the right order. And the puzzle element does enter in, and the wart on the nose; the wart sort of bounces from here to there. I don't think I have ever used a wart [smiles] but it could be something like that. All of those things have to come along logically and without boring people—there has be this quality of suspense and this sense of moving forward. And love. I put love in all of my stories. I don't know, maybe I shouldn't. Maybe its sentimental to have love stories. I feel like I'm always walking along a very narrow edge with my love stories. Are they going to be saccharine? Are they going to be silly?

Herbert   No, because there are other aspects of love going on in your books. I mean, when you say "love," one immediately thinks of Hope falling in love with Ananda Singh in *God in Concord*. But that is not the only kind of love that you explore. You show us the thwarted love that Mimi Pink experiences in her family. And then there is Oliver Frye's love for his daughter despite the fact that she is betraying all of his dearly held values. And isn't it so that it is often thwarted love, or love that's gone amiss, that causes people to become criminals?

Langton   Yes, that's true. And I use love as a thread of suspense, which means that my characters can't jump into bed with each other right away, as they are so prone to do in contemporary novels!

Herbert Good choice of word there, "prone!"

Langton (Laughs.) In my stories, it's not until the end that they come together, which means it has a kind of 1930-ish element. All those movies I saw in the 1930s and 40s! I think movies have a very strong impression on writers, much more than writers are aware of. And I can't escape those movies. Who, these days, would have a pair of lovers wait till the end to come together? But that was the pattern of movies in those days: they are all crossed in love all the way through; they never embraced until the end. And my story lines reflect that. But I think it does give more suspense than if they are having sex on page two. I did put a little sex in the end of this *Divine Inspiration*. I listened to some successful author talking on the radio, and it was his first novel, and he had sold hundreds of thousands copies, and he read a very torrid passage. And I said, "Well, you know, *I* could do that." So I put in a little passage. But it's very short. I could have gone on and on.

Herbert (Laughs.) Is this the demure Sunday school teacher of my acquaintance?

Langton But it really didn't fit in the book. But who knows? Maybe next time?

Herbert And humor is another very important element in your work. One always envisions that the person who writes humor just tosses it off. But when you describe your six drafts, and all of your hard work, I wonder how you keep the humor fresh? It certainly comes across as fresh.

Langton I think that if you can be funny, you should. So I grasp at any opportunity to be funny. I sometimes think it makes it too glib, that maybe they should sober up a little. And there are some people who perhaps one shouldn't poke fun at.

Herbert People whose "laughable" attributes are pitiful? For instance, we can snicker at Mimi Pink's predicament in the garbage dump, because her greed has brought her to this juncture, but we do not laugh at the pain of her childhood?

Langton Yes, that's it. It all comes back to what we were talking about earlier, the idea that "Character is fate." I wrote books for years before it dawned on me that the things that happen to people should flow from themselves.

Herbert From their essential nature?

Langton Yes, and from fate. Fate, it seems to me, is so much more interesting than a spread of cards all labeled with character names from which you pluck one out to fill a role. The character himself should determine his end. The result should have an unstoppable and inevitable quality.

Herbert   Like a Greek tragedy.

Langton   Like an arrow loosed that will sail in an inevitable direction.

▶ ROBERT BARNARD

In a suburb located between the industrial metropolis of Leeds, England, and the vast expanse of workingmen's homes built of stone a century or more ago in Bradford, Yorkshire, is nestled a substantial stone house fronted by a classic English garden where laburnum, flowering cherries, and roses bloom. Upstairs, behind a window overlooking the garden, Robert Barnard has spent most mornings for the last ten years composing crime novels and short stories full of slightly black humor, sharp irony, and a good measure of malicious fun.

According to the author, all it takes is a desk, ink, and blotting paper. Does this sound like the nineteenth century? Well, Barnard, who is now the chairman of the Brontë Society, does keep a photograph of Charlotte Brontë beside him as he works, but the photograph in question was discovered only ten years ago. Barnard, who has fought long and successfully to keep the Brontë residence free from extensive "theme park"–style development, lives a hop, skip, and a jump from Haworth Parsonage where the Brontë family resided.

As an author, former professor of English literature, and expert on Dickens, the Brontës, and Agatha Christie, Barnard can hardly fail to be an informed conversationalist on the subject of mystery writing and its place within the broader landscape of English literature. But his gleefully ironic outlook on life and his ready wit add to the pleasure of his company. On the page, sardonic humor is a forte; in person the cunning smile adds spark to the wry remark.

Born in Essex, England, in 1936, Barnard is the son of Leslie Barnard, a farm laborer, who built a career as a full-time author of popular fiction for lowbrow magazines for women. Barnard's mother was a housewife about whom the author guards his feelings. There is no doubt that the position of the child in uncertain family and societal circumstances preoccupies Barnard to good advantage in a number of his novels where he demonstrates his sharp eye for domestic detail. Barnard says he enjoys the juxtaposition of the fruitful and claustrophobic aspects of family and neighborhood life.

But Barnard is also able to look at professional relationships that take on a different kind of intimacy: his novels have focused on political machinations, a writers' conference, a literary society, an opera company, a monastery, a university club, and other fraternities of characters. Two of the more distant settings, the Australian outback and a Norwegian university, are drawn from places where Barnard has lived at length. He has taught English literature in New South Wales, Australia, and at the northernmost university in the world, in Tromsø, Norway. As an "exile" in his own country after twenty-two years abroad, Barnard is equally comfortable casting an objective eye on the contemporary scene, the relatively recent past (the World War II era), and the nineteenth century where he has set two of his latest works.

In a continued commitment to varying his tone and subject matter, Barnard employs series characters only where they are an advantage to the situation that inspires each book. If their personalities, location, and outlook will not enhance the story, Barnard has no fears of working without them. But his series characters, the Scotland Yard detective Perry Trethowan, and his more recent creation, the black police inspector Charlie Peace, are both professionals possessing laconic wit, which makes them memorable to readers.

Barnard is considered one of today's leading practitioners of the traditional detective story, but his insight into character is thoroughly modern. Over the years, Barnard's work has generally changed in hue from bright and witty to darker writing. But even when he treats his most somber themes and deviant characters, his sense of humor comes through. As he puts it, "No one is entirely without a sense of humor—except, perhaps, Margaret Thatcher."

More recently the author has developed increased subtlety in his characters with the result that the "grotesque" characters in the Dickensian mold who populated his earlier work are replaced by singular characters whose fatal flaws are thoroughly understood—if not admired—by their creator.

Herbert   The detective novel often takes a group of people and introduces
        something very stressful into their midst. So it talks about a segment

of society under stress. What do you enjoy about working with that kind of situation?

Barnard   Oh, it's just purely malicious fun. One always enjoys in the short term going to a party where there are all sorts of tensions pushing up to the surface, like geysers bubbling in the mud. That sort of thing is marvelous to observe, and I like dealing with it.

And I think you could say about my detective stories that I play down the stability part. Christie, for instance, tends to create the stable society threatened or undermined temporarily. My situations tend to be pretty uncertain from the beginning. I also try to bring the social class I portray closer to the working class.

Herbert   How is the notion of class particularly useful to the British crime writer?

Barnard   Well, it's a perennial source of friction and conflict. The English are obsessed with class. As a source of social observation, as a way of characterizing someone, these aspects of class are enormously useful to the crime writer. This is fertile ground for conflict. Perhaps the fact that Americans do not have this obsession with class to the same extent as we do accounts for the fact that your cozy mysteries are not so convincing.

Herbert   In order to understand how your wittiness and your eye for social commentary developed I'd love to learn a bit about your childhood and education.

Barnard   Yes. The only interesting thing, I suppose, is my father wrote. He wrote cheap and awful women's romance stories, of the lowest kind. I mean sub–Barbara Cartland. *Very* sub–Barbara Cartland. He wrote for cheap weekly women's magazines, sort of factory-girls' magazines, if one wants to be snobbish. His name was Leslie Barnard, but he very often wrote under the name Peter Burnham. Nobody would know him now. He also did some other work, including some children's things for the BBC. And he made a perfectly reasonable living most of his life. He'd been a farm laborer before he went on to writing fulltime, which I think is very remarkable.

So writing was in the family. The only time I wrote a story as a boy, I remember him taking it and I would guess altering it drastically. It was published in a children's annual 'round about 1948–49. That was the only time I thought about writing as a child. It was only much, much later that I really started writing. I was about thirty-three when I started thinking I might be able to write a whole book. (Smiles.) And it was quite a lot after that before I got the first one published.

Herbert   Often the artist or writer feels a little bit different, even during

253

childhood, than the average person. As a boy, did you feel set apart from your peers in any way?

Barnard (Smiles.) No! The only way in which I felt set apart was in that I was *supernaturally* boring. I was appallingly dull! I wasn't academically bright in any way. In class I was quiet. I didn't joke. I didn't make witty remarks. I was *so* boring until I went up to Oxford, I hate to think of it! (Chuckles.) And this is why I say, I think at one point in *School for Murder*, that childhood days are the most irrelevant days of your life. Contrary to what Wordsworth said, the child is *not* the father to the man.

   I was in a bookshop four or five years ago, and I heard a voice in the back of the shop, and I said to myself, "I know that voice." The voice was talking about English literature, Crabbe or Trollope or something. And I thought, "My God, doesn't he sound to be the most typically boring academic?" I mean just as you think the most *dreary* academic must be. And when he came out he was one of the boys in school who we all thought was the most wildly romantic and dashing and exciting.

Herbert So just as that boy turned out to be quite a different adult than one would expect, you, too, regard yourself today as quite different than you were as a boy?

Barnard Oh, yes. Thank God.

Herbert (Laughs.) Wasn't there even a trace of humor and wittiness in you then?

Barnard It must have been kept horribly quiet if there was. I can guarantee that none of my schoolfellows will ever remember any witticism from me. I can guarantee that absolutely.

Herbert Then what caused the change in you?

Barnard It must have been the liberating effect of Oxford. Everybody talks about it, as in *Brideshead Revisited*. There were perhaps two liberating effects for me. First of all, you know, the English school system is dominated by exams. Well, after I took the first of the major exams, that is the "G. C. Ordinary Levels," at the age of sixteen, I remember coming back to school. I had always been in the best form but I'd always been halfway down and terribly dull—so quiet and shy. But I remember getting the test results and finding that I'd done jolly good. And I suddenly realized that (a) I was so much better than I'd thought and (b) that I had that wonderful gift of doing better on exams than I deserved, rather than the reverse.

   But then, when I talk about the liberating effect of Oxford, I made no sort of *splash* at Oxford. It was just that one got a little like-minded group around one, and one enjoyed oneself much more. One had a bit of freedom and a bit of money in that beautiful place. I think that began the liberating process.

Herbert   But you didn't have any inklings of a desire to write, even when you were at Oxford?

Barnard   No. After I was at Oxford, I worked for the Fabian Society in England for a year. I wrote an academic article on Dickens; I think that was taking a wrong road in a way. And then I went out to an Australian university. You won't have heard of it; it is in New South Wales, up in the mountains north of Sydney. It is a very small university with a big Rural Science section and a very big External section which is marvelous, teaching adults via post. It was more or less the prototype of the English open university, and I enjoyed that part very much. But the trouble with Australia was that there was so little to *do*—except drink!

Both   (Laugh.)

Barnard   And I'm quite sure that if I'd stayed I'd be an absolutely *unredeemable* alcoholic, instead of only a fairly far gone one.

While in Australia I wrote a few articles, I think, but no fiction. And then I went to Norway. And when I found that I could lecture and do it well, that left me with an awful lot of time. Particularly because in Norway one didn't change the syllabus very often, so I tended to be lecturing on *Wuthering Heights* and *Pride and Prejudice* over and over and over again.

I first wrote a very bad novel about Norway that luckily was never published. But my English editor said she would like to see my next one.

I thought, "If I don't write something about Australia now, it will go." I thought I had to record the flavor of this hick university with the near alcoholism, the fighting, and the spite and the backbiting. And I think I did it fairly well, because somebody later told me that whenever somebody spoke of taking a job in an Australian university he would tell him, "Read *Death of an Old Goat* !"

It's about a very elderly, almost snuffed-out visiting academic going the rounds of the Australian universities and unfortunately getting murdered at a little outback university which was the equivalent of the one that I was at. It's very, very nasty. It's my nastiest, I suppose.

Herbert   I like the way you say that with a gleam in your eye! Are you fond of other detective fiction with an academic setting or tone?

Barnard   No, not really. I hate the way some writers just fling quotations backwards and forwards; it is so irritating. I mean, you would think that academics spent their *whole lives* throwing quotations back and forth! I have never lived in universities of that sort!

Herbert   Then I suppose you don't approve of the sort of novel in which recognition of a literary allusion is essential to solving the plot, to being on an equal footing with the detective?

Barnard   Quite. Quite. But I must admit I did that sort of thing once, by the way. In reading *Death of an Old Goat*, there would be an *enormous* advantage for an English reader who has had a university education. I will say no more. But I never expected that book to be published; I was writing the book for myself, for my wife, and a few friends. And so that would be my apology if any aspect of that book seems rather elitist or unfair to American readers.

Herbert   But you cannot entirely hide your literary bent, Bob.

Barnard   You *will* quite often find in my books quotations hidden under the surface. It's really terribly snobbish; it's a signaling to the educated reader, "All right, you've read Evelyn Waugh; you'll recognize the quote and I'll quote it for your benefit." But it won't disturb the other reader, he won't see that it's a quotation at all. And I like that much better.

Herbert   That seems the ideal manner in which to indulge in literary witticisms or allusions without the pretentiousness that often goes along with all that quoting. What writers have most influenced you? Previous to taking up writing, did you read lots of detective fiction?

Barnard   Oh, yes. And I do it now. I think that, when I went on from children's books, I began reading lots of Agatha Christie and Ngaio Marsh. And Margery Allingham really is my absolute favorite.

Herbert   In what regards did Allingham influence you?

Barnard   Oh, her humor and grotesque characters, without question! I can't agree with anyone, like for instance Mr. [Jacques] Barzun, who cannot find Lugg to be funny. He is enormously funny! It is Allingham's ability to produce characters who are so funny and quirky and individual that I admire so very much. But I won't hear anything nasty said about Agatha Christie.

Herbert   I think all crime writers are indebted to Christie even if they do not seek to follow in her footsteps.

Barnard   Enormously. I can't think of anybody who is like her in the wonderful ingenuity of clueing. We can most of us pull off the odd ambiguity in the course of our novels, but I don't think we have that supercharged ability to see ambiguity everywhere, that wonderful sense of, "*This* can mean *that* thing and if I present it in *that* way, it would seem to mean *that* thing, but in fact I can twist it to mean *another* thing.

Herbert　　You're not the first writer in this volume to produce conversation that sounds like something from *Alice in Wonderland* !

Barnard　　(Laughs.) But this wonderful ambiguity is something very peculiar to Christie. She must, all of her life, have been training herself to see these ambiguities in things, and yes, I think we are very indebted to her. I think we all "pinch" from her. That is the most obvious form of indebtedness you can have. She made the crime novel immensely popular. She made it intellectually respectable. An awful lot of very clever people have enjoyed reading her very much indeed.

Herbert　　Please tell me about how you came to write *A Talent to Deceive: An Appreciation of Agatha Christie.*

Barnard　　Well, the fiftieth anniversary of the Crime Club was coming up and I angled most definitely to do it for this occasion. The idea was to issue a work about Christie in connection with the anniversary. But by the time the publishers were definite about taking the project on, I had only four or five months to work on it. It came out in 1980 and it involved, of course, a tremendous amount of reading. I admire Christie enormously. I think she is absolutely the most professional detective story writer there has ever been. If you look at her books between 1930 and 1950, you've got, I would say a ninety-nine percent success rate.

Herbert　　And there were so many!

Barnard　　Sometimes three a year. I find that sort of professionalism admirable. So many first-rate, sparkling ones with wonderful endings.

　　The trouble is so many people come to the crime novel looking for the same sort of thing as they would look for in an ordinary middlebrow novel. Now Christie, as everybody knows, is slim on characterization, very slim on writing; but her whole emphasis is on miraculous plotting. She is dragging the novel back toward the storytelling element. And I don't think one should downgrade that and try to pretend that it's something that any fool can do, because they can't. Her books are so wonderfully planned. I can't do it myself. I wish I could. They're so beautifully planned that everything is going to slot into place.

Herbert　　I was wondering what you personally find appealing about that sort of novel?

Barnard　　I tell you, it's a confession of weakness, really. The only time I've tried to write real ordinary novels, I've come unstuck with the plot. I get the characters working nicely. And I get a nasty, ironic, witty—hopefully—atmosphere going. And then I think, "What are the characters going to do?" And I can't actually think of a plot. And the great saving for me has been to turn to writing detective stories where I know I've got to have a body at some point and a solution at another point. And I know the solution has got to be gradually worked 'round to.

Herbert   Are there any conventions of this kind of novel that you find confining?

Barnard   I've probably enjoyed all of them. We aren't really as confined now as Christie and others were in the 30s. I have felt that I could bring to the crime story more humor and irony and social comment than I think Christie or Marsh would have felt comfortable with.

Herbert   Yes, I think that's a very good assessment of what you have achieved.

Barnard   Well, other people have done it, of course. Another thing that was confining [for the earlier writers] was that people did tend to want a conclusion where the culprit was seized; he was probably going to be hanged, or else he would kill himself. But today you don't have this rather crude sort of justice, with a capital "J," coming at the end. I've enjoyed that.

Herbert   Would you agree that in mystery fiction today there is more of a feeling that characters are people whose lives continue after the puzzle is solved? That the reader can imagine them facing other situations?

Barnard   Yes. I think that often happens, especially when you have slightly grotesque characters as I sometimes do. I think grotesque characters are fine. As long as Dickens used grotesque characters—like, for example, Uriah Heep—it's all right for the rest of us! There's a touch of the grotesque in Hillary Frome [*A School for Murder*] and in Lil in *Death of a Perfect Mother*.

Herbert   I've noticed a fascinating growth and development in your treatment of grotesque characters in your fiction over the years. What have you done differently with Lydia, the childless writer who takes over the affections of two pairs of boys in *A Fatal Attachment*, than you did with Lil, the vulgar mother in *Death of a Perfect Mother*, for instance?

Barnard   Well, Lydia was entirely mine whereas Lil Hodsden was suggested by a character in a biography. In a manner of speaking I cribbed Lil. So Lil isn't the best of examples.

Herbert   Lil is a borrowed character, then, so to speak?

Barnard   As is my character who is based on Evelyn Waugh in *Death of a Mystery Writer*. But if you take *Sheer Torture*, the characters there were centered on the Dickensian kind of caricaturization end of the spectrum, where physical or vocal gestures—turns of phrase—characterize them. There was comparatively little emotional life behind those characters. Now with Lydia, there is a physical feel to the character, too. One does see her aging elegance, but it goes beyond that to reveal a twisted and mixed-up emotional life of an intelligent woman who does not see the extent to which she is destroying other people's emotional lives.

Herbert   Can you summarize some of the thinking that went into writing *A Fatal Attachment*? I think this is a particularly strong novel.

Barnard   Thank you. It concerns a woman who is a sort of lady historical biographer. Not Lady Antonia Fraser, I hasten to say, because I don't know her! But she is a sort of—you know, historically she knows her business. She's not a romantic biographer. She knows her business; she's a good researcher; but she has already taken over her sister's two boys. One of them died in the Falklands and Lydia's blamed for this—[for] giving him this slightly patriotic, romantic attitude—by the sister and by her husband. And the other boy has sort of conspicuously failed to live up to her ideals and has gone into a rather ridiculous career in commercial television. Anyway, one is now dead and the other is now living away and the interest at the beginning of the book is that Lydia starts talking to another pair of brothers and starts the process of taking them into her web, if you like to see it like that. So in a way, one has to say of her that her intentions are always perfectly good, but that she doesn't understand herself and she doesn't really understand other people's emotions and needs.

Herbert   Would you tell me something about where your ideas for the more grotesque characters stem from?

Barnard   Lil, in *Death of a Perfect Mother*, was suggested by the biography of Joe Orton, the English playwright who was murdered by his lover boyfriend. In the marvelous biography by John Lahr, called *Prick Up Your Ears*, you get a wonderful sense of the ghastly vulgarity of his mother. Lil didn't turn out to be a carbon copy, but I'd seen enough of these vulgar mothers to know that they exist.

Herbert   Yes, there is the selfish love of Mrs. Eastlake in *A City of Strangers*.

Barnard   I mean, I enjoyed doing Mrs. Eastlake with her obsession with the Royal Family and her love of her son, which is really a terrible selfishness—really quite awful and the ending with her in a sense casting him off as she comes back into reality. This is really very, very sad to my way of thinking. That sort of self-deception on the part of the son about the nature of the mother is—I enjoyed doing that.

259

Herbert   You've done quite a number of things with interesting mother figures.

Barnard   Many people have commented on this. Somebody said last night, "What was your mother like?" Just like that. I had to tell them that she was not the original of *Death of a Perfect Mother*.

Herbert   What sort of woman is she? What has she done in her life?

Barnard   Oh, nothing very much. It may be best not to talk about that. I'd had an unhappy childhood and that's really all I want to say. There is one thing about my mother that I've used in a book: she tends to take over other people's children.

Herbert   As Lydia does in *A Fatal Attachment* ?

Barnard   Yes, but Lydia is certainly not my mother.

Herbert   Have you always had a sharp eye for the domestic relationship?

Barnard   Yes. I should think it's true that probably seventy-five percent of my novels could be described as "domestic." There are others like the "monastery" one [*Blood Brotherhood*], for example, and perhaps the "opera company" one [*Death and the Chaste Apprentice*] where you're really in—you might almost say professional relationships. But probably seventy-five percent are domestic. After all, most people say that one gets most of one's valuable impressions in the first twenty-two or -three years. This is a period of relationships in the family and this probably made me reasonably observant of domestic details in friends' and colleagues' and so forth's lives. So I find the domestic situation an interesting one to use, because it's both fruitful and, to a degree, claustrophobic at the same time. So a relationship like Mrs. Eastlake with her son or indeed the man with his new wife or mistress or live-in lover or whatever she is—I find those certainly interesting to explore and also of course the relationship of neighbors with each other. Because often this is friendly, but quite often also it is a little bit touchy and neighbors are looking at each other to see whether they have the same sort of standard of living, whether they are getting out of their class, people move out and move up, and there's jealousy. So a neighborhood involves a lot of close looking at each other, which can be very tense, can be fraught.

Herbert   It seems to me that one of the things that you have done over the years is to wrestle with the significance of childhood experience. Would you address this?

Barnard   A lot of my books fairly recently have been concerned with children because I think really the modern age has invented its own way of making childhood horrifying. That includes child abuse. We do seem on the one hand to have stopped the hideous cruelties of the Victorian education system—or perhaps we shouldn't blame the Victorians; we should say the education system up to and including the Victorians. On the other hand we've filled childhood with new horrors and terrors. And so this is something that I think I would like to bring out in books these days.

Herbert   I'd love to know what has caused you to focus in on these questions about childhood in your work. And about parenting. Is there anything in your own life that has caused you to look at children who feel vulnerable to invasion by certain adults or to being abandoned, in fact?

Barnard   I've never been abandoned, but to the first half of your question will you let me just say "Yes" and leave it at that?

Herbert   Of course, I shall respect your privacy if you like. But even P. D. James, who is very protective of her personal life, admits that an author's body of work reveals the topography of his or her emotional landscape. In what regards do your books reveal their author?

Barnard   They wouldn't reveal me very much at all. I'm writing books for other people's enjoyment; I'm not using them as some sort of psychiatrist's couch. I loathe confessional books. Writing is about creating other people and other worlds and making people interested in this imaginary world, not about a sort of emotional diarrhea! No, certainly not. I don't usually use personal things at all. Because most of my novels are pretty objective anyway. Subjectivity in the crime novel is usually an awful trap if you are getting subjectively involved with somebody, for example, who is going to turn out to be the murderer or whatever. I don't, myself, use very much of my own experience unless it's fairly superficial experience like meeting people at a writers' conference, which I might use in something like *A Cherry Blossom Corpse*, but not people I know well.

Herbert   You have used your Australian experience in *Death of an Old Goat*.

Barnard   Yes. I think what I was really doing was just using types that I was familiar with—actual people that I was familiar with from my academic teaching—it wasn't anything that was very personal or close to me.

Herbert   Have you chosen this genre because you would wish to shield your own persona—and it is easier to do so here than in perhaps a "novel of character"?

Barnard   No, that's not the reason. I'm involved with crime novels because I've always enjoyed it; there's no second or more suspicious reason

261

than that. And I don't myself think literature very often tells you very much about the writer.

Herbert   I see.

Barnard   I mean, would somebody reading *Wuthering Heights* necessarily know what sort of a person Emily Brontë seemed to be to the people of Haworth who actually knew her?

Herbert   Good question. But of course no doubt she shielded herself.

Barnard   Well, she did, of course, but that doesn't necessarily mean that the self that wrote *Wuthering Heights* is the true self and the self that glided silently around Haworth is a false self. They're both her selves.

Herbert   I like the way you put that.

Barnard   I mean I'm simply not a subjective writer and I don't usually read for pleasure people who are very subjective writers like D. H. Lawrence—the only exception I can think of really is Charlotte Brontë. That's the only example I can think of really. I don't like people who indulge in endless self-analysis. I can't imagine what for!

Herbert   On the other hand, I believe I do see some of your attitudes reflected in your work, as well, of course, as your sense of humor.

Barnard   Attitudes, yes. Fair enough. And of course political things come in. But even though attitudes do come out in the novels, you also have to be able to disguise them in order to get into the skin of other people as well.

Herbert   But despite your desire to take the objective path, you do write the Perry Trethowan novels in the first person, do you not?

Barnard   Yes. Well, all the Perry Trethowan ones were written in the first person. But of course Perry is not in fact the important figure there. He's never analyzing himself. It's an observer figure, rather than somebody who is very closely involved, except in *Sheer Torture*, where the fact is that his own family is being investigated. Otherwise there is one book that is not written in the first person, but which is mainly the consciousness of one person and that is *Skeleton in the Grass*, where I do go rather deeper than usual into Sarah and her attitudes—her reactions to the family that she is nursery governess to. But that's the closest, I think. Probably somebody could prove me wrong by going and looking at the books but I think that's the closest I get. That one and *Out of the Blackout*, where I'm very closely involved with the consciousness of the boy and the grown-up man. The boy when he's grown up.

Herbert   I am sure readers will wish to know more about this novel, which is a departure from your other work.

Barnard   When I wrote it it was totally "un–Barnard" in that it has no humor. Of course since then, I've written others which have limited humorous elements. It's more a "who-am-I" than a "whodunit." I think it is fairly gripping. It's about a little boy in 1941 suddenly turning up with a party of evacuated children at a country railway station. This is the height of the Blitz. The other children are all accounted for on the list and given foster parents, but he's not on the list. He lies about his name, and he goes to a foster family, but he seems to have dreams of violence tormenting him.

Herbert   I can't help but feel that you must have felt a particular connection to this book because you so thoroughly involve the reader in the boy Simon's plight. Can you talk about how you crafted the book to achieve this?

Barnard   I brought the personal experience in periodically because I made him my own age, more or less. I sent him up to Oxford at the same time I went up to Oxford; so one used one's own experiences—at least for a time. By the time he got to adulthood I was off to Australia and he was a victim. And I think you've hit why I made the characters around Simon so *mean* and unpleasant. I mean, I think there's a difference between someone who is grandly unpleasant like the Dickens characters and those who are meanly unpleasant. You have to be very careful about [the latter]. But I think you had the pull of the sympathy for Simon and also the feeling in the reader, "I don't want him to be connected with this family too closely." And so readers remain interested in his well-being.

Herbert   I guess that betrays a point of view that environment really is very central to how a person develops. This is a little bit different than what you said earlier about the child not being the father to the man.

Barnard   Yes, well that was a generalization about my own personality as it developed. Environment is of course very important, but there is also, if you like, the spark from God, or *something*, a pure accident, that helps some people to survive despite incredibly awful parents.

Herbert   So apparently some people are destined to be survivors?

Barnard   Yes. I mean you can think of Oliver Twist growing up in a workhouse. Now, what chance has he? But of course it helps that he speaks the Queen's English.

Both   (Laugh.)

Barnard   But he does survive. And think of, for example, H. M. Stanley, the explorer, who also grew up in an even more brutal Victorian workhouse.

Herbert   So the child can overcome his circumstances. Was *Out of the Blackout* a turning point for you, leading you in the direction of the more psychologically preoccupied crime novel?

Barnard   Yes and no. It is a direction I like to take, but it is not the only direction I have chosen.

Herbert   I have noticed that one of the ways that you have updated the well-worn English scene is to introduce into it updated characters with very modern concerns.

Barnard   Yes, of course they *are* rather more modern types. I mean the academic [in *The Cherry Blossom Corpse*] who has left his wife and is with his graduate student/dolly bird. He's a much more modern type than anything in Christie, for instance.

Herbert   Yes, the ambiguity of his position in that marriage is very nicely done.

Barnard   On a very practical level he felt, "Of course it's right" that he should do the housework or, if he wants it cleared up he's got to clear it up because [his new young partner] doesn't mind living in mess and he has his yearning to go back to the security of the first marriage. That was meant as a sort of comment on the *messiness* of some peoples lives—that people often get themselves caught in an ideological twist in many ways.

Herbert   Another contemporary topic that you introduce is homosexuality. Or at least it is a topic that can be addressed in a crime novel today in a manner that was impossible in the old cozy whodunit.

Barnard   It is a great gain, the sexual ambiguity these days. People can, for example, be sexually ambidexterous. Or they can actually change sex, though I don't like that happening in crime novels!

Herbert   No! That's not playing fair with the reader.

Barnard   It's a cheat, really. But this is a big advance from the constraints upon the golden age people who could hardly mention the subject. There are very, very few treatments of this. There's a lesbian in Dorothy Sayers's *Unnatural Death*. But other than that, there's very, very little. So we have got a big advance there.

Herbert   How consciously do you seek to introduce contemporary issues and unusual and ambiguous characters?

Barnard   Very much so! Certainly that's true.

Herbert   Do you find it satisfying, in writing a detective novel, to be in the position of controlling the situation even though your characters may not be?

Barnard   I certainly think that writing crime stories may minister to your power lust in the sense that here are these people; one of them is going to be killed by the time page sixty comes along—my murders tend to occur 'round page sixty—and now I'm going to act like some sort of Thomas Hardy god. Perhaps even making the murderer be the character you have made most sympathetic to the readers! I'm never obsessed by evil, by the way. I'm much more interested in meanness.

Herbert   What do you think is the most fascinating human failing?

Barnard   From a writer's point of view, the human failing most useful for me is lack of self-knowledge. The general propagation of the ideas of Sigmund Freud has made everybody awfully self-conscious these days. People feel they are giving themselves away by all sorts of things, by expressing mother love, by neatness, even! So I rather value the person who gives himself away effortlessly. Whether it's money-meanness or vulgarity, or whatever.

Herbert   Would you hint at where people tend to give themselves away in your work?

Barnard   I think dialogue is very important. Characters give themselves away in dialogue. I like the fact that you can just write the dialogue and have the character condemn himself out of his own mouth.

Herbert   Not only do you take advantage of certain characters' failures in knowing themselves, but also in *A Fatal Attachment*, you do something much more sophisticated and complicated. Here you portray a character who is blind to the effect she is having on other people precisely because in many ways she *does* possess self-knowledge about smaller things. For instance, she is able to scrutinize her own motives regarding the librarian who helps her with research, to scold herself, and adjust her behavior accordingly. And as you pointed out, her intentions were basically good from her point of view.

Barnard   Yes, this is all the more insidious because it was very cruel to the parents.

Herbert   Can you address the usefulness to the crime writer of the individual who may possess self-knowledge but nevertheless fails to understand the effect of his or her actions on others?

Barnard   I think that is often the basis of a lot of crimes: that people are simply so wrapped up in themselves. You can just watch people. I said, for example, in *City of Strangers*, that you can learn a lot by watching people in the supermarket, how they wheel their trolleys, and how they behave in the aisles. Some behave as if they are the only people on the universe. Now Lydia is like this and she is also a rather political figure.

Herbert   Hmm. What do you mean by political?

Barnard   She likes ruling people, manipulating people, finding the right way to make people do what she wants them to do. And I think this is quite true of actual parents with their children, don't you? That they may have a great deal of self-awareness when it comes to dealing with other people, but when it comes to their own children and the ambitions that they form for them—it's the silliest ambition to have, ambition which is for other people and not for yourself. They almost ignore the fact that the children are other people, and are not themselves. But I have to add that I think Lydia was an emotional monster, that it was a dreadful day for both sets of boys when they got involved with her.

Herbert   You know, it takes a very good writer to take an emotional monster and show how she is not monstrous from her own point of view. This novel is a superb example of your darker work. I wonder if you would agree that the early part of your career featured books in which you engaged in malicious fun, and then there was a darkening with, perhaps, *Out of the Blackout* as the turning point. And in this more recent part of your career your books have become more ruminative, rich, and subtle.

Barnard   I think the darker period probably began with *Skeleton in the Grass*, really. I can't say that it was more meditative than the others but I think probably the more subtle, ambiguous view of character dates particularly from there because one has the view of the family in that book as being so wonderful and glamourous and so good and yet, by the end of the book, you're reversing that entirely.

Herbert   Your books do take into consideration the psychological *motivations* of the characters and really go a step beyond the Agatha Christie story, which looks much more at tangible, material *motive*. Do you agree with Julian Symons that the detective story is, in general, heading toward the psychological crime novel?

Barnard   I think the detective story ought to be happy to be the detective story. It's a jolly good, popular form, and if you try to write miniature *Crime and Punishment*s you will soon find out that you are not Dostoevsky!

It's funny that with the loss of religion we have embraced still further so many Puritan attitudes. The distrust of entertainment is quite pathetic. If you go from the detective story to the crime novel, you've got to be damned careful not the throw out the baby with the bath water. And the baby is entertainment.

Herbert   By saying that, you've played right into my hands regarding the hidden agenda of this book. The title, *The Fatal Art of Entertainment*, comes from a statement made to me by Brian Aldiss, who was wrestling conversationally with the question of just how entertainment might interfere with the highest of literary aspirations. Based on your twenty years of experience writing detective fiction, do you believe the crime novel can be the "undeniable book," the sort of book that, in the words of Pushkin, "lays waste the hearts of men"?

Barnard   No. Simple answer. It is popular fiction and that inevitably means it is formula fiction to quite a large extent. I think whether it can—I mean it might just occasionally happen, but I would say in general that it's extremely dangerous for the crime writer to aim in that direction. Very, very dangerous indeed. You can get too pretentious. You can get a view of yourself and what you're doing that starts removing it from the immediate need of popular fiction, which is to entertain and to arouse the interest and excitement, you know, that popular literature traditionally does, and I think that should remain our main aim. If in the process we write something that really is a bit original and unusual, well, that will be splendid, but don't forget that the first aim is to involve the reader very strongly or to entertain the reader, keep him happy. I think popular literature has kept storytelling alive during a rather dark age in the novel, and I think we should be proud of that and not seek to do other things.

Herbert   If you are saying that the crime novel is unable to soar to the heights of the greatest of literature, what is it that is lacking? What specifically does the crime novel need in order to take it further? I'd like you to speak here not only as a writer but as an English professor.

Barnard   Psychological complexity of the sort a George Eliot, or a Charlotte Brontë would have in the characters. We don't really have the space. And the whodunit genre doesn't allow the possibility of getting that deep into the character because we have to keep secrets from the reader—and one has to get into the *surface* of the mind and then only peers deeper down into the mind of the person who is the murderer toward the end.

But the reason that it can't is that it is a formula. The whodunit book is a formula book in a way that none of the great novels is. A lot of the great books fall into certain patterns, for example *Jane Eyre*—with Jane as the governess who eventually marries the master—follows a pattern that you can also see in [Samuel] Richardson's *Pamela*, with the servant girl whom the master attempts to rape and who eventually reforms him and marries him. There are lots of patterns like that and they existed even when my father was writing stories for women in cheap magazines in which the nurse got the great surgeon and the air hostess got the great pilot and so forth. But in good books, they're not really formulas.

Herbert   Or they are formulas that do not limit the writer to the same degree the mystery formula does; these formulas do not require the writer to keep secrets about character.

Barnard   Yes!

Herbert   So then you would agree with Catherine Aird, who has said that the crux of the issue is that you cannot in a crime novel tell "the whole truth and nothing but the truth" about character.

Barnard   That is pretty much what I mean to say. We *are* writing to a formula for a certain sort of audience. And it does restrict us.

Herbert   And one aspect of that formula is the need to center most mysteries around a puzzle concerning violent death. What is your personal attitude toward death? Do you have any religious convictions, or do you believe that death is final?

Barnard   I'm one of those fairly rare people in my generation who hasn't even been christened. I've grown up in a totally unreligious environment. On the other side, I'm somebody who is always taken up with churches. You know, Thomas Hardy called himself "churchy," not Christian or religious, but "churchy." And I'm definitely "churchy" in that sense.

Herbert   Do you consider yourself to be a person who is particularly sensitive to the fragility of life?

Barnard   Not at the moment. Whether I have been in the past I find it difficult to remember. If you are wondering if I've chosen crime writing due to some sort of preoccupation with death, this is not the case for me. This is just part of the formula; it is the puzzle that appeals to me and death is an incidental near-necessity for the formula.

Herbert   P. D. James has said that she thinks detective novelists and people who read detective fiction avidly are often especially aware of the tenuousness of life. Would you agree with her?

Barnard   Yes, I think that is true, but I also think detective fiction provides the reader with a particular thrill of excitement to think along these lines. I think the average person has a resentment about the fact that his life is bounded by so many rules and regulations. I mean, even the fact that we drive on the left-hand side of the road—you sort of resent it. I'd like to use the whole road, although I know it would be chaos. I think there is a sort of thrill in saying, "Here is a basically law-abiding community, but underneath the surface there is that instinct which results in the unpredictable destruction of a life." This is part of the appeal of the old-fashioned sort of detective fiction that I write. It gives a thrill and shock to the reader.

Herbert   Would you say that the type of novel that you write assumes that law and order have some basis that is sensible, sane, and desirable? I don't mean by this that you or your readers are necessarily politically conservative, but do you feel that there is something valid about justice administered by the law?

Barnard   Yes. It's an awful pity, I think, that the law-and-order thing has been hijacked by the politically conservative. For instance, I think it's very sad that many socialists in England have an absolute paranoid hatred of police. After all, any left-wing political ideology doesn't overlook a lot of rules and regulations and, if you like, taking away of people's freedom.

I'm sort of center-left politically. I don't regard the police as supernaturally good or virtuous. And though I often laugh at my policemen, I certainly would hate to think of myself as anti-police. I think that's rather disgusting unless you are living in a country where the police are *quite* appalling.

Herbert   When writing, the author must portray the characters convincingly. I wonder if when you're writing about the victim you ever experience a sense of *frisson*, if you feel identified with what is happening to him?

Barnard   Not so far, probably because, as I say, I've never been particularly preoccupied with death. And my feeling about the kind of detective story I write is that in fact it is only about death on a very superficial level.

Herbert   What about getting into the mind of the murderer? How do you go about this?

Barnard   Well, *I* create my characters in the first place! I don't think that getting into the mind of the murderer is very difficult. We all can imagine situations in which we would want to commit murder. (Smiles.) There are very few people who have led the sort of lives from which that is totally absent. I certainly have encountered people who—I would say just lightly, "I could cheerfully murder them."

Herbert   I love the choice of the word "cheerfully" there!

Barnard   If it came to the point, of course I *wouldn't*, but the fact is you can imagine the sort of emotions that lead to murder, particularly in domestic situations.

Herbert   What about violence? Have you experienced violence in your own life?

Barnard   No, not really. As you know, I live on the edge of a fairly tough area so one can see the effects of violence. We've had, in fact, two murders in the area since I came here in 1983. That's a lot for England. We've had a sort of council estate riot a few years ago. So, you know, there is violence around, but actual personal experience of violence in the sense of being beaten up, or even threatened: not really, no. Remember, I've lived a long time in Norway in which years go by and there is no murder at all.

Herbert   How very dull!

Barnard   (Laughs.) It doesn't give me much acquaintance with violence.

Herbert   This leads me to ask you about how it felt to return to England in 1983, after so many years away.

Barnard   I lived in Australia from '61 to '66 and in Norway through '66 to '83. So I am a foreigner; I'm an exile in my own country.

Herbert   What are the advantages of this for the writer?

Barnard   There are so many things about British life that I've had to renew acquaintanceship with and so many things that I find much more unpleasant then when I left England. These are things that happen in many other countries. I mean, noise pollution if you like, the appalling litter problems, that sort of thing. These are fairly universal. But it's rather sad. I mean, coming from Norway, which is a country where you never see a poor person whom you can label as poor—coming back to England is a bit of a shock where you not only do see poor people but you see an awful lot of them. And you see women—I mean the old stereotype of the working-class woman who is old before her time. I see lots of people in the estate just by me who I can see are of childbearing age, but who look closer to sixty. It happens all the time. And also finding that it is the sort of society where children of eleven and twelve can be begging and sleeping rough in London: I found that very shocking and everybody knows they are being involved in prostitution and sometimes getting horribly murdered. And nobody seems to care and certainly nobody's doing anything about it. I found that very, very shocking and I don't think it would have been like that under a different sort of Conservative government in the 50s. Give them their due, they would have seen the problem and said, "Something has got to be done."

Herbert   How is the exile's perspective useful to the writer?

Barnard   Because I've been so long away from England, I find a lot of things that have happened strange and foreign and reprehensible. Yet if I went back to Norway, I would be equally an exile there. Though I was there for seventeen years, I was never remotely accepted as a Norwegian. Anywhere I go I would be an exile now.

Herbert   Isn't it said that what a writer needs is "silence, exile, cunning"?

Barnard   Indeed. An exile is not a bad thing to be if you're a writer. It gives you a certain objectivity; you are distanced from the thing by being not part of it or even very emotionally involved with it. And as I've remarked before, I think objectivity is something that a crime writer—and especially a whodunit writer—is bound to find useful and can play with in a lot of ways. It means, for example, that I can sit back from the characters and the action and I can say to myself, "If I make my character react like this at this point, the reader will get emotionally involved with her and *really* start sympathizing with her and then she may be the murderer in the end!" I can be objective and stand back and quite cynically think of the means by which I will try to deceive the reader.

Herbert   So this objectivity, engendered by your sense of exile, is the clue to your talent to deceive?

Barnard   I would agree with this.

Herbert   Now that you've addressed many questions regarding the art of your writing, what about the physical process, your writing habits?

Barnard   I generally write from about ten to twelve-thirty in the mornings when I'm working on a novel. That would be from about October to March. Then I revise and work on other things that I've contracted for, like short stories, during the remaining months.

Herbert   I'm impressed that you accomplish so much in such a compact period of time! It must be very concentrated work. Have you any superstitions associated with the process?

Barnard   No. I don't have any superstitions. I do have the conviction that it is morally and, from a literary point of view, very much better to write longhand. I think there are very good and fairly rational reasons for this. [Writing by hand] does take much longer and it does involve more physical effort and because of this, I think, first of all, that people who write in longhand are very much less likely to overwrite. Secondly—say it's just a sentence like, "No, I shan't be coming out today after all." That takes several seconds to actually write down, but only a second to compose in your head, and while you're actually writing one sentence down quite often other good ideas, either for other lines of plot, for other possibilities—even a joke or whatever—will come to you which wouldn't come if you were whooshing away on a word processor. So I feel there are possibly some quite good rational reasons why it is a good thing for you to write in longhand, first draft.

Herbert   What sort of materials do you use?

271

Barnard   Lined exercise books.

Herbert   And then, does someone type this up for you?

Barnard   No. I type it up. That's the nicest part of the process. Typing up the first draft into the first typed draft. At that stage I'm more likely to be making additions rather than editing. Quite often on this side of the paper I will have put things that are possible insertions into the rather bald first draft and these insertions will probably come about at the second stage of the first typed script. I value the hard work of the first draft with the pen and I think that for short stories, where you've got to have an awful lot of concentration, and the words have got to be really weighed, I think it's very, very necessary to write in pen the first draft.

Herbert   That's a good point. The process of writing short stories does require something different. Would you like to comment on that a little bit?

Barnard   I find that when I get ideas and put them in the ideas book, I always know what is a short story idea and what is a novel idea. In other words, the ideas that require an awful lot of elaboration and deletions and additions, I can see at once that they are the novel ideas. The ideas that are interesting twists to a common situation, for example, are inevitably short story ideas and they can't be made into novels. Someone once said to me, "I don't write short stories because they don't pay; I just wait until I've got three short story ideas and turn them into a novel." That is absolutely inconceivable to me. Because they just wouldn't work at all. I couldn't imagine how the process could even *begin* to come about. It doesn't work at all. I've come, over the years now, to enjoy writing short stories. I never used to enjoy reading them, so I didn't write them very much. And so when I get the ideas, I would tend to put them down and leave them for a bit. A short story is always better for not being told in the head of the idea. Occasionally novels, I think, might be, but short stories almost always are better for being left to mature, and so what usually happens is that while I'm writing a novel, I will get one or two ideas for short stories. Quite skeletal ideas really. Then when I've finished writing the first draft of the novel I put it aside for two or three months before the final polishing up and setting in order, and that is the time when I'll be doing odd things for people that I've contracted for, if possible. And this would be when I'd write the odd short story.

Herbert   I see. Not only do you write both novels and short stories but you write series and nonseries works. What are the advantages and disadvantages that you have encountered in using the series character?

Barnard   Well, of course, somewhat recently I have developed a second series sleuth, Charlie Peace, and he is going to be in the next book that comes out, called *A Hovering of Vultures*.

Herbert   Oh, I love the title.

Barnard   This has sprung partly from my involvement with the Brontë Society and the big row stopping the extension to Haworth parsonage that was proposed.

Herbert   I'll bet there's a lot of biting commentary about that!

Barnard   Well, Charlie Peace is in that and he was in *A Fatal Attachment* and *Bodies*, and so forth. And I've taken him up to Yorkshire so that I can use him more often. It was a bit silly when he initially joined the police in London.

Herbert   Well, there's no accounting for what characters will get up to, is there? As John Mortimer puts it, you can construct a lovely plot but often the characters just won't behave!

Barnard   (Laughs.) Well, I had Perry Trethowan in the London area anyway so if I have any more London subjects, I may use Perry Trethowan again, but most of my subjects these days are Yorkshire subjects, since that is where I live. And so I won't use him too often because I find series detectives tend to dictate the tone of a book, and the Trethowan novel is always a certain sort of novel and I prefer to vary the tone of each book.

Herbert   And has this been part of the reason why you have written books that feature no series detective at all?

Barnard   Yes, the book I've just finished, which I'm just revising at the moment, has no sleuth at all.

Herbert   Is it a mystery?

Barnard   There is an element of detection in it, particularly on the part of the older boy. It's called *The Masters of the House*. There's mother who has died in childbirth and, while the father is going quietly mad upstairs, the children take over their own destiny.

Herbert   The circumstances of this book don't seem to demand one of your series sleuths. When you first get an idea for a book how do you decide whether or not to use a series sleuth and which series sleuth to use?

Barnard   I probably don't really decide until I'm into it. For example, if the setting comes early on and the setting is not either London or Yorkshire, it's quite difficult to use either of my series sleuths. And so that's one thing that determines it. If I had a subject that was really dark and serious—once again both my sleuths are fairly sardonic, humorous types—I would probably decide not to involve them because it would go against the darkness of the subject matter.

Herbert   I see. Your mention of setting leads me to ask how important the sense of place is to you.

Barnard   I don't think one can say that the place where the book is set is as vital as the character or the action, but it is something obviously which helps to *shade* the various characters or to *shape* the action. And I think it's really important to get a really good sense of the sort of place you're in. I'm a great admirer of the Yorkshire novels of Peter Robinson because he's got a splendid sense of Yorkshire; equally you could say that the Lindsay Davis novels set in ancient Rome give you a very jolly picture—I don't know how accurate but it's wonderfully convincing in its own right—of whatever date it is, A.D. 65 or something. So I do think, yes, place, or what Norwegians always call "milieu," is very important indeed.

Herbert   What you do with your work is to create a sense of place that is more than an array of props on which to place clues. Your scene is not just a flowerbed whose only purpose is to retain footprints.

Barnard   Yes, I hope that's true.

Herbert   Is there a symbolic dimension that you consciously seek to suggest?

Barnard   No, I don't think that is very suitable in the crime genre except in very exceptional circumstances. One could think of, for example, Ruth Rendell's *The Master of the Moor* where she gives her upland milieu sort of Hardyesque dimensions. But I think that's very rare.

Herbert   Thinking of Thomas Hardy, and of the man who inspired the title of this volume, Brian Aldiss once said to me that Thomas Hardy employed the first zoom lens in English literature when he described that vast landscape of Egdon Heath and then zoomed in on the individual. I wonder if you will accuse me of stretching this when I ask about the role of the crime writer in providing us with a well-wrought world—often a "great, good place," in the words of Auden—and then zooming in on the problems that underlie that landscape?

Barnard   No, I don't think you're stretching it. But of course sometimes that landscape is quaking to begin with, and not at all stable and secure! But it's interesting that you should mention Hardy because I've set my new pseudonymous novel in the nineteenth century.

Herbert   Oh, how wonderful! We can look forward to another new direction in your work. What is the pseudonym?

Barnard   Bernard Bastable. The book is *To Die Like a Gentleman*, and it is not a comedy. It also does not feature a series character but there is a second one set in the same period to come. It's called *Dead, Mr. Mozart*, and it is full of humor.

Herbert   So this is a series milieu or period, rather than a series sleuth. How is the nineteenth century particularly suitable for the crime writer?

Barnard   A lot of historical crime is actually set in quite different periods. This just happens to be my century; my great loves in reading have been Dickens and the Brontës.

Herbert   As we have discussed, your writing has taken several directions and evidently you are continuing to explore new ones. What do you think links the whole of your body of work, Bob? What can a reader look for in a Barnard volume?

Barnard   I have to presume that readers like the irony; they like the humor—the slightly black humor. And they like a good old-fashioned puzzle, which I'm not particularly good at. But at least I combine it with the other ingredients and I think I've got a nice little solid core of people, thank God, who like that combination.

276

▶ JEREMIAH HEALY

Fistfights, wry humor, rugged individualism. These are the trademarks of the fictional private eye. Author Jeremiah Healy's popular sleuth, John Francis Cuddy, follows in the best private eye tradition; he's a maverick who single-handedly "gets his man"—*and* gets to the truth of the matter in cases where the ordinary system of justice fails. But Cuddy is a private eye with a difference. This fictional sleuth has the advantages of his creator's real-life experience in law training, practice, and teaching, as well as Healy's hands-on involvement on crime scenes.

Healy will be the first one to tell you that his legal training and expertise has everything to do with his career as a novelist. In an interview in his suite in Boston's historic Back Bay neighborhood, an area where he lives and that he uses as a backdrop for some of his fictional scenes, Healy spoke about how the law and writing are intertwined on every level, from the philosophical to the practical. Kicking at the dead leaves fallen from the ornamental tree struggling to grow in his bay window, Healy said that he was born and raised in New Jersey where he attended a progressive public school that exposed talented students to an intensive writing program. In high school he wrote for the literary magazine, but then found that in Rutgers University, where he majored in political science, and at Harvard Law School, his writing efforts were focused on analytical rather than creative writing.

During his college summers, Healy worked for the Sheriff's Office in Bergen County, New Jersey, a job that required him to do everything from filing to fingerprinting to quelling race riots. In law school, Healy was a member of the Harvard Volunteer Defender Program, a student-run organization that provided criminal representation to indigent defendants. The experience persuaded him that he enjoyed courtroom work, but caused his orientation to change from criminal to civil law. After spending five years practicing civil litigation, Healy joined the faculty of the New England School of Law in 1978 where he is now a full professor. It was the leisure built into the academic year that allowed Healy the summers to try his hand at writing. After multiple rejections from publishers to whom he doggedly sent his manuscript, Healy's perseverence paid off when his first novel, *Blunt Darts*, was selected by *The New York Times* as one of the seven best mysteries of 1984.

Now in the process of writing his ninth novel, Healy composes his manuscripts in a no-nonsense manner on the word processor that he keeps in his small library in the Back Bay home. Revisions are undertaken, to the sounds of New Age music, in his living room. Sometimes Healy also works in his lakeside retreat in Maine.

Healy's conversation resonates with his classroom and courtroom experience. His thoughts are always carefully phrased, qualified with subordinate clauses whenever necessary, and he is particularly careful to use pronouns that reflect both genders. This "inclusive language," spoken in a strong voice, provides one with a first impression of formality. But the content of his conversation, often punctuated by bursts of laughter, convinces one that this is Healy's natural voice. Healy is not unlike his private eye: he projects a masculine toughness tempered with sensitivity. And he's a good sport. Asked to pose with the famous brass statues of the "Make Way for Ducklings" figures in the Boston Public Garden, he promptly strangled the sentimental objects, much to the horror of the small children being wheeled in strollers to see them. But when Healy saw an ill squirrel nearby, he warned the mothers to keep their children away from the animal. And then he charmed children and passersby alike as he demonstrated his ability to call squirrels from far and wide with an inimitable clicking sound made with the tongue and teeth.

Herbert   When you took up the pen to write your private eye novels you were established as a professor at the New England School of Law in Boston, Massachusetts. What inspired you to become a writer at that point in your life?

Healy   There was something about being a lawyer that led me to believe that you could right a lot of wrongs. As a full-time lawyer I learned [that] about ninety to ninety-eight percent of cases are handled very well by the existing dispute resolution mechanisms, whether it be criminal law, divorce law, or whatever. But I also learned, after awhile, about the cases that tended to slip through the cracks.

Herbert   And the fact that these were not resolved satisfactorily upset you?

Healy   Yes. And one of the real advantages, I think, of being a mystery writer who practiced law in the courtroom, is the ability to highlight realistically those cases that fall between the cracks of the system. And that, in effect, is when the private investigator is brought in in fiction.

Herbert   Did you become a private eye writer, then, because you had a mission to use fiction to right some of the wrongs that you had observed in real life?

Healy   No. But it was a good way to blow off steam about them. In fact, as a lawyer, you did the best you could, but there were some situations that simply were not very solvable using the legal system. And so, a good way to blow off steam is to create somebody who can obtain justice, if you will, outside the law. A private investigative character is a pretty good example, in a generic sense, of that sort of person who can deal with things outside the law.

Herbert   Was there a particular case or incident that inspired you to do this?

Healy   No. It was more like categories of cases, [for instance] noticing that a woman who had been battered by her husband basically could not very effectively get court help. This was so, particularly if she had children, because she needed the husband to continue to pay to keep the kids in food and shoes, and, as a result, the judge couldn't very well decide to send the breadwinner to jail. That's one category of what I mean by "categories of cases that trouble me" rather than individual cases.

Herbert   These types of cases outraged you.

Healy   Exactly. The problems of reporters and their confidential sources is another example, another categorical example.

Herbert   Have you got an agenda in mind of categories of cases that you would like to deal with in your fiction?

Healy   No. To be honest with you, it would be nice to paint myself as a crusader but I don't think it would be accurate. Basically it's fortunate for Jerry the mystery writer that he used to be Jerry the trial attorney and continues to be Jerry the law professor because the experiences as a trial attorney and the research facilities as a law professor allow me to use, in my mystery writing, themes, plot ideas that are different spins on the ball than most other mystery writers have had access to. Not all of them, but most other mystery writers.

Herbert   This leads me right into something that Massachusetts adventure novelist and vice dean of the Harvard Law School, David Smith, said: "As a lawyer, Jerry sees the various ways in which people come into conflict—and mysteries are about conflict and about the resolution of conflicts. Jerry is more conscious of making points of law in his writing than other writers who are not lawyers, but I think the familiarity with points of law is in some ways the least important part of a lawyer writing mysteries. More important is the lawyer's familiarity with many aspects with life." I wonder if you agree with this, Jerry?

Healy   I do. Definitely. The beauty of having been a trial attorney is that you are forced to learn about a lot of aspects of life that are not so pleasant that you would automatically delve into them as a researcher or as a writer who is simply in search of an idea. And because you have been forced to deal with grim reality, you're in a little bit better position to write about it. The law aspect is what gives you the spin on the ball, but the ball has to be there to start with.

Herbert   Can you provide us with a specific example of a case that had direct impact on your writing career?

Healy   Sure. When I was in full-time practice I represented a reporter who was investigating allegations of police brutality in a given Massachusetts city. The reporter wanted to protect confidential sources who had helped him in writing a series of articles. Given what I learned in that case, I was able, ten years later, to come up with the idea for *Yesterday's News*. The central question of *Yesterday's News* is: "What would happen if a reporter had a confidential source who was killed?" The reporter, perhaps suspecting police involvement in the killing, would not be likely to turn to the official authorities for help. Instead, he or she might turn to a private investigator. And from that spin on the ball grew the novel.

Herbert   What sort of courtroom work did you do, Jerry? Was it very varied?

Healy   I was what was called a general litigator, which basically means I did all kinds of noncriminal courtroom work. I was neither prosecuting nor defending criminal defendants. So, for example, on Monday I might be arguing a preliminary injunction in Federal Court involving reporters' rights; and Tuesday I might be taking a deposition in an environmental protection case; on Wednesday I might be arguing to a jury in a residential construction case; on Thursday I might be representing a wife in a divorce case; and on Friday I might be beginning the trial of a civil fraud case involving investment securities. I don't want to make this seem melodramatic but basically it requires you to understand boxing, judo, karate, sword fighting—

Herbert   (Laughs.)

Healy   —different ways of fighting in different arenas against different kinds of opponents.

Herbert   Wow, that gives you a window into people's private lives that is far different than the average person's. And in addition, you have the advantage of understanding justice from a legal standpoint.

Healy   I agree with that. John Lutz once said that a private investigator is the novelist within the novel because he or she goes through the course of the book much like the author has to, talking to the characters and so on. I think that a lawyer, or a doctor, or a social worker, or individuals in similar professions, get their own windows into the world and, through those windows, formulate their sense of how the world works. And here's why I think that a lot of readers find private investigative fiction particularly enjoyable to read: because most of us who write it used to be journalists, lawyers, police officers and have had the opportunity to see life basically as it's *lived* rather than as it's *dreamed*. And there's, I think, a real advantage in having had a rougher background. Bluntly, I've been in a room with a corpse for three hours.

Herbert   I'd like to know more about that!

Healy   There is something about that that focuses you in a way that you simply don't get if you've only seen a videotape of it, or you've done research and read books, and learned, "Here's what happens to a body a certain number of minutes after death, hours after death, and so forth."

Herbert   Why were you on the scene with a corpse?

Healy   When I was in college, I was a sheriff's officer as a summer job. Then, in the army, I was in the military police, but I didn't have to deal with any homicides there. The Sheriff's Department is, in New Jersey, basically similar to what the State Police is up here: they are the people who go in and investigate major crimes, especially murders, armed robbery—really significant matters. And so, as a result, even though I was basically a college student who had a summer job, I had the opportunity to be involved in jailbreaks, race riots—

281

Herbert   My goodness!

Healy   —half a dozen or eight homicides, including everything from domestic violence to gangland hits. This gave me a sense at a young age of how things worked.

Herbert   Of course domestic violence and gangland hits are features of many private eye novels. But I doubt that most P.I. novelists have experience of dealing with mobsters. How closely involved were you in the investigation of gangland-related crimes?

Healy   Most of the homicides I was involved in were not gangland hits. However, there were a couple that were never closed, meaning they were never solved. We were pretty sure who had ordered the hit but could never prove who had done the killing. In those days the actual person pulling the trigger would be called the "button man," as in the person who pushed the button, and the gangland mobsters ordering the hit were usually smart enough to use only very careful and loyal underlings or import from another city for a sort of cameo hit—

Herbert   I love your choice of words!

Healy   This would be a professional from another outfit who was functionally untraceable.

Herbert   What was your role in the investigation of a suspected "cameo hit," for example?

Healy   I would generally investigate the crime scene rather than engage in the interviewing of witnesses. I would take photographs at the crime scene, help in the search of the house for evidence, accompany the body to the morgue, and witness the autopsy.

Herbert   I still can't get over the extraordinary fact that this was a summer job! What was your role at the autopsy?

Healy   I would photograph the knife wound to the heart or whatever it would be. Once they buzzed off the chest plate.

Herbert   I love the matter-of-fact tone in which you added your last remark! What kind of background do you come from, Jerry? Until that time, had you lived a rather protected life?

Healy   I was your typical middle-class kid—lower middle-class in the sense of income level—but, you know, living in a detached house in a nice suburb, going to nice schools, and so forth.

Herbert   So this summer job must have been quite an education! How old were you when you first held this job?

Healy   Eighteen to twenty-two.

Herbert And you did this every summer?

Healy Five summers.

Herbert How did you even acquire a job like that?

Healy My desire as a senior in high school was to major in political science in college. My mother knew some people who were in the county administration, in the county I lived in. And so she said, "Let me see if I can get you a job in the county administration." I figured I'd work on a board of elections or something like that. Well, it turned out the opening they had the day that I arrived was in the Sheriff's Department. So I went down there, and [during] my first summer, I was basically just a file clerk. And then they said, "Are you interested in coming back next summer?" So the next summer I started to do some other things. I'd go out on homicide investigation scenes, and bank robberies, and so forth. And it just blossomed into basically a very interesting summer job.

Herbert I would say so!

Healy I saw a lot of stuff that people, certainly people my age, had never seen. So by the time I got to go to basic training in the army at age twenty-one as an ROTC cadet, I had already learned pretty much how to handle weapons, by going to the firing range, and qualifying with handguns, and so forth. And during the civil disturbances, which occurred in 1967 in New Jersey—Newark and Englewood and Hackensack basically blowing into flames—you had to go out with shotguns and machine guns and all that stuff.

Herbert Were you personally in physical danger?

Healy Yes, I was.

Herbert Did you have to perpetrate violence in order to protect yourself, or in the line of duty?

Healy I did have to level weapons at people from time to time.

Herbert And the county allowed you to do this as a summer job?

Healy Well, it probably wasn't the best judgment in the world, but they only had so many human beings and we were all doing twelve-hour shifts basically with no days off for three whole weeks.

Herbert So you really have considerable experience then, on crime scenes?

Healy Yes.

Herbert What you've just told me has anticipated my next question. I was going to ask you about the research you have done to bring a sense of verisimilitude to your crime scenes.

Healy   One of the real problems with providing a sense of reality is realizing that you are quickly out of date in an authenticity sense. And so, in my books, although I try to give the sense of what it would be like to be on a crime scene, I don't try to be detailed as to *exactly* what happens when you are there because, literally, things varied from county to county in New Jersey twenty years ago, so I know that they would vary state to state. And with the improvements in technology, things have changed significantly *everywhere* from what my real life experiences were. But, you know, you can stay reasonably in touch with developments in criminal investigation if you develop friends in the field who are willing to proofread things for you.

Herbert   What about the mind of the criminal? Did your summer work in any way help you to understand the workings of the criminal mind?

Healy   Well, I did become acquainted with a number of prisoners. We used to eat over in the jail, to kind of make a show of force, so the impression was created that there were an awful lot of us [in law enforcement]—though there were very few of us and an *awful lot* of them.

Herbert   Now, when you say you would eat at the jail, you mean you dined in the cafeteria with the people who were jailed?

Healy   Yes. Sometimes.

Herbert   And you would be in uniform?

Healy   Uh, yes. I was in plainclothes, but yes. It was very clear that I was not in a jail inmate uniform.

Herbert   Okay. You weren't in stripes and a ball and chain!

Healy   (Laughs.) It was fairly clear that the guys in green scrubs were the inmates, and then there were the guys in the blue uniforms who were the turnkeys—the jailers—and then there were other people, like me, from parts of the Sheriff's Department who were law enforcement, but not all in uniform—in a tie and a shirt in the summertime, let's say.

Herbert   When you were dining in the jail, did you actually strike up conversations with the prisoners?

Healy   Oh, yes. I got to be good friends—when I say good friends, I mean you wouldn't go out for drinks—but I did get to know some of the people. One guy I especially remember was the trustee who ran the kitchen one summer that I was there. Bear in mind this was a county jail, so they were in prison for up to, I think, a year at a time. I met this guy, and got to know him pretty well, and the next summer, I ended up holding a gun on him because he was arrested by city police and brought to our department, but he was huge, and really tough, and so there were several of us in the room with him at once. And he had just raped and murdered one eighty-seven-year-old woman, and raped and nearly killed her ninety-year-old sister, who was the one who identified him. The forensic evidence was overwhelming—no question that he did it. I still don't understand everything that happened in his mind, obviously, but you get the sense you really can't predict who would do what. You know, there is no scale of zero to ten on just how crazy a person is. You just never know who is going to do what.

Herbert   That's one of the things that I have noticed about your characterization: you understand that people are unpredictable.

Healy   I'm glad that comes through because, although I don't think I have a private agenda in writing, this *is* one of my conclusions about human nature.

Herbert   This brings to mind John Mortimer, who told me that life is "absolutely composed of plots," but the characters just won't behave. And so one might come up with the perfect plot, but the characters will do something surprising. Have you found that that's the case in your writing?

Healy   Less so, because I tend to start with the plot and I believe strongly that in a mystery the plot really has to be the master and everything else the servant. And so as a result, I tend to cast, as players in the mystery, characters who will stick to their roles. To a great extent, that gives you *more* flexibility rather than less flexibility.

Herbert   Oh, could you expand on that? That fascinates me.

Healy   I think it's pretty simple. You can't really have freedom without discipline because [without discipline] you don't appreciate what freedom is. Well, the beauty of plotting the book carefully first, and then casting it according to the plot, is that once you've imbued a character with what you require from him or her as a spear carrier in the opera, you can then personalize him or her in a very free way as regards characteristics that won't hurt the plot, won't drag the plot, won't injure the plot in some central way. I think most readers come to mysteries—and many readers of mainstream fiction find that they prefer mysteries—because there is a satisfaction sense in the resolution of mystery stories. You know, bluntly, the bad guy gets it in the neck in the end. That is something that, as a result, is missing from much mainstream fiction. With mysteries, I believe plot is king or master of everything. For example, in *Shallow Graves* I have a member of the mob who happens to love New Age music.

Herbert   There's a surprising character trait!

Healy   Once I made him what he needed to be for the plot, I had tremendous freedom in giving him a characteristic that would make him memorable and maybe interesting in a different way. But I could not have given him that characteristic until I determined what role he would play in the opera or what aspects of the plot he had to carry.

Herbert   While your characters may possess attributes that surprise us as readers, my impression is that you are fairly much in control of your characters.

Healy   Correct. But I'm convinced that this is a function to some extent of past experience. Let me give you the difference between Tony Hillerman and me, for example. Tony and I wrote articles about mystery writing that appeared in *The Writer* magazine. Tony said basically that he starts with an idea for a story, the characters start to talk with each other, and that's how he writes. Well, I start with a very determined destination, backstep from there inductively, from chapter thirty to chapter one, and then outline forward. So that before I sit down to do the first chapter in what you and I would think of as the manuscript, the first draft, I already have a thirty-page, one-page-per-chapter outline of what's going to happen. I decide who has to do what to whom, and then after that I can have people do what I want them to do.

Herbert   You mean, after you decide on the actions that they must take in order to forward the progress of a satisfying and logical plot, you can then endow them with various characteristics to make them memorable in terms of personality?

Healy   Precisely. This is where freedom operates for me: once the discipline's taken hold. I have the superstructure of that "building" down pretty solidly. I know it's going to be thirty stories; I know how wide its going to be, how long its going to be, and so on. Well, I think that the difference between Tony's and my approach [reflects] the difference between our backgrounds. Tony was a reporter who tended to follow events as part of his profession, not anticipate them.

Herbert   That's an excellent insight.

Healy   And he certainly could not try and control them. His job was the opposite of controlling events; his job was to report on events that other people were controlling. That was his credo, as a reporter, as I understand the concept of reporting.

Herbert   That's entirely true.

Healy   Well, as a trial attorney, you are trying to control everything. You're trying to control the audience's reaction to your players, to the props that you are having your players use in the play, and so as a result, it is not surprising that because the attorney is held accountable for what he or she can produce at the end—and accountable not just to the justice system as a participant but to the client who can sue for malpractice—I think it's pretty natural for an attorney who writes fiction to craft books in a similar manner. So I would think the reason why Tony and I write differently—though we had the same editor for four books, and the same editor liked both of our [work]—has a lot to do with the life experience that we each brought to the writing process.

Herbert   That makes a great deal of sense. Not only you and Tony, but most mystery writers manipulate character in order to surprise the reader with the solution to the crime. One way to do this, of course, is to use character stereotypes in order to cause your readers to make untrue assumptions about the suspects.

Healy   I think you put your finger on it. For example, a writer can say that a given character resembles Spencer Tracy, or resembles Katharine Hepburn. Now that saves you a tremendous amount of time—it's a shortcut—and will allow that character forever to be recognizable by the reader. But I'd like to think that if I use a stereotype, it's for a reason rather than because I am lazy. It has always seemed to me that the way to use the stereotype to its best advantage is for you to surprise the reader by having the "stereotypical character" break out of role, or sort of surprise the casting director. I think in that sense the writer uses the stereotypical character somewhat in the manipulative way.

Herbert   So, if we take the case of your gangland figure, the fact that the reader immediately forms an impression of a stereotyped character is useful to you in providing two different surprises. There's the unexpected taste in New Age music to delight us with the revelation of an unexpected aspect of character. And there's the fact that we may automatically assume that he must be involved in any gangland-style violence that occurs in the novel; this might deflect our attention from the actual criminal.

Healy   Yes. Basically, if the ultimate goal of the mystery is to keep the reader guessing about plot, a good way to keep the reader distracted from what you're really doing in the story line is to have other distractions or surprises, other ways in which the reader is kept guessing.

One way to do that is for the reader to be kept guessing as to how a character will behave, within certain bounds of reality. I think it's one thing to have a gangland figure like New Age music and otherwise be relatively consistent with the gangland stereotype. It would be another thing to have the gangland figure truly believe in flying saucers!

Herbert   (Laughs.)

Healy   Unless, that is, there was a particular reason why you were setting up that gangland character as being completely crazy so something he or she does later on is credible. However, to think that somebody with that degree of idiosyncracy would be kept on by the mob is probably incredible because basically the mob can't tolerate loose cannons, any more than a police force can.

Herbert   You've got a point there! So you are obviously conscious of what is going to make us stretch our disbelief to the point that the elasticity just breaks.

Healy   I hope so, anyway.

Herbert   Speaking of unearthly matters, one of the things I wish to know is whether or not you indulge in any superstitions connected with the writing process. For instance, Antonia Fraser told me that she has two paperweights. Under one, she puts work in progress, and under the other, she keeps work that is completed. She confided that if she ever puts something in progress under the other paperweight, something goes wrong, or there's a delay, or there's a problem with that manuscript. Do you have any quirks of this nature?

Healy   I don't think I have quirks that would rise to the level of superstitions. The point is, I'm not much involved with anything except the computer keyboard. There probably isn't a whole lot of room for superstition or for idiosyncracy in that process. However, once the first draft is done, meaning once I've got the 440 pages that represent the first draft of the manuscript, what I will do is go from the computer room to the living room, put on, in fact, New Age music, which I really enjoy, with no voice in it, which is important because you can't have words distracting you from the words on the page. And I go from first draft to second draft—in other words, I rewrite the first draft—with instrumental music behind me, in my mind, all around me. I don't know that this is superstitious, but I do find it tends to make the hours go by very quickly. And it's not at all infrequent [that] I'll go eight hours and realize that I am starving and have forgotten [to] eat lunch and forgotten to monitor the clock. I think that's more a function of concentration than superstition.

Herbert   Most likely.

Healy   I think [it] would be interesting to probe whether in writing fiction, if we create a kind of fantasy world—not necessarily a science fiction fantasy world but a chronology that is different from our real life—whether or not it is likely that we enter that chronology ourselves while we are writing. Then it might not be so surprising that if the character is not stopping to eat, the author forgets to eat.

Herbert   Unless you are Robert Parker, whose characters are eating all the time.

Healy   (Laughs.)

Herbert   That is something that you have certainly not emulated. Many other writers have done this "tossing up the pasta" while their characters are trying to puzzle out the case.

Healy   I have to tell you in *The Staked Goat*, which was the second book I ever wrote . . . Bob Parker was nice enough to give a blurb to it, and somebody afterward said to me, "You know, I was always surprised that Parker blurbed that book." And I said, "Why?" "Well, you were so obviously making fun of him." I said, "What do you mean?" And the person I was speaking to said, "Well, the scene where you have Nancy and Cuddy having dinner at Nancy's apartment, it's like chicken breasts and beans out of the can." And I looked at the person who asked me the question and said, "But that's how I eat." I mean, what I was doing was describing a meal that I knew stood up, because it was a meal that I typically have. I wasn't trying to make fun of Parker by undermining his gourmet aspect; I was simply stating, in my private investigator book, the kind of meal that I have because I knew it was meal I could rely on; I knew it was reasonably accurate for what someone could eat.

Herbert   Oh, I think it's much more accurate. The average private eye is not tossing up these gourmet dishes any more than the average mobster enjoys New Age music. And the New Age music reminds me of your rewriting process. Can you share with me the kind of preoccupations you have in mind as you focus on manuscript improvements?

Healy   I'm at the stage now of logging the book, meaning, going through all 440 manuscript pages, writing down on notecards every time I use action words, like "stumbled" or "arched" or anything like that, and making sure that I know every place that each one of those words appears, and then I go back and I eliminate them, or use synonyms, or whatever, so that the reader won't be subliminally bored by redundancy in the words that I've used.

Herbert   What a good idea.

Healy   I do this because I've read books [in which] an author will use "clatter" five times within ten pages. Now, there is nothing wrong with the word "clatter" and in fact it produces a great effect, but if you use it over and over again, it loses its effect as a word. It also gets, it seems to me, overused to the point where the reader loses interest in the sentence in which it appears.

Herbert   So this is a conscious technique that you employ to eliminate the possibility of subliminally boring the reader?

Healy   Yes. And what you will notice is that it is very self-instructive when you do it. You'll notice, for example, that for some reason, when you were writing those 100 pages of a given novel, that a given word must have really been on your mind. Because you used "swing" an awful lot. And then you suddenly realize, you'll find, by just objectively logging the book, you'll find that you didn't use it once in the next 100 pages, so what you do is just sprinkle it around. There are some words you can only use once in a book. You can't have somebody "dawdling" in every paragraph—

Herbert   —or you will find the reader dawdling on the way to picking up your book again!

Healy   (Laughs.) Or unless that is the subliminal signature of that character. But you can't have five different characters in that book being attached to the verb "dawdle."

Herbert   Especially in a private eye novel. "Lurk" might be a more believable verb for a multitude of characters. I wonder if, before you chose to write private eye novels, you had been a great reader of the genre. And if so, was it the dominance of plot and the satisfaction provided by the strong resolution that attracted you to this form of literature?

Healy   Yes, I read private eye fiction, and for the reasons you suggest, but not exclusively. I had read a lot of science fiction, a lot of historical novels, and so on. And it just happened that in 1978–79 I had discovered Robert B. Parker as somebody to read, John D. MacDonald, and a bunch of others whose extraordinary ability to express themselves in private investigator fiction really made an impression on me.

Herbert   What aspects of Parker's and MacDonald's work most appealed to you?

Healy   I thought John D. MacDonald was the best writer of the prose paragraph that I had ever read in terms of being able to describe a scene and put you in there. I would say that the current best practitioner of that, in prose, is Sue Grafton. And it wouldn't surprise me if that is because of Sue's background in producing movies. She has to have a sense of what the thing will look like to an audience when she's searching out a locale to use as the backdrop to the scene. I think Bob Parker wrote the best dialogue that I have ever read. And you know there are tricks to it probably in the sense that he uses mostly two-character scenes rather than three-character scenes.

Herbert   So you've analyzed that a little bit.

Healy   You don't have to give a lot of cues to the reader as to who's speaking now and it's much faster as a duet than it would be as a trio, and so on. But those are the two characteristics about MacDonald and Parker that I think stood out in my mind. I'm not sure I thought of them in that way at the time, and when I think back on them as influences, I try to describe a place as memorably as John D. MacDonald would describe it, and have dialogue move in the way Bob Parker would have done it.

Herbert   In other words, you are guided by their talents in keeping the reader thoroughly engaged in the narrative?

Healy   Definitely.

Herbert   Do you consciously set out to make certain that the reader is entertained by your work?

Healy   I think [the need to keep the reader entertained] serves as a good quality control. I think the problem for a lot of people who believe they are writing great literature is that they have self-indulgently explored only their own philosophy or attitude toward life in their work, but even if it's done in basically good writing, who is seriously going to be interested in a personal statement, in effect, of one guy's philosophy? No one would continue reading this after the first ten or twenty pages. And I think the requirement for entertainment in mystery stories [ensures] that the author is writing on several levels at once, like playing chess on several different vertical boards at once, that you are, in effect, making a move that if a pin were dropped vertically through that square on all the chessboards, would keep you square—it would keep you honest with respect to a move on any board. And you know, I think a story has to be entertaining. It has to have conflict, has to have someone you can root for, et cetera.

Herbert   I wonder if a literary form that is self-consciously entertaining might face any artistic limitations. This has been a criticism of mystery writing. What do you think about this?

Healy   Great literature that's not read to the end is wasted literature, and if you don't entertain the reader, he or she isn't going to read to the end.

Herbert   Julian Symons has pointed out an additional challenge that faces mystery writers, and that is the necessity to keep a secret from the reader for reasons of plot and structure and formula rather than for purely artistic reasons. Have you encountered that as a problem?

Healy   I don't think so. I think that the person who buys what is called a mystery pretty much understands that what he or she is buying is a ride that is partly in the dark. And the trick is to guess where we are when in the dark. And I don't think that in that sense the readers resent it. I think they find it as exciting as when you were a little kid and you went into the fun house, or when you were a teenager and you closed your eyes as the car's going down the road and tried to figure where the driver was taking you, by just the sounds and smells and so forth around you. I don't think there is anything that is dishonest about that so long as the writer plays fair with the reader. It's one thing to deceive the reader, it's another thing to deceive the reader without fair clues. In a book that goes on for 300 pages, and all of a sudden in the last twenty pages you realize the whole first 300 was a complete red herring and some new character who was never even mentioned earlier turns out to be the killer—that's unacceptable deceit. But I think most readers are prepared for some deception in much the same way that when they go to a magic show, they're prepared for some illusion, some distraction. And the trick is to try to spot the trick.

Herbert   But does the deception in any way limit the artistic potential of the mystery, if one is looking at it in comparison with the novel of character?

Healy   You can argue that Dostoevsky's *Crime and Punishment* is a police procedural! If you agree with my insistence on plot as the primary strength of a novel, then, if you have a strong plot, whether you are talking about a mystery, a western, or a romance, you'll have a strong book. And I think for a mystery or any other piece of fiction to ascend to the next level of what you and I might call "literature" requires additional characteristics: deeply drawn characters, clever dialogue, and prose that captures the subliminal signature of a setting. I think a number of mysteries have those additional characteristics and thus are what I would consider to be "literature."

Herbert   But some would argue that the necessity, in a mystery novel, for the author to make decisions based on formulaic needs provides a challenge that is greater than that faced by the ordinary "novelist of character." Is this your experience? Do you think that the mystery writer faces extra difficulties along the path to creating a work of real literary merit?

Healy   It's just the opposite. I think that the person who imposes on himself or herself the discipline inherent in writing a solid mystery— that is to say, a sensitivity to plot—is more than halfway to producing a work of literature in that he or she has already provided a necessary, though not independently sufficient, component of a great novel. I am very serious about my commitment to the centrality of plot in any decent work of fiction.

Herbert   And the law, too, is a very serious business. I've noticed that both personally and in your work there is often a lively sense of humor. Did you turn to writing in order to have an outlet for this part of your personality?

Healy   It's nice of you to say that. I think I realized fairly early on, prob- ably before I ever started to try to write the first book, that if one was not entertaining, one would have a very difficult time persuading a publisher to accept the book, much less persuade potential buyers to purchase the book.

Herbert   Tell us, please, about yourself as a boy. Have you always been a person who had both a serious side and a healthy sense of humor?

Healy   I had a good friend, when I was in about seventh grade, who took me aside and he said, "You know, you have to loosen up a little bit. You're too serious, you're too studious. If you see something that you think is funny, try to make a joke about it and see what happens." Now I remember that vividly: that was in adolescence; I was thirteen years old. Going back earlier than that, I used to play by myself a lot, creating little war scenes with toy soldiers, and, in that sense, I would often spend three hours imagining scenarios requiring a beginning, a middle, and an end. I mean I can remember thinking, "Why are the soldiers on one side in this situation? Why are the other soldiers lying in wait for them?" And so on. And so I think I tended as a kid, depending on what I found as an outlet for play, to focus on aspects of what we now think of as plot, structure, characterization, motiva- tion, and so forth. I thought of them without labels, just as answers to the simple question "W-h-y?"

Herbert   Were you a very observant kind of person?

Healy   Not as a kid, but in law enforcement you've got to be observant in order to pick up that which is necessary for identification purposes. Let's say, how somebody's ears looked is bound to identify someone easily because that is the hardest thing to change easily and quickly. You notice someone's style of walking so you can spot them more easily. And in terms of my legal work, I would read documents over and over, particularly depositions—which would be the transcribed recollections of people regarding a given event—to try and find inconsistencies, areas maybe where people weren't lying intentionally but were honestly mistaken. People tend to confabulate. For example, in *So Like Sleep*, I have a situation in which a question is asked: "Can someone who is hypnotized about an event be a competent witness later on in the courtroom to testify regarding the event that he or she experienced?" The problem is, in between the event and courtroom testimony was the hypnosis, in which the questioner encourages the person under hypnosis to confabulate, to fill gaps so that the events that really are remembered make sense. To make a longish answer a little shorter, I think powers of observation [are] something that I gained because of my work in law enforcement and as a trial attorney and not from being a little kid who looked around at the world.

Herbert   When you were younger did you have any notion that you would one day become a writer or did you always aspire to be a lawyer?

Healy   I think I had a sense I'd be a lawyer rather than a writer. I guess I pictured writers as a very rarified, lucky group of people who could be called writers because they could support themselves from the writing they sold. I can remember in fifth or sixth grade thinking that I wanted to be a lawyer; I can't really remember thinking about writing until probably the ninth grade when the public school that I attended in New Jersey had a fairly unusual progressive sort of English curriculum. Twenty or thirty of us were chosen—probably mostly based on grades—to have a five-day-a-week program in which three class hours were taught by a relatively rigid, drill-oriented older teacher on grammar, punctuation, syntax, spelling, et cetera, and the remaining two days of the week the class hours were taught by a twice-published general novelist. And as a result he focused on creative writing.

Herbert   Who was the novelist?

Healy   John Jurick. So you see, in the course of every week we had three hours of drill and then two hours of creative application of what we'd learned. And looking back on it, I think it was a remarkably clever way to both produce minimally competent writers, whatever field of endeavor they might eventually enter, and also to strike a little bit of a spark for becoming a creative writer for those of us who got a kick out of the second part of the program.

Herbert   Tell me, what led to your ambition to become a lawyer? Did you have family members who had been in the law?

Healy   No. I'm the first person in my family to go to law school. And I think I went on to law school really because I thought it was *acceptable*: at least when you were a little kid, at age ten or eleven, firemen tended to be dropping somewhat in appeal when relatives would ask you what you intended to do with your life.

Herbert   (Laughs.) That reminds me of Brian Aldiss saying that one of his early ambitions was to become a cattle rustler! I take it you never dreamed of becoming a private eye?

Healy   No.

Herbert   As an attorney, did you ever work personally with private eyes? Did any private eyes of your acquaintance form the role models for your sleuth, John Francis Cuddy?

Healy   Yes, I did work with private investigators, but Cuddy is not based on them. He is, rather, a composite of my dad and my uncle.

Herbert   In what regards?

Healy   My dad was a military police captain during World War II, and my uncle was an insurance investigator after the war, and so they are objectively the Cuddy character in the sense of what the Cuddy character's résumé would look like if updated to the Vietnam era. I would say that the Cuddy character is a composite of them in a true character-characteristic sense, in that, I think that if my dad or my uncle had lost his wife young to cancer, either would have stayed faithful to the memory of his dead wife as Cuddy does.

Herbert   Would you reveal what inspired you to make Cuddy a sensitive male character whose tough nature is balanced by his desire to hang onto the memory of his deceased wife? Many readers find Cuddy's graveside conversations to be one of the most memorable aspects of your books.

Healy   When I sat down to write the first book, I tried to say to myself, "How can I make the principal character, the private investigator John Cuddy, a striking one if not a unique one?" And I had shortly before that attended a funeral at which I was kind of a friend of a friend making an appearance, rather than somebody emotionally involved in the death of a loved one. And so, when we went out to the graveyard for the graveside ceremonies I found that I was looking around the cemetery a little bit as the ritual proceeded and I noticed an older man standing over a gravesite that was obviously long filled in and shuddering from emotion, crying, whatever—he was far enough away that I couldn't quite tell—but it wasn't so cold that I thought it was the elements. And it occurred to me that it would be different to have the principal character be someone who had lost his wife unexpectedly. And since in our generation cancer seems to be the classical culprit, I decided to have Beth be a victim of cancer. I

295

later found out that there was a side benefit to doing that, and that was that I could, through the conversations at the graveside, allow the principal investigator to talk about the case as a device for summarizing and transitioning from one section of the effort to the next section of the effort—which is a very helpful device to have. It saves a lot of awkward expositional prose.

Herbert   Yes, it succeeds not only in advancing the plot but in enhancing our understanding of your principal character. It seems to me, in knowing you to the degreee that I do, that you do have some of the same characteristics: you can be masculine and tough—I'd have hated to be your opponent in the courtroom—but you can charm squirrels and give someone a rose when she's feeling terrible.

Healy   I think that in fairness and honesty there is some of me in John Cuddy. There simply are aspects of my dad and my uncle that I would never really know about because I simply wouldn't be in a position to see them; they naturally, as elders, would hide their sensitive aspects of themselves from me. I suppose I rely on my dad and my uncle to provide the superstructure for the character, and then [use] quirks of my friends or even myself as kind of the fill-in between the superstructure—the bricks that are between the I-beams, so to speak.

Herbert   Can you think of an example of one of those bricks that comes from your own personality?

Healy   Yeah, the fact that I really can't stand kids. And Cuddy is obviously somebody who really doesn't enjoy being around children much.

Herbert   What about your attitude toward death? As you know, the puzzle at the heart of most mysteries centers around a question of death. And I have often wondered what draws some authors to write in a genre that requires them to deal with death in every book. Would you consider yourself to be a person who is particularly aware of the fragility of life?

Healy   No. It's the opposite. I would venture to say that I very rarely think about death. Basically my attitude toward death is that it's simply "light's out" and there really is no afterlife. Even though I was raised Catholic, it's very hard for me to believe that there is some sense of the spirit continuing after the organism dies. So, as a result, I find death to be interesting because of the consequences it visits on the living rather than because of some intrinsic interest in death and what might come after for the person who dies.

Herbert   So death is not an issue that preoccupies you?

Healy   I've come very close to having what I would assume would be fatal automobile accidents, for example.

Herbert   Oh, my goodness. More than one?

Healy   Oh, yeah, and not really given it much more than sort of a passing smile. The first jetliner I was ever on blew an engine in mid-air and went down.

Herbert   What! Oh, Jerry.

Healy   Ever since then, I have sort of joked about it, because I figure I'm not going to be taken by air. If the Big Fellow wanted to take me by air, that was his chance. Oh, I grant you, even thinking about the Big Fellow is somewhat inconsistent with my view that it's "lights out" when we die. But the fact is I don't give it a second thought.

Herbert   Turning from death to life, may I ask: How true to life is the detective work that Cuddy engages in as a private investigator?

Healy   Our image, derived from television and fiction, of what a private investigator does is not really reflective of the degree to which a private investigator is involved in the system.

Herbert   Yes, the fictional P.I. does seem to be more of a loner and outsider.

Healy   He's a kind of a gunslinger who comes in to clean up the town, whereas in fact, in real life, the private investigator is just an extension of the attorneys involved in most cases and rarely strikes out on his or her own, rather, follows directions to the letter and submits detailed reports and signed statements.

Herbert   I see.

Healy   I try to inject some of the actual work that a real-life private investigator would do. But one of the real problems is that if you truly wrote a 220-page novel about what a private investigator does most of the time, it would be *crashingly* boring and would not have much of a story line. It would be a series of very loosely strung together three-day to five-day vignettes much like you see as subplots in a Sue Grafton novel, for example, and I'd like to think that you see in the subplots of the books that I've written. But in fact an investigator would be hired by an insurance company to stake out a potential arson. And he would—or she would—sit there, for a week or two weeks at a time, with the telescope trained on the potential source. And that's what it's all about; it's not interesting. Most of the work is deadly, *crushingly* routine. Because that's the only way that so-called breaks ever really occur.

Herbert   That's hardly the stuff of dramatic fiction! But what about writing? Where does the "break" occur that inspires your fiction? Do your books stem from issues that you wish to address, ideas for twists in plot, a sense of place, or something entirely different?

Healy   I'm not sure they've all come from the same spark, or the same category of spark. As I think back on it, *Blunt Darts* came from an idea I had when I was sitting in the courtroom of a particularly authoritarian judge, saying to myself: "Gee, I wonder what it would be like to be the kid of that judge. It must not be a lot of fun." In *So Like Sleep*, it was different. That was sparked by being a law professor and teaching a course in evidence in which the issue of hypnosis, as we already discussed, comes up. So that book was sparked by an intellectual, rather than anecdotal, concept or idea.

Herbert   Some writers go from book to book always with a similar kind of start. It seems that in your case the common inspiration for each of your books lies in your postulating a question.

Healy   That's true. And as to the sense of place that you mention, New England is an author's dream in that it contains, in a fairly confined geographical area, all kinds of landscapes and socioeconomic groups, but although it is important to me to make my settings accurate and atmospheric, I don't think generally it is a sense of place that sparks off books for me.

Herbert   I wonder, Jerry, if you would say that your desire to see justice done is the other major link between your novels.

Healy   I think that's the kick for a lot of the writers, that you get to play God to some extent. You sit in front of a computer terminal and you create this fantasy world; you people it with the individuals you need to make the story—and the moral that you'd like to draw—credible. I think the satisfaction that the reader derives from reading a private investigator book is a sense that there *is* someone out there who does in fact cause justice to be produced in the relatively small percentage of cases that the formal system tends not to handle well. And what we're really talking about, of course, is justification for vigilantism, when you really come down to it. I think that's something that troubles, philosophically, a lot of people who've dedicated themselves to the law as a career. In effect, to the extent we cheer in a moviehouse at certain things being done on screen, what we are really doing is praising the individual who steps outside the system to do unto a bad person that which the system seems ill-equipped to do to that bad person. That's vigilantism.

Herbert Well, crime writing is on the whole a very conservative form. I mean in the end order is established—

Healy It's formulaic. And in that sense it is perhaps as structured as certain kinds of poems would be.

Herbert Is it fair to say then, that you have it both ways? As a law professor, you prepare students to work within the system for the greater good of society and as a private eye novelist, you step outside of the law to right the wrongs that the law doesn't handle to your satisfaction?

Healy You've put your finger on it, Rose. That about sums it up.

▶ CATHERINE AIRD

Perhaps more so than any individual interviewed in this volume, Catherine Aird fits the popular image of the female English detective writer of the traditional school. Residing in the substantial "doctor's house" located at a crossroads and railway crossing of a large English village two and a half miles from the cathedral city of Canterbury, Aird is a person who radiates keen intelligence, cheerful self-sufficiency, and marvelous wit, all articulated in a small voice speaking perfect Queen's English. Sitting in her bower of yellow roses, she quietly reveals that she possesses all the requisites for success as a detective novelist: an eye for domestic detail that turns a serving vessel into a poisoned chalice, staunch belief in law and order, uncompromising acceptance about the truth of people's circumstances and character—and the ability to uncover that truth—and even training similar to Agatha Christie's in dispensing drugs. She has even served on the burial committee of the parish council, experience "most useful to the crime writer," Aird admits with a smile.

Born Kinn H. McIntosh in an industrial town in Yorkshire, the girl who would later take the pseudonym Catherine Aird always dreamed of becoming a doctor. But before she could follow in the footsteps of her father, a family practitioner with a taste for forensic studies, Aird suffered a life-threatening illness that confined her to bed for several years. Following her recovery, she took on the clerical and dispensing duties of her father's country practice. In addition, she has engaged in considerable volunteer work connected with her church and for the Girl Guides Association, where she became chairman of the finance committee. In 1989 she was made a Member of the British Empire for her service to the Girl Guides.

She also devoted many years of her life to caring for her parents, who were invalided through ill health, and with whom she shared a home.

In 1964, while engaged in her medical and volunteer activities, Aird published her first detective novel, after writing and discarding three mainstream novels. Since then she has produced fifteen novels, all but one of which feature the series sleuth Inspector C. D. Sloan, inevitably nicknamed "Seedy," whom she modeled on those good-humored and ageless sleuths whom she admired from the pages of the golden age of the detective novel. Sloan investigates crimes in the company of his "defective" detective constable, William Crosby, in the fictional county of Calleshire, a locale that features familiar English settings such as stately homes and the cathedral close. Aird makes these memorable through juxtaposing the contemporary detail or character with the well-worn setting, and by interjecting highly humorous observations.

While Aird says that her sleuth does not speak for her or reflect her point of view, anyone who gets to know the character and author will respond to similar endearing qualities: a winning sense of humor often expressed in delightful understatement, dedication to the truth, and lack of pretentiousness. One imagines them both as possessing the same sparkle in the eye.

In 1991, the centennial year of Agatha Christie's birth, Aird was elected chairman of the British Crime Writers' Association and in that capacity arranged for Princess Margaret to present their annual awards. In 1992 she was presented with the first Golden Handcuffs Award by the Crime Writers' Association, honoring her lifetime achievement. She has also written nonfiction in the form of numerous articles, speeches, and some local history. She is also an editor of *The Oxford Companion to Crime and Mystery Writing*, a work in progress from Oxford University Press.

Herbert   I wonder what you would consider to be the most fascinating human flaw.

Aird   (Smiles.) I think I would have to ask you to amplify that question a bit.

Herbert   Well, I ask this because your novels look at very real human beings who seem to be flourishing within their communities and then you reveal to us a fatal flaw or failing that pushes them to commit the ultimate crime of murder.

Aird   Well, I suppose I would agree with F. Tennyson Jesse's reasons for crime. You are aware that she has listed six good classes of murder?

Herbert   Yes.

Aird   One is murder for gain; two is murder for revenge; three is murder for elimination; four is murder for jealousy; five is murder for lust of killing; and six is murder for conviction.

Herbert   When you say "murder for conviction," you mean murder motivated by one's belief, rather than murder with incarceration as it's goal?

Aird   (Laughs.) Yes, of course. And I think if you can find another good reason for murder other than those, then I would very much like to be made aware of it!

Herbert   Which of these reasons for murder most appeals to you as a writer?

Aird   I think I'd probably tackle that the other way 'round by saying that I don't think I've ever used lust as a reason for murder nor, in fact, conviction or the love of killing.

Herbert   When you say that you have not used love of killing as a motive, it makes me think of Patricia D. Cornwell. Her murderers may indulge themselves in a warped love of killing, yet she has very consciously decided not to show the murder from the point of view of the person who is getting a sick pleasure from perpetrating the crime.

Aird   Yes, I am very familiar with her work. And I would agree with her view absolutely. I think the crime writer has a positive duty not to write a *vade mecum* for murderers and not to facilitate crime or in any way glamorize it in a sense that anybody might use it or abuse it. I mean I can't speak for all crime writers; I can only speak for this one, but I myself feel very strongly about this—and I'm not above making a deliberate mistake in something that I am writing just so that somebody can't trot down to the chemist and make up something fatal.

Herbert   In other words, you might add an ingredient that would make the actual formula harmless?

Aird   I wouldn't make it harmless but I would describe something that wasn't as effective as it might seem to be. I would go out of my way not to write a sort of planning guide to easy murder.

Herbert   What typically occasions the start of each book for you? Is it an ingenious method of murder, or one of F. Tennyson Jesse's six motives, or a setting, perhaps, that inspires you?

Aird   The setting doesn't inspire my books but it certainly helps in constructing my mysteries. What inspires me much more is the situation which I would hope to explore within a definite sense of place.

Herbert   So your goal is to do more with your setting than to use it simply as a stage set within which to place clues?

Aird   I think one must obviously set the scene but I would like to go the second mile there and include a sense of place as an added extra —but not as the raison d'être.

Herbert   And when you take your setting that extra mile, is your purpose to give it a symbolic dimension?

Aird   No. I think I'm looking for accuracy rather than symbolism.

Herbert   Do you take particular delight in using a setting that is familiar to the seasoned reader of traditional English crime and mystery fiction and updating it? I am thinking of *The Stately Home Murder* in this context. In that novel you take the well-worn stately home setting and, with a marvelous sense of humor, you show that while such edifices do exist today, they do not continue in the private splendor of their heyday. Instead of using a well-off family dining in the company of numerous guests and servants, you populate your country house with assorted tourists who ramble through it in a poorly guided tour that supports the family retainers who continue to live there.

Aird   Well, yes. During the 1920s authors were able to write about country houses and describe conditions as they were then, but I am writing about stately homes as they are now. It provides the occasion for contrast of traditional and contemporary worlds.

Herbert   And, it provides the occasion for you to exercise your sense of humor while commenting on that changing and changed English scene. For instance, I just loved the scene where your sleuth, C. D. Sloan, arrives at the stately home in the company of his constable. "Two members of the county constabulary to see you, my Lord," the butler says. And then you remark, "As a way of introducing a country police inspector and his constable, Sloan couldn't have improved on it. It was the first time in Sloan's police career that he had ever been conducted anywhere by a butler."

Aird   I'm pleased you liked that little scene.

Herbert   Well, it illustrates two of your fortes: your sense of humor and your powers of writing brief vignettes that say a great deal—and it shows how the success of both rests on your toying with the reader's assumptions. How conscious are you of manipulating the reader's reaction through playing with his or her assumptions?

Aird   I think that comes along as part of the ride; it's not part of a conscious plan.

Herbert   What about our assumptions regarding certain characters? If you give us a vicar we may assume certain things.

Aird   Oh, yes! That's a legitimate use of archetypal characters: as seen through a mirror, perhaps.

Herbert   Would you embroider on that a little bit? Or perhaps I should say "reflect on that."

Aird   (Laughs.) Well I think probably the crime writer always has a stock of archetypal characters but they aren't in fact as archetypal as they seem; they are the reverse or slightly askew, as seen perhaps in a distorted mirror. They're there but they're not always what they seem, as, in fact, in crime writing nothing is what it seems.

Herbert   Returning to your skill at producing vignettes that say a great deal in a limited number of words—

Aird   I am curious to know what you see in that particular vignette.

Herbert   Well, of course, it tells us that these are contemporary policemen who, although they are undertaking an investigation at a stately home, are not accustomed to being formally introduced by the classic butler. It tells readers that although the lord in question is reduced to having tourist groups surge through his premises, he retains a sense of pride and superiority over his servant, who must refer to him as "my Lord." And Sloan's internal reflection endears him to us, since we enjoy his sense of humor and lack of pretentiousness.

Aird   I see.

Herbert   But returning to these vignettes, I wonder how much you have been influenced by Sir Arthur Conan Doyle, since he, too, was a master of establishing atmosphere and character through brief vignettes and short sections of description.

Aird   I always enjoyed the work of Conan Doyle enormously, yes. And I do admire the way he was able to tell you something about the sound of horses' hooves on the cobblestones and instantly give you the impression of fog, and the damp London night.

Herbert   In Conan Doyle you always get a wonderful picture of London but when you actually examine the stories you see that it's done very economically.

Aird   And it's nearly always the way in which it's said, you know.

Herbert   Do you mean in terms of what the *characters* say or in terms of how *Doyle* describes the scene, what he says?

Aird   It's the way in which he puts economy into the speech of his characters, the way in which *they* refer to the scene which gives you a very good picture. It is the speech of the character; it's not the authorial voice.

Herbert   That shows that you are truly a writer. Most of us read for the effect of the stories but you seem to naturally analyze their construction.

305

Aird　　You're too kind! Flattery will get you everywhere, you know. But I think Conan Doyle has a great gift in this regard.

Herbert　When you think about the description of the famous Sherlockian clue of the dog in the night, that is also provided in dialogue, isn't it?

Aird　　Yes, it is a marvelous line. The Inspector says to Holmes, "Is there any point to which you would wish to draw my attention?"

Herbert　And then Holmes replies, "To the curious incident if the dog in the night-time."

Aird　　And the Inspector says, "The dog did nothing in the night-time."

Herbert　Holmes says—

Aird　　"That was the curious incident."

Herbert　Did you read the Holmes stories in your early years?

Aird　　Yes. But I was brought up on the real-life tales of Dr. Joseph Bell, who was Holmes's original. Conan Doyle modeled Holmes on Dr. Joseph Bell of Edinburgh University.

Herbert　Can you tell me more about this? I understand your father was a medical doctor. Did he, or anybody of his acquaintance, actually come in contact with Dr. Joseph Bell?

Aird　　My father studied forensic medicine at Edinburgh University in the 1916 period when the name of Bell was still revered there. And he certainly heard him quoted on many occasions.

Herbert　Although your father studied forensic medicine, he became a general practitioner, didn't he?

Aird　　Yes. But they all had to do forensic medicine. It was a subject that always interested him and he always used to speak a lot about it.

Herbert　Do you think Dr. Bell's scientific approach to sleuthing influenced you when you came to create C. D. Sloan?

Aird　　It isn't so much a scientific approach; it's an approach of observation and deduction. This isn't quite the same thing. It was his powers of observation and deduction that were so remarkable. It was this that Conan Doyle was so taken with, not pure forensics, by any means.

Herbert　I see. That's an important distinction, isn't it? When you were creating Sloan was this deductive ability something that you wanted to endow him with?

Aird　　I have always tried to make him logical. Real life isn't as logical as fictional life shown in crime writing.

Herbert　That is certainly true!

Aird   In crime writing every problem has to be absolutely capable of solution and as we all know, real life isn't this way.

Herbert   Did you know from the start that Sloan would be a series detective?

Aird   Yes, I did. When he first appeared, so to speak, I felt, "Here was a good chap."

Herbert   What kind of decisions did you make in creating your series sleuth?

Aird   My chap is not limited because I set out quite consciously not to limit him. I've always liked series where the character doesn't get more and more distinguished and old as time goes on. I thought of the appeal of the sort of writer I read when I was young—where you had an absolutely ageless Bulldog Drummond or the Saint or any of these people—I think they were the ones who appealed to me, where you didn't have them getting older. I like it to be a snapshot, a timeless snapshot.

Herbert   What sort of pitfalls did you seek to avoid?

Aird   I've avoided using real dates and using money, which is equally dating. I've tried to keep the idiom up to date, but that is more difficult. I have consciously tried to keep it as dateless as possible.

Herbert   And with what strengths did you seek to endow your sleuth?

Aird   I wanted to make him an ordinary man, oppressed by his superiors and disappointed by those underneath; in other words, the common man. I should imagine his circumstances are part of the human condition! I want him to be the middle-of-the-road chap, a bit oppressed by life but not too much so.

Herbert   And it sounds like that was quite a conscious decision. What advantages do you see in having a series sleuth?

Aird   Well, the character develops from book to book and you see things through his eyes. With a series character, you don't have to start again fresh with every book through different eyes. It saves quite a lot of time if those eyes seem to work—which in Sloan's case they do.

Herbert   In what regards do you identify with your sleuth?

Aird   I'm not conscious of identifying with him at all, really.

Herbert   Doesn't he speak for you in any particular regard?

Aird   No, in fact none of my characters speaks for me. I think quite a lot of the authors who turn to crime writing do so because nobody speaks for them. In ordinary fiction you can pick out who is the author's spokesman, but I think crime writing is rather useful in that it doesn't actually lend itself to the author speaking in a personal sense.

Herbert   But even P. D. James admits that a body of work does reveal certain things about the writer's private landscape, as it were.

Aird   I'm not denying that, but I'm saying that none of my characters is speaking for me and my role is to be more of an observer than that, more detached.

Herbert   Well, I think I do see something about the topography of your private landscape revealed in your books.

Aird   Indeed?

Herbert   Yes, certainly a love of England.

Aird   Yes, but then that's true of all my characters.

Herbert   Well, not perhaps of the Sheikh of Lasserta who appears in *The Body Politic*.

Aird   (Laughs.)

Herbert   While of course Sloan is central to your work, your narration is always in the third person. I should add that it is a very delightful third person, particularly because this narrator is superb at engaging in amusing social commentary. To return to *The Stately Home Murder*, may we look at the scene where the working-class tourist, Mrs. Pearl Fisher, is described as having come from Paradise Row, Luston? Here this narrator remarks, "Any student of industrial philanthropy would immediately recognize this as a particularly grimy part of that particularly grimy town. By some Victorian quirk of self-righteousness the street names there varied in inverse proportion to their amenity."

Aird   Well, I was born in that sort of place, so I know a bit more about it.

Herbert   What was your home community like?

Aird   I grew up in industrial England, in the north of England. It was full of little chimneys, smoking. It was very dirty until the Clean Air Act came along. You know, you wouldn't run your hand over a wall without it getting fairly dirty. It would be quite different now in that regard. But it was a very, very busy industrial town with manufacturing and heavy engineering work there. My father's practice was in our home when I was very small.

Herbert   Even as a child did you feel yourself to be a keen observer?

Aird   I think probably so, but I was taught it. My father would come out of a house and say, "How many windows are there?" or that sort of thing. He was very keen on observation. I think there is a certain amount of observation that I would do in any situation—but some of this was taught.

Herbert So this was a rather fun challenge between you and your father?

Aird I don't suppose *he* thought of it like that!

Herbert He intended to instruct you, then?

Aird He thought, "Is the girl blind? Can't she notice?"

Both (Laugh.)

Herbert Did you always envision yourself becoming a writer? Or did you entertain other aspirations?

Aird I was always going to be a doctor.

Herbert Really? Why did you decide not to become one?

Aird Oh, yes, well, I collected a nasty disease called the Nephratic Syndrome and I spent the years I *would* have been in university in bed.

Herbert Oh, how awful!

Aird Well, it was very good training for a crime writer, or for any writer, I think. It forced one to organize one's thinking.

Herbert I've never heard of this disease.

Aird It's a kidney disease and [medical science] hadn't heard of it when I had it either! It was years afterwards that they identified it. So it was quite alarming. I think it must have been about five or six years after I had it that they suddenly said, "Ah! That's what you must have had."

Herbert So it was something that eventually corrects itself?

Aird Well, it *did*. (Pauses.) It doesn't always.

Herbert Was it for a matter of years that you suffered from this?

Aird Yes, it was quite a long time, actually. That's why I didn't do medicine.

Herbert Was it during that time that you started writing?

Aird No, not really. I started writing when I was about twenty-nine or thirty.

Herbert But you'd thought about writing earlier in your life?

Aird Yes, I'd thought about it when I was a child. I'd always enjoyed writing. So I finally set myself the challenge, "Can I really sit down and write a book?" And I did.

Herbert	Which one was this?
Aird	Oh, no, I threw it away.
Herbert	Did you destroy it?
Aird	Yes. *Rather!*
Herbert	What a pity!
Aird	Oh, I'm *sure* it was the right thing to do. I wrote two or three. And then I reached the point where I thought, "This is getting better," and I finally wrote one that I thought was all right to send for publication.
Herbert	Were the discarded books mystery novels?
Aird	No, this was before I turned to crime, so to speak. And then when I tried my hand at crime writing I felt I was in a medium that I could enjoy.
Herbert	Was there anything particular about the crime writing that immediately won your heart?
Aird	Yes, because I was a reader of crime stories, once I started to write one I felt at home. I was a reader of them always.
Herbert	And at this time you were working with your father in his medical practice? So that was a career in itself.
Aird	No, not particularly.
Herbert	I think I sense some modesty creeping in. Was your father's practice here, in Sturry? Would you describe the type of community Sturry is, particularly on behalf of the American reader?
Aird	I live in what is now a rather large English village two and a half miles outside of a cathedral city. It wasn't large when we came here. My father's was very much a country practice.
Herbert	Were your duties particularly useful to you when you decided to become a crime writer? Would you describe them for us?
Aird	I did a lot of the dispensing and the clerical work attached to a medical practice.
Herbert	I've noticed the bottles labeled "poison" on shelves in your home.
Aird	Yes, that's called the dispensary. The bottles are now empty but I've kept them just for old time's sake.
Herbert	When you do dispensing over here [in England], is that the same thing as a pharmacist would do in the States?

Aird   Yes. But when it's done in a doctor's surgery it's called "dispensing under supervision" and the doctor takes the responsibility for doing it and it happens in cases where you have a practice where the patient is more than a mile from the chemist. If the practice extends more than a mile away from the nearest chemist, then the doctor has an obligation to provide the medicine.

Herbert   Ah, so you were trained in potential poisoning or overdosing in the old Agatha Christie tradition, with hands-on experience dispensing medicines!

Aird   I won't answer that! (Laughs.) You can't force a pharmacist to come into the area but if you've got the doctor there then obviously the patients must have their drugs and therefore the obligation falls on the doctor.

Herbert   Did your work involve dispensing things that were already made up or did you have to mix them? It seems the responsibility of mixing medicines would provide much more useful experience for the mystery writer.

Aird   Well, once upon a time, you know, the mixing was de rigueur and one did the mixing of things. And then almost everything became tablets and capsules and as time went on it was really more a question of counting things out.

Herbert   Then it must have become a bit dull, when it was merely a matter of counting.

Aird   Well, there wasn't anything dull about it! (Laughs.)

Herbert   Well, one could always pass the time speculating about methods for murder!

Aird   Don't forget, you knew all the patients and what the medicine was for. No, I don't think I'd call dispensing dull.

Herbert   And as a result of this experience, you know a lot about drugs.

Aird   I think more important than knowing a lot about drugs is the fact that I know where to go to look it up.

Herbert   So you are better equipped than some to concoct a murder.

Aird   Yes, I've never used that as a particular theme. But I think that all information, however recondite, is useful to a crime writer, you know, rather than the specific knowledge of a particular thing. Any unusual knowledge *cannot help but be useful* to crime.

Herbert   Would you provide an example of the sort of experience that comes up in your ordinary life that might strike you as suitable for use in crime fiction?

Aird   Well, a young friend staying in my house, Kirsty McCormack, prepared a dessert by freezing a whole lot of rose petals in a bowl and then filling the resulting ice bowl with ice cream. It was absolutely lovely. But while rose petals are not poisonous, it does cause one to speculate on the results if something poisonous were to be imbedded in the ice instead.

Herbert   Oh, my goodness. I love the way you say that with a twinkle in your eye.

Aird   Yes, when you're looking at this you think, "Ah!" You can see possibilities in every situation from the crime writer's point of view.

Herbert   It's a frightening thought to imagine someone intentionally poisoning a person by this means but to consider that it might happen unintentionally is even more chilling somehow. This notion of the uneasy, uncozy aspect of crime writing leads me to ask you what you think of Julian Symons's belief that the detective story is gradually changing over to the more psychologically motivated crime novel.

Aird   I wouldn't have said that was entirely it, is it? It may be something he has observed but I can't say that I have. There's room for whodunits—with, obviously, updated social worries and social scene.

Herbert   Like the strawberry social in the grounds of the grand house that you portray in *The Body Politic*. In this classic setting we have a question of whodunit with international implications linked to mining concerns in a Middle Eastern sheikhdom.

Aird   That's right. I try to update the concerns in the novels, even if I use a traditional setting.

Herbert   But while you do write very much in the tradition of the classic whodunit, you are concerned to give some psychological depth to your characters.

Aird   I think probably regrettably my characters are stock characters, but if you take the stock character and it does something slightly out of the normal *then* you have something.

Herbert   I think Julian is trying to develop the idea that the crime novel today on the whole does offer deeper psychological development of the characters.

Aird   I take his point. But the problem sometimes comes—you've got to have your villain sane enough. I mean, I'm quite sure that in real life people are murdered for perfectly sound reasons like slurping or snoring or being rude—but in literature you have this great fiction that the murderer has to be sane to the extent that the reader can work out the rationality of his actions. The reader needs to be able to work them out.

Herbert   Yes, otherwise the author is not playing fair with the reader. This idea of fair play is one of the great tenets of the classical detective novel. Obviously, you are committed to this in your work. Are there other traditions of the classical detective story to which you are consciously committed?

Aird   Well, I think that it is a very satisfactory feeling when you've got a neatly all-loose-ends-tied conclusion. You can then feel, "That's all right; that job is properly done; I can go on to the next." I don't like leaving loose ends anywhere. I think I like to be outside of what I'm doing without any unfinished business. I think that way you sleep better and you know where you are.

Herbert   And so the uneasy ending is—

Aird   Not me! And sometimes—not always—it's a way of the author not having to work out a more satisfactory solution. But remember, one needn't be limited to the whodunit. This is one of the marvelous freedoms of the whole thing, isn't it? You can have a "whodunit," a "whydunit," a "howdunit." Or, you know, you can take something like Josephine Tey did—the Elizabeth Canning case in 1752—and write a brilliant book about it, updating it to your own present day.

Herbert   That was in *The Franchise Affair*, wasn't it? It treated the case of the missing young woman who, it seemed, had been kept as a household laborer against her will by two spinster ladies.

Aird   Yes. So you can go even farther backwards and take an ancient crime and put it into modern times, or you can do what Shakespeare did and you take the story of Sir Walter Raleigh and put that all into Roman times and call it *Coriolanus*—and you don't get your head chopped off. You know the variabilities are quite infinite.

Herbert   It doesn't sound as if you feel in any regard limited by the mystery story. Do you agree with P. D. James that the structure of the crime story is actually quite liberating?

Aird   Yes, I do. I think it's a great thing that you've got to have some parameters. If you take an ordinary novel, you've got no edges; with a detective novel you've got a framework ready-made within which convention requires you to work. The end product of which is that, in the last analysis, good triumphs over evil and if it doesn't, then it's not a detective story. You know that [the] end you're working toward is the solution to the mystery and the restitution of the rights of the individual, and a general sort of bringing together of everything, which

313

should tie up all loose ends. And you know when you set off that there must be a reason for everything in the book. Every book has to have a beginning, a middle, and an end. But there is always a *conclusion* in a crime story. You know it's going to be a satisfying read. I find it a marvelous framework and I wouldn't want to change it for any other.

Herbert   Would you say that you can do anything you like in a detective story?

Aird   It's quite a sensitive medium to work in because it's so elastic. I mean, there's absolutely nothing stopping you writing about anything you like.

Herbert   I see.

Aird   Within a crime story you don't even have to have a murder, but you do have to have some sort of conflict or rule-breaking, and I think that gives you all kinds of opportunities for developing characters and themes. Certainly I wouldn't want to exchange the framework for anything.

Herbert   But are there limitations regarding what you can say about human character, since there often is a need to keep secrets about character from the reader?

Aird   I think this is a technical challenge. You cannot reveal on page one everything about the personality of your murderer; you must hold back information. And I think that what you actually are able to reveal sets a great challenge for the crime writer. You are actually giving away judicious bits of information or misinformation. It's not "the whole truth and nothing but the truth"; it is some of the truth that you're telling about your murderer.

Herbert   I like the way you put that. Now, if you are only telling some of the truth about your character, does this in any way limit the potential literary achievement of the crime novel?

Aird   I don't think I'm writing for literary merit; I'm writing detective stories and that is part of the necessary luggage of the detective story—or some detective stories—that the identity of the murderer isn't apparent immediately and the only way that you can conceal it is by not painting the whole portrait of the murderer the first time he appears.

Herbert   Clearly, I believe that your work does have "literary merit." But are you then saying that if you personally wanted to write something to an even higher literary standard, that you would have to turn away from the detective story?

Aird   I am trying to write detective stories to my own highest personal standard. That is my objective.

Herbert   What I am asking is, if one doesn't tell the whole truth and nothing but the truth in a novel, can that novel succeed on the highest levels of literature?

Aird   (Pauses.) You're not painting a true picture of your main character. To that extent it can't be fair. I wouldn't disagree with Julian in this respect at all. If you're deliberately misrepresenting your principal character, it can't be to that extent absolutely true, can it?

Herbert   You have said that you are writing to your highest personal standard. What personal challenges do you set yourself in your writing?

Aird   Are you a golfer?

Herbert   No, I'm afraid not.

Aird   Now, when you're playing golf you can either play a match game against an opponent or you can do what is called playing bogey. Bogey is par for the course, when you challenge yourself to play the course and do your best at it.

Herbert   It's an individual challenge to yourself, then?

Aird   Yes. In a way. If you're asking me how I would view the writing process, I would say that I'm always trying to play bogey, so to speak, because I'm trying to do the best each time I take out a piece of paper. Because the reception to the writing comes so long and so late, you're playing a course; you're not really saying, "I wonder what people will think about this in eighteen months time when they read this?" I think it's much simpler than that. It's something between you and the paper and you're actually concentrating on that.

Herbert   I am curious to know about your choice of pseudonym.

Aird   Catherine Aird got her pseudonym at the request of her publishers because her Christian name is a very unusual one and it's very difficult to determine from it whether she is male or female. And her surname is a Scottish one beginning with "McI," which is a very difficult name for somebody to pronounce who is not familiar with the Scottish ways of writing surnames. And this of course would be true in very many countries where there is a translation question. So my publishers told me to go away and get myself a euphonious—nice to the ear—pseudonym. So I came home and I unfurled the family tree and I ran my finger up it until I came to the name Catherine Aird, which is, I think, my great-grandmother on my father's side. I could have chosen quite a few actually, out of the family tree, but it seemed to me to be just right. And as far as I could make out from family legend, I believe that she was a midwife. So this seemed to be the right one.

Herbert   I'm intrigued by this choice of a midwife's name for a pseudonym.

Aird   Well, I've never heard any other author mention this but I'm terribly conscious of it myself. There comes a stage in every book where I feel a definite quickening, a coming to life of the work. The same as in pregnancy. It suddenly gives a little kick, and you say, "Ah, this is going to be all right."

Herbert   And does this come in the idea stage or the writing stage?

Aird   Oh, definitely in the writing stage. I like to sit down, not being sure myself what is going to emerge during the day. And then one day the work just takes on a life of its own.

Herbert   Would you tell me more about the writing process for you, and perhaps comment on other life experiences that have directly influenced the process?

Aird   In my youth I edited a parish magazine—which everybody laughs about—but is, in fact, a very good discipline because whatever happens, it has to be published on a certain day of the month and you learn quite a bit about accuracy. The great thing about editing a parish magazine is if you put something in it that isn't right, well, you're centered in the middle of the people about which it is written and you *know* you have a series of critics. (Smiles.) And it teaches you about deadlines and accuracy. It is a bit like knowing you're about to be hanged in a fortnight; this does concentrate the mind!

Herbert   (Laughs.) And have you done other work that has influenced your writing?

Aird   I've done a lot of voluntary work. I was for many years the chairman of our local parish council and I was chairman of the burial committee, which was quite useful for a crime writer.

Herbert   I love the mild manner in which you tell me this! Please tell me about some of the information you gleaned as a part of this work.

Aird   Oh, yes, well, you had to be familiar with the laws regarding the running of cemeteries, which is quite a useful thing for background information. It can't be other than helpful.

Herbert   Have you ever used information that you learned on the burial committee in constructing a particular book?

Aird   Yes, there was one, where I had the burial by the water, in *Last Respects*. There the chap buries his wife near the edge of the river where it is subject to flooding. I did use a bit of knowledge there. He buried her in the corner of the cemetery that flooded a little bit so that the—I think it was arsenic in the body—gets washed away.

Herbert I would also imagine that as a member of the burial committee you would have considerable experience dealing with people facing grief and loss. This makes me think of P. D. James' reference to Graham Greene, who said that the author is essentially an observer with an icicle at the heart.

Aird Yes. You observe the process of grief in an intellectual manner. Yes. But this also happens when you yourself are experiencing something; you are experiencing it but above your shoulder you are noticing how you experience it. I don't think everybody does this at all, but I think most writers would. When you're undergoing an experience, however unpleasant or rapturous or whatever it is, somewhere above and behind your shoulder there's another part of your alter ego that is saying, "Ah!"

Herbert This makes me think of the expression "beside oneself."

Aird Yes. It is all pushed into a great big melting pot, everything that you see and hear and experience. Then it churns around for a bit and eventually you pull a book out of it.

Herbert What about death and the mystery writer? Since you choose to write books centered around puzzling death, I wonder if death itself is a subject that preoccupies you.

Aird I think that one of the reasons why death is so important a subject with writers of crime, and especially detective fiction, is that in all countries there are sufficient procedures and formalities attached to it to help the story along. It is also a rite of passage about which it is proper and seemly to ask intimate questions—which is not so in the case of birth and marriage. It is also a subject on which almost everyone has given some thought by the time they come to read this sort of fiction. John Donne wrote that "any man's death diminishes me." I think that the converse might also be true and that writers and readers are trying to diminish death by writing and reading about it.

Herbert It interests me that you are concerned with the propriety of asking questions. This seems terribly English to me. What do you think about P. D. James's point of view that the investigation of a crime invades the privacy and even damages the lives of those who are touched by the crime? How do you come to terms with this unseemly invasion of privacy in your work?

Aird Oh, yes, well, this is what it's all about, isn't it? This invasion of privacy is very useful to the crime writer. Murder provides the occasion to ask awkward questions at an awkward time.

Herbert   Talking of things happening at awkward times, several authors have told me that serendipity has played a rather large role in their work, causing them to change direction and enrich their books. Is this the case for you, too?

Aird   I don't know how much of this is genuine serendipity and how much is thematic apperception. You know, when you're writing a book about chimney sweeps, you begin to become an expert on chimneys. Once you have decided on your subject you are much more aware of it. You are alerted and attuned to be receptive to any information that comes your way. But, yes, information does sometimes come my way seemingly serendipitously. Perhaps because I've always kept active with things other than writing. I've always done something else. Writers should always have another form of work. Writing is a very dangerous occupation. And I think the other thing is, you cannot possibly spend eight hours every day working in good creative writing, unless you're very exceptional.

Herbert   When you are actively engaged in a novel, do you write for a typical span of hours each day?

Aird   Yes, but not a great deal. I usually write for a couple of hours first thing in the morning. I'm much more relaxed now than I used to be but I was very disciplined at one time and I would write for a couple of hours at sort of half-past six, seven in the morning, day in, day out, week in, week out. And I'm more inclined now to do it in a leisurely fashion. I've never *not* done anything interesting because I felt I ought to sit and write. You know life is for living and you're more likely to write better if you're engaged in things. Everything is grist for writers, though, really.

Herbert   And of course you had endured that isolating time in your life when you couldn't get out due to illness.

Aird   Yes, that was very helpful, I think.

Herbert   You certainly seem to possess the power of positive thinking!

Aird   But [pauses] at the time, of course, it was very, very daunting; but looking back, I realize that my habits of thinking were probably formed at that time, and my habit of reading. And also I think it does concentrate the mind a bit—I mean you sort out all sorts of things in your own mind that you can see other people coming to terms with perhaps twenty years later. Whereas if you've gotten through them in your own mind when you're quite young, it saves you a lot of time.

Herbert   Was your illness life-threatening?

Aird   Oh, yes. Oh, my, it was.

Herbert   How awful.

Aird   Oh, no—that's what I mean. In some senses it's quite a useful exercise; it concentrates the mind a bit and you sort out things.

Herbert   Major issues like coming to terms with possible death? I wonder if this caused you to become a person who is particularly aware of the fragility of life. After all, you have devoted your writing career to focusing on plots concerned with puzzling deaths.

Aird   Death comes to us all in the end, but perhaps for the crime writer it comes earlier, and more frequently.

Herbert   (Laughs.)

Aird   But I don't think I'm unusually preoccupied with death. I hope I'm mature and sensible enough to accept that it is something we must all face. Of course, I didn't feel quite this way when I was younger.

Herbert   What about when you were ill? Can you describe this experience a little bit more fully?

Aird   It was a long time ago. It was a period of years in which it was not physically possible to do anything else except read. This is probably a very good basis for a writer.

Herbert   And to think, there you were in the household of a doctor and still no one knew what the disease was.

Aird   And that didn't stop them from being pessimistic, you know. (Smiles.)

Herbert   Then you not only had to face your own mortality at an early age, but you were not especially coddled in terms of the dangerous reality of your illness.

Aird   I think both my parents were very much in that sort of way of living. They were both opposed to cloud-cuckoo-land and felt that it was important for patients and people to be able to know where they stood in order to be better able to cope with what faced them. They were very much, both of them, realists and, I think, both opposed to the sort of rose-tinted spectacles approach or the idea that if you swept it away it wouldn't come back. They were both of them inclined to deal with things in a very determined fashion. And I think probably I inherited this from them.

Herbert   And talking of habits of mind formed in those years and your writing today, do you bring any superstitions to the writing process?

Aird   No, not as far as I know. I always work better if I've got a pot of tea beside me. But I can work even without a pot of tea! I can write more or less anywhere and at any time. I mean, put down in a perfectly empty room with a piece of paper and pencil, I'm just as happy as I am sitting at my desk. And I can think well on the railway train. I find that that's quite a good place because nobody actually wants you to do anything—and the telephone can't ring.

Herbert   It sounds like you are a true professional who can just get on with it.

Aird   Yes, you just get on with it. I mean, you don't imagine that a dentist has a fetish when he goes to work.

Herbert   Well, there *was* Crippen.

Both   (Laugh.)

Aird   But I don't agree with Tchaikovsky—

Herbert   Mmm?

Aird   —who said that he went into his study every morning at nine o'clock, and every morning at nine o'clock he was punctually visited by the muse of music.

Herbert   Oh!

Aird   I think on that I would beg to differ. I don't think that you write to exactly the same degree every day.

Herbert   And sometimes you must not actually write anything at all.

Aird   Well, of course you don't. And sometimes what you write isn't as good one day as it might be another day. One is a human being, not a machine. And I don't think the muse of music was as punctual as all that.

Herbert   (Laughs.)

Aird   I could write at some length about the *un*puncutal muse. I agree more with Anthony Trollope, who wrote about the habit of industry, and I'm quite sure that that's more to the point. I've actually given a talk on the unpunctual muse and have some notes about this.

Herbert   I would love to know what to do to while away the time while the muse is late! What does one do to keep oneself going?

Aird   I think what I could do with most now is a tame archivist who can say to me where I have put this or that, so I would know what I have got and what I haven't got. Because it reaches a certain point when you've got so much material, so many old manuscripts, and so many notes that you can't actually remember where everything is, quite. And I occasionally come across people who do have everything exactly where they can find it and they in fact are not creative writers at all; they are people who are taxonomists, who actually enjoy codifying things and sorting, and their great pleasure comes from actually hanging everything in an orderly fashion. Which is quite a different sort of gift.

Herbert   I agree. And it is not a gift I possess, either!

Aird   I mean, I *could* do it. If you're a dispenser, obviously you have got to be able to be absolutely organized. My father used to insist that a good dispenser ought to be able to dispense blindfold—

Herbert   That gives me the shivers!

Aird   —because all of the things have been put back in the right place. If you're *really good*, then you ought to be able to do it blindfold. That's the sort of standard. And I'm quite sure if I did nothing else I could actually achieve that happy situation, but I have no wish to now.

Herbert   Can you share with me some of the changes and development that have occurred over the years for you in your writing?

Aird   You do learn something with each book you write, but what you've got to have is the absolute conviction that the piece of writing that you're doing *at this moment* is going to be the best that you have ever done. I don't mean that it *is actually* going to be, but I think while you're doing it, you want to feel that excited about it. "Oh, good, I'm really enjoying this. This is going to be good!" I mean, whether it is or not is quite a different matter. You need that feeling.

Herbert   Would you like to tease the readers with some remarks about your latest book published in the States?

Aird   *The Body Politic.* I'm afraid I would make an appalling mother, I think. I'd have a baby, have it adopted, and forget it! I find that once I've written a book and gone on to the next one, I completely forget everything else I've ever written, and I'd really be hard put to sit down and actually work out what my last book was about and in what book somebody appeared. It's like pulling the blind down. And I feel very strongly that one shouldn't be going over things [one has] written before; you should be concentrating on the one that you're doing at the moment.

Herbert   That would seem to mildly contradict your thought that each book teaches you something.

Aird   Well, you can take the lessons with you from book to book but not so much the specifics of the previous book. You are deeply involved in the next one; you really can't be bothered to focus on the earlier ones. In fact I never read the old books.

Herbert   I wonder how you manage to keep a fresh approach in each book.

Aird   What I try to do, which is perhaps the easy way out—I try to take a totally different subject and move into a different venue. In other words, you don't have a murder taking place in, say, the same school twice. Instead you have it taking place in perhaps a stately home on one occasion and a coastal town or an estuary on another or at a flower show in a third one. So in a sense you've gone halfway because you've got your rectory tea, so to speak, [and] you take it to a different location with a different set of people interested in a different vocabulary of expertise. That's half your battle, isn't it?

Herbert   What sort of research do you engage in to acquire your various "vocabularies of expertise"?

Aird   I think what I do is I go around and do as many things as I possibly can, you know. If somewhere interesting is open you go around and have a look at it without perhaps consciously knowing whether you are going to use it. It's rather like building up a computer bank of things that may or may not come in handy. I mean, for instance, our local sewage works was open over a labor day. I thought, "Oh, I must go along and see how a sewage works functions," not because I'm writing a book about it or am ever likely to.

Herbert   You and Jane Langton, then, are both becoming experts on plumbing!

Aird   (Laughs.) But you're never quite sure when the sort of slightly arcane pieces of information are going to come in handy.

Herbert   And such information can enrich a book considerably. I am thinking about the names of organ stops, which you used as chapter titles in the novel *Passing Strange*. I think the reader appreciates having a window on another world and gleaning information along the way in reading a mystery. Your organ stops and Dorothy L. Sayers's bell-ringing in *The Nine Tailors* and Jonathan Gash's antiques lore leap to mind here.

Aird   Yes.

Herbert   But how does one draw the line between offering the reader a view of another world and providing merely escapist entertainment, I wonder?

Aird   I think that depends upon the intention of the person who goes to them. If you are in fact going to [mystery novels] to, so to speak, go through wardrobes into another world, they may be a little bit escapist. But I think their appeal is to people in search of an *orderli-*

ness—although personally you may inhabit a world that is not reliable—within the hard covers of a book you know perfectly well that justice will be done. There is a distinction between this and escapism. You're looking perhaps for something that you would like to see there in real life.

Herbert   I think readers certainly do turn to your books with this desire for an orderly resolution of matters.

Aird   Yes. I hope they can count on me for this. It's confidence in the solution and right following upon the solution that I think is most important. I think we actually need this.

Herbert   Do you find this need on the reader's part for a reassuring solution to be a guiding principle for you in crafting your books?

Aird   I find it quite helpful, yes. [Ronald] Knox had the best description of writing detective fiction. He said it was like composing a crossword puzzle according to the rules of cricket.

Herbert   (Laughs.) Talking of cricket, I think American readers, in particular, turn to your books in order to enjoy your depiction of England.

Aird   I'm pleased that you say this because I'm very conscious of writing about my vision of England—my perception of England—perhaps "vision" is the wrong word. I mean I'm writing about the England that I see and live in and have been brought up in—and I feel I'd like other people to know about it.

Herbert   Would you consider this to be your mission in writing?

Aird   No, I haven't any missions in writing, actually. I'm not a missionary. I would prefer to think of myself as an observer rather than a missionary.

Herbert   A couple of your novels look to secrets of the past as being very significant. This strikes me as a way in which one can look at society's mores, contrasting the past and present.

Aird   I find this *very* interesting.

Herbert   Must you do considerable research in order to accomplish this?

Aird   I probably ought to! (Laughs.) I do quite a lot, actually. For *The Late Phoenix* I spent an enormous amount of time in the Imperial War Museum. But don't laugh if I say that research actually is something that you have to be careful not to confuse with writing. You can get very, very enchanted with research, which is easy, at the expense of writing, which is difficult.

Herbert   Do your books generally come about in a similar way?

323

Aird   Something strikes you. You hear something or you see something or you read something.

Herbert   Something evil, perhaps? That last remark reminds me of the three monkeys who hear, see, and speak no evil.

Aird   (Laughs.) I think you develop judgment. This judgment is rather the same as Lovejoy's, who can tell a good piece of furniture or a painting. I think after awhile a seasoned—not to say, long-in-the-tooth—

Herbert   (Laughs.)

Aird   —crime writer can look at an idea and know instantly whether or not it's going to be any use. And I think this sort of judgment *does* come with practice. I can hear somebody talking and think, "Ah, yes. I can use that." And I can look at an idea and know that somehow it isn't a good one.

Herbert   When suitable ideas strike you, do you have to write them down right away?

Aird   You can answer that in two different ways. If you were to give me a rather nice piece of dialogue or something quirky to quote, I would write it down straightaway. But if you were to give me an idea, then sometimes you lose it by writing it down. It gains a little bit by thinking about it.

Herbert   I see.

Aird   There was an occasion when I went into the East Station in Canterbury to collect a couple of friends who were coming down from Yorkshire. He was a retired newspaper editor and a quite prolific and very good writer himself. And the train was late. And his wife was becoming very agitated at the thought of me sitting at the station waiting for them. And he said, "Don't be silly, dear. Kinn's a writer. Writers are never bored. And she'll come to no harm sitting in her car waiting for us and she'll be thinking." And I think it's quite nice to have that *idea* that you will go on tossing 'round in your mind and letting it grow like a snowball with putting a little bit more on. But sometimes, if you put it down on a piece of paper, it's too bald somehow and you think, "Oh, it's not quite right" and you reject it. But if you keep it in your mind and you go on playing about with it while you're in the bath, or waiting at a railway crossing, or during very ordinary, routine domestic tasks, you'll say, "It's really not such a bad idea" because your mind is free while your hands are busy.

Herbert   I like that insight.

Aird   It's a little bit like these things that grow the coral. Each time you think about it a little more accretion is formed.

Herbert   That's a good way of putting it. So then by the time you are starting to write the book, in general, you have quite a strong idea of where the story is going?

Aird   Yes, yes. I have a strong idea of what I'm writing about if not exactly where it is going.

Herbert   So when you say you know what you're writing about, do you mean that you are acquainted with your characters, or do you mean you are certain of what the plot devices are going to be?

Aird   I don't really know much about them before I start. What I start with is the situation. And, for instance, in *Dead Liberty* I've got the situation that the girl suddenly finds herself the sole executrix for a remotely connected member of the family. Quite obviously she's been made the sole executrix for a reason.

Herbert   Yes. It's a very mysterious situation.

Aird   I've got an extremely good reason for this. Also, the old lady is convinced that she isn't going to die a natural death.

Herbert   Since you've allowed me the privilege of seeing the first pages of this manuscript, I can point out that while you introduce a mysterious situation you do it with a light humorous touch. You have also advised me to begin a talk I have to give in this way, in order to get the audience's attention.

Aird   I was thinking of *you* more than the audience when I said that. When you first stand up to give a talk you want a few lines in which you, yourself can hit your stride. And preferably make them laugh and take them with you. And then you take a deep breath and go into your real business.

Herbert   This sounds like a recipe for your success. Make them laugh, take them with you, and—

Aird   —get on with the business of the crime! Yes, that sums it up very nicely!

► BARBARA NEELY

Since African-American protagonists remain rare in detective fiction, Barbara Neely's work would be remarkable merely for the fact that it features the black domestic worker, ironically named Blanche White, as sleuth. But Neely has gone beyond simply choosing an African-American to act as heroine; she has endowed her character with a frank voice that speaks for an entire class of workers and individuals who are otherwise invisible in our society. Through Blanche, Neely also offers biting but humorous comments upon her character's oppressors. The result is mystery writing that is universally hailed as original, entertaining, and certainly enlightening.

A meeting with the author who has created Blanche's predicaments and her refreshing voice confirms the reader's expectations that this will be a person with a fine sense of humor who nevertheless does not suffer fools gladly, particularly those fools who indulge in racism and classism. Neely holds strong views on social issues, informed by her extensive work experience with women facing incarceration and/or drug addiction and her own harsh personal experience as a woman of color in our society. But in conversation, she eschews bitterness in favor of humor and great personal warmth.

Having published her first mystery at age fifty, Neely is a recent arrival on the crime-writing scene but her experience as a writer of "mainstream" short stories has served her well in writing the character-driven detective novel. Neely says she began her first novel, *Blanche on the Lam*, without being aware that it would become a mystery novel. Only when she saw the need for a murder did she decide that Blanche would play the dual roles of sleuth and main character. She admits that the mystery element at first surprised her, but says, "I've been reading mysteries all of my life and I suppose that there is a sense in which it was natural for me to flow into that. But I certainly hadn't planned to and hadn't expected to."

But throughout her life the author has often surpassed her expectations. Born in Lebanon, Pennsylvania, Neely faced poverty in a loving family of independent women and natural storytellers. Aware of the limited options available to her as a black female, Neely's career and educational aspirations were modest at first. But a secretarial job led to a rich variety of work including everything from office work to designing a program for the placement of incarcerated women in city communities. Neely even earned a masters degree without ever having received an undergraduate degree.

Currently she writes full time in a very private sanctuary in her frame house in suburban Boston. When publishers' advances are not forthcoming, she works as a consultant to various sociopolitical organizations and programs. When inspiration is not forthcoming, she draws upon the spiritual strength symbolized by the reminders of her female ancestors and African heritage that she keeps in her study.

Herbert   Your novel *Blanche on the Lam* succeeds not only as a mystery story but as a political statement that raises the reader's consciousness about the position of the African-American domestic worker Blanche White, who is your main character. What caused you to choose the mystery genre to explore this issue?

Neely   Now that's a question that I struggle with because I have spent a huge amount of my adult life working for causes in which the major goal is to save people. To be spending time sitting in my own room thinking of clever ways to kill people—

Herbert   Seems a little unusual ?

Neely   —sometimes seems absolutely bizarre! Totally bizarre. I only justify it by saying [that] although I don't understand the reasons for it, I do understand our fascination for murder as *the forbidden*. And therefore it is a wonderful clothesline on which to hang everything. And that is the only way I can really justify it, because I think there is something very weird about it.

Herbert   I understand that you worked in the field of criminal justice.

Neely   Oh, yes, that's true. My first job after [graduate] school was as the director of the Womens' Correction Center in Pittsburgh. The state of Pennsylvania had decided that it would try to move women who were serving sentences as felons into the community as an alternative to prison life. And the design for it was essentially based upon my master's thesis. It was wonderful. I met just tremendous women, amazing! Both as workers and women who were serving their time. We had everything from bank robbers to people who had killed their husbands.

Herbert   So in the course of your work you became acquainted with murderers?

Neely   Oh, yes. Definitely.

Herbert   Did it strike you that these people were ordinary people gone wrong, that any of us is capable of murder?

Neely   Well, ironically enough, most of the murderers that I came across in my work with women had done the right thing, as far as I was concerned, because they had killed abusive husbands. Every woman we had who had committed murder, that was the cause. And [I felt], "Well, of course they are just like everybody else, only better."

Herbert   Because they had the guts to assert themselves, to rescue themselves?

Neely   Mm hm.

Herbert   Do you feel we are all capable of murder if we are put in a situation like that?

Neely   Oh, absolutely. I don't think there is any thing that we are *not* capable of if our life is threatened, if our loved ones are threatened— for some people, if their *status* is threatened. For some folks, there are a lot of what I would consider very superficial reasons for killing people, like money. But I certainly think we are all absolutely capable of murder. If someone were to walk into this room and say [to me], "You are going to go next door and shoot that person there, or [else] we are going to take your partner out and kill him," the people who are related to the folks next door ought to start planning a funeral.

Herbert   (Laughs.)

Neely   The thing that worries me, quite frankly, as a woman, is that I would not have the courage to defend my life, even though it comes to that, and I think that that's a real important issue for every woman in this society to consider very, very seriously, because there are people out there who are prepared to kill us for no reason other than it makes them feel good. You know, I was listening to the news last night and they were talking about another young woman who has disappeared. Well, they will find some cuckoo guy who decided to kill her because he likes the way women scream when they die, or some nonsense. Our lives are very much on the line in this society, so I do think about that.

Herbert   I wonder if, because you are sensitive to the violence toward women in society, you tend to avoid identifying with a criminal or killer in your fiction.

Neely   I can think of any number of cases where I'd be delighted to enter the mind of the murderer!

Herbert   Ah!

Neely   I think the way the whole issue of women being battered plays out for me is that I find myself being very careful about *who* is killing *whom*. That's part of it for me; I am tired of books in which the woman is always the victim and the perpetrator is always male. I think that reinforces to us, as women readers, that we are always the victims, that *that* is our role in society. I don't think I would have difficulty identifying with a murderer, depending upon whom the murderer is murdering. That, to me, is the ultimate issue. I certainly believe that there are legitimate reasons why one person would kill another person. So no, I don't have any difficulty with that; I don't have any difficulty with [portraying] violence per se. I grew up in the sixties; I came through the Black Nationalist Movement where considerations of violence were things that we really had to think about with a great deal of clarity.

Herbert   I see. How *do* you come to your understanding of the criminals whom you portray in your books?

Neely   I don't have any difficulty being sympathetic to people who commit crimes, depending upon who the victim is.

Herbert   So the likelihood of your getting into the mind of a serial rapist would be very low, but you might be able to identify quite well with somebody who was putting an end to an abusive husband?

Neely   Absolutely, absolutely.

Herbert   I wonder if one of the reasons you have been drawn to write the mystery novel is because there is this marvelous control of matters of life and death?

Neely   Well, I think that's true for all writing. I can say *generally* that that is one of the things that attracts me to writing. It's just that omnipotence! I can decide who lives, and who dies, and who gets off, and who has to pay.

Herbert   It is a good feeling, isn't it?

Neely   For *writing in general*, that is the major attraction. You can make the world turn out the way you want it to turn out.

Herbert   Isn't that marvelous? Sue Grafton and Patricia D. Cornwell, among other mystery writers, have spoken about how the mystery novel personalizes death, since fictional murder is always inspired by well-thought-out motivation. There is usually, in fiction, a strong connection between the murderer and his or her victim: murder is not a random or glancing occurrence. How do you feel about this?

Neely   That's an interesting point. I had never really thought about that but in fact it does personalize it in a real way and it is the personalization of the murder that really draws the reader in: it's not the death of *somebody*, but it's the death of *this particular person*. And clearly, I must have agreed with that without having thought of it because, as I was writing the first Blanche book, when my writers' group read the manuscript as I was developing it, and they told me how much they loved a particular character, I knew that *that* character had to die!

Herbert   (Laughs.)

Neely   Then these folks would never let this book go! So that is it, of course! That it personalizes it.

Herbert   And in some ways it's reassuring when you compare this with what you might encounter in society.

Neely   Yes, because what we're all afraid of these days is random violence.

Herbert   On the other hand, P. D. James and others have said that fictional murder paradoxically distances death by making it a puzzle, an intellectual exercise. Sue Grafton said murder becomes another trip to the underworld from which we know that we will return unscathed, at least when it is within a mystery novel.

Neely   I would agree with that in essence but I would say it's much more an emotional than an intellectual experience.

Herbert   Hmm!

Neely   It is an emotional experience for people who read mysteries in which the puzzle is of less importance than the characters. I think in the character-driven books it's the emotional piece and not the intellectual piece that will come forward. You can get involved in all of these messy lives and decide who has killed whom and then you can go back to your family with clean hands! So I think it depends upon the type of book that you're reading, but intellectually or emotionally you are allowed to dabble, as Sue said, in the underworld and come away unscathed.

Herbert   Tell me about the usefulness to you, as the constructor of a mystery puzzle, of having a domestic worker as your sleuth. I was struck by Blanche's statement that one cannot have servants and secrets.

Neely   This is absolutely true. Both of my grandmothers did domestic work and I certainly remember the stories they used to tell about their employers, the way in which they would tell those stories, the lessons that came out of those stories.

Herbert   Have you used any of their anecdotes as you write about Blanche?

Neely   Not yet, but I talked to a friend who is a domestic worker now as I was writing this book, and she told me, "Don't forget the wastebaskets." Huge amounts of information are in those baskets. And of course [if you are a servant] people do talk in front of you as though you're the wallpaper.

Herbert   Isn't that amazing, in this day and age? This also reminds me of the way Agatha Christie determined that it would be a strength to have as her sleuth—in the Miss Marple character—a person who often would not be taken seriously because of her age.

Neely   Yes, absolutely. Yes, you know, it's interesting. One of the pains of being black in this country has now turned into something very useful to me. And that is that we are generally not seen. For example, I work in the feminist community in Boston. I was the director of Women for Economic Justice for two or three years. I am not an unknown person in that community. White women pass me every day who know me and *don't see me*, because they generally don't see black people. It happens all the time.

Herbert   That's appalling!

Neely   But what it has done for me is that I can now go [to] certain kinds of settings that I want to be able to describe with some understanding and be unobserved. So yesterday, for instance, I went to the Park Plaza Hotel and stood about, and was totally ignored.

Herbert   I hate to think of you being treated as a nonperson.

Neely   Well, it's perfectly ridiculous, but it's turned out to be useful to me at this point in my life. It's very, very true. So we as a people are invisible. And when you put us in a uniform, in a maid's uniform, we're definitely and totally *off the screen*. One of the inside jokes among black people is the way white people—particularly upper-class white folks—when we are on the same path of the street, the assumption is always that we are going to move out of their way—and they are constantly startled if we don't. I said to a friend yesterday, in fact [chuckles], that I'd gone to the Park Plaza to look around and jostled a couple of extremely well-dressed white males who'd expected me to step off the curb because they were headed in my direction.

Herbert   I admire you for being able to chuckle about that. And in your mysteries you are able to turn this painful experience into a strength. Not only does *Blanche on the Lam* empower the heroine, but readers see how helpless the employers are in running their own lives and in taking care of themselves—even down to whether or not they are clean.

Neely   Yes, exactly.

Herbert   And you are giving a voice to someone regarded as voiceless. I think it's very effective, and what an inventive way to use the detective story.

Neely   Good. I'm glad you think so.

Herbert   I notice that in conversation you can maintain a sense of humor regarding how you've been treated, but in *Blanche on the Lam* you evidence a far more angry attitude. Even the humor is fueled sometimes by the anger that must result from a daily round of such treatment.

Neely   Listen: count on it. Trust me: you would be full of rage, too. I am at a privileged point in my life. I don't have to go out in the world of work. I don't have to put up with that sort of crap that people of color and women have to put up with on their jobs. It's a luxury for me to be able to *use* discrimination to my own ends. And there are probably five black people in the country who have the luxury of doing that!

Herbert   A well-earned luxury, no doubt.

Neely   When I was in the world of work [I had] to confront this every day. You know, even folks who have their hearts and minds in the right place, who go out and work against discrimination and work for a better world are capable of viewing us in this way. You have no idea. You have *no idea*. It is an abstraction for other people. For us, it is a daily problem.

Herbert   When you decided to write your first mystery novel, did you consciously set out to bring empowerment to people of color?

Neely   Well, I really must try to remember. I am not totally positive that I started out to write this book *as a mystery*. I do remember that when it became clear to me that there was going to be a murder, that the mystery genre seemed like a very good place to talk about serious issues. The best way to talk about serious issues is to talk about them in a nonserious way, because people are not threatened by them. If you give people an opportunity to laugh at them, if you give folks an opportunity to see other people on the page acting in ways that are totally reprehensible—in fact, so reprehensible that they are really hilarious—then it's a lot easier for the reader to get the point. And it occurred to me that this is, in fact, a wonderful way to bring up these subjects. Readers have responded—a woman told me, "I would never have read anything on race and class, but I got the message through your mystery." So I think that because it is considered by so many ill-informed people to be just light entertainment, you can slip in a lot of very, very serious material and have it accepted in a way that you couldn't if you did a nonfiction treatment.

Herbert   So, when you began *Blanche on the Lam* you did not know that it would be mystery but you did set out consciously to talk about the uncomfortable relationship between the black and white worlds?

Neely   Yes. One of my major goals with this book was really to talk about the relationship between domestic workers and their employers in a way that gets at race and class in the United States, and to do that in a way that was both entertaining and amusing. A very interesting challenge was trying to figure out, then, where do you put the heavy stuff?

Herbert   And what conclusions did you come to about typically good places to provide this commentary?

Neely   (Smiles.) *Wrapped up in laughs*.

Herbert   Marvelous!

Neely   Give it to people with laughter; give it to them with irony; give it to them with sarcasm; give it to them with something that puts a sugar coating on the pill!

Herbert   And I've noticed that the commentary typically comes in Blanche's internal reflections.

Neely   Always, yes. I think that that's the thing that makes the difficult issues—the race-class issues—so much more attractive to folks, because you are hearing this through a voice and from a perspective that you rarely ever get in this society.

Herbert   I am fascinated by the balance you strike in being good-humored and personable while also having to deal on a daily basis with insulting or enraging situations. Does this have to do with your upbringing, perhaps?

Neely   Let me give you an example. When I was the director of Women for Economic Justice, we had a number of women from Roxbury on our board who would not come downtown to board meetings.

Herbert   These were women of color who were uncomfortable in the white enclaves?

Neely   Yes. They said that every time they came downtown, white people acted as if they had no right to the sidewalk. They were always getting jostled around. A young woman who worked for us—we went out to lunch one day together—she said, "Why, I love walking with you." I said, "Oh, yes, my mother taught me how to walk the streets." I would imagine I am not the only young black child whose mother explained how to walk the street, in that you don't move out of the way. You give space to people as they give space to you, but you can [learn to] judge whether this is a person who doesn't even see you. My mother's thing was, she would never jostle people, she would just stop in her tracks and make them go around her.

Herbert   What a tactful way to assert oneself.

Neely   That's right.

Herbert   I wonder, Barbara, if the daily round of facing people who will not acknowledge your equal need for personal space and right of way, as it were, has contributed to your desire as a writer to keep your work space very private. You are the only writer whom I am interviewing for this book who does not wish me to see her work area.

Neely   Yes, it does. It has something to do with the atmosphere I need for writing and something to do with me personally. That is, I am a very—for want of a better word—"superstitious" person. And I started to say "spiritual," which is the worst term. My space is very important to me. Rarely does anyone come in my room. Children are much more likely to get access than anyone else, and I'm not really quite sure all of what it's about, except that, sometimes I feel like the space is an extension of me, and being in it is having crossed my personal boundaries in some way.

Herbert   Like being in an elevator when somebody gets too close.

Neely   Exactly. I've had friends who have stepped into the room and stepped right back out again. It isn't really comfortable. Whether they are picking it up from the air or whether they are picking it up from my stiff back, it's hard to say. It seems that even before I have the opportunity to say, "Let's go to another room," they just back out.

Herbert   Isn't that interesting? What would be the worst that could happen as a result of having people invade your space?

Neely   I wonder sometimes if it has something to do with the way that I develop stories, you know. I wonder if that isn't it, because a story has to be pretty well developed before I can talk about it. Perhaps what is happening is all of my little bits of ideas are floating around in this room, and it feels like [I am] somehow exposing them to the outside world before they're ready. And I do, when I think about it, have things on my wall, over my desk, questions about new ideas, questions about relationships between the idea and the story.

Herbert   These ideas are written and posted on the wall?

Neely   Oh, yes. I discovered a wonderful new product, a tube of stuff and it makes anything stick. So I have different sizes and colors and shapes of papers.

Herbert   So that you can post your thoughts directly onto the wall?

Neely   Yes.

Herbert   I can see why you would like to keep the visitor from the work space, then, if your rough ideas are on display there. Would you be willing to describe the room in other regards?

Neely   It's covered with bookshelves, essentially, bookshelves and file cabinets. Essentially, it's devoted to writing—I mean, I don't do anything else there. You know, just talking with you about it, I also realize I've had this great need for privacy in general, and perhaps it's [a result of] growing up poor and never having had a room of my own until I was older.

Herbert   I can identify with that because I lived in a tiny house when I was growing up. I did have my own room but it was right beside the kitchen and all of the activity prevented me from having a sense of privacy.

Neely   I remember once my partner and I lived in a house that had two bedrooms only, and we slept on a sofa that opened in the living room, so that we could each have a room of our own.

Herbert   When you refer to your partner, I assume you mean the man in your life. Is he a writer, too?

Neely   He's an economist and he also writes. He is working now on a book about economic boycotts. His name is Jeremiah Cotton. But as to having our own rooms, it really is a luxury. When we think about how most of the people in the world live, you know, the idea, just the idea that we have a six- or seven-room dwelling for two people—it's an amazing luxury in the sort of universe of housing out there.

Herbert   You know, it really is. But for many artists, solitude and privacy are also a necessity. Just think about Virginia Woolf's famous essay "A Room of One's Own."

Neely   Well, also, it seems to me, when I'm writing—or even in that period when you are sort of staring at the wall with your finger up your nose when you're trying to figure out what comes next—there is a kind of nakedness, a kind of self-exposure. I can't imagine how I would get myself in that state with somebody at a desk next to me, or someone watching TV or reading in the room with me.

Herbert   Many writers feel this way.

Neely   I find that—and I certainly know that I am not original in this— that a lot of my best ideas, answers to questions, and new and more provocative questions come up when I am doing something else. Something else is often *writing* something else. You know, "Book A" may be my major project, but at the same time, I've got a short story I am playing with. And very often when I am working on a short story, I will get some grand idea about the book, or some question about the book. And so, I develop this idea of just sticking things on the wall because I used to do a very foolish thing—which I'm sure that many writers have done—and said, "Oh, I'll remember that, I'll remember that." *Wrong*! So the wall is a quick way to get it there, to get the idea down and get it some place at least semipermanent.

Herbert   So how does your writing day progress? Do you begin right at the start of the day? Does it vary from day to day?

Neely   Sometimes. When I first started writing seriously, I used to really give myself the blues about not having good habits. Finally, I realized that good habits are the habits that work for you. And I have a number of them, and I keep promising myself that someday I am going to try and chart them to find out, "Do they have any relationship to the phase of the new moon, season, or whatever?" As I said, there seems to be a couple [of approaches]. One is, I will get up at around three thirty–four o'clock in the morning and work—

Herbert   In the dark?

Neely   Yes. There's something about working in the dark that gives me extra courage. And so I will get up and work until nine-thirty or ten A.M. or so and go back to bed, get up around one P.M., and then start again. The other pattern is to get up around seven A.M., you know, exercise, drink my orange juice, and get right to work. After the coffee is made. I have to have a jug of water, a thermos of coffee; I essentially have to have no excuse to leave my room. I turn off my telephone, turn the machine down so I can't even hear voices coming in, and then work until three or four o'clock in the afternoon.

Herbert   That's a long day.

337

Neely   And then, other days, I get up and mess around, and mess around, and decide to take a nap and don't get to work until three or four o'clock in the afternoon, but then work until three or four in the morning. So I don't know why one habit kicks in at any particular time, but I've gotten to the point that I will take whatever comes.

Herbert   Well, fortunately, if you don't have children, and you have some flexibility, that's the way to do it.

Neely   Yes, yes, and I have an extremely supportive partner who expects me to have spent my time writing. So I don't have pressures to fix dinner or wash the bathtub. Those things become wonderfully attractive when I don't want to write.

Herbert   You can tell that things haven't been going well when the bathtub is sparkling!

Neely   That's exactly how it is.

Herbert   Going back to the idea of superstitions about the workplace—I am always intrigued by the objects that writers feel that they have to have around them.

Neely   I have to have my coffee in my thermos, the sort of thermos that guys take to work. I have to have my Palestine Women's Association cup. I generally light a candle. Within African religions, especially voodoo religions as they are practiced within the United States, there is color significance to certain kinds of candles. Orange is for concentration, I usually will light an orange candle. A white candle for clarity, a yellow candle for creativity.

Herbert   What a delightful ritual.

Neely   Sometimes I will keep them burning. I do have in my room—and it's interesting, I'm even feeling uncomfortable *talking* about this—because I have my little ancestor worship altar in my room that has some stones and soil and sand that I've collected from Africa and other places. [And there are] pictures of all of my female ancestors—all that I have pictures of—with my great-grandmother being the oldest. I generally sometimes during the day invoke the girls to give me a little assistance here.

Herbert   I like that. Thank you for sharing it with me. I feel as if I have been granted a little peek at your personal space.

Neely   Lots of times when I get up at three or four o'clock in the morning, I will work by candlelight. I have been known to close my blinds when it gets light if I am into what I am doing. I will just close the blinds and keep the candles going until whatever it is that I am writing is finished.

Herbert   It seems that you do have a very spiritual approach, Barbara, and although you said you don't particularly like the term, I think it is a better one than "superstition," which can be uncomplimentary.

Neely   Well, it's interesting that you should say that. I was quite shocked at myself when I came up with the term "superstitious." And, you know, at some point, when you went out of the room, I was trying to figure out why did I even use that term? It's like a blind: "Oh, this is just superstition. Don't look at this too carefully, don't touch my personal stuff." It's almost as though I didn't want you to know how serious and important this was to me.

Herbert   Actually for a writer to protect her work space seems quite natural to me.

Neely   So let's drop superstitions and get to the real thing. I have always considered myself very spiritual—not a relegous, but a very spiritual, person. And I don't know how you *cannot* be if you've got huge amounts of Africa in you. I mean it doesn't really matter what part of Africa you are from. I think that's one thing that the whole continent has in common is its spirituality. Especially around ancestors.

Herbert   You have suggested that you might call upon your ancestors for inspiration from time to time. This leads me to ask you which parts of the writing process are easiest for you and which provide the greatest challenges.

Neely   It's hard for me to say, you know, because, I can't look at it as an abstraction. (Pauses.) I guess one of the areas in which I have always felt my strength is dialogue. I am able to get voices very quickly; I've very clear ideas as to how people talk and what they *say* as opposed to what they *mean*. So dialogue is something that I always feel extremely comfortable with. [I'm] much more comfortable with dialogue than straight sort of description, which is something that I have to work at a little bit harder. Because I tend to be so internal, my focus tends to be on the character's internal self. One of the things that I always try to do in my fiction is to give voice to, and reveal the inner lives of, people that the general society assumes don't have any voice or inner light. And I am so focused on that that sometimes I forget to look out and see what they are seeing, as opposed to looking into them and seeing who they are.

Herbert   I am not surprised that you feel at ease with dialogue, or that you are fascinated by the inner lives of your characters. But I am a bit startled to learn that you must remind yourself to describe the environment in which the character is acting. You seem to have a natural ability to anchor your scenes in realistic domestic detail.

Neely   What I realized, as the book was beyond the middle, and I could see more of it, [was] that this is sort of a very female "take" on the world. We are rooted in reality. I mean, romanticism wasn't simply invented by males, it's carried on by males.

Herbert   Would you care to elaborate on that?

Neely   Men need romanticism in order to survive. The sharp edges of reality are very difficult for men to handle. And I don't necessarily mean *big* reality; I mean the reality of a rotten cucumber that they can't touch because it looks too horrible.

Herbert   (Laughs.) You see, I told you that you are a natural for domestic detail!

Neely   (Laughs.) And so, women are very rooted; we have lots of things going on in our minds at the same time; we're aware of things on the spiritual level and the material level, and [of] time as it progresses; yesterday and tomorrow are happening while we are trying to deal with today.

Herbert   I've noticed that with Blanche, she may be chopping asparagus and determining what aspects of a meal are likely to be useful as leftovers the next day while also reflecting about the behavior of her employers and—in the mystery context—coming up with some clues about character.

Neely   That's right.

Herbert   In recent years it seems that, particularly in the hands of female writers, readers are increasingly provided with information about the sleuth. As is the case in your work, we are privy to an inner monologue.

Neely   That's my sense, too, that most of the character-driven work is really being done by women. And I think [this is] probably because we are much more involved in the world than men, in the sense that we are the keepers of the children, we essentially keep the society going, and it is very hard to find women who are alone, have no family, have no community, have no ties. We're more like webs than anything else. We're really spread out over a wide area.

Herbert   And we're sensitive to subtleties in people and keeping people happy.

Neely   That's right. One of the things that I felt that I had to really discipline myself about in the book was the need to put in enough material for the whodunit aspect. I knew from the very beginning that this was Blanche's book, and I wanted to write about these characters. To me, the book was always a novel that has a murder in it, and I think that that's going to turn out to be true for all of the books in the Blanche series.

Herbert　Have you written others already?

Neely　I'm working on the second one now, which is called *Blanche at Amber Cove*. The themes in the second book are colorism and classism within the black community. Color has always been a big issue, and class is a growing issue, and so this book takes place at an upper-class, fictitious, I must say, black resort off the coast of Maine. Blanche uses the money that she gets from the folks at the end of this book [*Blanche on the Lam*] to send her kids to school, as she said she was going to do. And they are invited by friends from a private school to spend part of their summer at Amber Cove and Blanche is invited for a long weekend because it's one of the children's birthdays. This is a real issue for many people who are able to scrape the money together to send their kids to private schools: the child then comes home with a bunch of right-wing Republican ideas and are sort of out of sync with their community, and it's the tension between keeping your child rooted in African-American culture and heritage, and getting them an excellent education. And so this is part of the tension in the new book. And then the whole issue of dark skin versus light skin, which has been both a personal, political, and economic issue for black people and [is] something that we don't do a lot of talking about, don't do nearly as much talking about as we should. By the way, Blanche is extremely dark-skinned, and many of these folks who own cottages at Amber Cove are extremely light-skinned.

Herbert　That is certainly an unusual issue to address in a mystery novel.

Neely　Yes, well, friends have told me I should get myself in the FBI witness program and get a new identity before the book comes out! I'm just doing my job.

Herbert　Wow, *there* would be more grist for future mystery writing! And is there a murder in this one as well?

Neely　There is a murder in this one. And the third book is going to be called *Blanche in the 'Hood*, which is about the—you know that term, right?

Herbert　No, I don't.

Neely　It's short for "neighborhood." And will take place in Roxbury, and its issues will be the sort of myths that are floating around the inner city: that everybody is a crack addict, and there are no stable families, and everybody's miserable and unhappy, and all of that nonsense. I take a poke at some of that.

Herbert   There is no question that you have a mission in mystery writing. I would be curious to know about how you came to be a writer. Did you always, from a small child, think of yourself as wanting to be a writer, or were there other things you had in mind?

Neely   I think there was a point that I really wanted to be an actress. But I didn't start writing seriously until I was in my middle thirties. I've always been encouraged to write; I've always liked writing; I've always been good at it; and I've had professors who encouraged me to drop my major and become an English major and write fiction. You grow up poor, and you ask, "How am I going to pay my mother's mortgage as a fiction writer?" It's hard to take it seriously as a career. I also suffered from the sort of view that you understand society has of you. I'm supposed to *be* Blanche, I'm not supposed be writing *about* Blanche in a novel. And so you question whether in fact you have anything to say.

Herbert   You can stop questioning that!

Neely   I've always played around the edges, writing a little short story here for a friend's birthday, or some poetry that I'm very happy never got out to anyone else in the world, but as I got older, on the basis of what I saw happening with other women writers—Toni Morrison, for example—I began to see writing as an option. Toni Morrison arrived on the American literary scene, rose to heaven, and left all of this space underneath for the rest of us. Her work was especially important to me because of her woman's sensibility and because she was writing about the poeple that I wanted to write about, and she legitimized that in many ways. And so I began to say that I wanted to be a writer. And then I was in San Francisco, and saw an old black woman dancing in front of a street band. There was a street band, the sort of street band you can only find in California—an Asian woman on the drums, a Chicano guy playing the guitar, a white guy playing something else: it was like one of everything they had in town [was] in the band! And bunches of tourists standing around watching this. And I had just moved to San Francisco. And this old woman came up with sort of very straightened, almost patent leather hair and polyester pants and sort of dumpy shirt and she started dancing in front of this band. And there was a sort of semicircle of people around the band, and she's in the middle of the circle, and she started dancing. And people had different attitudes: a lot of them were sort of chuckling, you know, just on the verge of ridicule. And as she danced, she started pointing at people. It seemed almost at random, but [she] would make eye contact and point at people and just—it was almost like I could hear a voice saying, "You're gonna dance, darlin', and you're gonna do it *now*." I went back to San Francisco Residence Club, which is where I was staying, immediately started trying to write a short story about this woman's life. Today in my basement, I probably have two large cartons of notes and revisions and rewrites, and I never wrote that story, but it got me started in a very serious way. I think it was a year or two after that that I published my first short story. And Blanche is informed by any number of women that I have come across: both of my grandmothers, friends who do domestic work, women that I have met at various times. She is a very real person in that sense.

Herbert Readers are rooting for her the whole time, you know. I think this is in part because you're not afraid to show her vulnerabilities. For instance, when she goes into the broom closet and cries after having talked to her kids, the fact that she misses her children endears her to the reader.

Neely Right. She's a very everyday kind of woman. That's the thing that I really, really like about her.

Herbert But you don't seem like an "everyday kind of woman." I understand you've had wide-ranging educational and career experience.

Neely Yes. I have a master's degree in urban and regional planning. I did not go to undergraduate school.

Herbert How did you get the master's degree, then?

Neely People generally ask me that, and when I'm at parties and trying to be clever, I say, "Because I am brilliant." But I must have been in my late twenties . . . when I got out of high school, I went to business college. My major goal in life as a late teenager was to be independent, and it seemed to me that going to business college and getting a job as a secretary was the way to do that. I also think—I probably don't want to credit it now, so I don't have the real memory of it—but it seems to me that I *have to* have been affected by what were the horizons for young black women at that time, so the idea of going to business school may have been as high as my horizons were at that time.

Herbert And you did wish to be independent. That's certainly an admirable goal.

Neely Oh, yes, well, I didn't have any choice with that! I grew up with extremely independent women. That was *bound* to happen!

Herbert Did you work in the business world for awhile?

Neely My first job was as a clerk-typist at St. Agnes Hospital in Philadelphia. And my next job was sort of slightly higher-level secretary at Children's Hospital in the psychiatric unit for young children, which was fascinating work. And one year I did have a job in the real business world in a small corporation called the Auerbach Corporation, and I don't even remember now what it is they did.

Herbert   And then where did your social work come in?

Neely   I eventually found a job working for the Philadelphia Tutorial Project as a community organizer. This was in the early sixties and I quickly got involved in African-American liberation kind of activities. I was *not* an integrationist. I did not participate in the sort of integrationist aspect of the civil rights movement. While many people are shocked, I'm still not sure that [integration] wasn't one of the worst things that ever happened to us culturally and economically because, in every major city and most reasonably-sized towns, there was a viable black business community that was thriving before integration and died immediately after. But anyway I decided that I needed a degree because when my boss at the Philadelphia Tutorial Project decided to leave, the board decided that I couldn't have his job because the organization had never had a woman director. That's when I realized I needed both a degree *and* another job. I applied to Carnegie-Mellon for their master's program, not their undergraduate program. They told me, based on my experience, that I would have to take a semester of calculus before they let me into the master's program.

Herbert   They must have valued your work experience highly.

Neely   I went there; I lived in an undergraduate dorm; there were very few black people there; I was older, probably, than the president of the unversity. He was twenty-seven years old at the time. I truly hated it—loved the *idea* of school, but couldn't stand that particular university simply because of that. In other ways, it was wonderful: decent stipends, wonderful professors, all of that was great; but I just really did feel like a hippopotamus in a fishbowl. So I transferred down the street to the University of Pittsburgh. And then my first job after school was as director of the Women's Correction Center, as I mentioned before.

Herbert   And I understand you've done computer work for *Southern Exposure* magazine; you've worked in a research project focusing on women who were using methadone as an alternative to heroin addiction, and you've done other office work.

Neely   That's correct.

Herbert   What a varied career! Did you gain any experience in any of these jobs that you have put to direct use in mystery writing?

Neely   Not directly, but this is rich experience. I know I will draw on it in later books.

Herbert   What were you doing in California at the time that you observed the woman dancer and got your start in writing?

Neely   I directed a nonprofit consulting firm for awhile, did some consulting work for central California Department of Corrections around juvenile justice issues. Anyway, back to North Carolina. Worked for *Southern Exposure* and then left them to work for African News Service as a radio producer, doing news and feature pieces on Africa. I got to move, got to go to the International Women's Conference in Nairobi.

Herbert   Oh, how wonderful! That must have been a marvelous experience.

Neely   Unfortunately the organization had a little financial trouble. I stayed as long as I could manage it and then left. My partner was teaching in Boston at UMASS, and that's how I ended up coming here to Boston.

Herbert   How long have you been in the Boston area?

Neely   I guess, maybe five years, five or six years.

Herbert   I would love to know more about the child who went on to do all of these interesting things with her life.

Neely   Well, I was a fantastic liar, if that accounts for anything. (Smiles.) I kept a journal at a very early age. I have always been involved with the written word in some way. I was always a reader, as are both my parents, so books were always a huge part of my life. I credit fiction for keeping me out of therapy, and saving me from disastrous situations. I have always been a person who likes to be alone, which I think is something that is extremely useful if you turn out to be a writer.

Herbert   Yes, yes. You can be alone without being lonely.

Neely   Yes, and I always liked to imitate people, too. Particularly their speech patterns.

Herbert   There is the groundwork for your ease in writing dialogue! Was there a tradition of storytelling in your family?

Neely   Well, my maternal grandmother was quite an unusual woman. As I said, she spent her life working as a domestic worker. But she somehow managed to get a hold of a piece of land and have a house built for herself. And so I used to love and go visit her because she had plenty of room for me and she used to tell me wonderful stories.

I used to go in the evening and braid her hair for her. And all of her stories would begin with "Back in slavery days . . . ."

Herbert   Do you remember any of the stories?

Neely   No, they're all gone. But I grew up, like Blanche, among story-telling people. Today, it's one of the things that I love about going to family reunions: storytelling. We have many, many natural storytellers and comedians in our family with wonderful, sly wit. So I grew up among people who are verbally very creative.

Herbert   One of the things that Sue Grafton pointed out to me is that a mystery writer has to be a storyteller who knows how to deliver infor-mation in the right order.

Neely   Yes. It is very much a part of the storytelling condition to know how to do that, to get people [gasps] right there [in the heart] and then slap them over the ear.

Herbert   So you enjoy surprising the reader?

Neely   Yes!

Herbert   I'm curious to discover how you know when a novel is ready to be written. Do you do a lot of planning first?

Neely   I do both planning and writing at the same time. Very often . . . I actually do both at the same time. I'm making notes furiously, but scenes are also popping into my mind. Generally, I end up with lots of scenes that I don't know where they are going to go.

Herbert   That's unusual and rather surprising. Of the thirteen authors interviewed for this book, you are the fourth who admits to writing scenes out of strict chronological sequence. The others are P. D. James, Jonathan Gash, and Jane Langton. I would have expected the vast majority of writers to construct their crimes in perfect order.

Neely   No! How can you do that? How *can* you just sort of get every-thing *in* chronological order?

Herbert   Well, I think most writers do construct books chronologically.

Neely   The characters generally show up and have something to say in their own voices.

Herbert   They knock on your door?

Neely   Well, you know, you're walking along and then this scene appears in your mind and somebody's talking. Oh! And that—you asked me about my childhood. That happened *all* of my childhood, *all* of my life, before I started writing. There was always this business going on in my brain: people talking, having conversations.

Herbert   There's the first clue that you would become a writer. Now, would you narrate your own life to yourself, as well?

Neely   I know what you mean. Yes, that's true; there *is* that person.

Herbert   Watching your reaction to things?

Neely   Right, yes.

Herbert   But you just didn't pursue the writing until much later.

Neely   I do think that a lot of that has to do with growing up in poverty. There was nobody to say to me: "Honey, you need to be a writer." There were no writers in our neighborhood. There were no actresses. There were no folks who knew anything about publishing.

Herbert   And when you became a writer you decided to write about the very personal experience of being African-American in this society. You seem to be getting across things that are very personal concerns. This differs from some writers who have turned to mystery writing because they don't want to say anything that is autobiographical; they wish to shield their personal lives from the reader's gaze. They ask the reader to focus on the puzzle rather than on the author. Have you felt in any way that you are shielding yourself in this kind of writing more so than in the mainstream writing that you do?

Neely   It never occurred to me. My short stories, for example, are not mysteries.   I think that if I find some aspect of myself that is just clearly me that has some potential for fiction, I'll use it. I'll use any-thing. I'm shameless! (Laughs.) What I'm trying to say is, these are issues that are important to me politically. I consider myself to be a political writer, [focusing on] class, poverty. These are issues that not only have affected me personally, but are issues to which I have devoted a great deal of my life as a volunteer and as a member of my ethnic and racial group. And so I see it much more as expounding on my political position than I do as something personal. But as, of course, feminism taught us, the personal *is* the political.

Herbert   I wonder if you have any sense of why so few African-American writers have chosen to write mysteries?

Neely   It is something that I have to say puzzles me. A sort of sociologi-cal reason that pops easily to mind is that, because of the prejudice that's always reigned in this country, black people have always been associated with the criminal class. And I wonder if that doesn't dis-courage writers from actually writing about murder. Of course you know there has always been somebody [African-American] who's written mysteries: Chester Himes did it. Another reason that pops into my mind is that there is so much that we have to write about and because the sort of reputation of the genre is that it is not as "serious" and it is not as "literary" when African-Americans or other people of color get an opportunity to break into print, you know, they may tend to lean toward the heaviest and most weighty forms because opportunities are so rare. It's like, "Well, if a mystery isn't going to be taken seriously, then I'm not going to write a mystery because we are *so rarely* taken seriously in this society." But I think that what Walter Mosely has done, and certainly what I am trying to do, is to point out that you *can* bring the same kind of enlightenment and sharing of secret cultural knowledge to a wider reading public in a mystery.

Herbert   One thing that struck me is that mystery writing has tended to be a conservative form, especially if you think of the British tradition, in terms of justice and the portrayal of class.

Neely   Yes. Another piece that occurred to me is that so much of mystery work is really based upon the police as heros, and the police have *rarely* been heros in *our* community! I still don't read police procedurals. It is difficult for me to put the police in the role of hero. And that may be something else that stops people [of color from writing in the mystery genre]. And as you said, or as you implied, there is this issue of how justice has worked for us in this country. You know, if justice means that you have to turn someone over to a system that has been prejudiced against him, as a writer this puts you in a strange position.

Herbert   Yes, it does, and that's why I think we get the black antihero like Walter Mosely's Easy Rawlins.

Neely   You know, in the first Blanche book, the police are *not* a part of the solution.

Herbert   That's right! Julian Symons has said that he is particularly fascinated by the question of what causes an otherwise upstanding member of society to cross over the line and be driven to murder—the most heinous of crimes because there can be no reparation to the victim. Do you see political forces as causing this among some of your characters?

Neely   Well, that is fascinating. I guess I don't see people who commit murder as being these special people who have taken this big leap over this great chasm but, in fact . . . we are all on this continuum, and as I said before, I think we are all perfectly capable of it. To me, one of the things that is interesting is how *undifferent* people are after they've committed a murder. I mean, it seems that if somebody has just come in from committing a murder, we ought to be able to tell that! It ought to be obvious. But it's not. People *are not* different.

They may be different internally, but they are, as I said, undifferent. They act exactly the same. They interact with people the same. That, to me, is fascinating, that you can do that and just go on with your life as though nothing happened.

Herbert   This makes me think of Agatha Chrisite's fears that the trusted relative across the table might be harboring threatening thoughts. And I recall P. D. James asking herself, while hearing the story of Humpty-Dumpty, "Did he jump or was he pushed?" Do you consider yourself particularly sensitive to the fragility of life?

Neely   I don't think always, but I certainly am now. I'm sure that it has something to do with age. In the last five or six years, the whole older generation of my family, essentially with one or two exceptions, has died out. When I say "the older generation," I mean my grandmother's generation and not my mother's generation, thank goodness. I believe that my sort of confrontation with death after death in the family is one of the things that has moved me toward ancestor worship, for example, because these people, particularly the women, were the very roots of our family. My grandmother has been dead three or four years now. We have not recovered from that. You don't understand how central people are to the life of a family, sometimes, until they are not there anymore. So I am a little more aware of death, and I think I am developing, or trying, at least, to develop a sort of a natural attitude towards it. Sort of an attitude that: it is coming, it is coming, that it is a part of life—as strangely put as that may be. It doesn't mean that I am going out looking for it. But trying to be more accepting about it and wanting to do more reading on the subject. Wishing that we knew more about what it is! I have been doing more speculating about this lately.

Herbert   I'd love to hear you speculate on the question of detective fiction as an entertaining form. I am concerned to know whether the need to entertain in any manner diminishes the literary possibilities of the genre.

Neely   That's fascinating. First of all, I don't agree with this sort of pejorative that is attached to mysteries as "sheer entertainment." I think one of the things that is wrong with lots of areas of life, including education, is that we *haven't* learned how to make it entertaining. Information is often best dressed in entertaining clothes. When we read people like Ruth Rendell—[in] one of her early books the person who commits the murder . . . is a woman who is illiterate.

Herbert   Yes, that's a fascinating study.

Neely   I don't remember the title.

Herbert   It is *A Judgement in Stone*.

Neely   I *do* remember that I understood more about illiteracy and what it does to the person internally than ever I would have understood if I had a read a book on illiteracy or even if I had talked to someone who was illiterate who could talk about that a little bit. So I think there are ways and times in which the mystery novel can, in fact, reveal as much, if not more, about character than a straight literary kind of novel. I do have to accept that there are some things that you don't tell folks because you don't want them to know it yet—because that is going to give the entire game away. So there is that sort of artificial construct. [But] there are people, like P. D. James for example, whose character development is certainly just as rich and enriching as lots of work that is considered to be more literary.

Herbert   But some would argue that the pure "novelist of character" is not shackled, as the mystery novelist may be, by the convention of keeping secrets about character and motivation from the reader.

Neely   Well, I suppose it could be—except when you think about it, for what sort of character-driven writing is this not true? Does not *every* writer reveal bits of the character as she goes along? (Pauses.) But I think that you're right. I think that it does—in the current book that I am working on, there are certainly some things that I would like to reveal about the person who is the murderer that I cannot reveal now because that would give the whole game away.

Herbert   Would you consider that the mystery writer has to be coy with the reader at times?

Neely   That's true, but then life is coy. How many times have you said, or heard people say, "I had *no idea* she was like that"?

I'm trying to remember back to the first book. I *do* remember having to do rewrites because I had been too revelatory at some points. And it really is—I think that Grafton is absolutely right. I mean, a lot of what we're trying to figure out is where to put the information, and how much information to give people. But otherwise, it may be that I've always sort of felt that this was a false dichotomy. Again, look at the character development [achieved by] people like P. D. James! (Chuckles.) You know, it's hard to figure out what people are talking about when they say, "Mystery writing isn't really literary." You know, in terms of my own writing, I certainly don't feel as though I bring anything more or less to writing short stories that are not mysteries than I do to the Blanche work. For me, the major question, of course, is, "Whatever the genre, whatever the form, am I able to say what I want to say?" And when I'm working on Blanche and when I'm working on other things I'm still trying to write the best story I can.

And I think the other thing is that there are going to be more people like me who are sort of genre benders—

Herbert   I like that terminology.

Neely   —who are writng novels that have a mystery in them or have a murder or have some puzzle that is integral to the story. Writers are going to be doing more bending. [With] the kind of excellent writing that goes on in the genre, I don't know how you develop an argument that says, "This isn't as good as it would be if there wasn't a murder in it."

Herbert   Well, I agree. But I am concerned to discover whether mystery writers are frustrated in any way by the form and, in particular, by that requirement to keep secrets from the reader.

Neely   You're *always* keeping secrets from the reader, no matter what you're writing. *You* know where the book is going. *You* know where it ends. And you don't tell the reader that on page one. You keep it a secret.

Herbert   As Sue Grafton put it, "Tolstoy didn't start out by saying, 'Anna Karenina fell under a train.'"

Neely   That's right! You *cannot* write and *not* keep secrets from people, as far as I am concerned.

Herbert   As a writer of both mysteries and mainstream fiction, are you *certain* that there is equal potential for you to write a piece of literature, an *undeniable* book, in both kinds of work?

Neely   The mystery novel may do different things than the other kind of fiction. But it isn't going to be any more or less valid in literary terms Who *are* these people who make these decisions? They're not me; they're not my friends. I mean, who said that some guys sitting in Harvard get to decide what's "literary"? So for me, there's a level at which that is all a bunch of bullshit. What is important is: "Is it good writing? Does it give me something new? Does it open up new avenues of thought for me? Is it exciting? Is it insightful, does it tell me something I never knew?"

Herbert   And I'd say the questions that you just stated provide a fair definition of the literary experience.

Neely   All of those are much more interesting questions to me than, "Is it a mystery or is it 'literary'?" *Any* kind of literature has got to say "Yes!" to those questions.

Herbert   And mystery fiction can answer "Yes" as well as any other fiction?

Neely   Absolutely!